CEREMONIAL FOR PRIESTS

MSGR. MARC CARON, S.T.D.

CEREMONIAL *for* PRIESTS

SOPHIA INSTITUTE PRESS
Manchester, New Hampshire

Cover by Updatefordesign Studio

Cover image: On the Altar by Piermichele Malucchi (Alamy M4TFXX);
golden ornamental floral-background (Freepik 6967200)

Sophia Institute Press
Box 5284, Manchester, NH 03108
1-800-888-9344
www.SophiaInstitute.com

Sophia Institute Press is a registered trademark of Sophia Institute.

paperback ISBN 978-1-64413-934-9

ebook ISBN 978-1-64413-935-6

Library of Congress Control Number: 2023941112

2nd printing

In memory of my parents

Laurel G. Caron (1927–2004)
and
Ella M. Bonang Caron (1928–2020)

who first introduced me
to the school of the Lord's service

Table of Contents

PART 2

Matters Related to the Celebration of Mass

PART 3

Seasons and Days of the Liturgical Year

PART 4

Selected Sacraments and Sacramentals

Part 5

The Roles for Priests and Deacons at Parish Celebrations by a Bishop

Part 6

Ceremonial for Small Congregations Described

Appendix
Diagrams

Preface

THIS BOOK GREW out of my work at St. John's Seminary in Brighton, Massachusetts, training seminarians to celebrate the Mass and the sacraments. Prior to the assignment at St. John's, I had spent eleven years as the diocesan master of ceremonies. Both of those experiences convinced me of the need for a manual like this, since the liturgical books often fail to specify many of the details needed if one is to celebrate the rites attentively, devoutly, and gracefully. Finding nothing in print which would serve my purpose, I began to compile a series of descriptions of each of the rites I was asking my students to rehearse. While teaching the liturgical *practica* courses, I was also writing a regular column on the *ars celebrandi* of the postures and gestures of the Roman Missal for the *Adoremus Bulletin.* That effort, over the course of several years, helped clarify my thinking regarding how one might fill the *lacunae* in the rubrics of the various liturgical books.

The title of this work, *Ceremonial for Priests,* is meant to evoke the title of a similar work, the liturgical book known as the *Ceremonial of Bishops.* Like its namesake, the *Ceremonial for Priests* provides the directions and indications needed to carry out the various rites found in the liturgical books themselves. Its scope is limited to those sacraments and sacramentals which the typical parish clergy are most likely to celebrate on a regular basis.

It is my hope that this book will serve the needs of seminarians, deacons, and parish priests. My approach draws upon the traditional practice of the Roman Rite as it pertains to the postures and gestures of the various rites. It is not intended to be a comprehensive guide to all the options or choices found in each rite. Rather, it is meant to provide a picture of what the celebration of each sacrament or sacramental could look like when taking into consideration the immemorial customs which have grown up around the public worship of the Roman Catholic Church. My suggestions are by no means the only approach to any number of disputed questions. But I trust they are a reasonable and practical guide for the seminarian, the deacon, and the parish priest as they begin to develop a personal *ars celebrandi* which is marked by the sobriety, nobility, and dignity so characteristic of the long history of the Roman Rite.

In this effort, I am grateful to my colleagues at St. John's Seminary with whom I taught the various liturgical courses, namely, Fr. Raymond Van De Moortell, Fr. James Conn, S.J., and Fr. Jonathan Gaspar. Their comments and observations as we taught our courses together were extremely helpful. In addition, I owe a debt of gratitude to the *Adoremus Bulletin* and to its indefatigable editor, Christopher Carstens. Chris encouraged me greatly to pursue the project of creating sound principles for applying the traditional practice of the Roman Rite to the Roman Missal of Paul VI. I wish to acknowledge the insights offered by Fr. Ryan Ruiz and Fr. Kyle Doustou, which equally contributed to improving this work greatly. I am deeply indebted to one of my former students, Fr. Lucas LaRoche, for his painstaking proofreading of the manuscript. Finally, I am very grateful to Charlie McKinney of Sophia Institute Press for his unflagging interest in this project. I hope this *Ceremonial for Priests* makes a positive contribution to the ongoing liturgical formation of the parish clergy, a priority so ardently desired by the Second Vatican Council.

Abbreviations

AAS	*Acta Apostolicae Sedis* (1909–)
CB	*Ceremonial of Bishops*
CIC	*Code of Canon Law* 1983
DOL	*Documents of the Liturgy*, International Commission on English in the Liturgy, eds. (Collegeville, MN: Liturgical Press, 1982)
GILH	*General Instruction on the Liturgy of the Hours*
GIRM	*General Instruction of the Roman Missal*, 5th ed.
HCWEOM	*Holy Communion and Worship of the Eucharist outside Mass*
MR	*Missale Romanum* 1962
OBC	*Order of Baptism of Children*
OCF	*Order of Christian Funerals*
OCM	*Order of Celebrating Matrimony*
PCS	*Pastoral Care of the Sick*
RCIA	*Rite of Christian Initiation of Adults*
RM	Roman Missal 2002/2008 (*RM* 1965 for 1965 Missal)
RS	*Redemptionis Sacramentum*

CEREMONIAL FOR PRIESTS

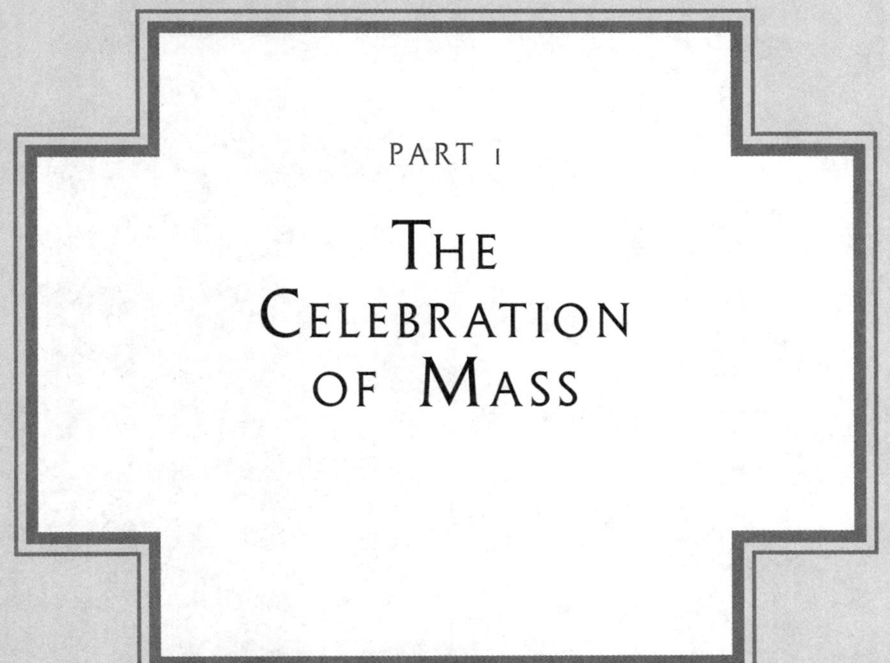

PART I

The Celebration of Mass

The Principles for a New *Ars Celebrandi*

In recent years, many priests and deacons directly involved in promoting the liturgical renewal launched by the Second Vatican Council have been left perplexed by how few indications the fifth edition *General Instruction of the Roman Missal* (2002) actually gives as to the manner one carries out the actions of the Mass. For example, how does the deacon hold his hands while he reads the Gospel? Or how is a priest meant to incense a freestanding altar? Since the promulgation of the first edition of the *General Instruction* in 1969, whenever questions of this kind were raised with the Congregation for Divine Worship and the Discipline of the Sacraments, the private responses published in *Notitiae,* the official publication of the Congregation, directed readers back to the same ambiguous wording in the liturgical documents which had given rise to the questions in the first place! These responses routinely asserted that no rubric, no practice, no custom from the previous Order for Mass and its *ritus servandus* could now be assumed to be illustrative or determinative in settling questions about the manner in which the new Order for Mass was to be celebrated.[1] This attitude effectively cut the celebration of Mass off from its past, and provided no context for understanding or implementing the gestures required by the revised *General Instruction.*

Unfortunately, this state of affairs has tended to create a situation in the Church where there are as many ways of performing a particular gesture of the liturgy as

[1] The origin of this way of thinking can be traced to two widely quoted responses from the Congregation for Divine Worship. See Congregation for Divine Worship and the Discipline of the Sacraments, Response, *Notitiae* 14 (1978): 301–302 (*DOL,* 481R11); Congregation for Divine Worship and the Discipline of the Sacraments, Response, *Notitiae* 14 (1978): 534–535 (*DOL,* 491R22).

there are celebrants. Because the current Order for Mass leaves many gestures and movements unspecified, the practice of the last fifty years has been to improvise a manner of celebrating Mass which fills in the holes left to the imagination by the *General Instruction of the Roman Missal.* Sometimes, that has meant adopting any number of practices uncritically from the Churches of the East. At other times, a mistaken or misunderstood recollection about a given rubric prior to the Second Vatican Council has provided the basis for acting today. Often, no single gesture is carried out in the same way by the same celebrant in successive Masses. Finally, this approach can easily lead to the conviction that "these details don't really matter." In the end, some arbitrary choice, invented on the spot or borrowed from here or there without much thought, becomes a localized custom that, in time, is eventually treated as an unchanging and unquestioned norm. This process has led to the fragmentation of the liturgy, so that the Mass as celebrated in this parish is quite different, if not radically so, from the Mass celebrated in that parish. This state of affairs cannot be good for the unity of the Church.

All of these scenarios weaken the celebration of the Eucharist, which depends, like all ritual does, on the elements of stability of form, predictability, and ritual repetition. Therefore, some reference to a common norm for behaving during the celebration of Mass can be both a source for and a stimulus to greater unity. The stated requirements of the *General Instruction* and Order for Mass, along with the traditional practice of the Roman liturgy, can be the sources for such a norm for acting. Therefore, it would seem that the optimal approach to the *ars celebrandi* demands a recourse to the tradition, so as to give the revised Roman Missal these necessary qualities of stability of form, predictability, and ritual repetition.

Thanks to the promulgation of the third typical edition of the missal in 2002, it is now indeed legitimate for celebrants to refer to the broad liturgical tradition when looking for direction on how to perform this or that gesture at Mass. This noteworthy change of attitude was signaled by a few words now found in one line which has no precedent in the previous editions of the *General Instruction*. Regarding the gestures and postures of the people and ministers, the *General Instruction* reads in part:

> Therefore, attention should be paid to what is determined by this General Instruction and *the traditional practice of the Roman Rite* and to what serves the common spiritual good of the People of God, rather than private inclination or arbitrary choice.[2]

2 *GIRM*, 42, emphasis added.

In addition, paragraph no. 44 of the same *General Instruction* goes on to make clear that the "actions and processions" of the ministers and faithful at various points in the celebration of Mass are among those gestures and postures which should be informed by the same "traditional practice of the Roman Rite." This tiny phrase in paragraph no. 42 has heralded a new approach to understanding the revised Order for Mass. That new approach to a more authentic implementation of the Order for Mass was seconded by the emphasis in nos. 38–40 of the post-synodal exhortation *Sacramentum Caritatis* (2007) on the value of recovering a proper *ars celebrandi* of the Mass in conveying the beauty and the holiness of the liturgical action taking place.[3]

What might the celebration of the Eucharist look like if the prescriptions of the latest edition of the *General Instruction* were to be implemented according to the "traditional practice of the Roman Rite?" What would this approach demand of the priest celebrant, concelebrants, deacons, other ministers, and of the assembled faithful themselves? Starting from the directives found in the *General Instruction* and in the Order for Mass itself, and relying on the previous liturgical tradition to fill in what may be either unspecified now, or simply assumed, how could this principle help the Church to better understand the manner in which one goes about celebrating Mass according to the Roman Missal of Paul VI? This work is an attempt to answer these important questions. It will examine the explicit directives of the *General Instruction* as to *what* is to be done, the ritual customs drawn from the tradition as *how* that is to be done, and the spiritual good of those worshipping as to *why* the liturgical action is taking place. It will attempt to show how keeping these three factors in mind helps to avoid shaping the celebration of Mass according to "private inclination or arbitrary choice."

At times, I have had to make a judgment and find a way to accomplish some gesture which now finds itself in a new ritual context, taking into account parallel circumstances found in the editions of the missal prior to 1969. For example, in the current Roman Missal, the priest imposes incense before the Gospel at the chair, not at the altar as in the past. That requires describing a way to accomplish this gesture which is in harmony, but not identical, to the historic practice. Naturally, there is room for interpretation in such an exercise. People of good will differ as to how the specific action might be carried out and which of the precedents from the liturgical tradition should be illustrative. What I have offered is *an* approach; it can never be *the* definitive approach to these matters. Nevertheless,

3 Benedict XVI, Apostolic Exhortation on the Eucharist *Sacramentum caritatis* (February 22, 2007), *AAS* 99 (2007): 136.

this book describes an approach which tries to avoid adding, deleting, or changing any element of the Order for Mass. A recent study confirms that it is indeed legitimate to implement *GIRM* 42 in this way.[4]

These chapters will also make clear how interpreting the provisions of the *General Instruction* according to the "traditional practice of the Roman Rite" and the spiritual good of all those participating can be accomplished while at the same time avoiding any mixing of elements between the two forms of the Roman Rite.[5] Nor is this manual intended to foster a "reform or the reform" of the current Roman Missal. Rather, the suggestions I make in the following chapters are part of the wider ongoing effort to actually implement the missal of Paul VI as it has been presented to the Church. After all, we cannot forget that the Roman Missal of 1969, and its successor, the Roman Missal of 2002/2008, have consistently been presented as being in continuity with Roman Missal of 1570.[6] Unfortunately, at times, it has become almost an unquestioned presupposition in liturgical circles that the current edition of the Roman Missal has almost nothing to do with the editions which preceded it. However, the fifth edition of the *General Instruction*, along with documents like *Redemptionis Sacramentum* and *Sacramentum caritatis*, rather places the *ars celebrandi* in the context of a tradition.[7] Any written text, even the Order for Mass, only makes sense in a given context. The context for the celebration of Mass as revised after the Second Vatican Council is the long tradition of the practice of the Roman Rite.

The main inspirations for this effort are the four best commentaries on the revised Order for Mass currently available. These are the very well-known trilogy by Bishop Peter Elliott, namely *Ceremonies of the Modern Roman Rite*,[8] its companion volume *Ceremonies of the Liturgy Year*,[9] and Elliott's most recent work, *Ceremonies Explained for Servers*.[10] The fourth source of inspiration for developing the *ars*

4 See Michael Casey Sanders, "An Interpretation of 1983 *CIC* Canon 846 § 1 in the Light of *GIRM* 42" (JCL thesis, The Catholic University of America, 2021).

5 Congregation for Divine Worship and the Discipline of the Sacraments, Letter *Quattuor adhinc annos* (October 3, 1984), *AAS* 76 (1984): 1089.

6 See Paul VI, Apostolic Constitution *Missale Romanum* (April 3, 1969), *AAS* 61 (1969): 217.

7 Congregation for Divine Worship and the Discipline of the Sacraments, Instruction *Redemptionis Sacramentum* (March 25, 2004), no. 9, *AAS* 96 (2004): 552; Benedict XVI, Apostolic Exhortation *Sacramentum caritatis* (February 22, 2007), *AAS* 99 (2007): 136. See also Benedict XVI, Letter to Bishops on *Summorum Pontificum*, no. 9, *AAS* 99 (2007): 797.

8 Peter J. Elliott, *Ceremonies of the Modern Roman Rite: The Eucharist and the Liturgy of the Hours*, rev. ed. (San Francisco: Ignatius Press, 1995).

9 Peter J. Elliott, *Ceremonies of the Liturgical Year According to the Modern Roman Rite: A Manual for Clergy and All Involved in Liturgical Ministries* (San Francisco: Ignatius Press, 2002).

10 Peter J. Elliott, *Ceremonies Explained for Servers According to the Roman Rite: A Manual for Altar Servers, Acolytes, Sacristans, and Masters of Ceremonies* (San Francisco: Ignatius Press, 2019).

celebrandi of the Roman Missal of Paul VI is the less well-known but equally impressive *Cérémonial de la Sainte Messe* by Fr. André Mutel and Peter Freeman.[11] Finally, when seeking a clear picture of the actions and gestures proper to the editions of the Roman Missal prior to 1969, the indispensable guide remains *The Ceremonies of the Roman Rite Described,*[12] edited most recently by Alcuin Reid. With these authorities as guides, the following chapters will offer a description of the *ars celebrandi* of the Roman Missal of Paul VI which draws upon the practical and spiritual wisdom found in the long tradition of the Roman Rite.

This work is necessarily more limited than the five references just mentioned. It does not address all the elements of the celebration of Mass such as sung texts, Scripture readings, choice of Mass texts, ritual objects, or the art and architecture associated with the eucharistic sacrifice. It also does not address any number of customs associated with the celebration of Mass which may not pertain directly to the gestures, actions, processions, and postures intended in the *General Instruction* 42 and 44. Some of these customs have died out for all intents and purposes, for example, the use of the *Sanctus* candle. Other customs contrary to the law continue to exist in rare locations without being corrected, such as a priest wearing a dalmatic while functioning as the deacon of the Mass. Other customs, such as the use of a burse to carry the corporal, while unspecified in the current *General Instruction*, continue to exist in a number of churches, but are not common. Regarding this last category, I have tried at least to acknowledge how even some of the less common, but not forbidden, customs might be carried out.

This manual is meant to serve as a kind of extended commentary on paragraphs nos. 42 and 44 of the *General Instruction*. Part 1 describes Mass celebrated by a priest *versus populum* in a typical parish on Sundays, with the assistance of a deacon. It also assumes a number of ministers fulfilling the various roles needed for Mass. It will take into account the possibility of one or more concelebrants. Part 2 deals with matters related to Mass such as eucharistic adoration. Part 3 illustrates the variations in the celebration of Mass according to the liturgical seasons and days of importance throughout the year. Part 4 offers a commentary on the postures and gestures of those sacraments and sacramentals which are most commonly celebrated by a priest in the parish church. Part 5 enumerates

[11] André Philippe M. Mutel and Peter Freeman, *Cérémonial de la sainte messe à l'usage ordinaire des paroisses suivant le missel romain de 2002 et la pratique léguée du rit romain,* 2nd ed. (Perpignan, France: Éditions Artège, 2012).

[12] Adrian Fortescue, J. B. O'Connell, and Alcuin Reid, eds., *The Ceremonies of the Roman Rite Described,* 15th ed. (New York: Bloomsbury, 2009).

the duties of the parish priests and deacon when the bishop celebrates Mass there, especially for the conferral of Confirmation. Finally, Part 6 describes how liturgies can be adapted in the case of small churches with limited resources.

This manual does not attempt, like the authorities mentioned above, to provide a comprehensive description of all the ceremonial elements of the Mass, of the Liturgy of the Hours, and every sacrament or sacramental celebrated by a priest or a bishop in every circumstance with the fullest range of ministers assisting. It is a more modest effort, therefore, designed for the priest or deacon who is just beginning to examine his own *ars celebrandi*. It is meant to be a straightforward and practical introduction to the celebration of Mass and those sacraments and sacramentals most commonly part of a parish priest's ministry that synthesizes and harmonizes the many directions given in the commentaries cited.

For some, it may seem exaggerated to pay such close attention to the details of the manner of celebrating the Church's rites. However, those details in the gestures, movements, and postures of the ministers of the liturgy are like the grammar which gives meaning to the body language which the Church uses to offer worship to God. When those gestures, movements, and postures take place in a coherent and consistent way, they help to make the entire liturgical action more intelligible. For the language of the body is simply one other way of communicating during the course of the liturgy. Together with the scriptural and liturgical texts, the music and song, the art and architecture of the place of celebration, the embodied nature of liturgical prayer itself communicates something important to those who participate in it. Seen in this light, attention to how the body is used to communicate meaning during the course of the liturgy is hardly unimportant. Exploring the Roman tradition's customs regarding the gestures, postures, and movements of the liturgical ministers is an act of liturgical retrieval, since a working knowledge of these traditions has nearly been lost in the usual celebration of the Mass and sacraments nowadays. Much like the instruction on the translation of liturgical texts *Liturgiam authenticam* (2001) has required the Church to seek a closer correspondence between the typical edition of the Latin texts of the Mass and their vernacular translations,[13] paragraph no. 42 of the *General Instruction* implies that some effort will be made to incorporate the historical manner of conducting oneself during Mass in the course of contemporary celebrations of the revised Order for Mass, for example. When celebrants are able to develop a habit of embodying the

[13] Congregation for Divine Worship and the Discipline of the Sacraments, Instruction *Liturgiam authenticam* (March 28, 2001), *AAS* 93 (2001): 685–726.

ars celebrandi, this frees the mind from constantly having to make decisions as to how to get from point A to point B, for example. By relying on an established pattern, one grounded in the norms and the tradition, the celebrant and other ministers can be free to enter more deeply in the mystery they are celebrating.

With all this in mind, this work is offered to priests, deacons, seminarians, and all those responsible for the careful preparation of parish liturgies and the training of the Church's liturgical ministers. In taking the approach outlined in these pages, may the beauty and grace of the Church's liturgical celebrations inspire more and more men and women to seek with their whole heart the One who is Beauty itself.

2

Common Gestures

BEFORE PROCEEDING WITH the specifics related to the celebration of Mass, the sacraments and sacramentals, it is necessary at the beginning of this manual to describe the various common gestures which are regularly repeated throughout the course of any liturgical rite. These are the building blocks of the grammar which make up the body language of the Roman liturgy. Celebrants and ministers will want to become so familiar with these gestures that they can be made effortlessly and without hesitation. They should be so internalized as to be second nature. At that point, the celebrant or the minister is free to pray without concern as to how something ought to be done.

Walking

All clergy and ministers walk at a slow and deliberate pace, neither too fast nor too slow. It should never appear that one is in a rush or a hurry. All take care to maintain a straight back, and look ahead, with eyes slightly downcast.[14] All walk with hands joined before them at the chest unless they are carrying some liturgical object. It may be necessary at times, especially at the altar, to take a single step back from one's position. However, in general, one never walks backwards in the sanctuary.[15] Apart from emergencies, all movement ceases during the time of the consecration of the elements during Mass. It is also best to observe this during the proclamation of the Gospel, and preferable during any other reading as well.

[14] Adrian Fortescue, J. B. O'Connell, and Alcuin Reid, eds., *The Ceremonies of the Roman Rite Described*, 15th ed. (New York: Bloomsbury, 2009), 46.

[15] Peter J. Elliott, *Ceremonies Explained for Servers According to the Roman Rite: A Manual for Altar Servers, Acolytes, Sacristans, and Masters of Ceremonies* (San Francisco: Ignatius Press, 2019), 50.

If two servers standing side by side must walk in the opposite direction, after washing the hands of the priest at the altar for example, they turn *toward* one another, and then walk away.[16] When turning in procession either to the left or to the right, the turn is made at a 45 degree angle, more or less, without any pause to turn in place toward the new direction. There should not be an inordinate amount of space between those walking in front or behind anyone in procession. The procession should move as one unit from its beginning to its end.

Walking up and down stairs, as in the case of the altar steps or the steps to the sanctuary, all ascend or descend the steps in a straight line, in the most direct manner. The center of the altar is approached by the center of the altar steps. One approaches the right or left side of the altar or departs from the altar from the right or left side by walking up or down the steps on either side. When going to the chair from the center of the altar, one descends the altar steps at the right-hand side. When departing from the center of the altar at the end of Mass, the celebrant turns and descends the steps at the middle. As an exception, if one is descending the altar steps on one side in order to ascend the altar steps on the opposite side, one walks down the steps from one side to the center on the floor of the sanctuary along the diagonal before ascending the altar steps from the center to the opposite side also along the diagonal.

Bowing

There are two kinds of bows: a bow of the head from the neck and a bow of the body from the waist.[17] One should face the person or object one will reverence in this way, while remaining stationary, with the head or the body lowered directly before oneself without leaning to one side or another. The legs and hips should not move when one bows. One straightens immediately after bowing. There is no pause made while bowing.

The bow of the body, or the profound bow, is made toward the altar when the Blessed Sacrament is not present there, when approaching it or departing from it, or passing in front of it. If one is walking between the altar and the celebrant, one bows to the altar if one is approaching it, or the celebrant if one is approaching him, but not to both. A better solution, depending on the circumstances, is to reverence both the altar and the celebrant with one bow, by passing in front of both the altar and the celebrant. A profound bow is always made whenever

16 Elliott, *Ceremonies Explained for Servers*, 53.
17 *CB*, 68.

approaching or departing the celebrant who is a bishop.[18] A profound bow is made before and after each person or thing incensed, except for the altar and the gifts at the Offertory.[19] When incensing the Blessed Sacrament, this profound bow is made from a kneeling position.[20]

The profound bow is required by the deacon seeking the blessing before the Gospel or by a priest is he is seeking the blessing from the bishop, by the priest preparing himself before the altar to proclaim the Gospel, and during the Creed, at the words, "And by the Holy Spirit was incarnate."[21] The celebrant bows profoundly at the Offertory prayer "With humble spirit and contrite heart" and during Eucharistic Prayer I at "In humble prayer, we ask you, almighty God." He also bows somewhat less profoundly at the words of consecration. The profound bow is required of concelebrants at each elevation. Historically, one customarily bowed profoundly before the one from whom the peace is received, then both parties bowed profoundly to each other after having exchanged the peace.[22] All bow profoundly when receiving the final blessing.

In any case, candle bearers and the cross bearer do not make the profound bow while they are holding their liturgical objects.[23] The deacon does not make a profound bow when carrying the Gospel book.[24]

According to tradition, the celebrant and ministers bow their heads to the crucifix in the sacristy before making their way to the altar. A bow of the head is required at the names of Jesus, Mary, and the saint commemorated at Mass that day whenever they occur in the course of the celebration.[25] One bows the head only once for the names of saints who are typically commemorated together, such as St. Peter and St. Paul, or St. Isaac Jogues, St. Jean de Brébeuf, and companions, for example. Customarily, one bows the head before the priest celebrant whenever approaching him or departing from him, or before and after reading at

18 André Philippe M. Mutel and Peter Freeman, *Cérémonial de la sainte messe à l'usage ordinaire des paroisses suivant le missel romain de 2002 et la pratique léguée du rit romain*, 2nd ed. (Perpignan, France: Éditions Artège, 2012), 40; Peter J. Elliott, *Ceremonies of the Modern Roman Rite: The Eucharist and the Liturgy of the Hours*, rev. ed. (San Francisco: Ignatius Press, 1995), 74.

19 *CB*, 91, *GIRM*, 277.

20 *CB*, 94.

21 On Christmas and on the Annunciation, all kneel on both knees at those same words of the Creed.

22 Fortescue, O'Connell, and Reid, *The Ceremonies of the Roman Rite Described*, 50.

23 *GIRM*, 274.

24 *GIRM*, 173.

25 *GIRM*, 275.

Mass,[26] or when passing before him.[27] The celebrant himself does not respond with a bow of the head, except after being incensed and after the washing of the hands.[28] The cross bearer and candle bearers bow their heads upon arriving at and departing from the sanctuary, rather than make a profound bow to the altar or genuflection.[29] The deacon carrying the Gospel book makes neither the profound bow nor even the bow of the head upon arriving at the sanctuary at the beginning of Mass.[30]

Kneeling

When changing from standing to kneeling, one goes down on one knee first, and then the other. One does not fall on both knees from standing to kneeling. When changing from sitting to kneeling, one stands first. Then one kneels from the standing position. One does not slide from a seated position to a kneeling position. When kneeling, one keeps the head and the back straight, without resting on one's heels.

Genuflecting

Genuflection is distinct from kneeling. Genuflection on one knee is an action of reverence or greeting directed to the Lord in the Blessed Sacrament by the one who comes into the Presence or departs from it. One should be attentive to have come to a complete stop and be oriented clearly in the direction of the Blessed Sacrament before attempting to genuflect. One never raises the front of the alb or cassock before genuflecting or kneeling. Genuflection is done by drawing the right leg back and bending the knee to the ground at the point where the right knee touches the ground momentarily, more or less at the location of the heel of the left foot.[31] One rises immediately, without rushing but without delay, and without any bowing of the head or of the body.[32] More importantly, the act of genuflection should be made with some attention so that the heart might bow before God as well as the knee.

26 Elliott, *Ceremonies of the Modern Roman Rite*, 96.
27 Mutel and Freeman, *Cérémonial de la sainte messe*, 41.
28 Mutel and Freeman, *Cérémonial de la sainte messe*, 42.
29 *GIRM*, 274.
30 *GIRM*, 173.
31 *CB*, 69.
32 Elliot, *Ceremonies of the Modern Roman Rite*, 73.

During the course of Mass, the celebrant makes three genuflections, at each elevation and before Communion.[33] If the priest celebrant is at the altar and has nothing in his hands, he genuflects by placing both hands flat on the altar.[34]

As a general rule, one reverences the Lord in the Most Blessed Sacrament by genuflecting every time one enters in His Presence and when one departs, as well as every time one passes before the Sacrament reserved or exposed. In addition, the Blessed Sacrament, when exposed on the altar in a monstrance or in a ciborium, is reverenced with a genuflection even when approaching it from the side. One genuflects on one knee whether the Blessed Sacrament is reserved in the tabernacle or exposed in a ciborium or monstrance.[35] When taking the Blessed Sacrament from the tabernacle, one opens the door first, and then genuflects. When reposing the Blessed Sacrament to the tabernacle, one genuflects before closing the door.[36] In general, one genuflects before taking the Blessed Sacrament in hand, and after placing it on the altar and departing.

One never genuflects to the Blessed Sacrament when carrying the Blessed Sacrament oneself under either species. In addition, those in procession do not make the genuflection when they pass the place of reservation during that procession.[37] Those carrying the cross and candles in a procession and the deacon carrying the Gospel book do not genuflect.[38] Finally, the *General Instruction* excludes genuflection during the course of Mass itself, other than at those times indicated for the celebrant and concelebrants: "If, however, the tabernacle with the Most Blessed Sacrament is situated in the sanctuary, the Priest, the Deacon, and the other ministers genuflect when they approach the altar and when they depart from it, but not during the celebration of Mass."[39] An exception to this rule exists on Holy Thursday and Corpus Christi, where everyone genuflects to the Blessed Sacrament resting on the altar after the distribution of Communion awaiting the beginning of the procession.[40] By extension, one could argue that the same gesture should be made toward the Blessed Sacrament during Mass on any occasion, whenever one approaches, departs, or passes before the Presence,

33 *GIRM*, 274.
34 Mutel and Freeman, *Cérémonial de la sainte messe*, 34.
35 *CB*, 69.
36 Mutel and Freeman *Cérémonial de la sainte messe*, 35.
37 *CB*, 71.
38 *GIRM*, 173.
39 *GIRM*, 274.
40 *CB*, 306, 389; Mutel and Freeman, *Cérémonial de la sainte messe*, 267–268.

even from the side, for the duration of the time the Blessed Sacrament rests on the altar until the Blessed Sacrament is placed in the tabernacle. *GIRM* 274 limits genuflections directed toward the Blessed Sacrament reserved in the tabernacle, not signs of reverence directed to the Blessed Sacrament exposed on the altar. In addition, the exclusion of genuflection directed to the tabernacle during the course of Mass as indicated in *GIRM* 274 need not be extended to other liturgies which are not the celebration of Mass. In those cases, it seems best to maintain the traditional practice of genuflecting whenever entering and departing the sanctuary where the Blessed Sacrament is reposed, as well as genuflecting whenever one passes before the tabernacle, even during the course of a sacrament or sacramental apart from Mass.

Finally, one genuflects before the cross exposed for the veneration of the faithful on Good Friday, until the beginning of the Easter Vigil.[41]

Placing the Hands

Hands joined means that the hands are held palm open, with the fingers joined, flat against each other, with the right thumb resting over the left thumb.[42] The hands are held this way whenever standing, walking, or kneeling during liturgical celebrations. The hands are held joined before the breast, with the upper arms hanging vertically from the shoulders, and the elbows resting lightly against the torso above the hips. The forearms are raised slightly to the wrist and the hands are raised slightly. The hands are kept joined even when making the genuflection or when bowing. The arms are not lowered when bowing profoundly. Likewise, the hands remain joined when going from standing to kneeling and when rising from kneeling. It is wise, *before rising,* to use the right hand to free the heels from the bottom of the cassock or the alb.

When seated, the open palms of the hand are placed on either knee with the fingers fully extended and joined. When wearing vestments in the sanctuary, one never crosses one's arms or one's legs or feet, nor should the hands be placed under the dalmatic or the chasuble.[43] When standing at the altar, when blessing with the right hand, the left hand rests on the altar. When standing elsewhere, when blessing with the right hand, the left hand rests on the chest.[44] Similarly,

41 *CB*, 69.

42 *CB*, 107, n. 80.

43 Mutel and Freeman, *Cérémonial de la sainte messe*, 43.

44 *CB*, 108.

when standing at the altar and using the left hand to turn the pages of the missal, for example, the right hand rests on the altar.

Making the Sign of the Cross on Oneself

The hands are joined before and after making the Sign of the Cross.[45] When making the Sign of the Cross, the left hand is placed on the chest. The right hand, with the palm open and the fingers extended and joined, begins by touching the forehead with the right hand before the face. Then one draws a vertical line with the right hand from the forehead to a point above where the left hand is held. Then, one makes a horizontal line from the left shoulder to the right shoulder before joining the hands once again.[46] One signs oneself with the cross when standing or kneeling.

Taking Holy Water

At the door of the church or of the sacristy, one takes holy water from the stoup by dipping the index and middle finger of the right hand, the left hand resting on the chest. If two persons are walking side by side in procession, the one closest to the stoup, before signing himself or herself, presents these same two fingers to the companion who touches them with the index and third finger of the right hand to receive the Holy Water.[47] Both then sign themselves as indicated above.

Signing Oneself at the Gospel

The hands are joined before the breast. The deacon or the priest who proclaims the Gospel first traces a Greek cross at the first word of the text with the thumb of the right hand, the left hand resting on the Gospel Book. He traces a Greek cross by moving the entire hand over the first word of the text, not simply moving the thumb. Then, with the left hand resting on the chest, he raises the right hand, fully extended with fingers together, and separates the thumb from the rest of the hand. Holding the hand parallel to the face, he traces a Greek cross with the right thumb on the forehead, the lips, and over the heart (customarily over the left breast) before joining the hands once again.[48] It is best to avoid signing the lips while one is speaking. The faithful do likewise.

45 Mutel and Freeman, *Cérémonial de la sainte messe*, 44.
46 Mutel and Freeman, *Cérémonial de la sainte messe*, 44.
47 Mutel and Freeman, *Cérémonial de la sainte messe*, 76.
48 Mutel and Freeman, *Cérémonial de la sainte messe*, 44.

Striking the Breast

Both hands are joined. Then the left hand is placed below the breast. With the right elbow near the body, the right forearm swings slightly away from the body before being drawn toward the chest. One strikes the chest with the open palm of the right hand, fingers extended and joined. The hand does not make a fist. Then one joins both hands.[49] When striking the breast at the altar, as during "To us, also, your servants," during Eucharistic Prayer I, the left hand rests on the corporal, not on the chest.[50]

[49] Mutel and Freeman, *Cérémonial de la sainte messe*, 45.

[50] Mutel and Freeman, *Cérémonial de la sainte messe*, 142.

3

Preparations before Mass

Even the humblest tasks associated with the preparations for Mass and those which follow the conclusion of Mass can be inspired by the traditional practice of the Roman Rite (see *GIRM*, 42). Many of these gestures, although entirely practical, can take on religious significance when done attentively, devoutly, and in a recollected manner. They can create an atmosphere of calm which is conducive to prayer, and can signal to all those involved that something out of the ordinary is about to take place. Attention even to these details can deepen the experience of Mass itself, especially in the young, who are most often charged with carrying out these necessary functions.

Requisites for the Celebration of Mass[51]

In the sacristy:

- Matching vestments in the color of the Mass for the priest and deacon(s)
- Matching vestments for concelebrants in the color of the Mass, or white if necessary
- Cassock and surplice or albs for ministers and servers
- Book of Gospels (unless it is placed flat on the altar prior to the beginning of Mass); the book is covered in cloth the same color and material as the vestments for Mass or with a precious cover

[51] See *CB*, 125; André Philippe M. Mutel and Peter Freeman, *Cérémonial de la sainte messe à l'usage ordinaire des paroisses suivant le missel romain de 2002 et la pratique léguée du rit romain*, 2nd ed. (Perpignan, France: Éditions Artège, 2012), 48–68; Peter J. Elliott, *Ceremonies of the Modern Roman Rite*, rev. ed. (San Francisco: Ignatius Press, 1995), 88–90.

- Censer and incense boat, charcoals, and incense
- Processional cross, unless it remains at the altar
- Two matching candlesticks with lighted candles
- Two, four, or six torches, all of the same design
- *At the ambo:*
- The lectionary for Mass open to the proper page; the lectionary is covered in cloth the color of the Mass
- The text of the Universal Prayer, unless it will be needed elsewhere in the sanctuary
- An antependium or fall in the color of the Mass

At the altar:

- One or more altar cloths, at least one of which reaches to the floor on both sides, the uppermost cloth being white
- Two, four, or six candles, all of the same design
- Crucifix on or near the altar, or stand for the processional cross near the altar
- An antependium or frontal in the color of the Mass in the same material as the fall at the ambo
- If the Gospel book is placed on the altar before the beginning of Mass, it is placed at the center, flat, face down so that the open edge of the book is on the left.[52]

At the tabernacle:

- Sanctuary lamp burning
- At least matching two candles burning during the course of Mass if the tabernacle is not located on the altar
- A corporal, unfolded on the ledge in front of the tabernacle or folded in a burse of the same color as the veil on the tabernacle
- The key, unless placed at the credence table
- An ablution cup or bowl with finger towel, unless placed at the credence table

52 Mutel and Freeman, *Cérémonial de la sainte messe*, 64.

- A veil, in white or the color of the Mass as at the ambo or the altar, covering the tabernacle or at least covering its door

At the chair:

- The Roman Missal open to the proper page, unless the missal is carried in procession by a server at the beginning of Mass on certain days; the missal is covered in cloth the color of the Mass
- The text of the Universal Prayer for the celebrant if needed instead of the missal
- The chants of the Mass for the celebrant and deacon
- The vessel(s) of water (and salt) to be blessed if used at the beginning of Mass
- Cloth cover for the chair, or at least the seat, in the color of the Mass as at the ambo and the altar

At the credence table:

- A white cloth covering the top of the credence table and falling to the floor on both sides
- The chalice, purificator, paten with host covered by the pall and by a chalice veil in the same color and material as the vestments of the Mass or white
- The burse in the same color and material as the chalice veil containing the corporal(s) and even the purificators needed at the altar, placed on the chalice and veil
- Another corporal, folded (and in a burse the color of the Mass), if the purifications will take place at the credence table
- Other ciboria, with or without covers, with hosts for the Communion of the faithful as needed
- Other cups with wine, with or without palls or placed behind the chalice and covered with the veil
- Purificators as needed, placed under the veil of the chalice or in the burse or unfolded over the main chalice itself
- The cruets of wine and water on their platter, unless these are located elsewhere

- Pitcher of water, basin, and towel
- Communion plate(s) for the Communion of the faithful
- White humeral veil,[53] if the tabernacle is located outside the sanctuary; the humeral veil can be folded on the credence table or placed over all the items at the credence table with the burse on top[54]
- Missal stand covered in cloth the same color as the Mass or a cushion for the missal made of cloth of the same color as the Mass
- A set of handbells, unless needed elsewhere
- An ablution cup or bowel with finger towel, unless it is placed at the tabernacle
- Key to the tabernacle, unless it is placed in the tabernacle prior to the beginning of Mass
- Room at the far corners of the credence table to place the processional candles

In a convenient place:

- Baskets for the offerings of the faithful
- Some of the bread and wine for presentation, perhaps along with the water and other gifts as circumstances suggest
- Microphones in the locations where they will be needed

The Preparation of the Priest

The *General Instruction of the Roman Missal* describes very little of what is intended to take place prior to the beginning of Mass. It recommends silence in the church and in the sacristy prior to the celebration.[55] If incense is used in the procession, it is blessed prior to the procession, either in the sacristy or some other suitable location.[56] The *General Instruction* does not describe the manner in which the sacred ministers vest, but an appendix to the missal provides several prayers for the preparation for Mass which the celebrant may use *ad libitum*. A fuller

53 *CB*, 328; Mutel and Freeman, *Cérémonial de la sainte messe*, 175, n. 315.

54 In this case, the chalice veil and burse used should also be white and made of the same material as the humeral veil, even if this is not the color of the Mass of that day.

55 *GIRM*, 45.

56 *GIRM*, 120.

description of the gestures and postures which accompany the preparation of the ordained ministers for Mass is found in the *Ritus servandus missae* of 1962.

The celebrant may spend some time in the church prior to Mass in prayer. He might pray one of the hours of the Divine Office, whichever hour is most suitable. He then goes to the sacristy where the vestments and everything needed for Mass have been prepared. He sets the ribbons of the missal to the appropriate texts, and then washes his hands, saying the prayer "Give strength to my hands, Lord," while doing so.[57] Then he prepares the chalice if necessary, and verifies that wine, water, and sufficient hosts have been prepared. He then proceeds to vest for Mass. The vestments for Mass are normally prepared on the vesting cabinet in front of the sacristy crucifix or on a table prepared for that purpose. They are placed on the cabinet in reverse order, meaning what will be worn first is uppermost and so on. Normally, the celebrant's vestments are in the middle of the vesting case, with the deacon's vestments to the right. The deacon may vest first in order to assist the celebrant in vesting. Or, the celebrant and deacon may vest simultaneously, assisted by servers.

First, taking up the amice at the two upper corners where the strings attach to the body of the amice, the celebrant kisses the amice in the middle where the cross is. Swinging his right arm over his head, he places the amice on his head momentarily, before bringing it down around the neck and shoulder. Meanwhile, he says the prayer "Lord, set the helmet of salvation." He arranges the amice at the neck to cover his collar entirely, placing the right side over the left side in front, and crosses the strings across his chest and under his arms, wraps them around his back, and then ties them in front before his chest. Then he puts on the alb, first putting it over his head if necessary, and then the right arm through the sleeve, followed by the left arm. As he does so, he prays, "Purify me, Lord." Using both hands, he girds himself with the cincture, which has been passed to him by the deacon or server standing behind him. Normally, the cincture is doubled, with its tassels held in the celebrant's right hand, and the other end held in his left hand. While taking the cincture, he prays, "Lord, gird me about." Making a loop in the left hand at the end of the doubled length of the cincture by folding the end upon itself, he passes the two tasseled ends through the loop with the right hand and tightens the knot at the front. Taking the stole with both hands, he kisses at the cross on the neck, and says, "Lord, restore the stole of

[57] Elliott, *Ceremonies of the Modern Roman Rite*, 332–333.

immortality." He adjusts the stole around his neck so that it hangs equally from both shoulders. The celebrant uses the two ends of the cincture to secure the stole on both sides. With the knot of the cincture at the front of his body, the celebrant takes the length of the cincture on either side and places it over the stole before passing a portion of each length (not the entire length) of the cincture under the portion of the cincture around his waist to create a loop below the waist. He passes the tassels of each end of the cincture through these loops on either side, and adjusts the knot in the front and the loops to each side. Finally, the takes the chasuble as he prays, "Lord, You said: My yoke is easy." The deacon or server may assist him so that the chasuble falls freely on all sides.[58] If a chasuble of Roman design is worn, the interior ribbons are worn in the following way. First, the celebrant crosses them before his chest. Then he passes them behind his back, and then brings the ribbons forward in order to tie them before the chest, just as he did with the amice.

A deacon vests in the same way as the celebrant. He also may say the appropriate prayers as he vests.

If time remains before Mass, the celebrant may remain standing in silence before the sacristy cross, or he may continue the prayers of preparation found in the missal.

Preparations of the Servers and Other Ministers

Historically, a sacristy separate from the vesting sacristy of the priest and deacon was set apart for the vesting of the servers. Today, such a space might also be set apart for the laypersons reading at Mass, or serving as cantors or extraordinary ministers of Holy Communion. Prior to the beginning of Mass, once the servers themselves are vested, they may assist the celebrant and deacon in vesting. Instituted acolytes and instituted lectors should vest during this time as well. Deputed readers and extraordinary ministers of Holy Communion might vest or not depending on local custom.[59]

The thurifer can prepare the burning charcoals if incense is used in the entrance procession. A server removes the dust cover from the altar and brings it into the sacristy. One of the last preparations prior to the beginning of Mass is lighting the candles of the altar. This is usually the responsibility of one of the older servers. During the Easter season, the Easter candle is located in the sanctuary, either next to the

58 See Fortescue, O'Connell, and Reid, *The Ceremonies of the Roman Rite Described*, 64–65.

59 *GIRM*, 339.

ambo or in the center of the sanctuary. The Easter candle is lit first, before lighting the candles of the altar. At the altar, the candlesticks are normally spaced equally on either side of the altar cross in a straight line at the back of the altar. The server customarily begins by lighting the candles on the right side of the altar as the server faces the altar, standing on the same side as the priest does during Mass.[60] The server begins by lighting the candle closest to the altar cross (or the center of the altar) first, and moving from the center of the altar to the right side, lights the other candles. The server then returns to the middle, bows, and begins lighting the candles on the left side of the altar, beginning with the candle closest to the altar cross or center of the altar, and working outward from the center to the left edge of the altar. After bowing once again to the center of the altar, the server returns to the sanctuary. If the altar candles are placed in two rows in either side of the altar rather than in a single row across the back of the altar, the server begins on the right side of the altar as one faces it, starting with the candle the furthest away. The server continues by lighting the candles progressively closer to himself or herself. The server bows to the altar at the center. Then, the server does the same on the left side of the altar. While lighting the Easter candle and the altar candles, whenever one passes before the Blessed Sacrament reserved in the sanctuary, one genuflects each time. Any other candles in the sanctuary are lit after the Easter candle and those at the altar. Finally, upon returning to the sacristy, the server lights the processional candles.

Meanwhile in the sacristy, if incense is used in the opening procession, the celebrant turns to his right to face the thurifer who presents the thurible with burning coals to him. The deacon holds the incense boat in his left hand. The deacon hands the spoon to the celebrant with his right hand, and transfers the incense boat from his left hand to his right hand. The celebrant receives the spoon in his right hand and imposes incense three times while his left hand rests on his chest. He returns the spoon to the deacon, who receives it in his right hand. Then he blesses the incense with his right hand in the shape of Greek cross, his left hand resting on his chest, saying nothing.

The priest says, "Let us go forth in peace," and all answer, "In the name of Christ. Amen." Then all face the sacristy crucifix and bow. At the door of the sacristy, a server may ring a bell to alert the faithful that Mass is about to begin. Also, all in the procession take holy water, using the index and middle fingers of

[60] Elliott, *Ceremonies of the Modern Roman Rite*, 317; Mutel and Freeman, *Céremonial de la sainte messe*, 63–64, 63 n. 37; Fortescue, O'Connell, and Reid, *The Ceremonies of the Roman Rite Described*, 115.

their right hands, as they enter the church two by two. The person closest to the holy water stoup extends the right hand and passes the holy water to the other server next to him or her. Both then make the Sign of the Cross before joining their hands once again.

If the celebrant and servers enter the sanctuary from the sacristy through doors on either side of the altar, as at a weekday Mass for example, normally they approach through doors on the Gospel side of the altar (the left side of the altar as one faces the from the nave), and depart from the altar at the end of Mass through doors on the epistle side of the altar (the right side of the altar as one faces it from the nave).[61] All face forward with eyes slightly downcast during the entrance procession.

[61] Fortescue, O'Connell, and Reid, *The Ceremonies of the Roman Rite Described*, 65.

4

The Use of Incense at Mass

THE *GENERAL INSTRUCTION OF THE ROMAN MISSAL* provides for the optional use of incense at any Mass. It identifies five points at which incense can be used: during the entrance procession, when honoring the altar and its cross at the beginning of Mass, at the proclamation of the Gospel, during the preparation of the gifts, and during the elevations of the eucharistic species.[62] In each case, the traditional gestures of the ministers involved can help to make each of these parts of Mass more graceful and more conducive to prayer. In part, the use incense symbolizes our prayers rising up to throne of God.

The traditional manuals often speak about single swings of the censer and double swings of the censer.[63] A single swing, as when incensing the altar, involves a simple lifting of the censer forward.[64] A double swing, as when incensing the Gospel book or a person for example, involves not only lifting the censer but giving it a forward thrust of energy such that it swings forward and backward on its own before returning to its still point.[65] The censer is swung back and forth two times for the incensation of relics and image of the saints exposed for public veneration.[66] Otherwise, the censer is swung back and forth three times for the incensation of all other objects or persons,[67] except the altar, which is incensed

62 *GIRM*, 276.

63 André Philippe M. Mutel and Peter Freeman, *Cérémonial de la sainte messe à l'usage ordinaire des paroisses suivant le missel romain de 2002 et la pratique léguée du rit romain*, 2nd ed. (Perpignan, France: Éditions Artège, 2012), 82, n. 28.

64 See *CB*, 93.

65 See *CB*, 92: "The censer is swung *back and forth*" (emphasis added).

66 *CB*, 92.

67 *CB*, 92.

with a series of single swings forward.[68] The Blessed Sacrament exposed in a ciborium or a monstrance is always incensed from a kneeling position.[69]

During the Entrance Procession

Historically, whenever incense was used at the beginning of Mass, the use of a processional cross and processional candles always accompanied it. According to the current *General Instruction,* incense can be used at any Mass celebrated by a priest. Nevertheless, its use still demands a sufficient number of ministers at any given celebration. Thus, there may be times when it is more practical to forego the use of incense at the opening procession of Mass even if one desires to use it at other points during the same Mass.

If incense is used during the opening procession of Mass, the celebrant imposes incense in the sacristy or in another location where the procession will actually begin. The thurifer opens the censer, holding the ring of the chain(s) in his left hand and the chain(s) close to bowl of the censer in his right hand. He holds the bowl of the censer up, slightly below eye level for the celebrant. Normally, the deacon or another server holds the open incense boat in his left hand and presents the spoon to the celebrant with his right hand. Then, transferring the boat to his right hand, the deacon holds the incense boat close to the bowl of the censer, with his left hand resting on his chest. The celebrant, meanwhile, holding the spoon in his right hand and with his left hand resting on his chest, imposes incense three times before returning the spoon to the deacon. The deacon then transfers the incense boat to his left hand once again in order to receive the spoon with his right. The celebrant joins his hands and then, with his left hand to his chest, makes the Sign of the Cross in the shape of a Greek cross toward the open censer with his right hand, saying nothing, before joining his hands once again. The thurifer closes the censer and holds the censer in his right hand at the ring of the chain(s). Meanwhile, the thurifer also holds the boat in his left hand before his chest, unless another server holds it for the thurifer. The thurifer and any server assisting as boat bearer walking to the thurifer's left then go to the head of the procession to await its beginning.

As the procession makes its way to the sanctuary, the thurifer, holding the censer from its ring in his right hand, gently swings the censer backwards and forwards. In some larger churches, depending on the circumstances, the thurifer

[68] *CB,* 93.

[69] *CB,* 94.

may swing the censer from right to the left as he goes forward, then from left to right before him. Whichever method is chosen should be proportionate to the size of the church and the importance of the occasion. Upon arriving at the sanctuary, the thurifer bows his head and proceeds to a position to the right of the location where the celebrant will stand at the altar. If the altar is oriented to the liturgical east, the thurifer will go the right; if the altar is oriented to the assembly, the thurifer will go to the left in order to arrive at the celebrant's right at the altar. If needed, the thurifer or another server can add more incense at this time.

At the Veneration of the Altar

Once the celebrant has kissed the altar at the center, the thurifer stands to his immediate right. If incense was not used in the entrance procession, either because of a lack of servers or some other practical reason, the server acting as thurifer can simply approach the celebrant at the altar from the sacristy or from an incense stand in the sanctuary where the censer with burning coals was left prior to the beginning of the entrance procession. At the center of the altar, the celebrant imposes incense for the first time if incense has not been used in the entrance procession. In this case, the celebrant rests his left hand on the altar while blessing the incense just imposed with his right hand. The thurifer passes the censer to a deacon or a master of ceremonies, who in turn passes it to the celebrant. The celebrant receives the ring of the chain(s) of the censer in his left hand and the chains near the bowl in his right hand. Historically, the rubrics have made no accommodation for celebrants who are left-handed. The deacon or the thurifer passing the censer to him makes sure to place the ring of the chains in the celebrant's left hand and the chains near the bowl of the censer in the celebrant's right hand. This means that the minister will need to hold the censer in the opposite manner so as to pass them directly to the celebrant without any confusion. The deacon, or in his absence a master of ceremonies or another server, may accompany the celebrant to his right as he incenses the altar, or the celebrant may do so unaccompanied.

Immediately after receiving the thurible, the celebrant begins by incensing the altar cross, if that cross is directly before him. The celebrant, with the left hand holding the ring at his chest, bows to the altar cross, and incenses the cross with three double swings, then bows to the cross once again. When swinging the censer, he holds the bowl elevated slightly above eye level. After incensing the altar cross, he begins to incense the altar with no further reverence.[70] Historically,

[70] *CB*, 91.

all the surfaces of the altar, both vertical (such as the faces of each side) and horizontal (the *mensa* of the altar itself) are incensed with single swings.

The incensation of a freestanding altar is carried out in the following way regardless of which direction the celebrant will be oriented for Mass. (See figure 1.) First, the celebrant incenses the right side of the altar top (the *mensa*) with three single swings as he walks from the middle of the side of the altar where he will stand for Mass to the right-hand edge of the altar. Arriving at the right corner of the altar, he drops his right hand to incense the vertical surface at the right-hand end of the altar with two swings. Continuing in a counterclockwise direction with a measured pace, he then incenses the entire vertical face of the long side of the altar, opposite from where he will stand for Mass. He incenses that entire vertical side of the altar opposite where he will stand with six single swings, equally spaced apart. He bows to the altar at its center.[71] He then turns again in a counterclockwise direction and incenses the other vertical end of the altar with two single swings. Arriving at the left-hand corner of the same side from which he began, that is, the side where he will stand for Mass, the celebrant remains stationary at the corner and from that position incenses the left-hand side of the top of the altar (the *mensa*) with three separate single swings of the censer from the left edge toward the center of the altar. Having completed the incensation of the entire top (the *mensa*) of the altar, he then resumes his measured pace along the entire side of the altar from which he began. The celebrant now incenses the entire vertical portion of the side where he will stand for Mass. He does so with six distinct single swings equally spaced apart, bowing to the altar at its center.[72] He concludes his circumambulation of the altar at the right-hand corner. There he hands the censer back to the deacon or thurifer, and proceeds directly to his chair.

If the altar cross is not located directly in front of the celebrant when standing at the altar, he begins by incensing the altar. When he arrives at a point at the altar closest to where the altar cross is positioned, he stops there, bows, incenses the cross with three double swings, bows again, and resumes the incensation of the altar where he left off.

At the Gospel

When incense is used in the Gospel procession, its use has also been accompanied by the presence of two servers bearing candles. Incense and candles can be used even if a separate Gospel book is not used, as was historically the case in a sung Mass

[71] Mutel and Freeman, *Cérémonial de la sainte messe,* 84.

[72] Mutel and Freeman, *Cérémonial de la sainte messe,* 84.

without deacon or subdeacon.[73] At other times, such as Palm Sunday or at funerals, two acolytes without candles accompanied the minister who proclaimed the Gospel, without the service of a thurifer.[74] Conversely, there seems to be no precedent for the minister of the Gospel to be accompanied by the thurifer alone without such servers, with or without processional candles.[75] In that case, it might be better to have at least one additional server assisting the deacon along with the thurifer when two additional servers are not available to serve as candle bearers.

The celebrant imposes incense for the Gospel procession at the chair. The *General Instruction* indicates that "all rise" as the Alleluia or other Gospel Acclamation is sung.[76] The *Ceremonial of Bishops* also confirms that "all rise, except the bishop, as the Alleluia begins."[77] Thus, if the celebrant imposes incense while the Alleluia is being sung, he clearly does so from a standing position. The thurifer will likewise be standing before him at the chair, as will the deacon, who assists him with the boat in his left hand after presenting him the spoon with his right hand.

However, the rubrics of the Order for Mass of 1965 made clear that the celebrant imposed incense while *seated*, and then rose to bless the deacon.[78] Thus it would seem that if incense is imposed during the time after the conclusion of the second reading and before the Gospel Acclamation begins, as is the custom in some churches, or during the singing of the Tract during Lent, for example, when there is no Gospel Acclamation properly speaking, then there is precedent for the celebrant, even one who is a priest, to remain seated to do so.[79] In that case, the thurifer, depending on his height and the arrangement of the chair, might either stand to present the censer, or kneel if this is more convenient.[80] The deacon could stand next to the celebrant to minister the spoon, or, depending on the circumstances, kneel before the celebrant to minister both the incense boat and spoon.

The thurifer opens the censer and, using his right hand, holds the bowl of the censer elevated before the celebrant, slightly below eye level. The celebrant imposes incense three times with the spoon in his right hand, saying nothing. If he is seated, his left hand rests on his left knee; if he is standing, his left hand rests

73 Adrian Fortescue, J. B. O'Connell, and Alcuin Reid, eds., *The Ceremonies of the Roman Rite Described,* 15th ed. (New York: Bloomsbury, 2009), 165.

74 Fortescue, O'Connell, and Reid, *The Ceremonies of the Roman Rite Described,* 158, 328.

75 Mutel and Freeman, *Cérémonial de la sainte messe,* 71.

76 *GIRM,* 131.

77 *CB,* 140.

78 *RM* 1965, "Order for Mass," no. 42.

79 Mutel and Freeman, *Cérémonial de la sainte messe,* 95.

80 Mutel and Freeman, *Cérémonial de la sainte messe,* 100.

on his chest. The celebrant returns the spoon to the deacon or master of ceremonies, who receives it in his right hand and places it in the incense boat he holds in his left hand. The thurifer closes the censer and hold the chain(s) at the ring in his right hand. If necessary, the deacon or the master of ceremonies, using the right hand, returns the boat to the thurifer, who holds it in his left hand. The thurifer joins the two servers with candles so as to accompany the deacon to the ambo. The celebrant blesses the deacon; the deacon may go to the altar to take up the Gospel book, if one is used. The thurifer leads the servers, who walk side by side, and the deacon to the ambo. The group does not stop to reverence the altar on the way to the ambo.[81]

Once at the ambo, the thurifer stands to the deacon's right. Once the deacon has announced the Gospel, the deacon turns to his right to receive the censer. The thurifer places the ring of the chain(s) in the deacon's left hand with his own right hand, and the chain(s) near the bowl in the deacon's right hand with his own left hand. The deacon, bowing to the Gospel book, incenses it with three double swings, one to the center, one to the left, and one to the right. He bows again to the Gospel book before returning the censer to the thurifer. The thurifer, holding the censer at the ring in his right hand, steps slightly back from the deacon to his right, and gently swings the censer to the left and right during the reading of the Gospel.[82] After the reading of the Gospel, the thurifer returns the censer to the sacristy or other location, pausing to bow to the altar with the servers. The same procedure is followed if a concelebrant, or even the celebrant himself, reads the Gospel in the absence of a deacon.

At the Preparation of the Gifts

While the Roman Missal enumerates five different occasions during Mass when incense can be used *ad libitum*, historically there have been two degrees of solemnity in the use of incense. Either incense was used at all the possible occasions when servers with candles could accompany the entrance and Gospel processions, or incense was simply used at the Offertory and at the elevations, without being used at any other point in Mass. Thus, it seems that if a choice has to be made as to when to use incense during Mass, priority should be given to the use of incense at the Offertory and the elevations above all.[83]

81 Mutel and Freeman, *Cérémonial de la sainte messe*, 102.
82 Mutel and Freeman, *Cérémonial de la sainte messe*, 104.
83 Mutel and Freeman, *Cérémonial de la sainte messe*, 71.

During the preparation of the altar, after the celebrant rises from saying the prayer "With humble spirit and contrite heart," he turns to his right, without stepping away from the center of the altar. The deacon takes a step back to receive the incense boat. The thurifer approaches the celebrant within an arm's length of him. The thurifer passes the incense boat to the deacon. The deacon holds the open incense boat in his left hand and presents the spoon to the celebrant with the right hand. The thurifer opens the censer and holds the bowl elevated so that the celebrant can impose incense while standing erect. The deacon holds the boat in his right hand close to the bowl of the censer. The celebrant imposes incense three times, holding his left hand to his chest. Then returning the spoon to the deacon, he places his left hand on the altar while blessing the incense with his open right hand in the shape of a Greek cross, saying nothing.[84] The deacon or the master of ceremonies first places the ring of the chain(s) of the censer in the celebrant's left hand with his own right hand, and then places the chain(s) near the bowl in the celebrant's right hand with his own left hand.

The celebrant begins by incensing the gifts, with no further sign of reverence to the altar.[85] Traditionally, while the celebrant is incensing the gifts, the deacon places the joined fingers of his right hand on the base of the chalice to steady it.[86] He keeps his left hand at his chest during this time. The celebrant holds the ring of the chain close to his chest with his left hand. He swings the censer from the wrist of his right hand, and controls its movements with the thumb, index, and third finger of his right hand. He may incense the gifts with three double swings or by making the Sign of the Cross with the censer over them.[87] (See figure 2.) He makes the Sign of the Cross by swinging the censer in the same way he would make the Sign of the Cross with his hand, always keeping the censer in the same horizontal plane. Authors are divided whether the rubrics means a single Sign of the Cross, or three Signs of the Cross, according to the traditional practice.[88]

Having incensed the gifts, the celebrant and deacon bow to the altar cross. The celebrant incenses it with three swings if the altar cross is directly before them. Customarily, the deacon moves the chalice to the right of the corporal when the celebrant incenses the altar cross in order to prevent any accidents.[89] The deacon

84 *CB*, 108.

85 *CB*, 91; *GIRM*, 277.

86 Mutel and Freeman, *Cérémonial de la sainte messe*, 120, n. 150.

87 *GIRM*, 277.

88 Mutel and Freeman, *Cérémonial de la sainte messe*, 120.

89 Fortescue, O'Connell, and Reid, *The Ceremonies of the Roman Rite Described*, 139.

replaces the chalice to the middle of the corporal, and the celebrant and the deacon bow after having incensed the altar cross. If the altar cross is not located directly in front of the celebrant when standing at the altar, he begins by incensing the altar. When he arrives at a point at the altar closest to where the altar cross is positioned, he stops there, bows, incenses the cross with three double swings, bows again, and resumes the incensation of the altar where he left off.

Having incensed the gifts and altar cross, the celebrant then begins to incense the altar in the same way he did at the beginning of Mass, by first turning to his right and circling the altar in a counterclockwise direction. (See figure 1.) All the surfaces of the altar, both vertical, such as the faces of each side, and horizontal, the *mensa* of the altar itself, are incensed. The deacon or the master of ceremonies may hold back the folds of the celebrant's chasuble if necessary with his left or right hand, depending on the circumstances, and accompany him as he incenses the altar, unless the celebrant prefers to do so unaccompanied. If the celebrant is accompanied by a deacon or server, this person bows with the celebrant whenever the celebrant bows. The incensation of a freestanding altar is carried out in the same manner described above at the beginning of Mass. Historically, a server or the master of ceremonies removed the missal from the altar at this time so that the celebrant could more easily incense the entire top (*mensa*) of the altar on the left side.[90] That person stands at some distance from the altar, facing its left-hand end. After the incensation of the entire *mensa* of the altar is completed, the server or the master of ceremonies then replaces the missal at an angle to the left of the corporal but off of the corporal. Having concluded his circumambulation of the altar, as already described, at the right corner of the same side where he began, the celebrant hands the censer to the deacon. The celebrant stands at the right-hand side of the altar, perpendicular to it.

The deacon or, in his absence, the thurifer, takes a step back and incenses the celebrant. The deacon or the thurifer holds the bowl of the censer elevated before the celebrant, slightly below eye level. He bows, incenses the celebrant with three double swings, and then bows again.[91] The celebrant, likewise, bows to the deacon each time.[92] The deacon or the thurifer then proceeds to incense those in the sanctuary, beginning with any concelebrants and proceeding with the remaining

90 Mutel and Freeman, *Cérémonial de la sainte messe*, 120.

91 *GIRM*, 277; *CB*, 91–92.

92 Although not specified in the rubrics, this is the historical practice. See Peter J. Elliott, *Ceremonies of the Modern Roman Rite*, rev. ed. (San Francisco: Ignatius Press, 1995), 146 and Fortescue, O'Connell, and Reid, *The Ceremonies of the Roman Rite Described*, 50.

ministers. He incenses the concelebrants, first those to his right and then those to his left, as he faces them standing in the middle of the sanctuary either before or behind the altar as the circumstances suggest. He first bows to the group on the right and incenses them with three double swings, one to the center of the group, one to the left, and one to the right, and then bows. He repeats the same gestures with the group to his left in the sanctuary. He then does the same with the ministers in the sanctuary, first to his right, and then to his left. Each group to be incensed stands in turn in order to receive this mark of respect, bowing before and after. The deacon or the thurifer then turns to the assembly and incenses them as a group. He bows to them and incenses with the double swings, one to the center of the assembly, one to the left, and one to the right before bowing and departing.

Traditionally, the deacon himself was incensed. After the deacon incenses the celebrant and concelebrants in the sanctuary, he may pass the censer to the thurifer. The thurifer bows, incenses the deacon with three swings, and bows again before proceeding to incense the remaining servers and the assembly as described above.[93] However, at Requiem Masses in the past, only the celebrant himself was incensed, not any of the ministers or the assembly. A celebrant might also follow this custom at Masses for the dead.

At the Elevations

Connected to the incensation of the gifts, altar, cross, and celebrant is the incensation of both the Sacred Host and Precious Blood after their respective consecrations. While the Roman Missal places this among those times when incense can be used at Mass *ad libitum*, the traditional practice has been to join the use of incense at the preparation of the gifts with the use of incense at the two elevations.[94] The form of the Requiem Mass found in the missals prior to 1969 establishes the precedent where incense can be used at the elevations even without two or four torches being used.[95]

When incense is used at the elevations, the thurifer exits the sacristy holding the censer by the length of its chain in his right hand. The thurifer or another server has already imposed incense in the sacristy or some other discreet place. The thurifer leads the torch bearers (two, four, or six depending on the circumstances) out of the sacristy during the singing of the *Sanctus*. Whenever possible, the torch bearers walk in pairs, carrying the torches in their outside hands, the

93 Mutel and Freeman, *Cérémonial de la sainte messe*, 121.

94 *GIRM*, 276; Mutel and Freeman, *Cérémonial de la sainte messe*, 71.

95 Fortescue, O'Connell, and Reid, *The Ceremonies of the Roman Rite Described*, 158–159.

other hand resting on the chest as usual. They form up in front of the altar in a straight line across the sanctuary, either within the sanctuary or just outside it, with the thurifer in the middle. Or, they can place themselves in two lines facing each other on either side of the sanctuary, again with the thurifer standing between the two lines in the middle of the sanctuary. (See figure 3.) All kneel when the assembly kneels, that is, at the conclusion of the *Sanctus*.

At the elevation of the Body of the Lord, the thurifer, still kneeling, bows from the waist and then incenses the Blessed Sacrament with three double swings using his right hand to elevate the censer to the height of his face. He bows profoundly once again at the waist. The same procedure is repeated after the consecration of the Precious Blood. At the doxology which concludes the Eucharistic Prayer, the thurifer leads the torch bearers back to the sacristy.[96] The censer is put away and the torches are extinguished.

An additional deacon might incense the Blessed Sacrament at the two elevations instead of the thurifer. This deacon leads the torch bearers to their places and incenses the Blessed Sacrament from their midst, or he might go to his place alone if torches are not used. If torches are not used at the elevations, the deacon could kneel directly in front of the altar to incense the Blessed Sacrament in the manner described above. Or, he could kneel facing the end of the altar to the right of the priest and incense the Blessed Sacrament from there. This is the customary position in the Requiem Mass found in the missals prior to 1969.[97] This position has the advantage of being closer to the sacristy where the censer will be loaded and brought to the deacon. It may also be less disruptive for the deacon to leave the right side of the priest to kneel at the right side of the altar than to walk around the altar in order to position himself in the middle of the sanctuary facing the altar.[98]

According to tradition, the censer is not carried out in procession at the end of Mass, unless some ceremony where it will be needed immediately follows Mass.[99]

96 Elliott, *Ceremonies of the Modern Roman Rite*, 149.

97 Fortescue, O'Connell, and Reid, *The Ceremonies of the Roman Rite Described*, 159.

98 Mutel and Freeman, *Cérémonial de la sainte messe*, 130.

99 Elliott, *Ceremonies of the Modern Roman Rite*, 152; Mutel and Freeman, *Cérémonial de la sainte messe*, 181.

5 The Introductory Rites

The entrance procession at Mass is described in four locations in the *General Instruction of the Roman Missal*: 1) nos. 120–123 for Mass celebrated without a deacon, 2) nos. 171–174 for Mass celebrated with a deacon, 3) nos. 210–211 in the case where Mass is concelebrated by a number of priests, and 4) no. 256 in a Mass at which only one minister participates. The entrance procession, like the other processions at Mass, is considered among those "gestures" and "actions" which are meant to be determined by the provisions of the *General Instruction* itself as well as by the traditional practice of the Roman Rite and by what serves "the common spiritual good" of those taking part.[100]

Entering the Church

Ordinarily, the procession begins when someone rings a bell at the door of the sacristy where the procession begins. If the vesting sacristy is in the back of the church, the procession can directly proceed down the center aisle. If the sacristy is located in the front of the church, the procession can make its way through the entire length of the church by the side aisle and then down the center aisle, or part way up the side aisle and across to the center aisle. Holy water is taken at the door of the sacristy, as described earlier in chapter 3, or at the church door.[101]

Two servers holding candles lead the procession, walking side by side. (See figure 4.) An instituted acolyte or another server may hold the processional cross

100 *GIRM*, 42, 44.

101 André Philippe M. Mutel and Peter Freeman, *Cérémonial de la sainte messe à l'usage ordinaire des paroisses suivant le missel romain de 2002 et la pratique léguée du rit romain*, 2nd ed. (Perpignan, France: Éditions Artège, 2012), 76–77.

between them, walking with the candle bearers side by side in one line. According to the traditional practice, the candle bearers do not walk several paces behind the processional cross, since their purpose is to the light the way for the procession. If the pathway of the procession becomes too narrow for the three servers to walk side by side, the candle bearers walk *ahead* of the cross for as long as needed.[102] If a sufficient number of servers is not available, it is possible to omit the processional cross and retain the two processional candles. In fact, this was formerly the common practice at any solemn Mass celebrated by a priest. Historically, the use of the processional cross was reserved to Masses celebrated by a bishop or to Masses celebrated by a priest which involved some kind of special procession, as on Palm Sunday or at a funeral, for example. Whenever used, the processional cross is always carried with the image of Jesus Crucified facing forward in the direction of the procession.[103]

The servers holding the candlesticks should be of the same height as much as possible in order to be able to hold the two candles at the same height. When holding the candlestick, the server on the right places his left hand on the foot of the candlestick and his right hand on the node at the middle of the candlestick. The server on the left does the opposite, placing his right hand on the foot of the candlestick and his left hand on the node.[104] The Roman custom is to hold the top of the candlestick directly before one's face in such a way as to be able to see where one is processing. In addition to accompanying the procession at the beginning and end of Mass, these same candlesticks are used for the proclamation of the Gospel reading.[105]

Other servers follow behind the cross and candles. They walk two by two according to their height or rank. If there is an odd number of such servers, the last one customarily walks alone behind and between the two in front of him. Instituted lectors or other readers may walk behind the servers, either side by side if there are more than one, or directly behind and between the two lines of servers if there is only one. The deacon, wearing the stole and dalmatic, and holding the Gospel book, walks directly in front of the priest celebrant and any other concelebrants. The Roman manner of holding the Gospel book is similar to the manner of the servers holding the processional candles. Customarily, the deacon carries the Gospel book with its front cover facing forward. He places his

102 Mutel and Freeman, *Cérémonial de la sainte messe*, 76.

103 *CB*, 128.

104 *CB*, 74, n. 67.

105 Mutel and Freeman, *Cérémonial de la sainte messe*, 74.

right hand close to the top of the spine of the book and his left hand close to the bottom of the opening of the book. He holds the Gospel book in front of him at chest height, no higher than eye level, so that he can peer over the top of the book and see where he is going.[106] The priest, vested in stole and chasuble, walks alone behind the deacon, with hands folded, holding nothing in his hands. If there are concelebrants, they walk two by two with hands joined, between the deacon holding the Gospel book and the principal celebrant. (See figure 4.)

If the deacon is not carrying the Gospel book, he walks with the priest celebrant at his right side. In this case, the Gospel book might be placed on the altar before Mass begins, unless the Gospel passage will be read from the lectionary instead. When the deacon is not carrying the Gospel book, concelebrants walk after the readers and before the celebrant with the deacon at his side.

As the procession makes its way to the sanctuary, everyone tries to walk two by two rather than in two distinct and independent lines. This is especially the case when turning left or right to exit or enter one of the aisles of the church. Everyone stands from the beginning of the entrance chant, or from the moment the priest leaves the sacristy, indicated by the ringing of the bell. All remain standing until the priest has concluded the opening Collect for Mass.

Entering the Sanctuary

Once the procession has made its way through the body of the church, some gesture of reverence is made upon arriving at the sanctuary. If the Blessed Sacrament is reserved in the tabernacle in the sanctuary, either directly behind the altar or to one side (but still in the sanctuary), one genuflects on the right knee in the direction of the tabernacle. If the Blessed Sacrament is not reserved in the sanctuary, one bows profoundly to the altar from the waist. Servers would make this reverence two by two, or even three at the same time if there is an odd number of servers. Concelebrants and instituted lectors or readers do the same. Those carrying some liturgical object in the procession do not make such a reverence, however. Therefore, the cross bearer and the candle bearers do not bow to the altar or genuflect to the tabernacle. Instead, they pause at the entrance of the sanctuary and simply bow their heads before proceeding.[107] The deacon carrying the Gospel book makes no reverence at all, neither to the altar nor to the Blessed Sacrament reserved in the sanctuary, but advances

106 See Adrian Fortescue, J. B. O'Connell, and Alcuin Reid, eds., *The Ceremonies of the Roman Rite Described*, 15th ed. (New York: Bloomsbury, 2009), 137, 207.

107 *GIRM*, 274.

directly toward the altar without interruption.[108] The sanctuary is generally raised one or more steps from the floor of the nave. Sacred ministers, historically, have entered the sanctuary by placing their right foot on the first step.[109] In addition, the altar itself is raised one or three steps above the floor of the sanctuary. The ministers customarily place their right foot on the first step of the altar as well.

The Roman Missal indicates that the processional cross may be placed on or near the altar in order to serve as the altar cross for Mass.[110] When the processional cross does not serve as the altar cross, it is placed in a discrete location to the side of the sanctuary or at the entrance of the sacristy itself. As with the processional cross, it is possible to place the candlesticks carried in the opening procession on or near the altar for Mass. Otherwise, it is preferable to place them aside. Traditionally, the candlesticks were placed on the credence table, on the rear corners. Usually, the credence table is placed against the wall of the sanctuary to the right of the location where the celebrant will stand at the altar and perpendicular to the altar. In other locations, the credence table is located against the east wall of the church, to the right of the altar and in line with it. The candle bearers who are also servers are usually seated on stools to either side of the credence table.[111] Other servers take their places on benches on the sides of the sanctuary. The instituted acolyte or the server who will hold the missal stands in a position near the priest celebrant, since no. 118 of the *General Instruction* calls for the missal to be prepared "next to the priest's chair" prior to Mass. It is always possible to place the missal on a second credence table in the sanctuary, opposite the main credence table if the principal credence table is located at some distance from the celebrant's chair. The deacon carrying the Gospel book places it reverently face down on the altar.[112] Then, standing slightly to the right side, he waits for the priest celebrant to join him in order to kiss the altar together with him.

Venerating the Altar

Meanwhile, concelebrants go up to the altar two by two to venerate it with a kiss. They may venerate the altar on either side, depending on the location of their seats in the sanctuary and whether candles and cross are placed on the altar. It is

108 *GIRM*, 173.

109 Fortescue, O'Connell, and Reid, *The Ceremonies of the Roman Rite Described*, 66.

110 This option is difficult to reconcile practically with two other instructions also from the missal which require only one altar cross, and require that such a cross remain on or near the altar when no liturgical rites are taking place. See *GIRM*, 122 and 308.

111 Mutel and Freeman, *Cérémonial de la sainte messe*, 79.

112 Mutel and Freeman, *Cérémonial de la sainte messe*, 64.

preferable to approach the altar in whichever way is most direct, avoiding unnecessary movements. For example, concelebrants approaching the altar should not have to meet concelebrants departing from the altar. Whenever possible, it seems easiest for concelebrants to approach the altar directly to venerate it on the side closest to the nave. They bow down to kiss the altar, touching it with their lips, holding their hands flat on the altar on either side.

Having made the required reverence either to the Blessed Sacrament in the tabernacle or to the altar, the celebrant now goes up to the altar to venerate it. If he will face the nave for the celebration of Mass, it is best if he walks to the right of the altar in order to join the deacon standing there, also facing the nave. If the deacon does not carry the Gospel book in the procession, he makes the required reverence with the priest at his right side and approaches the altar with him, taking care to remain on the priest's right side when both kiss the altar. Standing at the middle of the altar, with the palms of both hands placed flat on it to his sides, the priest reverences the altar with a kiss, that is, by lightly touching the altar with his closed lips without making any noise, and then joins his hands upon rising.[113] If there is a deacon, he kisses the altar at the same time as the priest, standing to his right, although traditionally the deacon does not place his hands on the altar when kissing it.[114]

If incense is used, the priest turns to his right after kissing the altar. Remaining at the center, he receives the censer from the deacon, or from the thurifer in the absence of the deacon. If necessary, the celebrant may impose more incense. When imposing incense, his left hand rests on his chest. With his right, he imposes incense three times, before returning the spoon to the deacon (or thurifer). He then blesses the incense, making a Greek cross with his right hand, saying nothing. Meanwhile, his left hand normally rests on the altar while blessing the incense with his right hand.[115] The celebrant then proceeds to incense the altar in the manner described in chapter 4. (See figure 1.) He concludes incensing the altar at the right-hand corner of the altar. The celebrant and the deacon proceed to their chairs in the sanctuary.

Historically, the seats of the sacred ministers for Mass were located to their right as they stood at the altar.[116] Their seats were placed on the floor of the

113 Peter J. Elliott, *Ceremonies of the Modern Roman Rite: The Eucharist and the Liturgy of the Hours*, rev. ed. (San Francisco: Ignatius Press, 1995), 92.

114 Fortescue, O'Connnell, and Reid, *The Ceremonies of the Roman Rite Described*, 141.

115 *CB*, 108.

116 Similarly, the credence table was historically placed to the priest's right side when he stood at the altar. In both cases, this may mean rearranging the position of the chair and the credence

sanctuary, at a right angle, perpendicular to the altar, either against the wall of the sanctuary or at some distance from it. Their seats might also be elevated on one step in the same position. Thus, as one faces the sanctuary, the chairs will be on the left side of the sanctuary if the priest normally stands at the altar facing the nave. Conversely, they will be placed on the right side of the sanctuary if he faces liturgical east when standing at the altar. While the *General Instruction* expresses a preference that the chair of the celebrant be located "facing the people at the head of the anctuaryy," it also recognizes that the tabernacle is often located in this position instead.[117] Often, the tabernacle is located at the head of the sanctuary because the church in question lacks any other location which is "truly noble, prominent, conspicuous, worthily decorated, and suitable for prayer" to receive it.[118] In these cases, the best solution to the placement of the celebrant's chair seems to be the traditional position perpendicular to the altar. The deacon's chair is placed to the right of the celebrant's chair. Therefore, having venerated and incensed the altar, both the priest and the deacon turn to their right to go to their chairs.

The Greeting and Penitential Act

Once the priest and the deacon have arrived at their seats, an instituted acolyte or a server brings the missal, open to the first words of the introductory rites for Mass, to the celebrant. The server should arrive at his position before the entrance chant ends and before the celebrant begins the Sign of the Cross. The server should hold the missal close to the body, with the hands at the bottom of each page. The server should not hold the missal out with arms fully extended. The upper portion of the missal usually rests on the chest. In the case of a very short server, the upper portion of the missal might rest on the server's forehead.[119] In any event, the server will endeavor to hold the book at the necessary height and at the necessary angle for the celebrant to read from it with ease. The server remains standing directly in front of the celebrant while holding the missal during the entire period of the introductory rites for Mass which concludes with the Collect for Mass. This will mean that the server should be old enough and strong enough to hold the missal motionless, regardless of its size, for that length of time. In that case, it is best if this function is entrusted to a server with more experience

table when the priest faces the nave for the celebration of Mass compared to the situation where the priest faces liturgical east.

117 *GIRM*, 310.

118 *GIRM*, 314.

119 Fortescue, O'Connell, and Reid, *The Ceremonies of the Roman Rite Described*, 203.

rather than a server with less experience. It may help if the server stands one step lower than the celebrant to hold the missal. In addition, if the presidential chair is oriented facing the assembly, it may be necessary for the server to stand slightly to the celebrant's left with his back to the faithful so that he does not completely obscure the celebrant from view.

Certainly, the priest may not need the missal in front of him for all the texts of the introductory rites, but traditionally, the celebrant always had the texts for Mass in front of him, either in the missal or on cards, even when praying some of those same texts from memory. At an early morning Sunday Mass or at a weekday Mass, when a server might not always be available, it seems that there is no alternative than to place a lectern in front of the celebrant's chair for the missal, since there is no provision in the *General Instruction* for beginning Mass with a congregation at the altar.

Once the entrance chant ends, the celebrant immediately begins the introductory rites with the Sign of the Cross, with the missal being held before his eyes. The missal itself gives two different indications for the orientation of the celebrant when making the Sign of the Cross. In one location (Order for Mass, no. 1), the missal directs him to face the people for the Sign of the Cross and the greeting that follow it. In another location (*GIRM*, 124), it directs him to turn to the people to offer the greeting, presumably after having made the Sign of Cross facing the missal. The first description is the most natural one. The second makes sense if the priest is reading the entrance antiphon from the missal when there is no singing, as is often the case in weekday Masses, for example. In that case, he concludes the entrance antiphon with the Sign of the Cross while facing the missal, just as in the past the priest faced the missal to make the Sign of the Cross as he began reading the Introit antiphon.

The celebrant begins with hands joined. The Sign of the Cross is made with the right hand. The hand is fully extended, with fingers joined, and touches the forehead, the breast, the left shoulder, and then the right shoulder in the dimensions of a Greek cross. Meanwhile, the left hand rests on the chest, below the ribs. His right hand does not extend lower than his left hand when making the Sign of the Cross.[120] Afterwards, he immediately joins his hands, before extending them toward the faithful and looking at them when offering the liturgical greeting. The priest joins his hands and receives the people's response, "And with your spirit."

[120] *CB*, 108, n. 81.

At each and every time the priest celebrant addresses the people and receives their response, it is important that he look at them. He is directing his words to them, after all. And he is expecting some kind of response from them as well. The eyes can communicate more than words or even gestures. By his demeanor, facial expression, and glance, the priest celebrant can establish an atmosphere of dialogue with the assembly which essential for the proper celebration of the Eucharist. For the Eucharist is always the action of Christ, head and members, lived out in the life of the Church hierarchically gathered.

Still facing the people, the celebrant offers the invitation to the penitential act with hands joined, glancing at the missal to his left if necessary. The priest may turn to face the missal, close his eyes for a moment and bow his head to allow for a brief examination of conscience in silence. In doing so, the priest and deacon indicate that they also are in need of purification at the beginning of Mass. In addition, they model for the assembly how to recollect oneself in order to examine one's conscience. When praying the *Confiteor* during the penitential act, the celebrant strikes his breast three times with his open hand, fingers joined.[121] He holds his left hand on his chest, below the location where he will strike his breast with the right hand. Still facing the missal, the priest concludes the penitential act with hands joined, and without making the Sign of the Cross while saying, "May almighty God have mercy on us."

In the missals issued prior to 1969, the *Confiteor* and verses to the prayers at the foot of the altar ("Have mercy on us, O Lord"), as well as the *Kyrie,* were recited facing the altar. Thus, in continuity with the past, the celebrant and the deacon might turn slightly toward the altar at their chairs unless it is manifestly awkward to do so, or at least face directly forward toward the altar from their chairs, when praying these parts of the introductory rites of Mass. The celebration of the Eucharist is an embodied act of worship. It is by its nature directed to God. Historically, this was represented by focusing one's attention toward the altar, which stands as the symbol of Christ in the midst of the praying community. As *Sacrosanctum concilium* no. 7 reminds us, Christ can also be found when the community gathers in prayer, in the proclamation of His Word, in the person of the ordained minister, and really, truly, and substantially in the eucharistic species.

121 Elliott, *Ceremonies of the Modern Roman Rite,* 93, n. 14. The missal does not indicate how many times the celebrant strikes his breast. The association of the gesture with the phrase, "through my fault," and the repetition of that phrase three times suggests that the gesture is repeated each time, as was the case historically.

Orienting one's prayer to the altar is another way of affirming spatially and bodily that Christ is in the Church's midst.

The Sprinkling Rite

On Sundays, and even at Masses on Saturday evening, the penitential act can be replaced by the sprinkling rite, found in appendix 2 of the missal. Historically, the principal sung Mass on Sunday was preceded by the rite of sprinkling with holy water. The third edition of the Roman Missal evokes this custom when it says, "From time to time on Sundays, especially in Easter time, instead of the customary Penitential Act, the blessing and sprinkling of water may take place as a reminder of Baptism."[122]

At the beginning of Mass, immediately following the Sign of the Cross and the greeting of the assembly, the celebrant, standing at the chair with hands joined and still turned toward the assembly, invites all to join him in the prayer of blessing. A server holds the missal in both hands from the Sign of the Cross to the conclusion of the opening Collect. If the celebrant is standing at the chair perpendicular to the altar, the server normally stands directly in front of the chair during this time. When addressing the assembly, the celebrant turns to his right to face them, with his eyes turning to the left as necessary to read the text of the invitation to prayer. If the celebrant is directly facing the people, either behind the altar or to one side of the altar, it is perhaps best for the server to stand slightly to his left. In so doing, the server will not block the celebrant from looking at the assembly when he addresses them.

After inviting the assembly to pray, the celebrant, if necessary, turns to face the missal once again. During this time, a server has been holding a vessel with water to be blessed. If the missal bearer is standing directly in front of the celebrant at the chair, the server with the vessel with water could stand facing the celebrant, on the celebrant's right. Another server with a vessel with salt on a tray could stand next to the missal bearer, on the celebrant's left. If the missal bearer is standing slightly to the celebrant's left because the celebrant's chair directly faces the assembly, both servers holding the vessels with water and with salt could stand slightly to the celebrant's right.

After inviting the faithful to pray, the celebrant, closing his eyes and bowing his head, pauses for a brief moment of silence. He then continues with the

[122] *GIRM*, 51.

blessing of the water with hands joined. He chooses a blessing prayer from among the three provided in the missal, one of which is reserved for the Easter season. With his right hand, his left hand resting on his chest, he makes the Sign of the Cross in the shape of a Greek cross over the water at the point indicated in the text. He does the same with the salt if he has decided to use it in the sprinkling rite. With his right hand, he then immediately pours the salt into the water, saying nothing.[123] Historically, the priest made the Sign of the Cross with the salt as he poured it into the water. The book bearer and the server holding the salt depart. The choir begins singing one of the appointed antiphons.

The deacon or a master of ceremonies dips the aspergillum in the water and presents the aspergillum to the celebrant in his right hand. The celebrant, still standing at the chair, sprinkles himself by touching his forehead with the aspergillum, making the Sign of the Cross. Alternatively, transferring the aspergillum from his right hand to his left, the celebrant touches the thumb of his right hand to the top of the aspergillum and traces the Sign of the Cross on his forehead before returning the aspergillum to his right hand. While holding the aspergillum in his right hand, his left hand always rests on his chest.

Still standing at the chair, the celebrant can then extend the aspergillum first to the deacon on his right, who touches the top of the aspergillum with the closed fingers of his right hand and makes the Sign of the Cross. The celebrant then can do the same for the server standing in front of him holding the vessel of water in his left hand. It is then perhaps best for the celebrant to proceed to the front of the altar to sprinkle the concelebrants and any others standing behind the altar in the sanctuary unless of course, at the chair, he is already standing directly behind the altar. Standing at the altar, the celebrant faces everyone in the sanctuary, with his back to the assembly. With the deacon now to his left and a server to his right holding the vessel with holy water, the celebrant begins with those to his right, then those to his left. The celebrant can sprinkle each group three times, first at their center, then to the left and then to the right. After sprinkling all those in the sanctuary, the celebrant, the deacon, and the server bow to the altar and turn to sprinkle the people. Upon turning to face the people, the deacon will now be on the celebrant's right and the server with the vessel of water will be on his left.[124] This position makes it easier for the celebrant to dip the

[123] *RM*, appendix 2, no. 3.

[124] Mutel and Freeman, *Cérémonial de la sainte messe*, 88.

aspergillum in the vessel with water as he sprinkles the people. The deacon can hold back the edge of the chasuble to facilitate this gesture.

Traditionally, the *asperges* rite began with the celebrant kneeling before the altar, sprinkling the altar three times, center, left, and right.[125] Still kneeling, he blessed himself with the holy water in the manner described above, then stood in order to sprinkle those next to him. The celebrant then proceeded to sprinkle all those in the sanctuary, going first to those on the right side and then to those on the left, bowing before and after. He then proceeded to sprinkle all those in the nave. Thus, as an alternative to beginning the sprinkling rite at the chair, the celebrant, the deacon, and the server holding the holy water may leave the chair immediately after the blessing of the water and salt and stand together facing the altar. In this position, the deacon stands to the celebrant's left and the server with the holy water stands to the celebrant's right. The celebrant blesses himself with the holy water and those next to him in the manner described above while standing before the altar. Then, the celebrant sprinkles those closest to him and those in the sanctuary. Turning away from the altar and toward the faithful, the server with the holy water is now on the celebrant's left and the deacon is on his right. The celebrant can then proceed to sprinkle the assembly.

The celebrant may stand at the entrance to the sanctuary and sprinkle the entire assembly from a stationary position, sprinkling first in the center, then to his left, then to his right, his left hand resting on his chest.[126] More appropriately, the celebrant may move through the church, sprinkling as he goes. When processing up the center aisle, he alternately sprinkles those on his right and then his left. Historically, the celebrant sprinkles others as he faces them, not from behind them.[127] This would exclude sprinkling one side of the center aisle as he walks to the back of the church and sprinkling the other side as he returns to the altar. Customarily, all make the Sign of the Cross as they are sprinkled.[128] Having reached the back of the church, the celebrant hands the aspergillum to the deacon, who returns the aspergillum to the vessel of water, and the celebrant joins his hands as he returns to the altar. At this point, the deacon and server may change sides in order to be on the celebrant's right and his left respectively once again.

125 Fortescue, O'Connell, and Reid, *The Ceremonies of the Roman Rite Described,* 110.

126 *CB* 133; Fortescue, O'Connell, and Reid, *The Ceremonies of the Roman Rite Described,* 110.

127 Elliot, *Ceremonies of the Modern Roman Rite,* 134.

128 Elliot, *Ceremonies of the Modern Roman Rite,* 134.

Upon arriving at the sanctuary, all bow to the altar, and the celebrant and deacon go to their seats. The server places the holy water on the credence table. After Mass, the holy water is added to the baptismal font or poured down the sacrarium if there is no need for it. The server with the missal approaches and stands before the celebrant once again. The celebrant, facing the missal, says the concluding prayer with hands joined.[129] Then the celebrant or the master of ceremonies turns the pages of the missal with his right hand to the Gloria, if required by the rubrics, or to the Collect for Mass.

The Gloria

The penitential act or the sprinkling rite concluded, the priest begins the Gloria by singing, or at least saying, its opening words with hands joined, turned at least slightly toward the altar or facing the missal. Again, this hymn is sung to glorify God in worship; it is not meant to be sung to each other as one would at some kind of festive social gathering. Making that distinction clear by one's posture helps to take the celebration of the Eucharist out of the profane realm and place it in the realm of sacred actions. The *General Instruction* indicates that all remain standing during the course of the Gloria.[130] Twice during the Gloria all bow their heads at the holy name, "Jesus Christ."

The master of ceremonies, a server, or the priest himself turns the pages of the missal to the texts needed for the penitential act, the Gloria, and the Collect. Normally, in order to turn the pages of the missal, or to make use of any liturgical object, the celebrant will use his right hand, holding his left hand on his chest at the same time.[131]

The Collect

Once the Gloria is concluded, the priest turns toward the people with hands joined to sing or say "Let us pray." He then turns toward the open missal and pauses in silence for a time. Again, he has invited people to pray; he should set the example by visibly praying silently himself. He may close his eyes and bow his head during this period. Then, extending his open hands with the fingers joined together, he prays the Collect. During the Collect, all bow their heads at the names of Jesus, Mary, or of the saint commemorated on that day. One bows

129 *RM*, appendix 2, no. 5.
130 *GIRM*, 43.
131 Mutel and Freeman, *Cérémonial de la sainte messe*, 81, n. 26.

the head only once for the names of saints commemorated together, such as St. Peter and St. Paul, for example. The celebrant joins his hands at the conclusion of the Collect, such as "Through Our Lord Jesus Christ your Son" or the other variants to this formula.[132] Once the people have responded "Amen," and not any sooner, the server bows his head to the celebrant, and returns the missal, still open, to its place near the celebrant's seat. Historically, the missal always lay open for use during Mass and was not closed again until the end of Mass. The open missal is placed near the celebrant and not at some distance away on the credence table, because the celebrant will eventually use the missal at the chair once again for the Creed and for the Universal Prayer.

Preparing to Listen to God's Word

All sit to listen to the Scriptures being proclaimed. All in the sanctuary sit with both feet flat on the ground and with the open palms of their hands resting on their lap.[133] Ministers in the sanctuary never cross their legs or their arms when sitting. By their manner of sitting, all in the sanctuary indicate their respect for God's Word, and the importance it holds in the life of faith. Casual postures can communicate that this portion of Mass is not to be taken very seriously. It also helps if those in the sanctuary look at the persons proclaiming the Scriptures from the ambo. In this way, they can give a good example to others to listen attentively and receptively to what is being proclaimed.

[132] *CB,* 136.
[133] *CB,* 109.

6

The Liturgy of the Word

THIS CHAPTER WILL examine how the Liturgy of the Word can be carried out according to the provisions of the *General Instruction of the Roman Missal* and the traditional practice of the Roman Rite. During the proclamation of the Gospel, we are reminded of the presence of Christ in the person of the minister announcing Christ's own words, living and active today. Following the homily, the words of the Creed summarize our Faith; we proclaim them with confidence and conviction. Finally, fulfilling their baptismal priesthood, the faithful intercede for the needs of the world and local needs, while the priest celebrant raises his own prayer of intercession to the Father.

Prior to the beginning of Mass, the lectionary has been placed on the ambo open to the proper page. After the opening Collect of Mass, all in the sanctuary and in the nave are seated to hear the Scripture readings proclaimed. The priest, deacon, servers, and other ministers in the sanctuary are expected to sit with both feet flat on the floor, with both hands resting open and flat on their knees or their lap.[134] They should be looking at the reader in a manner that communicates they are paying attention to what the reader is saying.

If the reader is not seated in the sanctuary, he or she goes to the center of the main aisle and makes a profound bow to the altar at the steps of the sanctuary before approaching the ambo. If the reader, however, is already seated in the sanctuary itself and must pass in front of the altar while crossing the sanctuary in order to approach the ambo, he or she makes a profound bow to the altar when doing so. In addition, either immediately after making this reverence to the altar or upon

[134] *CB*, 109.

arriving at the ambo, the reader makes a bow of the head toward the celebrant, and turns to the ambo to begin the reading.[135] Like the servers who acknowledge the celebrant with a bow of the head before and after approaching him to render some service, the reader at Mass does likewise. The bow indicates the reader's recognition that all ministries during Mass take place under the presidency of the priest celebrant. It is a gracious gesture to acknowledge the one who is moderating the exercise of various ministries into one harmonious act of worship.

The Readings before the Gospel

The reader places his or her hands on the edges of the lectionary while reading.[136] Historically, when a minister read the readings prior to the Gospel, he held the book in both hands to do so. In cases when the book rested on a stand, as when a priest read the same readings at the altar, he placed his hands on the edges of the book, as if he were still holding it in his hands to proclaim the reading. While the *General Instruction* gives no directions as to where to place one's hands when reading the Scripture passages prior to the Gospel, the traditional custom is to place both hands on the edges of the lectionary to do so.

After concluding the reading, the reader makes the necessary reverences once again, first to the celebrant, and then to the altar upon leaving the sanctuary. This process is repeated when the psalmist leads the responsorial psalm from the ambo,[137] and when there is a second reader. If any member of the faithful approaches the sanctuary from the nave, that person may be accompanied by a master of ceremonies or a server who walks with him or her at the left and stands near the ambo during the reading or the psalm. When the Gospel passage appointed for the occasion will be read from the Gospel book rather than from the lectionary, a master of ceremonies or the second reader removes the lectionary from the ambo after the second reading and places it on a nearby credence table or another suitable place.

[135] André Philippe M. Mutel and Peter Freeman, *Cérémonial de la sainte messe à l'usage ordinaire des paroisses suivant le missel romain de 2002 et la pratique léguée du rit romain,* 2nd ed. (Perpignan, France: Éditions Artège, 2012), 41–42, 95; Peter J. Elliott, *Ceremonies of the Modern Roman Rite,* rev. ed. (San Francisco: Ignatius Press, 1995), 96.

[136] Mutel and Freeman, *Cérémonial de la sainte messe,* 96.

[137] It is always possible for the psalmist or cantor to lead the psalm from "another suitable place." (*GIRM,* 61). If the schola sings the gradual response from the *Graduale Romanum* or the responsorial psalm *in directum* without any response from the people, they will almost always sing from another suitable place rather than from the ambo.

On Easter Sunday and on Pentecost Sunday, a sequence immediately follows the second reading and precedes the Alleluia. A sequence may be sung on Corpus Christi and Our Lady of Sorrows (September 15), according to the circumstances. All listen or join in singing the sequence while remaining seated.[138] During Lent, parishes may choose to sing the Tract from the Roman Gradual instead of the Gospel Verse or Gospel Acclamation from the lectionary. In that case, all remain seated as well during the singing of the Tract, then stand at the greeting "The Lord be with you," for the proclamation of the Gospel.[139]

The Preparation for the Proclamation of the Gospel

The high point of the Liturgy of the Word is the proclamation of the Gospel. All the gestures associated with this act should testify to this conviction. For example, as the Gospel Acclamation begins, all rise.[140] Servers should be reminded to stand attentively, not slouching or leaning to one side. Otherwise, they can give a strong counter-witness to the belief that Christ Himself is about to come and speak to His people as He once did. Normally, a deacon fulfills this ministerial function when he is present. Once again, as the Alleluia chant or Lenten acclamation begins, all stand. The deacon assisting at Mass bows profoundly with hands joined before the celebrant to ask for and to receive the priest's blessing. The celebrant, standing at the chair, prays the blessing with hands joined at first, and concludes by making the Sign of the Cross over the deacon with his right hand, his left hand resting on his chest, before joining his hands together before his chest once again. The deacon signs himself, responds, "Amen," and rises. The deacon then proceeds directly to the ambo with hands joined if there is no procession with the Gospel book. He bows profoundly when passing in front of the altar on the way to the ambo and upon returning to his chair.

If there is no deacon and concelebrants are present, preferably one of their number fulfills the office of proclaiming the Gospel. A concelebrant does not seek the celebrant's blessing as a deacon would, but proceeds directly to the altar to bow and say the prayer "Cleanse my heart." If there is no deacon and no concelebrant present, the celebrant himself proclaims the Gospel. At the Gospel Acclamation, he goes immediately to the middle of the altar. Since the silent prayer prayed before the altar, "Cleanse my heart," is addressed to God, the celebrant or one of the concelebrants,

138 Mutel and Freeman, *Cérémonial de la sainte messe*, 97, n. 87.

139 Mutel and Freeman, *Cérémonial de la sainte messe*, 98.

140 *GIRM*, 131.

according to the traditional practice, looks up momentarily to the altar cross before bowing profoundly with hands joined to say this prayer of preparation.[141] The priest then proceeds, with hands joined, to the ambo, unless there is a procession with the Gospel book, in which case he takes up the Gospel book in the manner described below. The celebrant or a concelebrant bows profoundly when passing in front of the altar on the way to the ambo and upon returning to his chair.

If there is a genuine procession with the Gospel book, the minister of the Gospel is led to the ambo by a thurifer with incense and two servers holding candles. In this case, just as the Alleluia chant or Lenten acclamation begins, all stand. The thurifer carries the censer in the left hand at the ring and the boat in the right hand. The thurifer hands the incense boat to the deacon or the master of ceremonies and then stands in front of the celebrant.[142] The thurifer presents the uncovered bowl of the censer to the celebrant with his right hand. Meanwhile, the deacon transfers the incense boat from his right hand to his left hand, he uses his right hand to offer the spoon to the celebrant, with the bowl of the spoon facing himself. Once the celebrant has taken the spoon, the deacon transfers the incense boat from his left hand to his right hand, his left hand resting on his chest. The deacon makes sure to hold the incense boat next to the bowl of the censer. Using his right hand, with his left hand resting on his chest, the celebrant now imposes incense three times on the coals. Meanwhile, the deacon once again transfers the incense boat from his right hand to his left hand. The celebrant returns the spoon to the deacon in his right hand. The deacon places the spoon in the boat, transfers the boat to his right hand, and passes it to the thurifer or to the master of ceremonies. The celebrant blesses the incense with his right hand, his left hand resting on his chest, saying nothing, then joins his hands together before his chest. The deacon then bows profoundly before the celebrant and asks for his blessing. The celebrant offers the blessing in the manner described above and the deacon signs himself and responds, "Amen."

The Alleluia chant with its verse is meant to accompany the procession of the ordained minister bearing the Gospel book from the altar to the ambo. Depending on whether the imposition of incense and blessing of the deacon can happen expeditiously when the Alleluia begins, as no. 132 of the *General Instruction* indicates, there are times when the brief Gospel chant ends prematurely before the

[141] Adrian Fortescue, J. B. O'Connell, and Alcuin Reid, eds., *The Ceremonies of the Roman Rite Described*, 15th ed. (New York: Bloomsbury, 2009), 70.

[142] *GIRM*, 212.

Gospel procession has even reached the ambo. To remedy this problem, some churches have added a second verse to the Alleluia chant, as the *Graduale Simplex* provides, in order to extend the singing of the Alleluia through the imposition of incense, the blessing of the deacon, and the procession to the ambo. Other churches simply anticipate the act of imposing incense to the moment immediately following the conclusion of the second reading, and delay beginning the Alleluia or Lenten acclamation with its single verse until the deacon has received the blessing. In that case, the celebrant imposes incense seated while the thurifer kneels before him and the deacon, standing or kneeling, holds the incense boat near the bowl of the censer.[143] While the celebrant blesses the incense with his right hand, his left hand rests on his knee. Then the priest stands. The deacon bows profoundly before the celebrant to ask for the blessing. The celebrant, standing at the chair, imparts the blessing to the deacon in the usual way. When the Alleluia or Lenten acclamation begins, everyone else stands.

The Procession to the Ambo

The Gospel procession, properly speaking, begins at the altar and concludes at the ambo. A Gospel procession may take place whether the Gospel book itself was carried in the entrance procession or simply placed flat on the altar prior to the beginning of Mass. In either case, the deacon, or the priest replacing him, bows to the altar upon arriving there and takes up the Gospel book in both hands. The deacon, or the priest replacing him, holds the Gospel book in the same manner as in the entrance procession. He holds the Gospel book with its front cover facing forward, his right hand near the top of the book's spine, and his left hand near the bottom of the book's opening.[144] He holds it at chest height, no higher than eye level.

The thurifer leads the way from the altar to the ambo, followed by the candle bearers walking side by side, followed by the ordained minister who will proclaim the Gospel. That priest or deacon follows the incense and candles with no further sign of reverence to the altar during the procession itself.[145] Once incense is imposed, the thurifer in the procession holds the censer in his right hand from

[143] Peter J. Elliott, *Ceremonies Explained for Servers According to the Roman Rite: A Manual for Altar Servers, Acolytes, Sacristans, and Masters of Ceremonies* (San Francisco: Ignatius Press, 2019), 91; Mutel and Freeman, *Cérémonial de la sainte messe*, 99–100. A dedicated boat bearer would kneel alongside the thurifer if the celebrant imposes incense seated.

[144] Mutel and Freeman, *Cérémonial de la sainte messe*, 102.

[145] *GIRM*, 173.

its ring rather than the left hand as he leads the procession to the ambo. He holds the incense boat in his left hand, unless this was taken from him by a master of ceremonies after the imposition of incense by the celebrant. The servers, walking side by side with candlesticks, hold them in the same manner as in the entrance procession. The server on the right side facing forward holds his right hand on the node at the middle of the candlestick and his left hand on its base. The server on the left side facing forward holds his right hand on the base of the candlestick and his left hand on the node.

According to the historical practice, the deacon in the Gospel procession could be accompanied to the ambo by an instituted acolyte, an instituted reader, or a server walking either to the deacon's left or ahead of him.[146] In addition, the master of ceremonies might accompany the thurifer at his left in order to direct the procession more effectively. This is not for the sake of additional ceremony itself but for the sake of a more gracious and dignified movement from the altar to the ambo, the place of proclamation.

Historically, the procession to the ambo with the Gospel book included the use of incense and candles. There were indeed some occasions, however, such as funerals, Palm Sunday, and Good Friday, when the Gospel procession did not include incense. In that case, the minister bearing the Gospel book was preceded by two servers only, both with hands joined, holding nothing. It would seem that today, if a thurifer and two candle bearers were not available, the use of the Gospel book in procession would demand at least two servers with or without candles or a thurifer with incense and one other server assisting the deacon in order to make it a true procession with the Gospel book.[147] Lacking these, the traditional custom would indicate that the appointed Gospel passage simply be read from the lectionary without any ceremony.

Having processed from the altar with the Gospel book, the deacon, or a concelebrant, or even the celebrant himself if necessary, arrives at the ambo and opens the Gospel book to the appointed reading. Or, a server, or the master of ceremonies who accompanies the deacon to the ambo, may take the Gospel book from his hands and do so for him instead. The servers stand on either side of the ambo with their candles in hand, facing each other.[148] (See figure 5.) The

[146] Fortescue, O'Connell, and Reid, *The Ceremonies of the Roman Rite Described*, 130, n. 58.

[147] Mutel and Freeman, *Cérémonies de la sainte messe*, 102.

[148] Elliott, *Ceremonies of the Modern Roman Rite*, 142; Mutel and Freeman, *Cérémonial de la sainte messe*, 102, n. 97.

thurifer stands to the deacon's right, ready to offer him the censer.[149] An instituted reader, or instituted acolyte, or some other server accompanying the deacon to the ambo may also stand to his right between the deacon and the thurifer in order to receive the censer from the thurifer and place it in the deacon's hands. This person may also turn the pages as needed and receive the Gospel book from the deacon at the conclusion of the proclamation.[150] Or, the master of ceremonies may stand to the deacon's left if he is going to assist the deacon by turning pages as needed.[151] Standardizing these positions is a service to the deacon. He should not have to guess at every Mass to which side he should turn in order to receive the censer, for example.

The Proclamation of the Gospel

All in the sanctuary and in the nave face the ambo from which the Gospel will be proclaimed, turning in their places if necessary.[152] This small gesture is often forgotten, but it can be a powerful witness to the belief that Christ is speaking and we should be listening. With hands joined, the deacon greets the people, saying, "The Lord be with you." A priest who proclaims the Gospel in the place of a deacon also greets the people with hands joined.[153]

While announcing the Gospel, the deacon or his replacement signs both the Gospel book and himself with his thumb. With his left hand resting on the book, the deacon or the priest who replaces him uses his right hand, opened flat with the fingers joined, to trace a Greek cross at the beginning of the Gospel text with the thumb, holding it separated from the rest of the fingers. Then, with his left hand resting on his chest, he traces the cross with the thumb of his right hand on his forehead, his lips, and his breast above the position where his left hand rests. He holds his right hand open, with the fingers joined, parallel to himself when making these crosses. At the words "A reading from," he makes the Sign of the Cross with the right thumb first on the text and then on the forehead, lips, and

149 Elliott, *Ceremonies of the Modern Roman Rite*, 142; Mutel and Freeman, *Cérémonial de la sainte messe*, 103.

150 Fortescue, O'Connell, and Reid, *The Ceremonies of the Roman Rite Described*, 130.

151 Elliott, *Ceremonies of the Modern Roman Rite*, 142.

152 *CB*, 141.

153 This is the only case during Mass where the people are greeted by an ordained minister with hands joined. The celebrant, who exercises a presidential function representing Christ as Head of the Body, extends his hands in greeting. The deacon (or his replacement) exercises a ministerial function when proclaiming the Gospel, not a properly presidential one; hence the difference in the gesture associated with this greeting at this point.

breast. One should avoid signing the lips while saying anything. One signs the breast when saying, "according to N.," then joins the hands when announcing the name of the evangelist.[154]

After joining his hands, he turns to his right and takes the censer in his right hand, bows, and incenses the Gospel book with three double swings: one to the center, one to his left, and one to his right.[155] He bows again and hands the censer back to the thurifer, or to the minister or server assisting him on his right.[156]

When giving the censer to the deacon, the thurifer or the minister or server assisting the deacon will take care to place the censer in the right hand of the deacon, and the ring to the chain of the censer in the left hand of the deacon facing him. Again, this is simply to render this action more graceful and to eliminate any awkward moments. Once he has received the censer back from the deacon or from the minister or server assisting him, the thurifer then continues to stand at the deacon's right, slightly behind him, holding the censer by the ring of the chain in his right hand. Some authors say that the thurifer can move the censer gently back and forth during the reading of the Gospel.[157] The thurifer's intention at this point is simply to generate some incense to accompany the proclamation of the Gospel; this gesture is not meant to become a distraction to those listening to the Gospel.

The deacon reads the Gospel with hands joined. During the reading, all bow their heads at the names of Jesus, Mary, or of the saint commemorated that day. When reading the Gospel, if he has to turn a page, he does so with the right hand, laying the left on the edge of the Gospel book. At the words "The Gospel of the Lord," the deacon does not raise the Gospel book in order to show it to the assembly. He pronounces those words with hands joined while looking at the faithful, since he is speaking to them. The deacon does not raise the Gospel book because the words just proclaimed, not the book which contains them, are the good news which the faithful are invited to acclaim. The gestures associated with the proclamation of the Gospel should not contradict this belief.

After the people have responded, "Praise to You, Lord Jesus Christ," the deacon picks up the Gospel book with both hands, raises it slightly, and bows his

[154] Mutel and Freeman, *Cérémonial de la sainte messe*, 103; Fortescue, O'Connell, and Reid, *The Ceremonies of the Roman Rite Described*, 71.

[155] Elliott, *Ceremonies of the Modern Roman Rite*, 143.

[156] *GIRM*, 277.

[157] Elliott, *Ceremonies Explained for Servers*, 92; Mutel and Freeman, *Cérémonial de la sainte messe*, 104.

head slightly to meet it.[158] He kisses the Gospel book, that is, touches the book lightly with his closed lips without making any noise, in the same location where he traced the Sign of the Cross at the beginning of the text, and then closes it. At the same time, he says quietly to himself the prayer "Through the words of the Gospel may our sins be wiped away."

The deacon, with the minister, server, or the master of ceremonies accompanying him walking to his left, may then carry the Gospel book back to the credence table or some other suitable location, where it remains for the rest of Mass. In this case, the deacon could simply hold the closed Gospel book with both hands at the bottom, with the top of the book resting on his chest. This is not a second Gospel procession; therefore, it should not appear as one. It is rather a purely practical gesture, that is, the movement of a group of ministers across the sanctuary in order to lay aside the Gospel book now that it has served its purpose and will not be used again. As an alternative, the deacon, standing at the ambo, may place the Gospel book in the hands of the person at his right who accompanied him. That person would carry the Gospel book in the same way, and the deacon would walk behind him with hands joined. The deacon and this minister or server then follow the candle bearers and thurifer back to the credence table, and eventually to their seats, pausing to reverence the altar as a group, with at least a bow of the head if they are carrying anything, if they pass in front of it.[159] If the deacon is preaching at Mass, this assistant may carry the Gospel book to a suitable location in the same manner while the deacon remains at the ambo to preach.

The Homily

After the Gospel, the priest celebrant may preach "standing at the chair or at the ambo itself or, when appropriate, in another suitable place."[160] Historically, "another suitable place" could designate either a raised pulpit in the nave, or the entrance to the sanctuary as at the gates of the altar rail, or before the altar itself toward the side of the sanctuary where the Gospel was proclaimed.[161] In any of these locations, the homilist is intended to preach standing. A priest concelebrant might

[158] Mutel and Freeman, *Cérémonial de la sainte messe*, 105.

[159] Elliott, *Ceremonies Explained for Servers*, 92.

[160] *GIRM*, 136. It appears that the option for the priest celebrant to preach seated at his chair has been eliminated by the fifth edition of the *General Instruction* (2000). See *Introduction to the Lectionary for Mass* (2nd edition, 1981), no. 26, and Elliott, *Ceremonies of the Modern Roman Rite*, 98.

[161] Fortescue, O'Connell, and Reid, *The Ceremonies of the Roman Rite Described*, 71.

preach either at the ambo or at "another suitable place." While a deacon might preach the homily during Mass at the ambo or even at "another suitable place," he would not preach standing at his chair.[162]

If the priest celebrant or a concelebrant preaches from the ambo, he makes a profound bow to the altar with hands joined whenever passing in front of it in order to arrive at the ambo. After preaching, the homilist returns to his chair. The deacon rises as the priest celebrant approaches the presidential chair as a mark of respect for him.[163] All sit for some time in silence to ponder what has been proclaimed in God's Word and in the homily. It is important that this time be free of fidgeting or wandering glances, as if one is anxious to have the silence end quickly. The Holy Spirit speaks to the heart in silence, and this takes a few moments of uninterrupted silence, being careful not to prolong it unnecessarily, such that it might become wearisome or burdensome to those gathered.

The Creed

The celebrant then rises to lead the assembly in the profession of faith by singing, or at least by reciting, the opening words of the Creed, either in the form of the Nicene Creed or the Apostles' Creed. Historically, the Nicene Creed was recited facing the altar, since it is a profession of faith made to God. The profession of faith is a public act done in common to be sure, but the gathered faithful, priest and people together, profess their faith before God first and foremost as an act of thanksgiving and praise to Him who has granted the gift of faith itself while all were still in unbelief. Therefore, the celebrant could face the faithful momentarily in order to elicit their participation and then turn his gaze toward the altar, which remains the focus of the entire assembly's worship throughout the course of Mass. If at all possible, the missal is held directly in front of the celebrant at the chair by a server for the Creed and what follows. The server should arrive in front of the celebrant before the celebrant begins the first words of the Creed.

During the Creed, all bow their heads at the names of Jesus and Mary. All bow from the waist at the words "and by the Holy Spirit . . . and became man." At all the Masses of Christmas and Christmas Eve, as well as on the Solemnity of the Annunciation (March 25), all kneel on both knees at the same words.[164]

[162] Elliot, *Ceremonies of the Modern Roman Rite*, 98; Mutel and Freeman, *Cérémonial de la sainte messe*, 106.

[163] Mutel and Freeman, *Cérémonial de la sainte messe*, 106.

[164] Mutel and Freeman, *Cérémonial de la sainte messe*, 106.

The Universal Prayer or the Prayer of the Faithful

After the Creed, all remain standing. The celebrant turns to face the people to introduce the Universal Prayer using one of the formulas found in appendix 5 of the missal or simply by saying, "Let us pray." The celebrant faces the altar if possible, with hands joined, while the intentions are read or sung. The deacon, a reader, or a cantor offers the intentions. He faces the people to do so whether he is standing at the ambo or at some other suitable place.[165] For the deacon, this suitable place may be his seat next to the celebrant. For the reader or the cantor, the suitable place may be a lectern, even one outside the sanctuary, which nevertheless faces the assembly. While the intentions are being read out, the celebrant may close his eyes and bow his head in order to signify that he is indeed praying. Again, he will be leading the assembly by example in doing so. All are meant to prayerfully ponder in their hearts those needs spoken by the deacon. Their vocal response to the deacon's intentions will be authentic to the degree that all have taken the time to pray with him internally first. The celebrant, still standing in the same position, now with hands extended, concludes the Universal Prayer with an appropriate Collect from the missal taken either from the Masses for Various Needs and Occasions or from appendix 5 of the missal. A server holds the missal in both hands before him.[166] The person who offered the intentions remains in position until the conclusion of the Collect. After the concluding Collect with the short ending "through Christ Our Lord," all sit, and the preparation of the gifts and the altar begins.

165 *GIRM*, 138.

166 After a period of improvisation in the earliest centuries, the spoken parts of Mass itself have traditionally been read from printed texts or spoken from memorized fixed forms. Currently, the celebrant may compose the texts to the Universal Prayer himself. In such a case, the server may hold that text before the celebrant for the opening invocation and its concluding Collect. These texts are not intended to be improvised on the spot.

7

The Preparation of the Gifts and the Altar

THIS CHAPTER WILL describe the postures and gestures involved in carrying out the prayers of preparation for the bread and the wine. The preparation of the altar and the gifts in the Roman Missal of Paul VI differs significantly in theology and in ritual elements from the Offertory prayers of the *Missale Romanum* of John XXIII. Nevertheless, many, though not all, of the directives found in the *ritus servandus* of the missal of 1962 can help structure this part of Mass in a way which is both dignified and graceful. In so doing, the "traditional practice of the Roman Rite" mentioned in no. 42 of the *General Instruction of the Roman Missal* can enrich contemporary celebrations of the Mass.

The Preparation of the Altar with the Gifts

After the conclusion to the Universal Prayer, the celebrant sits and the deacon goes directly from the place where he offered the intentions to the credence table or to the altar to begin the preparation of the gifts. According to long-standing custom, the credence table will be placed to the celebrant's right as he faces the altar whether celebrating *ad orientem* or *versus populum*. The deacon is joined at the credence table by servers. If convenient, the deacon may bring the chalice from the credence table to the altar,[167] or he may wait at the altar for an instituted acolyte or other server to brings it to him there.[168] Customarily, the chalice is vested, that is, the chalice has with it a purificator with the fold of the purificator pointing downward into the chalice, a paten with a host, a pall, a veil of the same

[167] *GIRM*, 171b, 171e, 178.

[168] *GIRM*, 190.

material and color as the vestments of the day or white,[169] and a burse containing a corporal. In the absence of a burse, which is not mentioned in the *General Instruction* or in the *Order for Mass*, although its use is eminently practical, the corporal lays on the pall under the veil.[170] When carrying the veiled chalice, the deacon or the acolyte holds it by the node in his left hand, with his entire right hand resting flat on top of the veil or burse so that nothing falls. He carries it with the front of the veil and the closed edge of the burse facing outward. He carries nothing else in his hands. The deacon, carrying the chalice in both hands, goes up the steps of the altar at the center. In contrast, the instituted acolyte or server who approaches the altar holding the chalice in both hands goes up the steps on the right-hand side.

The deacon or the server places the chalice on the right-hand corner of the altar, with the front of the chalice (denoted by a cross) and the front of the veil facing the faithful regardless of the orientation of the priest at the altar. If there is a burse, a server may take it off of the chalice, holding it open with both hands on either side of the burse so that the deacon can more easily retrieve the corporal.[171] The deacon, or in his absence a server, then unfolds the corporal in the middle of the altar such that its bottom edge will be an inch or two from the edge of the altar. With the folded corporal lying flat at the center of the altar, the deacon begins by unfolding a portion toward the left like a book, then to the right, then the top portion, and finally the bottom portion. (See figure 6.) The corporal is always unfolded and folded while it lays flat on the altar; it is never unfolded or folded while held up in both hands over the altar. Alternatively, the deacon takes the burse and lays it flat on the altar with its opening facing to the right. With his left hand, he lifts the left flap of the burse, and with his right hand he extracts the corporal from the burse and then proceeds to unfold the corporal as described above. The server holds the empty burse in both hands until he has received the veil as well.

The deacon then turns to his right and goes to the chalice. He removes the veil by lifting the veil from behind the chalice toward himself, folds it in half, and then folds it again in thirds. The deacon folds the veil while it lays flat on the altar; it is never folded while held in both hands above the altar. He places the

[169] *GIRM*, 118. The burse and veil may also always be white.

[170] André Philippe M. Mutel and Peter Freeman, *Cérémonial de la sainte messe à l'usage ordinaire des paroisses suivant le missel romain de 2002 et la pratique léguée du rit romain*, 2nd ed. (Perpignan, France: Éditions Artège, 2012), 110.

[171] Mutel and Freeman, *Cérémonial de la sainte messe*, 111.

folded veil in the hands of the server holding the empty burse. The deacon then places the pall near the top right corner of the corporal. He leaves the purificator draped over the chalice to the right side of the altar. The paten with the large host and perhaps other hosts as well can remain on the chalice and purificator, or it may be placed directly on the altar between the chalice and the central corporal.[172] Neither the paten with the host nor the empty chalice are placed on any corporal by the deacon.

If only one additional chalice or ciborium is needed, it is brought from the credence table to the altar by a server. The deacon places it on the corporal at the top right corner. If additional vessels beyond a single ciborium or chalice are needed, these can be arranged in a row across the top portion of the corporal. If even more space is needed, additional corporals might be placed on the altar, at first to the right-hand side, either at the edge of the main corporal or at some distance from it, and then on the left-hand side, away from the missal.[173] All the necessary corporals, purificators, and palls might be brought to the altar with the principal chalice either in a burse or under the chalice veil. Servers can bring additional vessels to the altar in a kind of procession, one behind the other, as the deacon places them in their proper locations. Older servers can carry a vessel in each hand; younger servers may need to carry only one vessel in both hands. These servers bow their heads to the deacon or celebrant before handing him a vessel or vessels and again before departing from him. The celebrant or the deacon does not reciprocate with a bow.[174] If two servers approach the altar at the same time, they make their reverences together and turn toward each other to depart from the altar.

Additional cups are brought to the altar uncovered, without any purificator or pall over the cup. If they are numerous, the cups could be conveniently placed to the right side of the altar on a corporal and the patens or ciboria to the left side of the altar on a corporal. The required purificators and palls are placed near their corresponding cups, along the edge of the corporal on which they rest. Customarily, the purificator is laid on the altar with its entire length touching the edge of the corporal and with its fold closest to edge of the altar. The additional chalices, ciboria, or

172 Mutel and Freeman, *Cérémonial de la sainte messe,* 111.

173 Peter J. Elliott, *Ceremonies of the Modern Roman Rite: The Eucharist and the Liturgy of the Hours,* rev. ed. (San Francisco: Ignatius Press, 1995), 101, 102.

174 Mutel and Freeman, *Cérémonial de la sainte messe,* 115.

patens already contain the elements which will be consecrated.[175] Ciboria can be brought to the altar with their covers. During Mass, the deacon will have to attend to uncovering the ciboria and cups and covering them at the proper time. Each time, the covers are placed outside the corporal.[176] However, the ciboria can also be brought to the altar without their covers, which remain at the credence table.

Once all the vessels needed have been placed on the altar, a server then brings the missal from the celebrant's chair or from the credence table to the altar. Or, he may have brought it to the credence table first in order to place it on its stand or cushion and then proceeded to take both to the altar once the preparation of the altar and the gifts is completed. The server carries the open missal on its stand or cushion to the altar. Arriving at the center, the server bows his head. Going to the left-hand side of the altar as one faces it, the server goes up the steps to the altar on that side. The server places the missal and its stand or cushion at an angle to the left of the main corporal, and insofar as is possible, off the corporal. The deacon or the server may turn the missal to the preparation of the gifts, if it is not already open to that page.

If there is no deacon assisting the priest for the celebration of Mass, an instituted acolyte or other properly trained server may take the role of the deacon described above. If there is no server suitable for these tasks available, perhaps because of age or stature, the priest himself should go to the altar at the conclusion of the Universal Prayer. Upon arriving at the center of the altar, he bows and then goes up the steps. Turning to his right, he begins to prepare the chalice, corporal, and other vessels with the assistance of servers as described above.

The Offertory Procession

If the faithful are to present the gifts of bread and wine, and even the water,[177] the deacon, who has been at the altar preparing it and the gifts, may remain at the right-hand side of the altar until such members of the faithful are ready to proceed, or he may return to his seat by the priest to stand there to wait for them to be ready. When the faithful are ready to present the gifts of bread, wine, and even water and monetary contributions, the celebrant and the deacon, or even the deacon alone, joined by one or more servers, go to "an appropriate place" designated to receive

[175] Peter J. Elliott, *Ceremonies Explained for Servers According to the Roman Rite: A Manual for Altar Servers, Acolytes, Sacristans, and Masters of Ceremonies* (San Francisco: Ignatius Press, 2019), 102.

[176] Fortescue, O'Connell, and Reid, *The Ceremonies of the Roman Rite Described*, 76.

[177] *GIRM*, 73, 140; *Order for Mass*, no. 22.

the gifts.[178] That place may be at the entrance to the sanctuary, or at the chair, as is often the case in the Mass celebrated by a bishop, or at the altar itself. A master of ceremonies or a server may accompany the faithful from their places and back, generally walking to their left.

The gifts are received individually by the celebrant and handed to the deacon, who stands on the celebrant's right. The deacon in turn may hand them to waiting servers. The celebrant may acknowledge those who presented the gifts with a bow of the head. Those who presented gifts would bow to the celebrant upon arriving before him and before departing from him. When all the gifts have been presented, the celebrant should have nothing in his hands. Standing before the altar and facing the people, the celebrant now turns to his right with hands joined and makes his way to the altar, bowing to the altar when passing in front of it or upon arriving there.[179] All who assisted the celebrant bow to the altar if they happen to pass in front of it.

If there is no procession with the gifts, or if the deacon alone receives the gifts from the faithful, the celebrant goes directly from his chair to the altar after it has been prepared. At the center, he bows to the altar upon arriving, and then goes up the steps.[180]

The Prayers of Preparation

At the altar, the deacon, standing to the right of the celebrant and using both hands, places the paten with the host or hosts in the priest's hands. If there is no deacon, a concelebrant can properly assume the duties of the deacon described below. The priest holds the paten with the thumbs and index fingers of each hand touching its edge, with the other fingers joined under it. He holds the paten over the corporal slightly elevated, at the height of the width of a hand, and says the prayer. According to the traditional practice, he raises his eyes, at least momentarily, to address the prayer to God. The celebrant then places on the paten at the center of the front portion of the corporal.[181] Meanwhile, at the right-hand side of the altar, the deacon simultaneously begins to prepare the chalice if there is music or singing to accompany the preparation. If the celebrant is saying the prayers of preparation out loud, it is fitting for the deacon to wait for the prayer over the

[178] *GIRM*, 73.

[179] Elliot, *Ceremonies of the Modern Roman Rite*, 102.

[180] Elliott, *Ceremonies of the Modern Roman Rite*, 102.

[181] Elliott, *Ceremonies of the Modern Roman Rite*, 102.

bread to be concluded, and to respond with the faithful, before proceeding to prepare the chalice. Depending on the circumstances, the deacon can also carry out the preparation of the chalice at the credence table.

First, holding the chalice by its node in his left hand on the altar at the right side and not away from the altar or above the altar, the deacon holds the fingers of his right hand together and lowers the purificator resting on top of the chalice with the fold facing downward into the bottom of the cup and wipes with interior of the cup of the chalice. He turns the chalice once to remove any dust from its interior. Then the deacon drapes the purificator over the thumb of his left hand at the node of the chalice, so that the inside of the folded purificator falls over his thumb onto the table of the altar. A server stands before the deacon, at the right side of the altar, with the cruet of wine in his right hand and the cruet of water in his left hand. Both cruets are held with their handles facing outward. Neither of them is brought to the altar with their stoppers in place; those are left at the credence table if they are used. With his right hand and facing the altar, the deacon takes the cruet of wine presented him by the server, who holds it in his right hand with the handle facing out, and pours a portion of the wine into the chalice. The deacon wipes the mouth of the cruet on the purificator and returns it to the server. In the meantime, the server has transferred the cruet of water from his left hand to his right hand. The server receives the cruet of wine in his left hand and offers the cruet of water, with handle facing out, with his right hand. The deacon does not make the Sign of the Cross over the cruet of water, and neither does the priest if he prepares the chalice in the absence of a deacon. The deacon takes the cruet of water and adds a little water, merely a few drops, to the wine, wipes the mouth of the cruet on the purificator, and returns the cruet to the server. The server bows to the deacon and returns to the credence table with the two cruets. At no point is either cruet placed on the altar. Each cruet is held either by the server or the deacon or the celebrant at all times.

The deacon then wraps the interior of the purificator at the fold around the index finger of his right hand at its center, folding over any excess material against the index finger itself and holding it there with the thumb of his right hand. With the index finger of his right hand wrapped in the corporal, the deacon wipes the drops of wine or water from the interior of the cup of the chalice. He refolds the purificator with its outer side facing outward once again. The deacon puts the purificator down next to the edge of the corporal along its length, the open end of the purificator toward the back of the altar and the fold of the purificator toward the front edge of the altar. Taking the chalice in both hands, with the right hand at the node and the left hand at the base, the deacon hands it to the priest. When handing the chalice to the celebrant, the deacon orients the chalice such that the cross at the base of the chalice will face the celebrant. The celebrant raises the chalice slightly, with his right hand at the node and his left hand at its base, with the base of the chalice a hand's breadth above the corporal. The celebrant says the prayer regarding the wine. According to the traditional practice, he raises his eyes, at least momentarily, to address the prayer to God. The celebrant then places the chalice down on the corporal, at the center of the back portion of the corporal. The deacon covers it with the pall using his right hand, his left hand resting on his chest. In order to prevent any accident at this moment, the celebrant places his left hand on the base of the chalice while his right hand rests on the altar outside the corporal.[182]

If there is no deacon or a concelebrant, the celebrant himself prepares the chalice in the same way, standing at the right-hand side of the altar. Having completed the preparation of the chalice, he may place it closer to the corporal with his left hand. Holding the purificator with the index finger of his right hand under the center fold, the celebrant joins his hands and returns to the center of the altar. There he puts the purificator down, the folded edge closest to him, with its length along the corporal. Then, still standing at the center, he reaches for the chalice at its node with his right hand, and holds it over the corporal with the left hand at its base as indicated above and says the appropriate prayer.[183] The celebrant places the chalice down at the center of the back portion of the corporal with the cross on the base of the chalice facing him. With his right hand, he covers the chalice with the pall. The fingers of his left hand rest on the foot of the chalice while he does so. The celebrant then steps back slightly and bows deeply with hands joined to say the prayer "With humble spirit."[184] Traditionally, the celebrant rests the extended fingers of his joined hands on the edge of the altar, with the fifth fingers of his joined hands touching the edge of the altar.[185] The joined hands rest on the table of the altar near the corporal but not on it. Rising, the celebrant turns to his right and goes to the right side of the altar with hands joined.

If incense is used, it is imposed and blessed according to the description found in chapter 4. The gifts, altar cross, and altar are incensed first. (See figure

[182] Elliott, *Ceremonies of the Modern Roman Rite*, 103; Mutel and Freeman, *Cérémonial de la sainte messe*, 112–114.

[183] Mutel and Freeman, *Cérémonial de la sainte messe*, 115.

[184] Order for Mass, no. 26.

[185] Mutel and Freeman, *Cérémonial de la sainte messe*, 114.

2.) The celebrant concludes the incensation of the cross, gifts and altar at the right-hand side of the altar. The celebrant and concelebrants, ministers, servers, and faithful are incensed afterward as described in chapter 4.

At the right-hand side of the altar, a server holds a basin in his left hand and the cruet or a pitcher of water in his right hand with which to wash the celebrant's hands. A towel or finger towel is draped on the server's left arm. Or, in the absence of a deacon, one server may hold the pitcher and basin and another server may hold the towel by its two corners. The celebrant stands perpendicular to the altar at the right-hand side and holds his joined hands over the vessel. The server pours water over the celebrant's hands into the bowl or basin. The deacon may take the towel from the server, open it, and hold it in both hands at its two corners in order to present it to the priest. The priest takes it from him and wipes his hands. The celebrant dries his hands facing the altar, not holding his hands over the altar, but outside it.[186] Turning again to his right, away from the altar, the celebrant then returns the towel to the deacon, who folds it and places it on the left arm of the server once again. The server bows to the celebrant. The celebrant, with hands joined, bows to the server as an expression of gratitude.[187] The server returns to the credence table. The deacon may now stand at the priest's left in order to turn the pages of the missal, or he may remain at his right for the entire Eucharistic Prayer. In this case, a master of ceremonies or the priest himself will turn the pages of the missal.

With hands joined, the celebrant turns to his left and returns to the center of the altar. There he extends and joins his hands as he says, "Pray brethren (brothers and sisters)," while looking at the people. Unless the deacon or a master of ceremonies does so, the celebrant then turns the pages of the missal to the prayer over the gifts with his left hand, his right hand resting on the altar outside the corporal. He says the prayer of the gifts with hands outstretched. He joins his hands at the concluding formula "through Christ Our Lord." Then begins the Eucharistic Prayer itself, the heart of the Liturgy of the Eucharist.

[186] Fortescue, O'Connell, and Reid, *The Ceremonies of the Roman Rite Described*, 74.

[187] Elliott, *Ceremonies of the Modern Roman Rite*, 104; Mutel and Freeman, *Cérémonial de la sainte messe*, 124.

8

The Eucharistic Prayer

While the Roman Missal of Paul VI greatly simplified the gestures associated with the Eucharistic Prayer, the traditional practice of the Roman Rite can still inform much of the manner in which the gestures which remain are carried out, as foreseen in no. 42 of the *General Instruction of the Roman Missal*. In addition, the missal often gives no indications at all about a range of gestures which, over the centuries, had become associated with the celebration of the Canon of the Mass. These too can help enrich the celebration of the Eucharist today. It is perhaps best to begin with the gestures and postures which are common to the celebration of all the Eucharistic Prayers before indicating those which are specific to Eucharistic Prayer I, in the Roman Canon. This chapter will first describe the gestures and postures of the celebrant alone, without an assisting minister, during the course of the Eucharistic Prayer. Then, in subsequent sections, the gestures and postures of a deacon who may be assisting or of other priests who may be concelebrating will be described as well.

The Gestures of the Celebrant

Following the prayer over the gifts, the celebrant will find the Preface selected by using his left hand, since the missal is historically placed to the left of the corporal at an angle. It is best to find the Preface desired before actually beginning the Preface dialogue, "The Lord be with you." At the same time, the right hand is placed flat on the altar outside the corporal. This was a consistent principle in the traditional celebration of the Roman Rite. Whenever a hand or both hands were placed on the altar prior to the consecration, the hand or hands were placed flat on the altar outside the corporal. Whenever the hand or hands were on the altar after the consecration had taken place, the hand or hands were placed on the corporal. While the missal makes no mention of this custom, it seems a worthwhile principle to foster, in continuity with the traditional practice.

When beginning the Preface dialogue, the celebrant extends his hands toward the assembly and looks at them, just as he does at the beginning of Mass itself. The celebrant continues to look at the assembly through the next two dialogues. He then raises his hands at the second invitation "Lift up your hearts." He then lowers his hands to the *orans* position, for "Let us give thanks to the Lord our God." The *orans* position of the hands can be expressed in a variety of ways. In general, it seems best to keep the fingers of the hand together and allow the palm to fall into an open position which seems natural and not tense. The hands can be kept slightly before the shoulders, with the elbows near the body.[188] The celebrant should avoid moving the hands up and down while reading. He should remain stationary at the altar, standing erect, without rocking back and forth or from one side to the other. One hand never remains raised in the *orans* position when another hand is resting on the altar or occupied. In that case, the free hand always rests on the altar during the time the other hand is occupied. The celebrant keeps his hands in the *orans* position as he begins the Preface. Whenever the names of Jesus, Mary, or the saint commemorated on that day are mentioned during the Preface, he bows his head. Only at the conclusion of the Preface does he eventually join his hands to join in singing the *Sanctus*. The celebrant may wish to keep his eyes downcast in a recollected way during the singing.

The *Sanctus* concluded, the celebrant extends his hands, once again in the *orans* position, and continues with the Eucharistic Prayer. Just prior to the epiclesis, if the chalice is covered with a pall, the celebrant places his left hand at the base and removes the pall with his right hand, placing it near the top right edge of the corporal. Similarly, the celebrant removes any covers to the ciboria at this point with the right hand, the fingers of the left hand steadying the base of the ciboria. The covers can be placed outside the corporal.

At the epiclesis, the celebrant joins his hands together first, then opens them flat, keeping the right thumb locked over the left thumb. He extends both hands over the gifts to be consecrated, neither immediately over them nor too high, with the elbows slightly bent in a relaxed position.[189] In some churches, the

[188] Peter J. Elliott, *Ceremonies of the Modern Roman Rite: The Eucharist and the Liturgy of the Hours*, rev. ed. (San Francisco: Ignatius Press, 1995), 70.

[189] Elliot, *Ceremonies of the Modern Roman Rite*, 70.

server rings the bells while the priest prays the epiclesis.[190] In all the Eucharistic Prayers except Eucharistic Prayer I, the celebrant makes the Sign of the Cross at the conclusion of the epiclesis. He begins by drawing both hands to himself and joining them. He then makes the Sign of the Cross with his right hand over the gifts, his left hand resting flat on the altar outside the corporal. The right hand with fingers joined is held perpendicular to the table of the altar. The Sign of the Cross is made over the gifts, from the center of the chalice to the center of principal host, and laterally between the chalice and host, from left to right, in the shape of a Greek cross. The dimensions of the Greek cross should not extend beyond the size of the pall, for example. The celebrant makes the Sign of the Cross without lowering the hand or the fingers, but keeping them in the same horizontal plane at all times.[191] As the celebrant concludes the epiclesis, the celebrant draws the hands together and toward himself. They remain joined until he is about to take the elements in his hands.

When the celebrant is about to take up the host, he might wipe his thumbs and index fingers on the corporal by drawing them across the corporal from the center to the edges once.[192] He holds the host with the thumbs and index fingers of both hands, keeping the other fingers of both hands extended and joined to each other. He does not rest his hands on the altar. He holds the host raised slightly over the altar (about nine inches) and bows slightly toward it to recite the words of consecration.[193] Historically, he directs his gaze toward the host while saying the words of institution. The celebrant then stands upright and raises the consecrated Host in both hands directly over the corporal at eye level whenever he is facing the people. The celebrant does not move his body or his feet from side to side when elevating the consecrated Host, but rather holds it motionless for a time, extending the Host toward the assembly somewhat so as to be clearly showing it to them. He joins the assembly in directing his gaze toward the elevated Host. This period of adoration is not meant to be extended disproportionately.

190 *GIRM*, 150; One commentary says the server rings the bells once or twice at the epiclesis. See André Philippe M. Mutel and Peter Freeman, *Cérémonial de la sainte messe à l'usage ordinaire des paroisses suivant le missel romain de 2002 et la pratique léguée du rit romain*, 2nd ed. (Perpignan, France: Éditions Artège, 2012), 136.

191 Mutel and Freeman, *Cérémonial de la sainte messe*, 133.

192 Elliott, *Ceremonies of the Modern Roman Rite*, 111.

193 Adrian Fortescue, J. B. O'Connell, and Alcuin Reid, eds., *The Ceremonies of the Roman Rite Described*, 15th ed. (New York: Bloomsbury, 2009), 76.

During this time, a server customarily rings the bells.[194] In some locations, the three swings of the censer toward the elements coincide with the three times the bells are rung. In other locations, the swings of the censer alternate with the ringing of the bells.[195] Using both hands, the celebrant then lowers the consecrated Host, and eventually places it directly onto the paten with the right hand alone. Then, the celebrant places his hands flat within the edges of the corporal and genuflects without bowing his head or his body.

The celebrant then takes up the chalice in both hands, the fingers of the right hand grasping the node of the chalice and the fingers of the left hand holding the base of the chalice. He holds the chalice slightly raised over the altar and bows slightly toward it as he says the words of consecration. He does not tilt the chalice toward himself or breathe into it as he says the words of consecration. According to the traditional practice, he directs his gaze toward the wine to be consecrated, at least for part of the words of institution. Standing upright, he then immediately raises the chalice with both hands over the corporal, holding the cup at about eye level whenever he is facing the people. He extends the chalice toward the assembly somewhat so as to be clearly showing it to them. Like those in the assembly, the celebrant too directs his eyes toward the chalice. Again, a server customarily rings the bells. After a moment, the celebrant lowers the chalice directly onto the corporal. The celebrant then places both hands flat within the corporal and genuflects, keeping his head and body erect. Upon rising, the celebrant replaces the pall on the chalice with the right hand, placing his left hand on the base of the chalice to steady it. He may replace the covers to the ciboria at this point as well.[196] He replaces the covers with his right hand, his left hand on the base of each ciborium. With hands joined, he looks at the people and says, "The mystery of faith." The celebrant then keeps his hands joined while the faithful sing the memorial acclamation.

The celebrant then extends his hands to continue the rest of the Eucharistic Prayer. The celebrant bows his head at the names of Jesus, Mary, and of the saint

194 One commentator says that the server rings the bells three distinct times at each elevation or continuously during the brief period of adoration. See Mutel and Freeman, *Cérémonial de la sainte messe*, 139, n. 211. Another says that the server rings the bells once or three times at each elevation. See Peter J. Elliott, *Ceremonies Explained for Servers According to the Roman Rite: A Manual for Altar Servers, Acolytes, Sacristans, and Masters of Ceremonies* (San Francisco: Ignatius Press, 2019), 65.

195 Mutel and Freeman, *Cérémonial de la sainte messe*, 139.

196 *CB*, 155.

commemorated that day whenever they occur in any of the Eucharistic Prayers. Just before the doxology, the celebrant may once again uncover the chalice in the same manner described above. The celebrant then takes the chalice in his right hand at the node and the paten, with the Host lying flat upon it, in his left hand to elevate.[197] The elements are elevated above eye level, since the doxology is addressed to God the Father, not to the assembly. The celebrant will make sure that he does not direct his gaze to the assembly, but rather in a direction which indicates he is addressing God the Father. Once the assembly has responded "Amen," the elements are then placed directly and reverently back on the altar in the same position they occupied prior to the elevation. If a pall is used, the celebrant places it once again on the chalice in the manner described above.

Gestures of the Celebrant Specific to Eucharistic Prayer I

In the specific case of Eucharistic Prayer I, the Sign of the Cross over the gifts is made some time prior to the epiclesis, at the portion of the Eucharistic Prayer which begins, "To You, therefore, most merciful Father." The celebrant joins both hands momentarily prior to making the Sign of the Cross. He lowers his left hand flat on the altar outside the corporal, while making the Sign of the Cross with his right. The right hand is held perpendicular to the altar, fingers joined, the hand extended straight. The Sign of the Cross is made from the center of the chalice to the center of the host, and then laterally between the chalice and the host from left to right in the shape of a Greek cross. The dimensions of the Greek cross should not extend beyond the size of the pall, for example. The celebrant makes the Sign of the Cross without lowering the hand or the fingers, but keeping them in the same horizontal plane at all times.[198] The entire Sign of the Cross is made in the same horizontal plane, without lowering the hand or the fingers. After making the Sign of the Cross, the celebrant joins both hands before extending them to continue with the prayer.

Where the celebrant exercises the option to conclude portions of the Roman Canon with "Through Christ Our Lord. Amen," he joins his hands together at each occasion before continuing.[199] In any event, even if he does not exercise this option throughout the prayer, he always joins his hands at the conclusion of the

197 Elliot, *Ceremonies of the Modern Roman Rite*, 117; Mutel and Freeman, *Cérémonial de la sainte messe*, 143.

198 Mutel and Freeman, *Cérémonial de la sainte messe*, 133.

199 Mutel and Freeman, *Cérémonial de la sainte messe*, 135.

section which begins, "Therefore Lord we pray," since he will then open his joined hands over the gifts for the epiclesis at "Be pleased, O Lord, we pray." The same is true at the end of the section "Remember also, Lord Your servants N. and N.," since the celebrant is about to strike his breast.

At the section which begins, "In humble prayer, we ask you," the celebrant bows with hands joined. Historically, the tips of the fingers of the joined hands were placed on the top of the altar, with the tips of the fifth fingers touching the edge of the altar. At the conclusion of the section, the celebrant stands erect and signs himself with his right hand, opened flat with fingers joined, his left hand resting on his chest. The celebrant will take care that his right hand extends no lower than the position of his left hand on his chest. Having made the Sign of the Cross, he joins both hands momentarily before proceeding with "Remember also Lord, Your servants N. and N."

When commemorating both the living ("Remember Lord Your servants") and the dead ("Remember also, Lord, Your servants N. and N."), the celebrant has traditionally drawn his joined hands toward his face for the time spent in silent prayer before proceeding with hands extended in the usual *orans* position. When holding his hands before his face, the fingers do not touch the lips. The celebrant bows his head and looks at the Blessed Sacrament before him when praying silently for the faithful departed whom he wishes to commemorate. At the words "Through Christ Our Lord," which conclude the commemoration of the dead, the celebrant has historically joined his hands and bowed his head.[200] This is the only time in Eucharistic Prayer I when the celebrant bows his head at the short conclusions to various portions of the Canon.

At the words, "To us, also Your servants," the celebrant strikes his breast with the right hand held open with the fingers joined. The right hand is not held clenched in a fist. The gesture is made with the elbow close to the body with the entire forearm rotating smoothly toward the breast without any exertion. During this time, the left hand is placed flat on the altar on the corporal. The celebrant then continues with hands in the *orans* position until the end of this section, when he always joins both hands at "Through Christ Our Lord."

The celebrant begins saying, "Through whom You continue," with hands joined. Before concluding that part of the Eucharistic Prayer, he may uncover the chalice in the usual manner in anticipation of the doxology. The celebrant then

[200] Fortescue, O'Connell, and Reid, *The Ceremonies of the Roman Rite Described*, 78–79.

begins to take the chalice at the node with his right hand and takes the paten in his left hand, ready to elevate them both at "Through him, and with him, and in him," without any delay. He holds both vessels elevated above eye level until the people have responded, "Amen." Then he slowly lowers both vessels to the position on the corporal they held before the elevation. He places the tips of his fingers of his left hand on the base of the chalice while he covers the chalice with the pall using his right hand.

The Deacon Assisting the Celebrant

When the celebrant is joined by a deacon during the Eucharistic Prayer, there are any number of additional gestures relating to them which also need to be described. Learning from the traditional practice of the Roman Rite can make the complex gestures and actions of the Eucharistic Prayer more graceful and therefore more prayerful. During the Eucharistic Prayer, the deacon assists the celebrant with the chalice and the missal.[201] Thus, the postures of the deacon will depend on whether he fulfills both functions or simply one of them. If there is more than one deacon, one deacon can remain at the celebrant's left and turn the pages of the missal, while the other deacon remains at the celebrant's right to assist with the pall and chalice. Or, if there is a master of ceremonies to turn the pages of the missal, one deacon could remain at the celebrant's right, while the second deacon, carrying the censer, joins the torch bearers before the altar during the Eucharistic Prayer and incenses the Blessed Sacrament at each elevation from a kneeling position.[202] (See figure 3.)

If, however, the same deacon does in fact fulfill both functions at the altar, as is usually the case in most parishes, he can go from the right side of the priest to the left side of the celebrant after the washing of the hands in order to turn the pages of the missal to the prayer over the gifts and the Preface. He stands close enough to the missal in order to turn the pages with his right hand, his left hand resting on his chest, without taking any steps forward or backward. During the commemorations of the living and the dead in Eucharistic Prayer I, the Roman Canon, the deacon historically has taken a step back from his position in order not to overhear the priest pronouncing the particular intentions for which he is praying. He remains at the celebrant's left side until just before the epiclesis when he returns to the right side to remove the pall from the chalice and uncover any ciboria. In Eucharistic Prayer I, the epiclesis begins, "Be pleased, O God, we

201 *GIRM*, 179.
202 Elliott, *Ceremonies of the Modern Roman Rite*, 149.

pray." In Eucharistic Prayer II, it begins, "Make holy, therefore, these gifts." The epiclesis for Eucharistic Prayer III begins, "Therefore, O Lord, we humbly implore You," and in Eucharistic Prayer IV, the text begins with "Therefore, O Lord we pray." The practice in some churches of the deacon removing the pall at an earlier point, as at the end of the *Sanctus*, for example, is without foundation. Just prior to the epiclesis, the deacon takes the pall from the chalice with his right hand, his left hand resting on his chest. He removes the covers from the ciboria with his right hand, his left hand resting on the base of each ciborium. Whenever he is standing at the altar or nearby, the deacon directs his gaze to the missal and to the actions taking place at the altar. After removing the pall and the covers just before the epiclesis, the deacon kneels in position, at the right side of the priest.

During the words of institution, according to tradition, he may bow slightly from the kneeling position. At each elevation, the deacon might lift the back of the celebrant's chasuble with his left hand, his right hand resting on his chest, if this is necessary.[203] During each elevation, the deacon directs his gaze to the consecrated Host and to the chalice. After the elevation of the chalice, the deacon rises at the same time as the celebrant rises from the second genuflection. The deacon covers the ciboria and chalice once again before passing to the celebrant's left side to turn the pages of the missal from a standing position for the remainder of the Eucharistic Prayer. He does not mirror any of the gestures of the celebrant during the course of the Eucharistic Prayer.

Just prior to the doxology, the deacon once again moves from the left side of the celebrant to his right side in order to elevate the chalice. The deacon removes the pall from the chalice in the usual way. It may be more gracious for the celebrant to hand the deacon the chalice. The deacon takes the chalice with the fingers of his right hand at the node, with the fingers of his left hand on its base. The celebrant holds the paten in both hands, somewhat above eye level. He directs his gaze toward God the Father, whom he is addressing. The deacon holds the bowl of the chalice roughly at the same height as the paten in the hands of the priest, and he is turned slightly to the left in the direction of the priest. The deacon brings the chalice close to, but not touching the paten.[204] The deacon directs his gaze toward the elements. He lowers the chalice at the same time as the celebrant lowers the paten. He may place the chalice with his right hand in the same position on the corporal that it occupied prior to the doxology, or he may hand the chalice back to the

[203] Fortescue, O'Connell, and Reid, *The Ceremonies of the Roman Rite Described*, 140.

[204] Mutel and Freeman, *Cérémonial de la sainte messe*, 143.

celebrant to place it there. He covers the chalice with the pall in the usual way. The deacon waits with hands joined for the invitation to the Our Father.

Then one of the deacons of the Mass may be charged with incensing the Blessed Sacrament at the two elevations. As the *Sanctus* begins, the deacon leaves the altar to stand at the center of the sanctuary, in front of the altar. The torch bearers follow the thurifer from the sacristy or the sanctuary to their positions in front of the altar as the *Sanctus* begins as well.[205] In the center of the sanctuary before the altar, the deacon receives the censer from the thurifer and stands with the censer in his right hand until the conclusion of the *Sanctus*. At the conclusion of the *Sanctus*, all kneel. Before and after the triple incensation of each element with double swings, he bows from the kneeling position. At the conclusion of the Eucharistic Prayer, the deacon hands the censer to the thurifer, who leads the servers back to the sacristy or to their places in the sanctuary. The deacon immediately takes his place once again at the altar. Or, the deacon may receive the censer from the thurifer at the right-hand side of the altar and kneel there, facing across the altar to incense both elements, bowing from a kneeling position before or after each incensation. This may be preferable if there are no torch bearers to accompany him, for example, or if Mass is celebrated *ad orientem*.

Concelebrants during the Eucharistic Prayer

At any given Sunday Mass in a parish, there may be one or more concelebrants joining the principal celebrant. Ideally, all the concelebrants are seated in the sanctuary for Mass. A single concelebrant could be seated to the celebrant's left, since the single deacon will be seated at the celebrant's right. Two or more concelebrants could be seated apart from the main celebrant in the sanctuary. If possible, they could be seated in two choirs facing each other across the sanctuary, rather than in a long row at the back of the sanctuary facing the nave. If the concelebrants are relatively few and the sanctuary is very small, the concelebrants might simply remain standing at their seats in the sanctuary for the entire Eucharistic Prayer in order to leave room for the deacon to exercise his ministry. At times, the number of the concelebrants and the size of the sanctuary may not make it possible for most or all of the concelebrants to be seated in the sanctuary. When seated in the nave instead, they are seated together as a group, with no other person seated in front of them, between them and the sanctuary.

[205] Mutel and Freeman, *Cérémonial de la sainte messe*, 129–130.

Even if it is not possible to seat the concelebrants entirely in the sanctuary, perhaps it is possible for all the concelebrants to stand in the sanctuary for the Eucharistic Prayer. This is greatly to be preferred. In that case, the concelebrants approach the altar from their seats with hands joined after the prayer over the gifts and prior to the Preface dialogue. If they are seated at some distance from the altar and will gather in the sanctuary closer to the altar, the celebrant may want to wait for them to take their places around the altar prior to beginning the Preface dialogue. While waiting for the concelebrants to take their places, the celebrant may keep his hands joined, or may rest both hands flat on either side of the corporal.

Once at the altar, one or two concelebrants might stand to the left and to the right of the principal celebrant, facing the altar with him, leaving room for the deacon to exercise his ministry at the celebrant's side. If they are somewhat more numerous, two might stand on either side of the celebrant and others might stand at either end of the altar, facing each other across the altar, as in the manner of concelebration in the Eastern Churches. If there are more than six concelebrants, for example, it may be best for all the concelebrants to stand in a semi-circle, rather than in a straight line, behind the main celebrant, again, leaving room for the deacon to exercise his ministry. (See figure 3.) In this way, they manifest that they are truly *circumstantes* during the course of the eucharistic sacrifice. Whenever the concelebrants are standing at the altar or nearby, they direct their gaze to the missal and to the actions taking place at the altar. Ideally, the concelebrants are sufficiently familiar with the Eucharistic Prayer so that they can participate from memory. Additional copies of the text of the Eucharistic Prayer can be placed on the altar to the right and to the left of the celebrant, perhaps at the sides of the altar, for those concelebrants who may have a speaking part. If the prayer used is very unfamiliar to most concelebrants, or if the Eucharistic Prayer is in a language which is not well known by the concelebrants, it may be necessary to distribute the text of the Eucharistic Prayer to each concelebrant. Once the concelebrants arrive at their places near the altar, the master of ceremonies, perhaps assisted by a senior server, can distribute the texts. Or, the texts may have been placed beforehand at their seats. The concelebrants bring the text with them when they approach the altar. After the doxology which concludes the Eucharistic Prayer, the concelebrants could pass the texts from one to the other to return them to the master of ceremonies and senior server so as to have both hands free during the Our Father.

During the parts of the Eucharistic Prayer read by the celebrant alone or by a concelebrant alone, the other concelebrants hold their hands joined, except where noted below. As they speak the epiclesis in a low voice with the celebrant, for example, the concelebrants extend both hands toward the elements, palms down, fingers joined, right thumbs locked over the left thumbs, for the duration of the entire epiclesis. They do not make the Sign of the Cross over the elements with the celebrant. During the words of institution, as they speak the words of consecration in a low voice with the principal celebrant, they may extend their open right hands toward each of the elements with the palms facing left, fingers joined in a pointing gesture, their left hands resting on their chests. They do not repeat at the consecrations the same gesture made during the epiclesis.[206] During the elevation of each species, with hands joined once again, they direct their gaze to the elevated elements.[207] Each time the principal celebrant genuflects, they bow profoundly from the waist. The celebrant and concelebrants join their hands while the faithful sing the memorial acclamation. Following the memorial acclamation, all the concelebrants hold their hands in the *orans* position as they join the celebrant in reciting the *anamnesis* section in a low voice.

If one or more of the concelebrants is selected to read aloud a portion of the Eucharistic Prayer which follows, that concelebrant alone does so with hands outstretched in the *orans* position. Obviously, this gesture will only be possible if he is reading his portion of the Eucharistic Prayer from the altar missal itself or from a card or booklet placed beforehand where he is standing at the altar. All other concelebrants, including the principal celebrant, join their hands during this time.

During Eucharistic Prayer I, in particular, the concelebrants do not lift their eyes to the Father at the beginning of the words of consecration as the principal celebrant does.[208] However, they bow with the principal celebrant with hands joined at "In humble prayer we ask You almighty God," and stand up straight to make the Sign of the Cross on themselves at its conclusion, resting their left hands on their chests. At the words "To us also Your servants," they strike their breasts with the right hands open, fingers joined together. The entire forearm pivots from the elbow in a smooth and relaxed gesture. The left hand is held on the chest below the point where the right hand will strike the chest. Then, the concelebrants join both hands once again. During the doxology, the concelebrants keep their hands joined and look at the elevated elements. Mass then continues with the Communion rite.

206 Elliott, *Ceremonies of the Modern Roman Rite*, 162.

207 *GIRM*, 222c.

208 *GIRM*, 222; Mutel and Freeman, *Cérémonial de la sainte messe*, 196.

9

The Communion Rite and the Concluding Rites

While the Communion rite and the concluding rites in the current missal are considerably simplified compared to the same points in Mass according to the editions of the missal prior to 1969, the traditional practice of the Roman liturgy can still provide celebrants with helpful directions as to how to accomplish the various gestures demanded by the preparation for Communion and the conclusion of Mass.

The Our Father

After the doxology which concludes the Eucharistic Prayer, the priest and the deacon place the paten and chalice down on the corporal. The deacon, with his left hand resting on his chest, covers the chalice with the pall using the right hand. The celebrant places his left hand on the base of the chalice and his right hand flat on the corporal. With hands joined, the celebrant looks at the assembly and invites them to pray the Our Father with the invitation "At the Savior's command." The celebrant then extends his hands in the *orans* position during the Our Father and keeps his hands in that same position for the embolism to the Our Father, "Deliver us Lord we pray," bowing his head at the name of Jesus at the end of the prayer. Then the celebrant joins his hands for the doxology, "For the kingdom, the power, and the glory." The deacon keeps his hands joined throughout. Concelebrants present extend their hands in the *orans* position during the recitation of the Our Father and join their hands at its conclusion. They do not continue to extend their hands during the embolism which follows the Our Father.

Traditionally, during the Our Father, the celebrant directs his gaze to the Host before him. Unless a deacon, the master of ceremonies, or a server is turning the pages of the missal for the celebrant, it might be more graceful for the celebrant to turn the page with his left hand just before he begins to recite the Our Father from memory, so as to be able to continue immediately with the embolism which follows without lowering his hands in order to turn the page in the missal. When singing the Our Father, the celebrant looks at the missal in order to follow the musical notation. In this case, after singing the Our Father, the celebrant will lower his right hand flat on the altar inside the edge of the corporal before turning the page of the missal with his left hand.

The Sign of Peace

Having concluded the doxology, the celebrant begins the prayer for peace, "Lord Jesus Christ," holding his hands once again the *orans* position. Again, the traditional practice has been to look at the Host when praying this prayer, bowing the head slightly toward the Host. Standing erect and facing the assembly, the celebrant extends and joins his hands, saying, "The peace of the Lord be with you always." The deacon keeps his hands joined when facing the assembly and inviting them to offer each other a sign of peace. Similarly, the celebrant, in the absence of a deacon, invites all to share a sign of peace with hands joined. He too faces the faithful and looks at them when speaking this invitation. The celebrant himself then turns to his right and gives the peace to the deacon or to one of the servers.[209] If concelebrants are present, the principal celebrant would offer the peace to those concelebrants closest to him at the altar before offering the peace to the deacon.[210]

The historical Roman manner of giving the peace is stylized.[211] Both parties are standing. The person to receive the peace first bows to the person who is giving him the peace. For example, the deacon would bow to the celebrant first. Both parties have their hands joined during this time. Then, the one giving the peace places both hands on the shoulders or forearms of the person receiving the peace. The one receiving the peace places his hands under the forearms of the person giving the peace. In the meantime, both parties bow their heads forward slightly, each bowing to the right of the other such that their left cheeks nearly touch. Standing erect once again, both parties join their hands and bow to each other. The process is repeated as often as the peace is exchanged. The missal

209 *GIRM*, 154; *RM*, Order of Mass, no. 128.

210 *GIRM*, 239.

211 Peter J. Elliott, *Ceremonies of the Modern Roman Rite: The Eucharist and the Liturgy of the Hours*, rev. ed. (San Francisco: Ignatius Press, 1995), 119.

does not indicate what, if anything, is said as the peace is exchanged.[212] Servers do not leave the sanctuary and move about the church to give the sign of peace to the faithful. They exchange the sign of peace with the servers closest to them on their right and left only.

The Fraction and Comingling

While the Lamb of God is sung, the deacon uncovers the chalice with his right hand, while his left hand rests on his chest. The celebrant places his left hand on the base of the chalice, while his right hand rests flat on the corporal. Then the celebrant first breaks the Host over the paten in at least two pieces using the thumbs and index fingers of both hands. He breaks the Host along the line scored down the center of the Host, beginning at the top of the Host and concluding at the bottom. He reverently puts the portion of the Host in his right hand down on the paten. While holding the remaining portion of the Host with the thumb and index finger of the left hand, he may remove the particles from that portion by running down its edge from top to bottom with the thumb and index finger of his right hand. Arriving at the bottom of the portion held in his left hand, he breaks off a small particle of the Host with his right hand, and lays the larger portion down on the paten with his left hand. Holding the chalice by the node with the fingers of his left hand, the celebrant holds the particle in his right hand over the chalice. He says the prayer "May this mingling" in a low voice as he reverently drops the particle into the chalice without making the Sign of the Cross. If the celebrant will eventually elevate the Host over the paten at "Behold the Lamb of God," the deacon now covers the chalice once again with his right hand, his left hand resting on his chest. Meanwhile the celebrant places his left hand on the base of the chalice, while his right hand rests on the corporal. He then joins his hands before him to continue singing the Lamb of God with the assembly. If, on the other hand, the celebrant chooses to elevate the Host over the chalice instead at the invitation to Communion, the chalice can remain uncovered for this brief period.

If concelebrants are present, the main celebrant or one of the concelebrants, but not the deacon, may bring a paten or ciborium of Hosts consecrated at that Mass directly from the altar to each of the concelebrants prior to the Communion

[212] *RM*, Order of Mass, no. 127. For the United States, *GIRM* 154 suggests the formula "The peace of the Lord be with you always. Amen." A commentator notes that "Peace be with you. And with your spirit," or "The peace of Christ. Amen," are common. See André Philippe M. Mutel and Peter Freeman, *Cérémonial de la sainte messe à l'usage ordinaire des paroisses suivant le missel romain de 2002 et la pratique léguée du rit romain*, 2nd ed. (Perpignan, France: Éditions Artège, 2012), 150, n. 251.

of the celebrant, for example, when the assembly begins to sing, "Lamb of God."[213] This priest says nothing as he approaches each concelebrant. Each concelebrant takes a Host consecrated at that Mass in his right hand with his index finger and thumb. He holds his left hand open under his right hand if he will be holding the Host in his right hand for some time before consuming it, for example, when all the concelebrants consume at the same time as the celebrant.

The Communion of the Celebrant(s) and Ministers

After the conclusion of the Lamb of God, the celebrant says one of the two prayers of preparation for Communion which follow, either "Lord Jesus Christ, Son of the living God," or "May the receiving of Your Body and Blood, Lord Jesus Christ," with hands joined. As far as possible, the celebrant directs his gaze to the elements while saying the prayer. Traditionally, these prayers were said bowing slightly to the elements, with hands joined, the ends of the fingers of his joined hands resting on top of the altar, and the tips of the fifth fingers of each hand touching the edge of the altar.

The celebrant then genuflects, resting both hands flat on the corporal, then rises and takes up a portion of the Host in the right hand and the paten or chalice in his left hand. He holds the portion of the Host directly over the paten or chalice. Or, while holding the paten or chalice in his left hand, he may hold both portions of the Host at the bottom in the thumb and index finger of his right hand, side by side and together in such a way that the Host appears unbroken.[214] He holds the elements at eye level, and extends them toward those present. The celebrant looks at the assembly as he addresses them, "Behold the Lamb of God." With the assembly, he says, "Lord I am not worthy," while looking at the elements. Then, placing the paten or chalice down on the altar, he uses both hands to place the half portion of the Host to the right over the half portion of the Host to the left, and holding both in his right hand at the bottom, consumes them reverently, bowing slightly to do so.[215] Traditionally, the celebrant held the paten under his chin while consuming the Host. Historically, those assisting the priest at the altar, deacons and servers, bowed low when the celebrant consumed the

[213] *GIRM*, 242.

[214] Mutel and Freeman, *Cérémonial de la sainte messe*, 154; Adrian Fortescue, J. B. O'Connell, and Alcuin Reid, eds., *The Ceremonies of the Roman Rite Described*, 15th ed. (New York: Bloomsbury, 2009), 81.

[215] Fortescue, O'Connell, and Reid, *The Ceremonies of the Roman Rite Described*, 81.

Host.[216] Standing erect, he joins his hands before his face as he reverently consumes the Body of the Lord. He may close his eyes in prayer. The joined fingers of his hands do not touch the lips. Meanwhile the concelebrants do likewise, giving themselves Communion simultaneously with the celebrant.[217]

Without delay, the deacon uncovers the chalice with his right hand (unless the chalice has remained uncovered since the fraction and the comingling), the left hand resting on his chest. The celebrant holds his left hand on the base of the chalice while his right hand rests on the corporal. According to the most common practice, the celebrant takes the purificator in his right hand and transfers it to his left hand. He then takes the chalice in his right hand, holding the purificator in his left hand under his chin, and reverently consumes the Precious Blood.[218] If he intends to consume the entire contents of the chalice, he does so in one draught, without raising the chalice high. Again, all those assisting the celebrant at the altar, deacons and servers, bow low when he consumes the Precious Blood. Although it is not mentioned in the missal, in some locations a server rings the bells once after the priest has consumed the Precious Blood to signify the beginning of Communion.[219]

The celebrant transfers the purificator from his left hand to his right hand and wipes the rim of the chalice with the purificator in his right hand, holding the chalice on the altar at the node with the fingers of his left hand. Depending on the location on the corporal of additional vessels, the celebrant places the empty chalice down on the back portion of the corporal, away from the center, either to the left or to the right. Only if the celebrant has consumed all the Precious Blood, or if he will not minister any of the Precious Blood which remains to anyone else, does the deacon then cover the chalice with the pall in his right hand, his left hand resting on his chest. If others will receive some of the Precious Blood from the principal chalice, the celebrant places the chalice with the Precious Blood which remains on the back portion of the corporal at the center.

[216] Fortescue, O'Connell, and Reid, *The Ceremonies of the Roman Rite Described*, 118, 126, 133, 141.

[217] *GIRM*, 244; Mutel and Freeman, *Cérémonial de la sainte messe*, 206.

[218] In the traditional practice, the celebrant purifies the paten over the chalice with his right thumb first. He then holds the paten under his chin in his left hand while using his right hand to consume the Precious Blood from the chalice. See *Ritus servandus* 1962, 10, no. 5.

[219] Peter J. Elliott, *Ceremonies Explained for Servers According to the Roman Rite: A Manual for Altar Servers, Acolytes, Sacristans, and Masters of Ceremonies* (San Francisco: Ignatius Press, 2019), 65. Fortescue, O'Connell, and Reid, *The Ceremonies of the Roman Rite Described*, 102.

The celebrant then proceeds to minister both species to the deacon by turning to his right, first for the Body of the Lord, and then again for the Blood of the Lord. He may do so from the principal chalice or from an auxiliary chalice. Traditionally, the Host is always ministered by the right hand, the left hand holding the ciborium at the node. The minister holds the Host slightly elevated over the vessel and looks at the communicant when saying, "The Body of Christ." Conversely, the chalice is held in the right hand in order to be offered to the communicants, with a purificator in the left in order to wipe the rim of the chalice after each communicant. Again, the chalice is held slightly elevated as the minister looks at the communicant and says, "The Blood of Christ."

Each concelebrant approaches the altar, genuflects, and takes the chalice by the node in his right hand, holding a purificator under his chin in his left hand. After consuming some of the Precious Blood, he returns the chalice to the corporal. He transfers the purificator from his left hand to his right hand and wipes the rim of the chalice with the right hand, the fingers of the left hand holding the node of the chalice. He replaces the purificator along the edge of the corporal. In many locations, each concelebrant turns the chalice a quarter turn or a half turn for the next concelebrant and returns to his place. The concelebrants can also receive from the chalice by remaining in their places. A deacon or a concelebrant may present each of them with the chalice, saying nothing, or they may pass the chalice and purificator among themselves.

Concelebrants may instead receive both species by approaching the altar after the Communion of the celebrant. Upon arriving at the altar, they genuflect, and take a Host in their right hands, and then receive from the chalice as indicated above for the principal celebrant. Alternately, if concelebrants are intended to receive Communion by intinction, they approach the altar, genuflect, take a half portion of a usual celebrant's Host in their right hands and the paten or purificator in their left. They intinct the portion of the Host in the chalice, holding the paten or purificator under their chin in their right hand, between the chalice and themselves. They replace the purificator along the edge of the corporal each time.

Finally, the concelebrants, if they are very numerous, may receive both species in procession in the nave during the Communion of the faithful, coming forward first to take a Host in their right hands from a paten held by a concelebrant, and to receive from the chalice extended to them by one or more deacons or concelebrants. Those ministering Communion to the concelebrants say nothing as each concelebrant approaches.[220] Generally, Communion is not received by intinction when distributed to the concelebrants in this way unless provision is made for the concelebrant himself or for a server to hold a paten under the Host and Precious Blood as both are received.

After the Communion of the celebrant, concelebrants, and the deacon, the distribution of Holy Communion to the servers and the assembly begins. If the number of priests and deacons available will not be sufficient for the number of people who will be receiving Communion, extraordinary lay ministers, either delegated by the bishop for a term or delegated for the occasion by the celebrant, can assist in the distribution of Communion. The *General Instruction of the Roman Missal* provides no indications as to the manner in which they approach the altar and receive the elements. One commentator has suggested that they approach the altar during the Communion of the celebrant, as the first among the faithful to receive Holy Communion along with the servers of the Mass.[221] The extraordinary ministers genuflect to the Blessed Sacrament upon the altar when they enter the sanctuary. They may go the credence table to cleanse their hands if necessary. They join the servers to receive Holy Communion from the celebrant. With either the ciborium or paten in the left hand, the celebrant gives the servers and extraordinary ministers Communion. They may approach the celebrant two at a time or four at a time.[222] Or, they may stand together, shoulder to shoulder in a line before the altar. The celebrant traditionally gives Communion by moving from left to right. The deacon might do the same when ministering the chalice immediately following the celebrant. Meanwhile, the Communion of the concelebrants may continue during this time if necessary. Extraordinary ministers never give themselves Communion, nor do they take the eucharistic vessels from the altar. The vessels needed are placed into their hands by the priest or the deacon.

The Communion of the Faithful

The missal urges the celebrant to minister Communion to all those present from elements consecrated at the same Mass they are attending.[223] This injunction is very often disregarded. Its observance can be made very simple. First, the determination needs to be made as to how many people actually attend the Mass in

[220] See *GIRM*, 246–249.

[221] Elliott, *Ceremonies of the Modern Roman Rite*, 289–292.

[222] Fortescue, O'Connell, and Reid, *The Ceremonies of the Roman Rite Described*, 149.

[223] *GIRM*, 85.

question. Over time, that number can usually be ascertained without difficulty. Then, a slightly larger number of hosts, perhaps by 10 percent for example, is habitually prepared. A sufficient, but not excessive amount of wine is also prepared if Communion under both species will be offered. After Communion, the Hosts which remain are reposed in the tabernacle. If during the distribution of Communion, the number of Hosts consecrated is insufficient for some reason, the distribution of Communion is temporarily halted while the celebrant retrieves the ciborium from the tabernacle and continues with the distribution of Communion. The ciborium in the tabernacle should be large enough to contain, when full, slightly more than the total number of persons attending any one Mass. Once the ciborium in the tabernacle is full and not able to receive any more Hosts remaining from the distribution of Communion, no hosts need to be prepared for consecration at the next Mass. All those present on that one occasion receive Communion from the reserved Sacrament. At the following Mass, the celebrant will once again consecrate the total number of hosts plus a few more needed to give Communion to everyone present. And the process begins again, until the ciborium in the tabernacle is full once more. Thus, the sacristan is instructed to prepare either the total number of hosts plus a few more needed to communicate everyone attending the specific Mass, or to refrain from preparing any hosts for the Communion of the people, since they will all be receiving from the ciborium sized to contain the number of hosts needed for the Communion of everyone present for that same Mass.

If the celebrant is obliged to minister the Communion from Hosts reserved in the tabernacle, he ordinarily approaches the tabernacle immediately after his own Communion under both species, not before.[224] The celebrant may instead prefer that a concelebrant, or even the deacon, accomplish this some time prior to the celebrant's own Communion, for example, while the *Agnus Dei* is being sung. That minister approaches the tabernacle, opens the door, and genuflects. He takes the vessel needed out of the tabernacle with his right hand. If the tabernacle will be completely empty when he removes the vessel(s), he leaves the door open. Otherwise, if any portion of the Blessed Sacrament remains in the tabernacle during the time of Communion, he closes the door without locking it. He can place the Blessed Sacrament on a corporal in front of the tabernacle while he closes the door. He takes the vessel in both hands and goes to the place where he will distribute

[224] Mutel and Freeman, *Cérémonial de la sainte messe*, 228; Elliott, *Ceremonies of the Modern Roman Rite*, 125.

Communion or to the altar without any further reverence. According to the traditional practice, if the tabernacle is located outside the sanctuary at some distance, the deacon or concelebrant assumes a white humeral veil to transfer the Blessed Sacrament from the place of reservation to the altar.[225] The priest or deacon is accompanied by two servers, or at least one, with burning candles.[226]

In the United States, the faithful stand to receive Communion.[227] They bow the head before receiving either species as a sign of reverence. When distributing Communion to the faithful who approach in a kind of procession, the celebrant remains stationary in one place, preferably standing at the edge of the sanctuary, or at least on its lowest step, to do so. Each Host is grasped by the index finger and thumb of the right hand. As he gives Communion, the celebrant may rub his fingers over the ciborium or paten to cleanse them of any particles which may adhere.[228] The Instruction *Redemptionis Sacramentum* recommends that the use of the chin paten for the Communion of the faithful be retained.[229] In that case, a server holding a paten in the right hand stands to the right of the celebrant distributing Holy Communion. The server holds the paten under the chin of the person receiving on the tongue, and under the hands of the person receiving in the hand. If the celebrant is distributing Communion to two lines of the faithful in alternation, it is often more convenient to have two servers with patens assisting him, each one standing on either side of the celebrant. Other servers may hold torches on either side of each station.[230]

Once the Communion of the faithful is over, any Precious Blood which remains is consumed while standing at the altar, facing any side of the altar. Any hosts which remain may be brought directly to the tabernacle for reservation or may more conveniently be combined into one vessel over a corporal at the altar. All genuflect after placing a vessel containing the Blessed Sacrament on the altar.[231] This single vessel is then brought to the tabernacle. If the tabernacle is located in the sanctuary, the celebrant himself or a concelebrant may reserve the Blessed Sacrament,[232] or the deacon may even do so on his behalf. Upon arriving

225 *CB*, 328; Mutel and Freeman, *Cérémonial de la sainte messe*, 175, n. 315.

226 Mutel and Freeman, *Cérémonial de la sainte messe*, 162, n. 289.

227 *GIRM*, 160.

228 *GIRM*, 278.

229 *RS*, 93.

230 Mutel and Freeman, *Cérémonial de la sainte messe*, 301, n. 209.

231 Elliott, *Ceremonies of the Modern Roman Rite*, 290.

232 *GIRM*, 163.

at the tabernacle, the priest or deacon places the ciborium in the tabernacle and genuflects, then closes and locks the door. Normally, the key is removed and eventually placed with the purified and vested chalice, on top of the veil or the burse. Ministers who distributed Holy Communion will often want to cleanse their fingers of any particles of the Host. They can do so by rubbing their fingers over the ciborium prior to reposition or by washing their fingers in an ablution cup placed near the tabernacle or at the credence table.[233]

If the tabernacle where reservation will take place is located outside the sanctuary, it is preferable for the deacon or a concelebrant to repose the Blessed Sacrament so that the celebrant is able to remain in the sanctuary.[234] When reserving the Blessed Sacrament in a tabernacle outside the sanctuary, the priest or deacon assumes a humeral veil to do so.[235] He is accompanied by two servers with candles, or by at least one. In that case, placing the Blessed Sacrament on the altar before the tabernacle, the priest or deacon kneels and then gives up the humeral veil. He rises, places the ciborium in the tabernacle, genuflects, and then closes and locks its door.

The Purification of the Vessels

The celebrant, assisted by concelebrants, the deacon, or an instituted acolyte, may then proceed to the purification of the vessels.[236] The celebrant or one of the concelebrants may purify the vessels at the altar or at the credence table. The deacon or an instituted acolyte purifies the vessels solely at the credence table.[237] If a concelebrant or deacon is available, it is perhaps more fitting for that minister

[233] *GIRM*, 278; Mutel and Freeman, *Cérémonial de la sainte messe*, 172, n. 309.

[234] *CB*, 165.

[235] *Caeremoniale Episcoporum*, no. 328. The English translation of the same in *CB* 328 omits the reference to the humeral veil found in the Latin edition. The humeral veil is worn only when an ordained minister transfers the Blessed Sacrament to and from one altar to another altar. See Mutel and Freeman, *Cérémonial de la sainte messe*, 175, n.315. It is not worn when an ordained minister or a lay minister brings the Blessed Sacrament to the tabernacle directly from a Communion station. In that case, at least one server with a torch may accompany each of the ministers from their stations to the place of reservation. If the humeral veil will be used at some point during Mass, it can be prepared before the beginning of Mass and draped over all the items on the credence table, following the traditional practice. See Fortescue, O'Connell, and Reid, *The Ceremonies of the Roman Rite Described*, 108.

[236] It is permissible to purify the vessels, suitably covered, and placed on a corporal at the credence table, after Mass, in accord with *GIRM* 183. There is always the risk with this approach that vessels which have not been purified may be put away prematurely by sacristans who may believe they have already been purified.

[237] *GIRM* 183, 192; Mutel and Freeman, *Cérémonial de la sainte messe*, 173.

to carry out the purification of the vessels, while the celebrant returns to the chair and sits. While carrying out the purification of the vessels, the priest celebrant or a concelebrant says the prayer "What has passed our lips," in a low voice.[238] At the altar or at the credence table, the celebrant or a concelebrant may remove particles from the paten by wiping it over the chalice with a purificator,[239] or by wiping it over the chalice with the thumb of his right hand. Historically, the paten was held upright in the left hand over the chalice. The fingers of the right hand were extended and held together, with the thumb separated from the rest of the hand. With the thumb, the celebrant brushed any particles which remained on the right half of the paten into the chalice. Then, rotating the paten 180 degrees, the celebrant repeated the gesture once again on the right half of the paten. The celebrant placed the paten on the corporal until it could be washed and wiped.

Then, the chalice is purified with wine and water, or water alone. If wine is used first, the celebrant, standing at the center of the altar, for example, holds the chalice by the node in his right hand over the corporal to the right while a server pours the wine. The same could take place over a corporal on the credence table as well. Then, holding a purificator or a purified scale paten in his left hand under his chin, the celebrant purifies his mouth with the wine. He puts the paten down on the corporal to the left and sets the chalice down on the corporal in the middle.[240] Then, as the celebrant holds the thumbs and index fingers of both hands over the mouth of the chalice while using the other fingers to hold the chalice by its cup, he turns to his right and steps toward the right side of the altar. He continues to hold the chalice in this way as he sets the chalice down on the right edge of the altar. The celebrant stands at the right-hand side of the altar and facing it. There a server pours a little wine and a much larger amount of water over the fingers into the chalice. If the server is short in stature, the celebrant may need to hold the chalice off of the altar and face the server in order to receive the wine and then the water. Having received the wine and the water in the chalice, the celebrant stands to the right of the corporal with the purificator at his left side.[241] The celebrant can sprinkle water from his fin-

238 *RM,* Order for Mass, no. 137. One commentator points out that the celebrant or concelebrant alone says this prayer even if others join him in purifying the vessels. The same commentator suggests that the priest celebrant may even say this prayer while others who are not concelebrants are purifying the vessels in his stead. See Mutel and Freeman, *Cérémonial de la sainte messe,* 173.

239 *GIRM,* 279.

240 Fortescue, O'Connell, and Reid, *The Ceremonies of the Roman Rite Described,* 85.

241 Mutel and Freeman, *Cérémonial de la sainte messe,* 172.

gers onto the paten before drying the fingers with the purificator. The celebrant turns the chalice gently in order to purify the entire interior of the chalice with the ablution. Then, holding the purificator in his left hand under his chin, he takes the chalice by the node with the fingers of his right hand and consumes the ablution. He then wipes the chalice with the purificator using the extended fingers of his right hand while holding the chalice by the node with the fingers of his left hand. Having dried the interior of the chalice, and put it down on the altar to the right of the corporal, he then uses the same purificator to wipe the paten a final time. The front of the chalice, indicated by a cross, should face the assembly.

The celebrant spreads the purificator open over the chalice, places the paten on top as at the beginning of Mass, and then places the pall. Moving the corporal slightly to the right, away from the missal, the celebrant folds it in reverse order to opening it, that is, folding the bottom portion up first, then the top, then the right-hand portion, followed finally by the left-hand portion. (See figure 6.) A server carries the empty burse to the altar. With the left hand, the celebrant holds the burse open and upright, with its edge on the altar. Holding the burse open in this way, he inserts the corporal into the burse with the right hand, the fold of the corporal at the bottom of the burse. If the burse is not used, the celebrant simply places the folded corporal on the pall under the veil. Another server brings the chalice veil to the altar, holding it in both hands by the top corners or back portion of the veil. The celebrant receives the veil in both hands, taking it by the two bottom corners of the front portion of the veil. Using a clockwise motion beginning to the left of the chalice, he veils it from behind the chalice toward himself. The front of the veil should touch the altar and eventually face the assembly, regardless of the orientation of the celebrant at the altar. The celebrant then places the burse with the corporal inside on top of the veiled chalice, with its opening facing away from the assembly. If the tabernacle key was brought to the altar, it is usually placed on top of the burse.

A deacon or a server then removes the veiled chalice from the altar to the credence table by carrying it in his left hand at the node, the long side of the veil and the closed edge of the burse facing forward, with his right hand with fingers joined resting on top of the veil or burse to hold the tabernacle key. It is worth noting that once the chalice and paten have been purified and the celebrant has consumed the ablutions, a deacon, an instituted acolyte, or even a simple server can also accomplish all the remaining actions mentioned above in his place.[242]

[242] *GIRM*, 183, 192; Mutel and Freeman, *Cérémonial de la sainte messe*, 176.

When multiple vessels have been used for the distribution of Holy Communion, they can be purified at the altar if they are few in number. A server pours water into ciboria or into patens with a raised edge. This ablution should then be poured into a chalice to drink. Ciboria or patens are not the kind of vessels meant for drinking. Auxiliary chalices, if they are few, can be purified at the altar with a little wine and water, or only water. The celebrant or a concelebrant pours the ablution from the first ciborium or paten into the other ciboria or patens in turn, then successively into each chalice, concluding with the principal chalice. The ablution is consumed once, from the principal chalice.

Numerous auxiliary vessels for Communion can more easily be purified on corporals placed at the credence table. At the conclusion of the Communion of the faithful, a server unfolds a corporal or corporals at the credence table in the usual manner. (See figure 6.) The empty vessels are brought to the credence table by the ministers who used them for the distribution of Communion. Unpurified vessels are not traditionally carried by servers. The server can begin by pouring water into one ciborium or paten. Then the celebrant, the deacon, or an instituted acolyte pours the ablution into each successive ciborium, and then into each successive chalice and consumes the ablution only once, from the last chalice to be purified. The vessels can be wiped by the minister(s) doing the purifying or by one of the servers as the ablutions are consumed. Depending on their number, the purified auxiliary chalices and ciboria can be placed in a line behind the principal chalice on the credence table. The celebrant, the deacon, an instituted acolyte, or even a server folds the corporal(s) on which the unpurified vessels were placed, and places the corporal(s) in the burse.[243] Then, the minister or the server drapes the principal chalice and the auxiliary chalices directly behind it with the chalice veil, provided the veil is large enough to cover all the vessels used. The minister or the server places the burse on top of the veiled chalice. Ciboria with their covers can also be placed to either side of the chalice if necessary, beginning on the right side.

Finally, it is also possible for the celebrant to purify the principal chalice and paten at the altar, while the deacon or instituted acolyte simultaneously purifies auxiliary chalices and ciboria at the credence table. In that case, it is best for two sets of servers to utilize two sets of cruets so that the purifications can truly be carried out simultaneously in the manner described above.

[243] *GIRM*, 183, 192; Mutel and Freeman, *Cérémonial de la sainte messe*, 176.

The Post-Communion Prayer

The missal can be brought near the chair if the Post-Communion prayer is to be said at the chair. The missal, open to the appropriate page, is carried from the altar to the credence table on its stand or cushion with both hands, with the open pages facing the server. The server then takes up the missal, facing away from him, with both hands placed on the bottom of the missal ready to approach the celebrant at the chair prior to the words "Let us pray." If the Post-Communion prayer is to be said at the altar, the deacon or a server may reposition the missal, open to the appropriate page, in the middle of the altar, parallel to the edge of the altar, and several inches away from the edge of the altar in order to leave room for the celebrant and deacon to kiss the altar at the conclusion of Mass.[244] If the size of the missal with its stand makes this awkward when facing the people, the missal can remain to the left of center, at an angle, instead.

At the chair, a server stands directly in front of the celebrant, unless it is necessary for the server to stand slightly to the celebrant's left, holding the missal with both hands at the bottom of each page. The server remains there through the blessing and dismissal, in the event that the celebrant wishes to use a solemn blessing or a blessing over the people, or wishes to sing the blessing or the dismissal. The celebrant faces the assembly, looks at them, and holds his hands joined when saying, "Let us pray." The celebrant holds his hands in the *orans* position during the Post-Communion prayer until its conclusion, when he joins his hands. If the chair is arranged perpendicular to the altar, the celebrant normally faces the altar when praying the Post-Communion prayer.

When the celebrant elects to pray the Post-Communion prayer at the altar, he leaves the chair and goes to the altar with his hands joined. He says, "Let us pray," once he has arrived at the altar; he does not say, "Let us pray," at the chair before moving to the altar for the Post-Communion prayer. He prays the Post-Communion prayer in the manner described above. If he wishes then to make some kind of announcements, it is best for him, or the deacon who accompanied him to the altar, to step away from the altar to its side to do so. It is unseemly to address the mundane while standing at the place of the eucharistic sacrifice. After making any announcement, the celebrant or the deacon may then return to the center of the altar for the final blessing and dismissal. If this is a regular occurrence, it may be advisable to conclude Mass consistently at the chair.

[244] Peter J. Elliott, *Ceremonies Explained for Servers According to the Roman Rite: A Manual for Altar Servers, Acolytes, Sacristans, and Masters of Ceremonies* (San Francisco: Ignatius Press, 2019), 254; Mutel and Freeman, *Cérémonial de la sainte messe*, 177.

The Concluding Rites

Afterwards, the priest faces the assembly, and extends and joins his hands while saying, "The Lord be with you." He blesses the assembly with his right hand. He holds the fingers of his right hand together with the hand fully extended, pointing upwards. He makes the Sign of the Cross in the shape of a Greek cross over the people, at the height of his face and within the width of his shoulders. When blessing the faithful at the chair, the celebrant's left hand rests on his chest. When giving the blessing at the altar and facing the assembly, the traditional practice instructs the celebrant to lay his hand on the altar while blessing with his right.[245] Traditionally, those receiving the blessing bow slightly to receive the blessing. As much as possible, the deacon should orient himself toward the celebrant to receive the blessing.

In the case where the celebrant will impart the solemn blessing or the blessing over the people, he turns toward the people, looks at them, and extends and joins his hands, saying, "The Lord be with you." The deacon, or even a concelebrant, with hands joined and facing the assembly, invites them to bow down. All bow slightly for the duration of the invocations or Collect and for the blessing itself, including the deacon. The priest extends his arms with the palms of his hands over the people, fingers joined, for the invocation(s) or Collect prior to the blessing itself. He imparts the blessing according to the alternative formula noted in the missal, in the manner described above, either at the chair or at the altar.

It is perhaps easiest for the celebrant to impart the solemn blessing or blessing over the people at the altar, facing the assembly, since the missal will likewise be resting on the altar directly in front of him. However, if the celebrant remains at the chair, he will have to turn his head slightly to the left to read the invocations from the missal, while keeping his arms directed forward toward the assembly. The server remains in the same position throughout the Post-Communion prayer and blessing; he does not change position based on the movements of the celebrant at the chair.

The celebrant or deacon both join their hands before them during the dismissal and its response. The deacon or a concelebrant or the celebrant himself faces the assembly and looks at them to dismiss them. After the response to the dismissal, the server returns the missal to its stand at the credence table if he has been standing at the chair. If the celebrant is at the altar, having finished with the

[245] *CB*, 108.

missal, the celebrant may close it with his right hand, his left hand resting on the altar or steadying the book.

After the dismissal, the celebrant goes to the altar if he has been at the chair. At the altar, he places both hands flat on the altar and kisses the altar with his lips closed and without making any sound, as at the beginning of Mass. The deacon, standing to the celebrant's right, kisses the altar with his lips closed and without making any sound. Traditionally, he has kept his hands joined without placing them on the altar. Concelebrants are not expected to kiss the altar at the conclusion of Mass.[246] If one or two concelebrants are already at the altar for the concluding rites of Mass, and can kiss the altar without any inconvenience, there seems to be nothing to prevent that gesture.[247] Having kissed the altar, both the celebrant and the deacon turn to their right, go to the steps of the sanctuary, and face the altar. Since the deacon will walk to the priest's right at the end of Mass, it is perhaps more convenient for him to be standing to the left of the celebrant as they face the altar.

Meanwhile, the servers and ministers can place themselves in the center aisle and face the altar in reverse order from what they will occupy in the final procession. The concelebrants can do the same between the servers and the principal celebrant, or in two lines, shoulder to shoulder, on either side of him. Concelebrants may also bow to the altar or genuflect to the Blessed Sacrament from their places if this allows for the recessional to begin more easily. In the case where there is not sufficient space for the concelebrants to genuflect in their places, they can substitute a profound bow for the genuflection to the Blessed Sacrament, as they do at both elevations of the species during Mass. Once all the ministers and concelebrants are in the proper position, the celebrant leads the entire group in genuflecting to the tabernacle if it is in the sanctuary, or simply bows profoundly to the altar if the Blessed Sacrament is reserved outside the sanctuary.[248] Servers holding anything in their hands do not genuflect or bow profoundly. They simply bow their heads. Then both the celebrant and the deacon turn toward each other to process out side by side in the proper positions. The servers, standing in two rows before the sanctuary, likewise turn toward each other in order to face the opposite direction and process out. When more

[246] *CB*, 170; Elliot, *Ceremonies of the Modern Roman Rite*, 169; Mutel and Freeman, *Cérémonial de la sainte messe*, 209.

[247] Mutel and Freeman, *Cérémonial de la sainte messe*, 209.

[248] *GIRM*, 251.

than two servers stand together in a line before the sanctuary, as in the case of the cross bearer and candle bearers, all three turn on their right in order to face the opposite direction and process out.

The Recessional

The procession at the end of Mass is conducted in the same way as the entrance procession, except that neither the Gospel book nor the censer are carried out.[249] If cross and candles were used at the entrance procession, the same three servers walk together in a line with other servers behind them two by two. If there is an odd number of servers, the final server walks last between the two lines of servers. Upon arriving at the location where the procession will end, as in the rear vestibule of the church, for example, it is customary for the servers carrying the cross and candles to turn around to face the celebrant. The two lines of servers part and stand in two rows facing each other. First, they turn slightly and bow with the celebrant to the processional cross standing at the head of the two rows in the middle. Then they turn slightly toward him and bow to him. The celebrant may bless the servers, who kneel, or at least bow, to receive the blessing, before thanking them. Afterward, the celebrant may remove his chasuble, and even the stole, in order to greet the faithful and then make his thanksgiving.[250] The recessional may also end in the sacristy in the same way.

After the Conclusion of Mass

In the sacristy, the celebrant bows his head to the sacristy cross. He removes his vestments in silence, assisted by the deacon or a server. The celebrant kisses the cross on the stole and the amice as he removes them, just as he did when he vested for Mass. After removing all his vestments, the celebrant may remain standing facing the sacristy cross to offer the prayers of thanksgiving found in the appendix to the missal. Or he may return to the church for a period of thanksgiving. After assisting the priest, the deacon removes his own vestments. All maintain silence in the sacristy during this time.

One of the first duties of the oldest among the servers is to extinguish the altar candles. The candles are extinguished in the reverse order in which they were lit. Therefore, the server now begins on the left side of the altar as he or she faces it, standing on the same side of the altar as the priest stood for Mass. The

[249] Mutel and Freeman, *Cérémonial de la sainte messe*, 181, 209, n. 80.

[250] Mutel and Freeman, *Cérémonial de la sainte messe*, 182.

server extinguishes first the candle closest to the left edge of the altar, and extinguishes each candle moving progressively closer to the altar cross or the middle of the altar. Bowing at the center of the altar, the server then continues by extinguishing first the candle at the right edge of the altar, and then each candle progressively closer to the altar cross or middle of the altar.[251] The server bows to the altar each time when passing at its center. If the altar candles are placed in two rows in either side of the altar rather than in a row across the altar, the server begins on the left side of the altar as he or she faces it, with the nearest candle and continues by extinguishing the candles progressively farther away. The server bows at the center of the altar and then does the same on the right side of the altar. If the Easter candle is burning in the sanctuary, as during the Easter season, the server then proceeds to extinguish the Easter candle last. Whenever passing before the Blessed Sacrament reserved in the sanctuary, the server genuflects each time, before finally returning to the sacristy.

After servers have made their own thanksgiving, removed all the items necessary for Mass from the sanctuary, and placed these same items away in the sacristy, they too remove their vestments in silence.

[251] Elliott, *Ceremonies of the Modern Roman Rite,* 318; Mutel and Freeman, *Cérémonial de la sainte messe,* 63–64, 63, n. 37; Fortescue, O'Connell, and Reid, *The Ceremonies of the Roman Rite Described,* 119.

PART 2

Matters Related to the Celebration of Mass

10

Celebration of Mass *Ad Orientem*

WHILE THE MISSAL of Paul VI clearly provides for the celebration of Mass *ad orientem*, there are relatively few indications as how this is to be carried out. Few commentators have provided direction to celebrants desiring this form of celebration. Therefore, much has been left to the improvisation of individual celebrants. At times, this can leave much to be desired if it is not informed by the traditional practice of the Roman Rite, as suggested by paragraph 42 of the *General Instruction of the Roman Missal*.

This chapter will assume the celebration of Mass *ad orientem* with the participation of ministers and the faithful. It will assume that the sanctuary where Mass is celebrated conforms to the provisions of the *General Instruction*, namely, that there is a seat for the celebrant and ministers, an ambo for the proclamation of the Scriptures, and a suitable credence table. These are oriented in the traditional manner, that is, the ambo is to the left as one faces the altar (what was formerly known as the Gospel side), and the credence table and chair for the celebrant are placed to the right of the altar as one faces it (what was formerly known as the epistle side).

The manner of incensing a freestanding altar is described in chapter 4. In the event that the altar at which the *ad orientem* celebration is taking place is not separated from the wall, such that the celebrant is not able to walk around it in order to incense it, the traditional practice offers guidance on how this can be done gracefully.[252] (See figure 7.) Standing at the middle of the altar after kissing it, the celebrant turns to his right. With his left hand on his chest, he imposes

[252] André Philippe M. Mutel and Peter Freeman, *Cérémonial de la sainte messe à l'usage ordinaire des paroisses suivant le missel romain de 2002 et la pratique léguée du rit romain*, 2nd ed. (Perpignan, France: Éditions Artège, 2012), 83–84.

incense three times with his right hand. He returns the spoon to the deacon. Then, with his left hand on the altar, he blesses the incense with his right hand, saying nothing.[253] He makes a Greek cross over the incense before joining his hands and receiving the thurible from the deacon. He takes the ring of the chain in his left hand, and the chain(s) near the bowl of the thurible in his right. Beginning at the center of the altar, the celebrant incenses the back portion of the *mensa* of the altar to his right with three swings. Arriving at the right side of the altar, he lowers his arm to incense the right-hand, vertical side of the altar with two swings. He then raises his arm to incense the front portion of the right side of the *mensa* of the altar with three swings, walking toward the middle. At the middle of the altar, he once again incenses the back portion of the left side of the *mensa* of the altar with three swings. At the left side of the altar, he drops his arm to incense the left-hand vertical side with two swings. Standing stationary in the same position, he incenses the front of the *mensa* of the left side of the altar with three swings from the edge of the altar to the center. He then lowers his arms to incense the vertical portion across the front of the altar with six swings, beginning at the left edge of the altar and concluding the incensation at the right edge of the altar. Returning the thurible to the deacon, the celebrant descends the altar steps from the side and goes to the chair.

If the altar cross is on the middle of the altar, the celebrant incenses the cross before incensing the altar. He bows, incenses it three times, and bows again, before beginning to incense the altar in the manner described above. Otherwise, he interrupts the incensation of the altar when he reaches the point closest to the altar cross and incenses it in the usual way before resuming to incense the altar.[254]

Whether or not the altar is separated from the wall, there are relatively few modifications to the celebration of Mass *ad orientem* compared to celebration *versus populum*. Upon arriving at the altar and then kissing it in the usual way, and after incensing it, the celebrant turns to his right and descends to the chair by the steps on the right side. He remains at the chair for the course of the introductory rites and the entire Liturgy of the Word. During the *Confiteor*, *Kyrie*, Gloria, Collect, Creed, and conclusion to the Prayer of the Faithful, he could orient himself, at least partially, in the direction of the altar, if this can be done gracefully. This will depend on the placement of the chair and its relationship to the altar, as well

[253] *CB*, 108.

[254] Peter J. Elliott, *Ceremonies of the Modern Roman Rite: The Eucharist and the Liturgy of the Hours*, rev. ed. (San Francisco: Ignatius Press, 1995), 140.

as the ability of the servers to hold the missal in the proper position. Historically, all of those parts of Mass were said facing the altar. It would be an expression of the continuity of the celebration with the past to respect this principle whenever reasonable. Standing at the chair, the celebrant turns to face the people when saying, "The Lord be with you," extending and joining his hands. He faces them with hands joined to say, "Let us pray," and to introduce the penitential act, the *asperges* rite, or the Universal Prayer.

A number of differences between celebrations *ad orientem* and *versus populum*, however, arise during the Liturgy of the Eucharist. After receiving the gifts or when going to the altar directly from the chair, the celebrant and the deacon approach the altar from the middle and bow to it upon arriving. The celebrant stands at the right side of the altar in a line with its far-right edge facing away from the altar in order to be incensed by the deacon or the thurifer and to wash his hands. He faces the altar at its right side for the preparation of the chalice and to dry his hands. He faces the altar at the center for the other parts of the preparation of the gifts. If incense is used, the gifts are incensed first in the usual way, then the altar cross if it is before the celebrant, and then the altar in the same manner as at the beginning of Mass. The deacon proceeds with the incensation of the celebrant and others as described in chapter 4.

The invitation "Pray brethren" is the only part of the preparation rite addressed to the faithful. Standing at the center of altar, the celebrant turns to his right to say the invitation. It seems proper that the celebrant remains facing the faithful while they answer him. He then continues to turn to his right, completing the circle, in order to face the missal placed to his left at the altar and to offer the prayer over the gifts.

After offering the prayer over the gifts, the celebrant begins the Eucharistic Prayer with the dialogue. According to tradition, the celebrant does not turn to face the assembly at this point.[255] When facing liturgical east, the traditional practice is for the celebrant to remain facing east throughout the entire Preface dialogue, since he will need the missal before his eyes for the three lines of the dialogue and for the musical notation if these dialogues are sung.[256] Since he does not say, "The Lord be with you," facing the people, he does not extend his hands, but places them flat on either side of the corporal, outside its edge. He raises his hands at "Lift up your hearts." He extends them in the *orans* position at "Let us

[255] Mutel and Freeman, *Cérémonial de la sainte messe*, 131.

[256] Elliot, *Ceremonies of the Modern Roman Rite*, 282, n. 43.

give thanks to the Lord our God." Without joining his hands, he continues with the Preface with hands extended in the *orans* position. The other gestures of the various Eucharistic Prayers are unchanged.

During the elevations, the celebrant does not turn around to show the consecrated species to the faithful. Rather, he lifts them high enough above his head so that they can be seen while he remains facing the altar. The deacon or thurifer usually kneels, facing the altar at its right side, to incense both species as they are elevated.[257] Alternatively, the deacon or the thurifer may kneel at the center of the sanctuary, between torch bearers kneeling on either side of him to his right and to his left, or facing each other across the sanctuary in two rows on either side, to incense the Blessed Sacrament.[258] The deacon or thurifer bows profoundly from the kneeling position before and after incensing both species with three double swings of the censer.

The celebrant consistently avoids turning his back directly to the Blessed Sacrament on the altar. Therefore, the celebrant does not turn to face the people when saying, "The mystery of faith," or "Through Him, with Him, and in Him." Neither does he turn to the people when saying, "At the Savior's command." The celebrant does turn to his right and faces people to say, "The peace of the Lord be with you always," and remains facing them during their response. When turning to his right, he steps slightly away from the center of the altar so as to avoid turning his back to the Blessed Sacrament on the altar. He stands with his back to the missal rather than with his back toward the Blessed Sacrament at the center of the altar. The celebrant then continues to face the people to say, "Let us offer each other the sign of peace." Or, if this is said by the deacon, the celebrant turns to his left to face the center of the altar again while the deacon now turns to his right and addresses the faithful. The celebrant then turns to his right slightly to offer the deacon the peace. He may offer the deacon the peace according to the traditional manner.

After the conclusion of the *Agnus Dei*, the celebrant, holding the Host in his right hand over the chalice or the paten, turns to his right to face people at the center of the altar and says, "Behold the Lamb of God." He continues to face them as he joins them in responding. He then turns to his left and faces the altar to reverently consume the Host. He consumes the Precious Blood facing the

257 Adrian Fortescue, J. B. O'Connell, and Alcuin Reid, eds., *The Ceremonies of the Roman Rite Described*, 15th ed. (New York: Bloomsbury, 2009), 114.

258 Mutel and Freeman, *Cérémonial de la sainte messe*, 130.

altar. He turns to his right to give the deacon Communion under both species. He descends the altar from the center and distributes Holy Communion to the servers and the faithful.

After the distribution of Holy Communion, the celebrant consumes what is left of the Precious Blood and the Hosts at the altar at the center, or collects the remaining Hosts at the altar and brings them to the place of reposition. Then, he may proceed to purify the vessels at the credence table or at the altar. If there is a deacon or an instituted acolyte, that minister may purify the vessels at the credence table.[259] The celebrant may then sit at the chair for a period of silence. He stands at the chair for the Post-Communion prayer and what follows, a server holding the missal directly in front of him or slightly to his left, as circumstances suggest. He turns to the people with hands joined to say, "Let us pray." He faces the missal for the Post-Communion prayer. He turns to the people and extends and joins his hands to say, "The Lord be with you," and to impart the blessing. The deacon stands in such a way as to face the people in order to say, "Bow down for the blessing," and the dismissal. The celebrant and deacon approach the altar at the middle to kiss it. The deacon stands to the celebrant's right in order to kiss the altar. The celebrant places both hands on the altar when he kisses it; the deacon does not. Then both the celebrant and the deacon turn toward each other and descend the steps, with the deacon at the celebrant's left side. At the entrance to the sanctuary, the celebrant and the deacon turn toward each other to face the altar once again. The deacon moves from the celebrant's right side to his left side as they face the altar. The celebrant and the deacon bow to the altar or genuflect to the Blessed Sacrament reserved in the sanctuary. They turn toward each other again, this time with the deacon on the celebrant's right, and depart.

After reserving the Blessed Sacrament and completing the purifications which follow, the celebrant may wish to remain at the altar rather than go to the chair for the concluding rites. In that case, the celebrant should step to the left-hand side of the altar and face it to allow for the deacon to retrieve the vessels and for others to remove the corporal, purificator, and pall. A server could reorient the missal to the center of the altar, parallel to the edge of the altar.[260] Then the celebrant may return to the center of the altar for silent prayer and the Post-Communion prayer and all that follows. Alternatively, after the purifications, the celebrant descends the altar steps by the right side in order to sit at the presidential chair for a time.

[259] *GIRM*, 183, 192; Mutel and Freeman, *Cérémonial de la sainte messe*, 173.

[260] Elliott, *Ceremonies of the Modern Roman Rite*, 128.

During this time, the deacon and servers approach the altar to remove everything used for Mass. After a time of silence seated at the chair, the celebrant approaches the altar by the center for the Post-Communion prayer. If the deacon has been seated next to the celebrant during this time, he approaches the altar with him at the center and stands to the celebrant's right. If the deacon remains at the altar to await the celebrant, he likewise stands to the right of the center of the altar and faces it until the celebrant joins him there.

Once at the altar for the Post-Communion prayer, the celebrant turns to his right to face the people and to say, with hands joined, "Let us pray." Presuming that the missal is placed directly in the middle of the altar and parallel to its edge, the celebrant then turns to his left to face the altar once again. If the missal is placed to the left of the center of the altar, as at the prayer "Pray brethren that my sacrifice and yours," the celebrant completes the circle by turning to his right instead in order to face the missal. He prays the Post-Communion prayer with hands extended. At its conclusion, the celebrant can close the missal. After the prayer, he then turns to his right once again to say, "The Lord be with you," while extending his hands. He remains facing the people to bless them. The deacon faces the celebrant to receive the blessing; he does not turn to the face the people during the celebrant's blessing. When the celebrant blesses the people, he places his left hand on his chest while using the fully extended right hand, fingers joined, to bless the faithful in the shape of a Greek cross. The gesture of blessing does extend higher than eye level, lower than the left hand held on the chest, but no wider than the width of the shoulders. The deacon and all those present bow slightly to receive the celebrant's blessing. Afterward, the deacon, standing to the right of the celebrant, then turns to his left to face the people and dismiss them.[261] While the deacon dismisses the faithful, the celebrant turns toward the altar by his left to face it once again. The deacon remains facing the people until they have responded, "Thanks be to God," to the dismissal formula. The deacon then turns to his right to face the altar once again and to kiss it with the celebrant. Having kissed the altar, the celebrant and the deacon turn toward one another and descend from the altar at the center. The deacon accompanies the celebrant at his left side at this point. At the entrance to the sanctuary, the celebrant and the deacon turn toward one another once again to face the altar. The deacon moves from the celebrant's right to his left side. The celebrant and the deacon reverence the altar with a profound bow or the

[261] Fortescue, O'Connell, and Reid, *The Ceremonies of the Roman Rite Described*, 142.

Blessed Sacrament reserved in the tabernacle with a genuflection. They turn toward one another a final time to join the procession to the sacristy, the deacon now walking to the celebrant's right side.

If the celebrant offers the solemn blessing or the prayer over the people, as on the Sundays of Lent, for example, while standing at the altar, a server will need to remove the missal from the altar and hold it in both hands directly in front of him while the celebrant faces the people for the blessing. Similarly, the deacon turns to his left to face the people to say, "Bow down for the blessing." Having said this, the deacon turns to his right to face the altar once again and bows while the invocation(s) to the blessing are read by the celebrant. After receiving the blessing, the deacon turns to his left again to face the people to dismiss them. He then turns to his right to kiss the altar with the celebrant. The celebrant reverences the altar with both hands placed flat upon it. The deacon kisses the altar while keeping his hands joined. Both celebrant and deacon, with hands joined, turn toward each other, descend the steps of the altar from the center, and depart as described above.

Whether the celebrant uses the solemn blessing, the prayer over the people, or the customary formula, and no deacon is present, the celebrant remains facing the faithful after the Post-Communion prayer until they have responded to the dismissal. He turns to his right to face the faithful after the Post-Communion prayer and then turns to his left after the response to the dismissal to face the altar. The celebrant kisses the altar, with both hands resting flat upon it, before joining his hands and descending the altar steps to reverence the altar with a profound bow or the Blessed Sacrament with a genuflection before departing.

11

The Celebration of Mass in Unusual Circumstances

IDEALLY, MASS IS always celebrated with the presence and participation of the lay faithful, and the assistance of designated ministers. As the *General Instruction of the Roman Missal* no. 91 points out, "All, therefore, whether ordained ministers or lay Christian faithful, in fulfilling their function or their duty, should carry out solely but totally that which pertains to them." Thus, at a bare minimum, a priest celebrant should normally be assisted by a server, and perhaps a reader. Joining them will be one or more members of the faithful who will respond to the celebrant throughout. At other times, a deacon, one or more concelebrants, or an additional server might also be present and ministering. The celebrant himself may be capable of singing the dialogues and acclamations of Mass without assistance. Or, perhaps those present might even be able to sing together the ordinary of the Mass according to some simple setting without assistance. But a cantor, if not a schola, will generally be necessary if the proper texts of the Mass are to be sung. These functions are perhaps the minimum needed to assure the celebration of the Mass according to some measure of dignity and decorum according to the provisions of the *General Instruction of the Roman Missal.*

In this chapter, we will examine circumstances where the conditions for the celebration of Mass are not ideal, and the celebration of Mass cannot be carried out even in the minimal way described above because of the absence of ministers or the absence of an assembly of the faithful. Three such cases are possible: 1) Mass celebrated with only one minister, 2) Mass celebrated with the participation of the faithful, but with no liturgical minister among them, and 3) Mass celebrated by the priest completely alone. None of these circumstances are ideal, but they can occur with some frequency, and then demand a measure of care to be celebrated with whatever measure of grace can be mustered. Finally, this chapter will also examine the cases where standard sanctuary furnishings may be missing. It will offer advice on the reverent celebration of Mass in those cases where there may not be a chair for the presider, or a lectern from which to proclaim the readings, or even a credence table on which to place everything needed for the celebration.

Mass with One Minister

The *General Instruction of the Roman Missal* nos. 252–272 describes the situation where only one minister assists the celebrant and offers the responses for Mass. This minister may both proclaim the Scripture readings and serve at the altar.[262] Provided that an ambo, a credence table, and a chair for the celebrant are located near the altar, this form of Mass involves relatively few changes to any postures or gestures of the celebrant. When one minister assists, the celebrant, after kissing the altar, may remain at the center of the altar, rather than at the chair, for all the introductory rites.[263] If the celebrant remains at the altar, the missal can be placed there directly before him, at the center of the altar, parallel to the edge of the altar.[264] If this does not allow enough space for the celebrant to kiss the altar, there is nothing to prevent the missal from being placed at an angle, slightly to the left of the center of the altar, in the position it will occupy during the Liturgy of the Eucharist. This form of Mass does not include the introduction to the penitential act, "Let us acknowledge our sins."

Later during the course of Mass, if the priest wishes to extend the sign of peace, he does so directly after saying, "The peace of the Lord be with you always," and its response. He omits "Let us offer each other the sign of peace," but proceeds directly to offer a gesture of peace. Of course, if the celebrant alone is to receive Communion, he does not say, "Behold the Lamb of God." Rather, he simply says, "Lord, I am not worthy," while facing the altar. Since the server will want to sign himself at the concluding blessing of Mass, it is perhaps preferable

262 *GIRM*, 110.

263 *GIRM*, 256.

264 The *General Instruction* does not specify the position of the missal at the center of the altar. Commentators recommend this position for the Post-Communion prayer when prayed at the altar. See André Philippe M. Mutel and Peter Freeman, *Cérémonial de la sainte messe à l'usage ordinaire des paroisses suivant le missel romain de 2002 et la pratique léquée du rit romain*, 2nd ed. (Perpignan, France: Éditions Artège, 2012), 177, and Peter J. Elliott, *Ceremonies Explained for Servers According to the Roman Rite: A Manual for Altar Servers, Acolytes, Sacristans, and Masters of Ceremonies* (San Francisco: Ignatius Press, 2019), 254.

for the celebrant to remain at the altar for the Post-Communion prayer and dismissal rite. In this case, the server does not need to hold the missal before the celebrant at the chair and will have the right hand free to make the Sign of the Cross. The celebrant will turn at least slightly toward the server whenever greeting, addressing, or blessing that person. In the celebration of Mass with one minister, the dismissal, "Go in peace," is always omitted.[265] Apart from these distinctions, Mass with the participation of one minister is celebrated in exactly the same manner as Mass celebrated with the assistance of the faithful.

Mass with the Faithful and No Minister Participating

The situation can also arise were one or more members of the faithful are present and responding, but none of them is able to proclaim the readings or assist the priest as a server. This specific case is not foreseen at all by the *General Instruction*. However, it can happen with some frequency, at times at a small weekday Mass or even in situations like a nursing home when none of those present can assure the specific ministries required for the celebration of Mass. Therefore, one must make some hypothetical conjectures regarding postures and gestures which are in conformity both with the overall principles of the Roman Missal of Paul VI and the traditional practice of the Roman Rite.

Since the celebrant is not assisted by any minister, it would be best if he made his way from the sacristy to the altar by the most direct route. The celebrant making his way from the back of the nave to the sanctuary entirely alone appears incongruous to the circumstances. If there are doors on either side of the altar leading from the sacristy to the sanctuary, the celebrant historically has exited the sacristy by the door to his right and thus entered the sanctuary on the Gospel side (left side as one faces the sanctuary from the nave). Similarly, at the end of Mass in the past, the celebrant exited the sanctuary by the door on the right side of the sanctuary, on what was considered the epistle side (right hand side as one faces the sanctuary from the nave). This would appear to be a more reasonable approach in this case.

It would also be best if the credence table could be moved closer to the altar, at the celebrant's immediate right as he is standing at the altar. A lectern of some kind will need to be placed in front of the celebrant's chair for the missal, since Mass is being celebrated in the presence of an assembly. After the Universal

[265] *GIRM*, 272.

Prayer, or even after the opening Collect on his way to the ambo for the readings, the celebrant will need to bring the missal from the lectern in front of his chair to the altar. In conformity with no. 135 of the *General Instruction of the Roman Missal*, the celebrant will proclaim all the readings of the Liturgy of the Word himself at the ambo since "no reader is present." Prior to the Gospel and its acclamation, while still standing at the ambo, he will turn toward the altar and bow to say quietly, "Cleanse my heart and my lips." He then proceeds with the proclamation of the Gospel in the usual way. If there is a Prayer of the Faithful, the celebrant leads and concludes this at the chair.

Returning to the center of the altar, he carries out the preparation of the altar and the gifts, turning to the right to the credence table as necessary. In the event that no credence table can be moved closer to the altar, the celebrant may even place the chalice, and everything needed for Mass, at the right-hand side of the altar itself.[266] After purifying the vessels, the chalice may return to this position once again.[267] It seems preferable for the celebrant to conclude Mass at the altar rather than at the chair, directly facing any of the faithful who may be present in order to offer the final blessing and dismissal.

Mass without the Participation of Even One Member of the Faithful

Even greater uncertainty arises when the priest, for some just cause and reasonable cause, celebrates Mass without the participation of even one member of the faithful.[268] In this case, the *General Instruction* indicates that the priest is to omit the greetings, instructions, and final blessing of Mass.[269] There is no unanimity among commentators whether this applies indiscriminately to all such texts consistently. One commentator has argued that it is simply not practical to follow the indication in the *General Instruction* without qualification.[270] A more nuanced approach would take into consideration the nature of the texts themselves as well as the traditional practice of the Roman Rite.

266 *GIRM*, 255. Normally, the chalice is placed closest to the edge of the altar, with the cruets on a metal tray or glass dish behind it. The cloth for drying the hands can be draped over the edge of the altar, under the cruets.

267 *GIRM*, 270.

268 *CIC*, 906.

269 *GIRM*, 254.

270 Peter J. Elliott, *Ceremonies of the Modern Roman Rite: The Eucharist and the Liturgy of the Hours*, rev. ed. (San Francisco: Ignatius Press, 1995), 198, n. 5.

The introduction to the penitential act, "Let us acknowledge our sins," is omitted in the form of Mass with one minister. The same is true of the invitation to exchange the sign of peace and the dismissal formula. Therefore, these three are likewise omitted when no minister is present. The plain reading of the *General Instruction* would appear to require the omission of all the greetings and instructions such as "Let us pray," "The Lord be with you," "The Word of the Lord," "The Gospel of the Lord," "Pray brethren that my sacrifice and yours," the Preface dialogue, "At the Savior's command," "The peace of the Lord be with you always," and "Behold the Lamb of God," since the celebrant is in fact speaking to no one. If these are omitted, then the corresponding gestures are omitted. The celebrant also omits the Universal Prayer, since this is meant as an exercise of priestly intercession by the faithful. The memorial acclamation itself is intended to offer the faithful a way to participate vocally in the Eucharistic Prayer. It appears to be one of those elements which a celebrant might also omit in the solitary celebration of Mass. It would appear that the celebrant could omit "Behold the Lamb of God," since this was never part of the preparation for the priest's own Communion historically. Finally, the celebrant is directed to omit the final blessing and dismissal of the faithful, again since there is no one present to bless or dismiss.[271]

On the other hand, the same commentator cited above has pointed out how all these forms of address were always included in the celebration of Mass without a server in the past, since every Mass is always an action of whole Body of Christ, Head and members.[272] Historically, even in Masses celebrated without the participation of the faithful, the celebrant always introduced these dialogues and answered himself.[273] A more nuanced approached today could include the following. The celebrant can pray the *Confiteor* alone, omitting the two occurrences of the phrase, "and [to] you my brothers and sisters."[274] The celebrant might say to himself the acclamations "Thanks be to God" and "Praise to You, Lord Jesus Christ," after the readings. After omitting the invitation "Pray brethren," the celebrant could say, "May the Lord accept the sacrifice at *my* hands," as was done in the past when the priest celebrated alone.[275] In addition, the beginning of every Preface, "It is truly right and just," makes little sense without the

271 *GIRM*, 254.

272 Elliot, *Ceremonies of the Modern Roman Rite*, 198, n. 5.

273 Adrian Fortescue, J. B. O'Connell, and Alcuin Reid, eds., *The Ceremonies of the Roman Rite Described*, 15th ed. (New York: Bloomsbury, 2009), 89, n. 90.

274 Fortescue, O'Connell, and Reid, *The Ceremonies of the Roman Rite Described*, 89.

275 Fortescue, O'Connell, and Reid, *The Ceremonies of the Roman Rite Described*, 89.

dialogue which comes before it, even if the celebrant is alone. Perhaps it is best to include the Preface dialogue for the sake of coherence with the Preface which follows it. The celebrant should, at the same time, retain the words "The mystery of faith," since this always constituted part of the Canon spoken by the celebrant.[276] The celebrant would pray, "Lord I am not worthy," while facing the altar, without its introduction. This too was always included historically in the celebrant's own preparation for Communion at every Mass. Finally, the celebrant could bless himself, using the same formula proposed at Morning or Evening Prayer when praying these alone, "May the Lord bless us, protect us from all evil, etc." Otherwise, Mass simply ends abruptly with the Post-Communion prayer and the signs of reverence to the altar and to the Blessed Sacrament reserved in the sanctuary. While the literal application of no. 254 in the *General Instruction* permits the celebrant to omit these various dialogues that are normally intended for the faithful, the long-standing practice of the Roman Rite and the nature of these dialogues themselves would argue for the retention of at least some of them even in the solitary celebration of Mass.

When offering Mass without the participation of even one member of the faithful, the celebrant should consider what his orientation at the altar will be. Offering Mass *versus populum* is intended to facilitate the actual participation of the faithful. When there are no members of the faithful present at all, it would seem that the celebrant should adopt the traditional orientation of the celebrant at the altar whereby he directs his gaze to liturgical east. This change in orientation when offering Mass alone may or may not be possible given the placement of the altar in the sanctuary, especially its placement with respect to the altar steps. It may mean relocating the credence table to the right of the celebrant when he stands at the altar facing liturgical east. Similarly, during the course of the celebration of Mass itself, the celebrant normally elevates the species after each consecration in order to show them to the faithful. If no member of the faithful is present, this gesture may seem out of place. Instead, the celebrant

[276] A *responsum ad dubium* published in *Notitiae* contradicts this advice. See *Notitae* 5 (1969): 324–335, no. 3. The response considers the words *mysterium fidei* to be an invitation of the celebrant addressed to the faithful when it is really an acclamation by the celebrant. This is clearer now that the Latin words are translated as "The mystery of faith," rather than "Let us proclaim the mystery of faith." In the case where no members of the faithful are present to respond, perhaps *mysterium fidei* can immediately follow the words of institution over the chalice and precede the genuflection of the celebrant, locating the acclamation closer to its original historical context.

might adopt the manner of adoration prescribed for the celebrant alone by the traditional practice of the Roman Rite. In that case, after the consecration of the bread, the celebrant genuflects while still holding the Host on the altar in both hands. After rising, the places the Host on the paten. After the consecration of the wine, he sets the chalice down on the corporal and genuflects. Upon rising, he covers the chalice with the pall once again and continues the Eucharistic Prayer. Modifying both the spoken parts of Mass and its gestures when no member of the Christian faithful is present is a way to respect the truth of the circumstances of a specific celebration.

Finally, there is the scenario whereby several priests concelebrate Mass among themselves without the participation of even one member of the faithful present. This can occur on the occasion of priests' retreats or conferences. It is a set of circumstances which is completely unforeseen by the *General Instruction of the Roman Missal* or by the *Rite of Concelebration*. The *General Instruction* is quite clear that when celebrating Mass with one member of the faithful, or even no member of the faithful, the celebrant needs to take into consideration the truth of the circumstances. These means modifying various words and gestures in order to correspond to the reality before him. The same should be true in the case of concelebration among priests. The principal celebrant will need to take into account the presence of other concelebrants with him.

In this case, it should be assumed that the concelebrants will say all the same parts of Mass which the principal celebrant himself will say, unless the missal itself directs them to listen in silence or recite the same words merely mentally. In contrast, the concelebrants would not speak those parts of Mass which the faithful alone recite without the celebrant.[277] For example, whenever the missal indicates that "the people" of the "the faithful" answer, one could assume that this means that the lay faithful respond without the celebrant. On the other hand, where the missal indicates "all" respond, one can assume that the celebrant and lay faithful together respond. In practice, what would this mean for a group of concelebrants gathered for Mass?

Even among a group of concelebrants, it would appear that the greetings and instructions such as "Let us acknowledge our sins," "Let us pray," "The Lord be with you," "Pray brethren that my sacrifice and yours," "At the Savior's command,"

[277] See *Notitae* 5 (1969): 324–335, no. 3. This response appears to indicate that concelebrating priests do not necessarily take on the responses of the faithful, but act in their proper role as concelebrants.

"The peace of the Lord be with you always," "Let us offer each other the sign of peace," and "Behold the Lamb of God" remain omitted, since they are normally directed to the people, not to concelebrants. An exception to this general rule could be the greeting at the beginning of the Gospel. Normally, the celebrant at Mass responds along with the faithful to the greeting of the deacon proclaiming the Gospel. Likewise, concelebrants might respond in the same way to the one among them who proclaims the Gospel in the place of a deacon. Another exception might be the Preface dialogue, for the reasons mentioned above.

When praying the *Confiteor*, concelebrants will retain the words "my brothers" and omit the words "and sisters." In contrast to the celebration of Mass by a single priest alone, one of the concelebrants serving as a reader might say, "The Word of the Lord," and "The Gospel of the Lord," with all responding, since celebrants normally respond this way whenever the Scriptures are read at Mass. Prior to the prayer over the gifts, all the concelebrants pray together that the Lord will accept the sacrifice "at *my* hands," according to the traditional practice mentioned above. While the principal concelebrant alone might say, "The mystery of faith," during the Eucharistic Prayer because of its association with the words of consecration, the concelebrants would not respond, since the memorial acclamation is proper to the faithful during the anaphora. The missal itself indicates that concelebrants pray the doxology to the Lord's Prayer, beginning with "For the kingdom."[278] Since a concelebrant serving as deacon is not blessed by the principal celebrant before proclaiming the Gospel, it is perhaps more consistent for Mass to end without the principal concelebrant imparting the final blessing upon the concelebrants. The dismissal formula is likewise omitted.

Adding a Missing Chair, Credence Table, or Lectern

At times, Mass is offered with the participation of the faithful at an altar with there is no ambo, credence table, or presidential chair available nearby. This can happen in rectory chapels or in nursing home common rooms, or even at side altars where Mass is offered *ad orientem*. Sometimes, the shelf serving as a credence table in such circumstances is not sufficient for all of the items needed for Mass. Masses celebrated with the presence of the faithful demand the use of a presidential chair, credence table, and lectern. Regarding the items necessary for Mass, the *General Instruction* reads, "Before Mass, the necessary vessels are prepared ... at the credence table."[279]

[278] *GIRM*, 238.
[279] *GIRM*, 118c.

The *General Instruction* also expects that "the readings should, in so far as possible, be proclaimed from the ambo or a lectern."[280] In the celebration of Mass with more than one member of the faithful, the celebrant leads the introductory rites of Mass at the chair. By adding these articles of furniture, even temporarily, the relevant prescriptions of the *General Instruction* can be carried out faithfully, whether the celebrant is accompanied by several members of the faithful or only by one.

A first step could be to obtain a more adequate credence table and place it to the right of the altar from the position where the celebrant will stand for the Liturgy of the Eucharist. Sometimes a small wooden stool is sufficient to function as a chair for the celebrant during the Liturgy of the Word. This too is placed to the right of the altar from the perspective of the priest when he is standing at the altar. A server holds the missal for the celebrant there, or the missal is placed on a stand in front of the chair if no server is available. Similarly, another lectern could be placed immediately to the left of the position where the celebrant will stand at the altar, on the opposite side from the chair. In that way, the reader, or in his absence, the celebrant will be able to fulfill the directions indicated in the *General Instruction of the Roman Missal* during the Liturgy of the Word.

Mass Celebrated without the Chair, Credence Table, or Lectern

An even more challenging case arises when the priest will offer Mass without an adequate credence table or chair, and without even a portable lectern. Perhaps these items of liturgical furniture are not available. Perhaps there is no room to introduce any of them next to the altar. When the priest celebrates Mass in such a location, with or without the assistance of one or more members of the faithful, the traditional practice of the Roman Rite can be helpful in establishing the adaptations to the *General Instruction* which are required by the circumstances. The following description attempts to account for the instances when a presidential chair, an ambo, and an adequate credence table are missing.

Without the use of a chair, an ambo, or a sufficient credence table, several modifications must take place to the usual manner of celebrating Mass. For example, when Mass is offered with only one member of the faithful present, or even without the participation of any member of the faithful, the missal can be placed before Mass at the center of the altar, open to the proper page, parallel with the

[280] *GIRM*, 260.

edge of the altar, since all of the introductory rites can take place there.[281] If there is no room for a chair near the altar, or no server or lectern to hold the missal before the chair, the missal may need to be placed at the center of the altar in any case, even if Mass is celebrated with more than one member of the faithful. The missal may also be placed at an angle, slightly to the left of the center of the altar, in the position it will occupy during the Liturgy of the Eucharist. This is the preferable position for the missal and its stand if there is no room to kiss the altar with the missal and its stand in a central position. Prior to the beginning of Mass, the chalice, preferably veiled with the burse on top,[282] can be placed on the far-right side of the altar if there is no adequate credence table or shelf nearby.[283] The chalice should be placed on the altar such that it is completely veiled when facing it. If there is no credence table at all, the other vessels needed for Mass can be placed on the far-right side of the altar as well, behind the chalice.[284] The priest approaches the altar, bows, kisses it, and begins the introductory rites as usual at the center of the altar, or omitting certain instructions normally addressed to the faithful if he is alone. After the Collect, the readings follow.

The readings for Mass are now generally found in a separate lectionary rather than in the missal itself. Therefore, if there is no ambo from which to proclaim the readings, the closed lectionary could be placed flat on the altar, on the far-right side in front of the chalice, with the edges of its pages toward the center of the altar. Or, if the altar is equipped with a gradine, the lectionary could stand upright, facing forward, leaning against the gradine on the right-hand side of the altar, behind the chalice. After the Collect, the celebrant moves to his right, takes the lectionary into both hands, and hands it to a reader. When the faithful are present, the reader holds the lectionary in both hands and faces them to proclaim the reading and psalm. When the celebrant alone is present, the reader faces the altar to read the reading and its psalm. The celebrant stands at the far-right side of the altar facing the reader to listen to the reading and respond. On certain days, the reader, or in his absence, the celebrant would also read a second Scripture reading. The psalm can be read without any intervening antiphon, since it is not sung.[285] The Alleluia or other Gospel Acclamation, if not sung, may be

[281] *GIRM*, 256. See the position of the missal for the Post-Communion prayer in Mutel and Freeman, *Cérémonial de la sainte messe*, 177 and Elliott, *Ceremonies Explained for Servers*, 254.

[282] *GIRM*, 118; *CB*, 125.

[283] *GIRM*, 255.

[284] Fortescue, O'Connell, and Reid, *The Ceremonies of the Roman Rite Described*, 89.

[285] *GIRM*, 61.

omitted when only one reading precedes the Gospel.[286] If no reader and no members of the faithful are present, the celebrant can rest the lectionary on the altar while he reads. He reads the reading(s), the psalm, and the Gospel Acclamation, if any, with both hands resting on the edges of the lectionary.

In preparation for reading the Gospel, the celebrant moves toward to the opposite side of the altar. At the center of the altar, he says the prayer "Cleanse my heart and my lips," bowing profoundly. The reader follows him, carrying the lectionary, open, in both hands. At the far-left side of the altar, the celebrant turns to face the reader, who holds the lectionary open before him. The celebrant faces those present, greets them, announces the Gospel, and reads the Gospel in the usual way. At the conclusion of the Gospel, he picks up the lectionary with both hands from the reader to kiss it, close it, and place it flat at the left side of the altar, with its open edge facing the center of the altar. If there is no one present to hold the lectionary before him, the celebrant carries the open lectionary in both hands from the right-hand side of the altar to the left-hand side, bowing at the center of the altar. After putting down the lectionary open on the far-left side of the altar, he returns to the center with hands joined to say the prayer of preparation, bowing profoundly. Upon returning to the left-hand side of the altar once again, he begins with hands joined, and then signs the book and himself, and reads the Gospel in the usual way. He then raises the lectionary in both hands to kiss the book at the beginning of the passage he just read, that is, at the cross printed on the page. He can then place the closed lectionary flat at the far-left side of the altar, with the edges of its pages facing the center of the altar. Or, if the altar is equipped with a gradine, the celebrant can lean the lectionary against the gradine on the left-hand side of the altar, with its open edge facing the center of the altar.

Returning to the center of the altar, the celebrant recites the Creed with those present in the usual manner, as required. He can turn to face those present to introduce the Prayer of the Faithful before turning to his left to face the altar for the intentions, which a minister will offer, and for the Collect, which he will pray from the missal with hands in the *orans* position. If necessary, the celebrant then moves the missal from the center of the altar to a position slightly to the left of the center of the altar, beyond the point where the edge of the corporal will eventually be. Then, he proceeds to the right-hand side of the altar.

[286] *GIRM*, 63.

At the right-hand side of the altar, taking the chalice in the left hand at the node, with the right hand placed on top, the celebrant moves the chalice closer toward the center of the altar first. Standing at the center, he reaches with his right hand and takes the burse off the chalice, placing it flat in front of him. With his left hand, he holds the left flap of the burse open, while extracting the corporal with his right hand. He sets the folded corporal on the altar. With his right hand, he places the empty burse to the left of the center of the altar; he stands it up in the open position against the gradine of the altar or against a candlestick. He then opens the corporal directly in front of him in the usual manner. (See figure 6.) Standing before the chalice, he removes the veil from behind the chalice toward himself, folds it in two and then again in three parts, and places it away from the chalice on the right-hand side of the altar, toward the back of the altar. Returning to the center of the altar, he removes the pall from the chalice and places it to the right of the top portion of the corporal, against the gradine if there is one, or lying flat on the altar.

If there is no burse, and the corporal is instead placed on top of the pall and under the chalice veil, the celebrant can simply remove the veil from back to front at the right-hand side of the altar, in the position where the chalice was placed at the beginning of Mass. There he folds the veil while it lays flat on the altar, and leaves it at the right-hand side of the altar toward the back. He then moves the entire chalice closer to the center of the altar with both hands to begin placing the corporal and pall.

The celebrant then takes the paten from the chalice to begin the prayer of preparation. He holds it up with the thumbs and index fingers of both hands above the corporal. The paten is raised slightly above the corporal, no more than the breadth of his hand. After the prayer, he places the paten on the center portion of the front of the corporal. Then, turning to his left, he takes the chalice in his left hand as he moves to the right edge of the altar. The cruets of water and wine may be on the altar if necessary, or they may be placed on the gradine at the right edge of the altar. A server, if present, offers the celebrant the wine and then the water. The celebrant prepares the chalice in the usual way at the right-hand side of the altar. Once the chalice is prepared, the celebrant moves the chalice closer to the corporal with his left hand. With the purificator draped over the index fingers of his joined hands, he returns to the center of the altar, and places the purificator along the edge of the corporal with its folded end toward the edge of the altar.

Standing at the center of the altar, the celebrant takes the chalice with his right hand and draws it over the corporal. Holding it at the node with his right hand and at the base with his left hand, he says the prayer of preparation. He holds the chalice slightly above the corporal, at the height of the breadth of his hand. After the prayer, he places the chalice down on the center portion of the back of the corporal. He covers the chalice with the pall using his right hand, while he holds the fingers of his left hand on the base of the chalice. Standing erect, the celebrant returns to the right side of the altar. There a server assists him to wash and dry his hands. The celebrant faces the altar to dry his hands. If the celebrant is completely alone, water can be poured in advance into a dish or bowl for this purpose, for example after adding the water to the wine in the chalice, or even before Mass itself. The celebrant then dries his hands on the towel hanging from the server's left arm, or hanging down under the lavabo bowl on the side of the gradine of the altar or even the side of the altar itself if necessary.[287] With hands joined, he returns to the center of the altar. The entire Liturgy of the Eucharist and Communion rite are carried out at the center of the altar.

After having received Communion and then given Communion to any who may be present, the celebrant, standing at the center of the altar, purifies the paten over the chalice with the purificator,[288] or with the thumb of his right hand, according to the traditional practice. If he wishes to purify the chalice with wine first, he holds the chalice over the altar to the right of the corporal while remaining at the center of the altar. A server reaches over and pours some wine into the chalice. In the absence of a server, the celebrant leaves the chalice on the top-right edge of the corporal and walks to the right side of the altar with hands joined to retrieve the cruet of wine. Returning to the center, he pours wine into the chalice. He might hold the node of the chalice with the left hand while doing this, or hold his left hand on his chest. He then returns the cruet to the right side of the altar before returning once again at the center to consume the ablution of wine. Traditionally, the celebrant held the purified paten under his chin while doing so. Then holding the cup of the chalice in both hands, and with the thumbs and index fingers of both hands over the mouth of the chalice if he purified the paten with his thumb, he goes toward the right side of the altar. There a server pours a small amount of wine and a greater amount of water into the chalice. If the celebrant is alone, he puts the chalice down and pours into the chalice a small amount of wine and then a greater amount of water, or simply water. He might keep the thumb and the index finger of his left hand over the

[287] *GIRM*, 255.

[288] *GIRM*, 279.

mouth of the chalice while pouring the water with his right hand. Holding the chalice in both hands in the same manner as before, he turns to his left to face the altar closer to the right edge of the corporal.[289] He turns the chalice gently to purify the entire interior of the chalice with the ablution. He purifies his fingers in the ablution. He can sprinkle some of the ablution on the paten to complete its purification. Standing slightly to the right of the corporal, the celebrant dries his fingers on the purificator, and then consumes the ablution, holding the purificator under his chin.

He wipes the chalice, putting it down to the right of the corporal. He takes the paten off of the corporal with his left hand. Then he wipes the paten with the purificator one final time with his right hand and places it on the chalice, over the purificator. With his right hand, he places the pall on top. He moves corporal away from the missal to the right slightly. He then folds the corporal, leaving it at the center. He takes the burse in his right hand and stands it upright, to the left of the corporal. Holding the left side open with his left hand, he places the corporal in the burse with his right hand, leaving the burse at the center of the altar with the open edge facing away from himself Standing before the chalice, slightly to the right of the center of the altar, the celebrant then veils it from behind the chalice toward himself and places the burse on top. Placing his right hand on the top of the veil and burse, and his left hand on the node, the celebrant moves the chalice to the far-right side of the altar where it was originally placed before the beginning of Mass. He places it in such a way that when it is in its final position, the long portion of the chalice veil and the closed edge of the burse will face those present. The celebrant holds the chalice, however, from the opposite side whenever moving it.

The celebrant returns to the center of the altar. If possible, he may move the missal to the center for the Post-Communion prayer. If necessary, he turns to his right to face those present when he says, "Let us pray," "The Lord be with you," and to impart the blessing to those present. He omits the dismissal if only one person is present.[290] Finally, the celebrant closes the missal and kisses the altar. He turns to his right, descends from the altar, and bows before departing.

Even under these very restricted conditions, Mass still deserves to be offered with as much dignity and care as possible. The adaptations described above, drawing from the traditional practice of the Roman Rite wherever applicable,

[289] Mutel and Freeman, *Cérémonial de la sainte messe*, 172.

[290] *GIRM*, 272.

can make it possible for all priests to continue to offer Mass worthily, attentively, and devoutly. Over time, rectors of churches will take the necessary steps to provide a celebrant with sufficient ministers to carry out the celebration of Mass according to all the provisions found in the liturgical books, as well as all the necessary appointments for each altar. But from time to time, when this is not possible, the adaptations described above can strive to come as close as possible to fulfilling the vision for the Church's worship found in the *General Instruction*, drawing from the traditional practice of the Roman Rite.

12

Defects of the Mass and Accidents That May Occur

THE *GENERAL INSTRUCTION of the Roman Missal* mentions three accidents which may occur during the celebration of Mass, along with the proper remedies for each. These are 1) when a Host or particle falls to the ground,[291] 2) when some of the Precious Blood is spilled,[292] and 3) when the priest notices after the consecration that only water and no wine has been poured into the chalice.[293] While these provisions of the *General Instruction* are helpful in themselves, what should one do in the case of the many other errors and omissions that can easily take place during the course of the celebration of Mass? For a broader perspective on the necessary remedies, recourse to the section of the *Missale Romanum* of 1962 called "De defectibus Missae" would be helpful. Modern commentators have often turned to this portion of the *Missale Romanum* to offer solutions to the many emergencies that arise in the course of the celebration of Mass.[294] This chapter will summarize the advice offered by the modern commentators of the traditional practice of the Roman Rite.

[291] *GIRM*, 280.

[292] *GIRM*, 280.

[293] *GIRM*, 324.

[294] See "Accidents," in Peter J. Elliott, *Ceremonies of the Modern Roman Rite: The Eucharist and the Liturgy of the Hours*, rev. ed. (San Francisco: Ignatius Press, 1995), 314–316; See "Les accidents qui peuvent se produire," in André Philippe M. Mutel and Peter Freeman, *Cérémonial de la sainte messe à l'usage ordinaire des paroisses suivant le missel romain de 2002 et la pratique léguée du rit romain*, 2nd ed. (Perpignan, France: Éditions Artège, 2012), 213–228.

Matter, Form, Intention, and Minister

"There is no Sacrament if any of these are missing: The proper matter, the form, including the intention, and the priestly ordination of the celebrant."[295] The proper matter is bread made from wheat flour and wine made from grapes. With regard to the bread for consecration, if so much other grain or other ingredients are added such that in the common estimation of most people it is no longer wheat bread, then it is not suitable matter for the celebration of the Eucharist. No-gluten hosts prepared from rice or other products constitute invalid matter for the Eucharist. Low-gluten hosts prepared from wheat flour that has been treated are valid matter and can be licitly used for the benefit of those who have received the necessary permission of the diocesan bishop. The wine made from grapes must be "natural, and unadulterated, that is, without admixture of extraneous substances."[296] For example, the wine should not be fortified by the addition of alcohol, nor rendered sparkling by the addition of carbon dioxide. If the wine made from grapes has become vinegar or become sour, or if so much water has been mixed with it that, in the common estimation of most people, it is no longer wine, then it is no longer useable for the eucharistic sacrifice.[297] If it is discovered at the Offertory that there is either no bread or no wine available, and the missing element cannot be obtained without a reasonable delay (even one as long as an hour), then Mass cannot proceed any further; it must be abandoned. Grape juice which has just begun to ferment (*mustum*) can be licitly used by those celebrants who receive the permission of the local ordinary. Again, this *mustum* must be unadulterated; therefore the trace amounts of alcohol cannot be removed by any process.

With respect to the form of the Sacrament, if the priest were to change the words of the consecration of the Body and the Blood so that the words did not mean the same thing, then the action is invalid.[298] At times, the celebrant can be distracted. If he does not remember having said the usual words of the consecration, he should not repeat anything. If, however, he is sure that he omitted something necessary to the Sacrament, namely the institution narrative and consecration, or if someone trustworthy points this out to him with moral certainty, he is to repeat the formula omitted and continue from there.[299] The same is

[295] *MR, De defect.*, 1.
[296] *GIRM*, 322.
[297] *MR, De defect.*, 4, 1.
[298] *MR, De defect.*, 5, 1.
[299] *MR, De defect.*, 5, 1.

true for concelebrants. If the celebrant thinks it is very likely that he omitted something essential, he is to repeat the formula conditionally, though the condition need not be expressed. If what he omitted is not necessary to the Sacrament, he is not to repeat anything, but should simply continue the Mass.[300] If the celebrant notices that he has chosen the wrong text for the day and occasion while he is singing or saying it, it is best for him to stop, find the correct text, and begin again. On the other hands, if the celebrant has already moved on to the next part of Mass when he realizes that he previously spoke the wrong text, it seems preferable for him to continue without correcting himself.[301]

Moreover, the intention of consecrating is required. The priest should have the habitual intention of consecrating everything placed on a corporal on the altar for the celebration of Mass. If necessary, more than one corporal can be placed on the altar in order that all the vessels used for Mass can be placed upon one of them. Whenever celebrating Mass, the priest should be careful to make his intention actual and not merely virtual, that is, merely coming to the altar intending to do what the Church does without having an actual intention at the time of consecration because he has allowed his mind to wander.[302] The priest should also be clear about his own intention regarding the elements to be consecrated. Any elements inadvertently left on the credence table or left in the sacristy that were meant for Mass, but are obviously not in the mind of the celebrant at the time of consecration, are in no way consecrated. The priest cannot have an intention to consecrate elements he does not know exist, as when they are hidden from his sight behind the missal on its stand or under a corporal, for example. It is best for the celebrant to habitually have the intention to consecrate the elements he will hold in his hands or that will placed on the corporal(s) on the altar. Any elements lying on the altar outside the corporals have not been consecrated, although they should be consumed to avoid scandal. It is sufficient to fulfill the intention of the celebrant if one or more vessels touch the edge of the corporal rather than fully rest on it. If the priest should fail to notice the placement of the vessels, the deacon should make sure that all the vessels of bread and wine to be consecrated rest on a corporal. He must place them in the proper position during the time of the preparation of the gifts.

300 *MR, De defect.*, 5, 2.

301 Mutel and Freeman, *Cérémonial de la sainte messe*, 225.

302 *MR, De defect.*, 7, 4.

Finally, it is necessary for the one who is to offer Mass to have received priestly ordination. The celebration of Mass is not possible otherwise.

Accidents before the Consecration

If the priest falls ill or dies before the consecration, Mass is discontinued.[303]

At the preparation of the gifts, if the priest notices that water, and not wine, has been poured into the chalice, he is to empty the chalice into a dish or a bowl. If there is no wine in the other cruet, the deacon or server brings one of the cruets to the sacristy and empties it of water, and then fills it with wine. The priest then fills the chalice with wine and adds a small amount of water, saying the necessary words, before resuming Mass where he left off.

At the preparation, while pouring in wine, the celebrant may notice that it contains an insect or some other impurity. He should empty the chalice of wine into a bowl or dish. The cruet of wine should be brought to the sacristy and emptied, rinsed, and filled with wine once again. Meanwhile, the priest may wish to rinse the chalice with water at the credence table, pouring the ablution into a bowl or dish, and wiping it dry there with a purificator before proceeding as usual with the newly refilled cruet of wine. Once again, he says the words for adding the water and offering the wine. The same procedure is followed if the celebrant notices any impurity in the wine after the preparation of the chalice but before the consecration. Saying the words for adding water and offering the wine (at least mentally), he resumes Mass where he left off.

When pouring the wine into the chalice, if the priest or deacon notices that a few drops fall on the altar cloth, outside the corporal, it is not necessary to remedy the situation during Mass.

If the celebrant forgets to add the drop of water to the wine at the preparation, and realizes it before the consecration, he should halt the Mass at a convenient point and remedy the situation by adding a drop of water and saying the formula (at least mentally). He then continues with Mass where he left off.[304] If he remembers this after the consecration of the chalice, he is not to add water, because the water is not necessary for the Sacrament.[305]

If the chalice is knocked over prior to the consecration of the bread, everything that is dry can be taken off the altar and placed on the credence table. Everything

[303] *MR, De defect.*, 10, 3.

[304] *MR, De defect.*, 3, 4.

[305] *MR, De defect.*, 4, 8.

that the wine has touched can be removed and brought to the sacristy if unusable, or dried and placed once again on the altar. It may be necessary to dry part of the altar with towels before placing an entirely new altar cloth and linens on the altar once again. If the bread has been replaced, the priest begins with the prayer of preparation of the bread; if the bread has not been replaced, the priest begins with the preparation of the chalice, before continuing where he left off.

Accidents after the Consecration

If the celebrant falls ill or is otherwise incapacitated after the consecration, even the consecration of only one of the two elements, another priest is to complete the Mass from the place where the first priest stopped. If possible, the first priest as well as the second priest are both to communicate from the Host and wine consecrated at that same Mass.[306]

If the chalice is knocked over *after* the consecration of the bread but *before* the consecration of the wine, it is best for priest and deacon to remain at the altar and hold in their hands the consecrated bread, while others remove everything from the altar, and then prepare it once again. When this is not possible, because perhaps the celebrant and deacon are needed to remedy the situation, the patens and ciboria with the consecrated bread can be brought to the credence table or to another altar in the church and placed on a corporal. At least one candle should burn and one server remain kneeling there at all times until the elements are returned to the altar. When the Blessed Sacrament rests on the credence table temporarily in this way, the credence table cannot receive any other items from the altar. These will have to be brought to the sacristy instead. And so, after the Blessed Sacrament has been removed from the altar temporarily, servers remove everything that the wine has touched. They will be careful to gather up the corporal in the altar cloth such that any particles may not fall to the ground. The altar and its cross and candles may need to be washed and wiped as described above. A new altar cloth and new altar linens, along with everything else needed for Mass, is placed on the altar. The priest and the deacon go to the credence table, genuflect, and transfer the consecrated Hosts from the credence table to the altar, genuflecting again once they have placed the Hosts on the altar. The priest will prepare the chalice with wine and water, saying the appropriate prayers, before proceeding immediately to the point where Mass was interrupted.

[306] *MR, De defect.*, 10, 3.

In the extreme case when the chalice is knocked over after the consecration of the wine, first the celebrant must immediately place the chalice upright once again in order to save as much of the Precious Blood as possible. A server needs to place a corporal on another altar with two lit candles or on the credence table. In that case of the latter, the processional candles can remain on the credence table, but all other items are removed. The priest and the deacon remove the consecrated elements from the main altar to a secondary altar or to the credence table and genuflect. A server remains at hand at all times, kneeling. Meanwhile, everything touched by the Previous Blood is removed from altar. The priest and the deacon fold up the corporal(s) and altar cloth(s) such that the outer surfaces remain on the interior of the cloths. One does not genuflect to altar cloths soaked with the Precious Blood. Everything that has been touched by the Precious Blood is wiped with purificators, washed with water, and wiped. These purificators are placed in a decent location of the sacristy along with the altar cloths and linens. Servers place entirely new altar cloths and linens along with the items needed for Mass on the altar. The priest and the deacon reverently return the consecrated Elements from the place where they were reposed to the altar, genuflecting after placing them on the altar. If even a minimal amount of the Precious Blood remains in the chalice for the celebrant to consume at Communion, the celebrant continues where he left off.[307] If no Precious Blood at all remains for him to consume at Communion, and he has not yet received both species, he puts wine, and a little water, in the chalice, says the prayer of preparation for the wine (at least mentally), and proceeds immediately to the consecration of the wine, omitting the elevation, before proceeding from the point where Mass was interrupted.[308] If the Host has been moistened by the Precious Blood, the priest is to consume both species together.[309] After the conclusion of Mass, all the altar cloths and linens removed from the altar are immediately soaked in a basin of water. The water from that rinsing can be poured into the ground or into the sacrarium. Depending on the amount of Precious Blood that was spilled on them, it may be prudent to repeat the process two or three times before setting aside the cloths for laundering.

During the course of Mass, after the consecration, something may fall into the Precious Blood. It may be possible to remove the object with a corner of the

[307] *MR, De defect.*, 10, 13.

[308] *MR, De defect.*, 4, 6 and 10, 13.

[309] *MR, De defect.*, 10, 10.

purificator, or, if necessary, even a pin. If the nature of the object which fell into the Precious Blood demands it, the consecrated wine is to be poured into another chalice and water added until the chalice is full, so that the species of wine is dissolved. This water can be poured into the sacrarium. If this occurred in a chalice intended for the Communion of the people, the celebrant proceeds with Mass where he left off; more wine is not consecrated. If this occurred in the celebrant's chalice, and there is no other chalice of Precious Blood on the altar from which the priest could receive at his Communion, other wine, with a little water, is to be brought out, offered, and consecrated before continuing from the point when Mass was interrupted.[310]

At the time of Communion, the priest is bound to consume both elements of bread and wine consecrated at the same Mass at which he is the celebrant. Otherwise, the integrity of the Mass has been harmed. This also holds true for concelebrants. If the priest discovers at Communion that there is only water in the chalice and not wine, he is to pour the water into another dish or bowl, put wine with a little water into the chalice, say the prayer of preparation (at least mentally), and proceed immediately with the words of consecration over the chalice. Omitting the elevation, he communicates from the chalice, without having to consecrate a new host.[311]

If the Host falls to the ground, it is to be taken up reverently by the minister, not the communicant. If there is reason to believe that particles from the Host may remain on the ground, the priest or deacon will wash the spot with water and dry it with a purificator. The water from the washing is poured into the sacrarium. If the Host should fall onto clothing, there is no need to wash the clothing. If the particles fall on a woman's clothing, however, the woman herself is to take the Host and consume it.[312] The use of the Communion paten can reduce the chances of a Host falling to the ground or onto someone's person. In addition, it is imprudent to distribute Holy Communion from a ciborium which is too full. It would be better to divide the Hosts between two ciboria rather than use one which is so full that a Host may fall out while Communion is being distributed.

Prior to the distribution of Communion or during the distribution of Communion, if drops of the Precious Blood should fall to the ground, the minister

310 *MR, De defect.*, 10, 6.

311 *GIRM*, 324.

312 *MR, De defect.*, 10, 15.

should mark the spot, perhaps with the purificator, while reposing the chalice on a corporal. Meanwhile, some water should be poured over the spot, and the spot dried with a purificator. The water from the washing is poured into the sacrarium. A new purificator should be brought so that the distribution of Communion can resume. If more has been spilled, corporals or even towels may be needed, as in the cases described above. If the Precious Blood spills onto clothing, the person should retire to the sacristy to apply water to the spot and dry it as best as possible.

Prior to Communion, if the priest should realize that the number of Hosts consecrated will not be sufficient for the number of persons intended to receive, and other Hosts are not available in the tabernacle, he can break the Hosts into smaller particles during the Lamb of God. The same can be done during the distribution of Communion if the priest realizes only then that the number of Hosts will be insufficient. He can return to the altar to fraction the Hosts, or can do so while distributing Communion. When there are simply no Hosts available for the communicants who remain, they can always receive Communion under the species of wine alone. But if there are no Hosts left, no Precious Blood left, and no way to bring Hosts from a tabernacle elsewhere in a reasonable period of time, the celebrant will have to conclude Mass without communicating the remaining faithful who present themselves. The celebrant cannot consecrate more Hosts simply to give Communion. Other than the cases mentioned above where a celebrant must act to ensure the integrity of the eucharistic sacrifice, it is strictly forbidden to consecrate one or the other element outside the celebration of an entire Mass.[313] Nor can wine become "consecrated" simply by adding more wine to the Precious Blood in the chalice. After the conclusion of the Mass, it may be possible, after the interval of some time, for the celebrant to bring Hosts reserved in a distant place to the church in order to provide for the Communion of those who would otherwise be deprived. This dilemma points out the need to accurately anticipate the number of hosts and the amount of wine which need to be prepared for any given celebration of Mass.

Finally, what is one to do if consecrated Hosts cannot be reposed in the tabernacle? This situation arises most often when Mass is celebrated outside a church. But it can also arise if the tabernacle cannot receive one more vessel, or if the key to the tabernacle has been misplaced during the celebration of Mass. If the number

[313] *CIC*, 927.

of consecrated Hosts is small, they can be consumed by the celebrant, deacons, and concelebrants. If the number is large, another solution must be found. Until that solution can be realized, the Hosts can be left in a ciborium on a corporal either on the altar, or in front of the tabernacle, or on another altar. In each case, candles will burn around it and at least one server will remain nearby, kneeling, until the situation is resolved. If the ciborium is missing its cover, it can be covered with the pall or even a portion of the corporal on which it rests. While the ciborium rests on the altar, all who pass before it, or enter or depart from the sanctuary, will genuflect toward the Blessed Sacrament.

13

Eucharist Worship outside Mass

THE RITES FOR the distribution of Holy Communion outside Mass and for exposition and benediction can be found in *Holy Communion and Worship of the Eucharist outside Mass*. However, the indications given there are minimal. They can be amplified by the descriptions found in the *Ceremonial of Bishops*, as well as in two contemporary commentaries on both these sources.[314]

Distribution of Holy Communion outside Mass

The rite indicated in paragraphs 26–53 of *Holy Communion and Worship of the Eucharist outside Mass* is intended for use in the church, for the distribution of Holy Communion to those individuals who have requested it or at the set times established for the benefit of the faithful. Depending on the circumstances, the number of readings can be limited to one brief reading, or to a Liturgy of the Word similar to Mass. Most often, this may occur on a weekday. The form of distribution of Holy Communion on a Sunday instead of the celebration of Mass, in contrast, has its own proper ritual in the United States.[315] Such Sunday celebrations in the absence of a priest, whether they include the distribution of Communion or not, require the permission of the diocesan bishop in order to regularly replace the Sunday Mass. The following items need to be prepared:

[314] See Peter J. Elliott, *Ceremonies of the Modern Roman Rite: The Eucharist and the Liturgy of the Hours*, rev. ed. (San Francisco: Ignatius Press, 1995) 245–264, and Elliott, *Ceremonies Explained for Servers According to the Roman Rite: A Manual for Altar Servers, Acolytes, Sacristans, and Masters of Ceremonies* (San Francisco: Ignatius Press, 2019), 138–147.

[315] See Committee on Divine Worship, *Sunday Celebrations in the Absence of a Priest* (Washington, DC: United States Conference of Catholic Bishops, 2012).

At the altar:

- Two candles burning
- A folded corporal (in a burse), unless this is placed on the credence table

At the tabernacle:

- Key
- An open corporal before the tabernacle

At the ambo:

- The Lectionary for Mass, volume 4, *Votive Masses of the Holy Eucharist*, unless the reading or readings are proclaimed from the ritual elsewhere
- The text for the Prayer of the Faithful, unless these are offered elsewhere

At the chair:

- The ritual, *Holy Communion and Worship of the Eucharist outside Mass*

At the credence table:

- The tabernacle key, unless it is already placed in the tabernacle
- White humeral veil, if the Blessed Sacrament is reserved outside the sanctuary
- Two torches, if the Blessed Sacrament is reserved outside the sanctuary

The candles at the altar and at the tabernacle should be lit prior to the beginning of the rite. A burse with a corporal can rest at the center of the altar with its opening facing away from the people.

The priest approaches the sanctuary and bows to the altar or genuflects to the tabernacle depending on the circumstances. The priest then goes to his chair. He greets the people with hands extended and then leads them in the penitential rite. Standing at his place or at the ambo, the priest may then read the brief Scripture passage. If multiple readings are proclaimed, the priest sits and listens. He may then lead the assembly in the universal prayer as usual.

The priest goes to the altar, bows to it, and unfolds the corporal. He may leave the burse flat on the altar toward the right, rear portion of the altar, its opening facing away from the people. The priest should also place the ritual on the altar, to the left of the corporal, at an angle. He then goes to the tabernacle, opens it, genuflects, and takes a ciborium out of the tabernacle. If there are other ciboria or pyxes which remain, he closes the door of the tabernacle; if the tabernacle is entirely empty, he leaves the door to the tabernacle open. If the tabernacle is located outside the sanctuary, the priest goes there with two servers, or at least one. Upon arrival, a server places the humeral veil on his shoulders. The servers light candles to carry. The priest covers the ciborium and both hands in the humeral veil, and follows the servers to the altar.

Upon arriving at the altar, the priest puts the ciborium down on the corporal, uncovers it, places the cover outside the corporal, and then genuflects with both hands resting on the altar. The server removes the humeral veil from his shoulders. The priest stands at the altar and invites everyone to pray the Our Father. The priest prays with hands extended, as at Mass. In the longer form of the rite, the priest may invite those present to exchange a sign of peace. Then the priest genuflects, takes a Host in his right hand, and raises it slightly over the vessel or pyx he holds in his left hand. Facing the people, he invites them to Communion. Meanwhile, all kneel, as at Mass. After distributing Holy Communion, the priest returns to the altar, covers the ciborium, and returns it to the tabernacle. After placing the ciborium in the tabernacle, he genuflects before closing its door. He wears the humeral veil and is accompanied by two servers with candles if the tabernacle is located outside the sanctuary. He may want to purify the thumb and index finger of the right hand in the ablution cup at the tabernacle or at the credence table. The priest folds the corporal on the altar and places it in the burse before returning both to the credence table. The priest prays the concluding prayer at the altar along with the specific blessing and dismissal indicated. The minister then bows to the altar or genuflects to the tabernacle, and returns to the sacristy as at the beginning.

If a deacon is leading this prayer in the place of a priest, he does so from his own chair in the sanctuary. A lay minister by the bishop delegated to distribute Holy Communion who leads this prayer does so from his or her own place in the nave. Both the deacon and the lay minister may proclaim the readings from the ambo or their seat. The deacon brings the ciborium from the chapel of reservation with the humeral veil like the priest, but the lay minister does not.[316] The deacon and the lay

[316] There is no provision for the minister to self-communicate. In the case of a deacon or a lay extraordinary minister who wishes to receive Communion and is leading the prayer, another

minister pray with hands joined. The deacon may bless and dismiss those present. The layperson uses the proper form of the concluding blessing.

The Rite of Eucharistic Exposition following Mass

In some cases, exposition of the Blessed Sacrament begins immediately at the conclusion of Mass. If so, the host to be used for exposition is consecrated during the course of that same Mass along with the hosts for the Communion of the faithful. In addition to what is usually needed for the celebration of Mass, the following items need to be prepared:

At the credence table:

- A lunette with the host to be consecrated for adoration
- A censer, eventually with burning coals, and an incense boat and stand, unless it is located somewhere more convenient
- A monstrance veiled in white
- Eucharistic throne, if used

Normally, the host to be consecrated for adoration is placed in the lunette prior to the beginning of Mass and brought to the altar with the other gifts at the preparation of the altar.[317] If the host to be consecrated is placed in the lunette from the beginning of the preparation of the gifts, the lunette is opened and closed by the deacon or the celebrant at the same time as the covers to the ciboria are removed and replaced during the course of Mass. Or, the host to be consecrated can be placed on the paten with the hosts intended for the Communion of the faithful. At the fraction rite or some other time prior to Communion, a server brings the empty lunette from the credence table and the priest then reverently places the Host consecrated for adoration in the lunette. In either scenario, the Host and lunette are left on the corporal during the time of Communion.[318]

During the distribution of Communion, the server brings the eucharistic throne to the altar, if it is being used, and places it on the corporal toward the back. The server unfolds a second corporal on the throne itself. The server also

deacon or delegated layperson should minister Communion to the leader and to others with the leader.

317 Adrian Fortescue, J. B. O'Connell, and Alcuin Reid, eds., *The Ceremonies of the Roman Rite Described*, 15th ed. (New York: Bloomsbury, 2009), 389.

318 Elliott, *Ceremonies of the Modern Roman Rite*, 258.

brings the veiled monstrance to the altar and places it off the corporal to the left, perpendicular to the front of the altar. The server removes the veil and leaves the door to the monstrance open. The server genuflects and returns to the credence table with the veil. Everyone approaching or departing from the altar during this time genuflects each time, unless they are carrying the Blessed Sacrament in their hands. After the distribution of Communion is completed, any remaining Precious Blood is consumed at the altar and any particles left after the Communion of the faithful are returned to the tabernacle. After the purifications have been completed, preferably at the credence table, the deacon, or the celebrant in his absence, goes to the altar, genuflects, and reverently places the lunette in the monstrance. He closes the door to the monstrance and places it on the throne, if used, or on the center of the corporal. The front of the monstrance faces the assembly. Genuflecting again, he returns to his chair. The celebrant, standing at his chair, says the Post-Communion prayer there. A server holds the missal before him. At such a Mass, it is not permitted to say the Post-Communion prayer standing at the altar with the Blessed Sacrament exposed.[319] Also, everyone avoids turning their back directly to the Blessed Sacrament during this time. The dismissal rites are omitted completely.

After the Post-Communion prayer, the celebrant, deacon, and thurifer go to the altar and genuflect before the lowest step. All present in the church kneel. The celebrant then stands to impose incense.[320] The thurifer stands to the celebrant's right. The deacon, also standing to the celebrant's right between the celebrant and the thurifer, receives the incense boat from the thurifer and offers the celebrant the spoon using his right hand. The deacon then transfers the incense boat to his right hand from his left hand and offers the incense to the celebrant, holding the boat close to the bowl of the censer. The thurifer opens the censer and holds the bowl of the censer up before the celebrant, slightly below eye level. The celebrant imposes incense on the burning coals three times, saying nothing, with his left hand resting on his chest. The deacon transfers the incense boat to his left hand once again and receives the spoon from the celebrant in his right hand. The celebrant blesses the incense in the

[319] *CB*, 389.

[320] Incense is used at exposition whenever a monstrance is used (*HCWEOM*, 85, 93). Whenever a ciborium is used for exposition, incense may be used (*HCWEOM*, 85). It appears that the use of incense may be omitted when exposition in the monstrance takes place at the conclusion of Mass (*HCWEOM*, 94). It may be that the ritual presumes that the Blessed Sacrament was incensed during the course of Mass itself at the elevations; therefore the gesture does not need to be repeated during exposition following Mass.

form of a Greek cross with his right hand, saying nothing, his left hand resting on his chest.[321] The deacon returns the boat and spoon to the thurifer or even to the incense stand so that his own hands will be free. The celebrant, deacon, and thurifer kneel. The thurifer can hold the incense boat in the left hand with the ring of the chains of the censer or the thurifer can place it temporarily on the altar step so as to have both hands free. The thurifer holds the ring of the chains of the censer, and perhaps the boat, in the left hand. The thurifer holds the chains near the bowl of the censer in the right hand. The deacon, using both hands, receives the censer from the thurifer in the kneeling position. The celebrant receives the censer from the deacon in the kneeling position. The deacon takes care to use his right hand to place the ring of the censer in the celebrant's left hand, and to use his left hand to place the bowl of the censer in the celebrant's right hand. Raising the bowl of the censer to eye level, the celebrant incenses the Blessed Sacrament in silence with three double swings from the kneeling position, bowing profoundly before and after.[322] All who are kneeling with the celebrant bow when he bows. If necessary, the deacon may hold the edge of the celebrant's chasuble, his right hand resting on his chest. The celebrant, kneeling, hands the censer back to the deacon, who is also kneeling. The deacon hands the censer to the thurifer, who also receives it while kneeling. All remain kneeling for a period of adoration. That adoration may be silent or may include a hymn. When the celebrant signals it is time to depart, all stand and then genuflect in place before returning to the sacristy in procession.

The Rite of Eucharistic Exposition apart from Mass

When eucharistic exposition, adoration, and benediction take place using a Host consecrated at a prior Mass, the following items are needed:

In the sacristy:

- Cope and stole for the priest celebrant, dalmatic and stole for the deacon, stole for the assisting priest or deacon if there is one
- Processional cross and candles, if these lead the procession from the sacristy to the sanctuary

[321] *CB*, 306, 391, 1109; Peter J. Elliott, *Ceremonies of the Liturgical Year According to the Modern Roman Rite* (San Francisco: Ignatius Press, 2002), 105; Elliott, *Ceremonies of the Modern Roman Rite*, 250. Formerly, incense was not blessed in the presence of the Blessed Sacrament exposed.

[322] *HCWEOM*, 93.

On or near the altar:

- Six candles, or at least four
- White burse with one or two corporals as needed
- Monstrance veiled in white
- Exposition throne, if used

At the steps of the altar or nearby:

- Censer with burning coals, incense boat and stand
- White humeral veil, if the Blessed Sacrament is reserved outside the sanctuary
- Two torches, if the Blessed Sacrament is reserved outside the sanctuary

The priest celebrant wears a white stole and cope[323] unless a portion of the Liturgy of the Hours is to be celebrated before or during exposition, in which case he wears a stole and cope of the color of the Office.[324] The celebrant may also wear only the stole without the cope for exposition, not benediction.[325] The celebrant can be assisted by a deacon walking to his right side, vested in stole and dalmatic of the same color as the cope the celebrant is wearing, or by two deacons similarly vested, walking on either side of the celebrant. If no deacon is available, the celebrant can be assisted by another priest, who wears a stole of the same color as the celebrant over the surplice or alb and walks immediately ahead of the celebrant.[326] A deacon who assists only with exposition and reposition, without assisting the celebrant at his side during the entire time of exposition, adoration, and benediction, may also vest in this way instead and walk ahead of the celebrant.

A burse with one or two corporals, depending on the circumstances, is placed at the center of the altar, its opening facing away from the assembly. To the left of the center of the altar, perpendicular to its front edge, is the monstrance,

[323] *CB*, 1105.

[324] Fortescue, O'Connell, and Reid, *The Ceremonies of the Roman Rite Described*, 296.

[325] *HCWEOM*, 92. The celebrant must wear a cope and white humeral veil to impart the benediction with the monstrance at the conclusion of adoration.

[326] Elliott, *Ceremonies of the Modern Roman Rite*, 248; Fortescue, O'Connell, and Reid, *The Ceremonies if the Roman Rite Described*, 301. Formerly, the assisting priest or deacon only wore the stole at the moment of exposition and reposition. He carried the stole on his left arm, or the stole was placed on the credence table beforehand. See Fortescue, O'Connell, and Reid, *The Ceremonies of the Roman Rite Described*, 296.

veiled in white.[327] If a throne is used for exposition, it can be placed at the center of the altar. A stand holding a censer with burning coals and incense is placed to the far-right of the center of the steps of the altar. Normally, the celebrant kneels on the bare steps. The use of a cushion or kneeler at adoration was formerly reserved to bishops and prelates.[328]

The rite of exposition begins as the ministers make their way from the sacristy to the sanctuary. Instrumental music or singing may accompany the procession to the altar.[329] Two servers lead the way, carrying nothing in their hands. On more solemn occasions, these two servers with candles may flank the processional cross and its bearer. These servers carry the candlesticks in their outside hands at the nodes, with their other hands resting on the bases of the candlesticks, walking immediately before the assisting priest or the celebrant and deacon.[330] Upon arriving in the sanctuary, these servers place their candles on either side of the lowest step of the altar or, if necessary, on either side of the lowest step of the sanctuary.[331] If this is impractical, they can place their candles at the rear corners of the credence table, as at Mass. The cross bearer places the processional cross aside. The ministers and servers genuflect before the steps of the sanctuary to the Blessed Sacrament reserved there, and then kneel on the first step of the altar. All kneel. The assisting deacon or priest, or the celebrant himself in his absence, does not kneel after genuflecting but goes first to the altar and unfolds the corporal(s) from the burse in the same way one would do at Mass, leaving the burse flat on the right-hand side of the altar. The opening of the burse faces away from the assembly. If a throne is used for exposition, a second corporal is placed on the throne itself, in addition to the corporal placed on the altar.[332] The throne with its corporal is placed at the far edge of the corporal on the altar. Then the assisting deacon or priest unveils the monstrance, placing it on the corporal on the altar, perpendicular to the front of the altar and to the left side of the corporal, with its door open. In some churches, the unveiled monstrance is already placed on the altar in this position before the entrance of the ministers.

The assisting deacon or priest then proceeds to the tabernacle in the sanctuary. He opens the door and genuflects. He takes the custodia and places it on the

327 Fortescue, O'Connell, and Reid, *The Ceremonies of the Roman Rite Described*, 297.

328 Fortescue, O'Connell, and Reid, *The Ceremonies of the Roman Rite Described*, 295.

329 *HCWEOM*, 93.

330 Elliott, *Ceremonies of the Modern Roman Rite*, 248.

331 Elliott, *Ceremonies Explained for Servers*, 188; Elliott, *Ceremonies of the Modern Roman Rite*, 268.

332 Fortescue, O'Connell, and Reid, *The Ceremonies of the Roman Rite Described*, 295.

corporal outside the tabernacle in order to close the door, provided the Blessed Sacrament continues to be reserved in the tabernacle in some other vessel or vessels. In contrast, if the tabernacle will be completely empty when he removes the custodia, he leaves the door open. He then takes the custodia in both hands and makes his way to the altar. Once at the altar, he places the custodia down on the corporal on the altar and opens it. He reverently places the lunette with his right hand into the monstrance and closes the door. He then closes the empty custodia and sets it aside to the right of the corporal.[333] He then reverently places the monstrance at the center of the corporal on the altar or on the throne on the altar, facing the assembly. He genuflects on one knee.[334] If he is a priest, he genuflects with both hands resting on the altar outside the corporal. A deacon genuflects with hands joined off of the altar. The minister of exposition returns to his place in the sanctuary or at the bottom step of the altar and kneels.

Additional accommodations must be made if the Blessed Sacrament is reserved in a location outside the sanctuary where exposition is to take place. There will need to be at least two servers in the initial procession to the sanctuary. Upon arriving, all bow to the altar and kneel. All in the assembly kneel. The assistant deacon or priest prepares the corporal(s) and monstrance as indicated above, and then returns to kneel in front of the altar. Standing behind the assisting minister, a server places the white humeral veil on his shoulders. The assistant and the two servers then stand. The two servers with torches then flank the assisting minister as he goes to the place of reservation to retrieve the Blessed Sacrament and brings the Host to the altar in the custodia. After placing the Host in the monstrance in the manner described above, genuflecting, and returning to his place at the bottom step, the assisting deacon or priest gives up the humeral veil from a kneeling position.

At once, the celebrant and those kneeling with him bow from the waist and stand. The celebrant turns to his right. The deacon receives the incense boat from the thurifer. The thurifer faces the celebrant and presents him the open censer, holding the bowl of the censer up in his right hand, slightly below eye level. The deacon offers the celebrant the spoon in his right hand while holding the incense boat in his left. He then transfers the incense boat to his right hand

333 Elliott, *Ceremonies of the Modern Roman Rite,* 249.

334 *CB,* 1103. According to the revised liturgical books, all genuflections, either during Mass, or made to the Blessed Sacrament in the tabernacle, or made to the Blessed Sacrament exposed, are made on one knee (*HCWEOM,* 84). Some churches have preserved the custom of genuflecting momentarily on both knees in the presence of the Blessed Sacrament exposed.

and holds it close to the bowl of the censer. The celebrant imposes incense three times on the burning coals with the right hand, his left hand resting on his chest. The celebrant returns the spoon to the deacon. The celebrant blesses the incense in the form of a Greek cross with his right hand, saying nothing, his left hand resting on his chest. The deacon returns the boat and spoon to the thurifer or even to the incense stand so that his own hands will be free. The celebrant, deacon, and thurifer kneel. The thurifer can hold the incense boat in the left hand with the ring of the chains of the censer or the thurifer can place it temporarily on the altar step so as to have both hands free. The thurifer hands the censer to the deacon kneeling at the celebrant's right. From a kneeling position, the deacon places the rings of the chain in the left hand of the celebrant by using his own right hand. The deacon places the chains near the bowl of the censer into the right hand of the celebrant with his own left hand. If necessary, the deacon may then hold back the edge of the celebrant's cope with his left hand, his right hand resting on his chest. Raising the bowl of the censer to eye level, the celebrant incenses the Blessed Sacrament with three double swings in silence, bowing before and after from a kneeling position. All those kneeling bow with the celebrant from a kneeling position, at the same time as he does. The celebrant then returns the censer to the deacon, who returns it to the thurifer. In many churches, a eucharistic chant is often sung during the incensation.[335] This chant is not mentioned in the revised liturgical books,[336] nor was it the custom formerly.[337] Rather a hymn, like "O Salutaris," was sung after the incensation, during the period of adoration, often immediately *after* the incensation.

All remain kneeling for a time of silent prayer. For periods of extended adoration, the celebrant may kneel or sit at the chair in the sanctuary, or at the first place in choir.[338] A kneeler can be provided for him at the chair. The assisting deacon or priest may remove the stole during the time of adoration. The ministers and servers stand and genuflect before taking their places in the sanctuary or in choir. During the time of exposition, no one sits or stands with his or her back to the monstrance. A genuflection is made whenever passing in front of the monstrance or upon entering or leaving the sanctuary, even at the side. All gestures of reverence normally made to the altar or to the celebrant or to the Blessed Sacrament

[335] Elliott, *Ceremonies of the Modern Roman Rite*, 249.

[336] *CB*, 1109; *HCWEOM*, 93.

[337] Fortescue, O'Connell, and Reid, *The Ceremonies of the Roman Rite Described*, 298.

[338] Fortescue, O'Connell, and Reid, *The Ceremonies of the Roman Rite Described*, 301; Elliott, *Ceremonies of the Modern Roman Rite*, 250; *CB*, 1110.

reserved in the tabernacle are instead directed solely to the Blessed Sacrament exposed on the altar. During the time of adoration, there may be prayers, song, readings, silence, or even a homily.[339]

The Rite of Eucharistic Benediction

Benediction can take place at the conclusion of a brief period of adoration, or it can take place after a rather extended period of adoration. When the rite of benediction takes place some span of time after the time of exposition, the following items are needed:

In the sacristy:

- Cope and stole for the priest celebrant, dalmatic and stole for the deacon, stole for the assisting priest or deacon if there is one
- Processional cross and candles, if these lead the procession from the sacristy to the sanctuary

At the steps of the altar or nearby:

- Censer with burning coals, incense boat and stand
- White humeral veil
- *Holy Communion and Worship of the Eucharist Outside Mass,* or at least a card with the necessary prayers
- Two torches, if the Blessed Sacrament is reserved outside the sanctuary
- Handbells, if used

The priest celebrant wears a white stole and cope.[340] When the time of adoration is concluded, the ministers and servers make their way either from the sacristy or from their places in the sanctuary and genuflect together before the altar. They then kneel on the lowest step of the altar, as they did at exposition. All in the assembly kneel in their places. Normally, the Blessed Sacrament is incensed during the final verse of the hymn "Pange Lingua," that is, at *Genitori genitoque,* or during some other eucharistic chant.[341] During the preceding verse, which begins with

[339] *CB*, 1111; *HCWEOM*, 95, 96.
[340] *CB*, 1105.
[341] *CB*, 1113; *HCWEOM*, 97.

tantum ergo, it is customary to bow together from a kneeling position at the words *veneremur cernui*, after which the priest celebrant, the deacon, and the thurifer stand; the deacon and thurifer assist the celebrant in preparing the incense.[342] The Blessed Sacrament is incensed in the same manner described above as at exposition. The hymn and the incensation concluded, the celebrant alone rises, without bowing or genuflecting. If he does not know one of the Collects from memory, one of the servers may rise with him to hold the book for him, preferably to his left. With hands joined and bowing his head, he sings, "Let us pray."[343] Then he sings one of the Collects provided, with hands extended.[344]

After the Collect, the celebrant kneels, and a server with the humeral veil comes behind him to place it over his shoulders. The server, holding the clasps of the humeral veil in his hands, makes sure to place the clasps into the hands of the celebrant as he places the veil on the celebrant's shoulders. The celebrant secures it in the front and stands to go up directly to the altar without any further reverence. The assisting deacon or priest may accompany him. It is often easiest to give the blessing from the side of the altar closest to the assembly. The celebrant may also go around the altar to face the assembly and give the blessing from there if he prefers. As he approaches the altar, the celebrant may enfold his joined hands in the humeral veil in order to lift its edges and avoiding tripping on it while climbing the steps to the altar.

Once at the altar, the celebrant and the assisting priest or deacon genuflect. The celebrant frees his hands and places them flat on the altar outside the corporal in order to genuflect. The assisting priest or deacon or the celebrant himself takes the monstrance with unveiled hands from the throne and places it on the corporal on the altar. Depending on at which side of the altar he is standing, he may need to rotate the monstrance first, so that it faces forward when the celebrant imparts the blessing over the assembly. The celebrant rises and covers his hands with the humeral veil to take the monstrance with its front facing forward. Alternatively, the assisting deacon or priest, after accompanying the celebrant to the altar and genuflecting and rising with him, may place the monstrance directly in the celebrant's veiled hands such that the front

342 Fortescue, O'Connell, and Reid, *The Ceremonies of the Roman Rite Described*, 299; Elliott, *Ceremonies of the Modern Roman Rite*, 251, n. 14.

343 Although it is not indicated in the revised ritual, some churches preserve the custom of singing the versicle, "You have given them bread from heaven," and its response prior to "Let us pray." See Elliott, *Ceremonies of the Modern Roman Rite*, 251, n. 15.

344 *CB*, 1113.

of the monstrance will be facing the assembly as the celebrant holds it. The celebrant can hold the monstrance with the right hand at the node, and the left hand steadying its base, or he can take it at the node with both hands. The assisting priest or deacon kneels to receive the blessing, as everyone in the church also does.

The celebrant turns to his right if he is not already facing the assembly and makes the Sign of the Cross once over the people, saying nothing. He keeps his eyes fixed on the Blessed Sacrament throughout this action. He begins by raising the monstrance slightly above eye level.[345] He lowers the monstrance, with its base no lower than the table of the altar, and raises it again halfway, at about eye level. Turning to the left but not beyond the extremity his left shoulder, he makes a straight line to the right, again not beyond the extremity of his right shoulder. The celebrant does not move his feet while he moves his arms.[346] He returns the monstrance to the center and pauses before lowering the monstrance onto the corporal on the altar or giving it to the assisting deacon or priest. If the celebrant is standing with his back to the altar to give the blessing, he turns to his right after giving the blessing to complete the circle, before setting the monstrance down on the altar or giving it to the assisting priest or deacon. Unless reposition follows immediately, the monstrance is positioned on the corporal on the altar so that the front of the monstrance is facing the assembly once again. The celebrant or the assisting priest or deacon may need to rotate the monstrance once again so that its front may face the assembly as before.

During the time of the blessing, a server may ring a set of handbells three times. Historically, it was usual to ring the bells once as the celebrant turned to the people, once at the middle of the blessing, and once as he turned back to the altar.[347] If the celebrant is already facing the assembly when he imparts the blessing, perhaps this custom could be adapted. The server could first ring the handbells to accompany the raising of the monstrance for the blessing. The server could ring them a second time when the monstrance moves from the center to the left, and a third time when the monstrance moves from the center to the right. Although it is not indicated in the rubrics, many churches maintain the practice of incensing the Blessed Sacrament during the benediction. The thurifer may incense the Blessed Sacrament with three double swings, bowing from a kneeling position

345 Elliott, *Ceremonies of the Modern Roman Rite*, 252.

346 Fortescue, O'Connell, and Reid, *The Ceremonies of the Roman Rite Described*, 299–300.

347 Fortescue, O'Connell, and Reid, *The Ceremonies of the Roman Rite Described*, 300.

before and after. He may do so either at the center of the sanctuary steps or at the right-hand end of the altar.[348] The thurifer will make sure that the timing of the swings of the censer correspond to the moments when the server rings the handbells during the benediction.[349] In some locations, all those present bow while kneeling at their places in order to receive the blessing. They may also sign themselves once with the Sign of the Cross.

After genuflecting at the altar, the celebrant and his assistant return to their places at the center of the sanctuary steps and kneel. A server, standing behind the celebrant, removes the humeral veil from him. Many locations observe the custom of praying the Divine Praises at this point, while all remain kneeling, rather than proceeding immediately with reposition.[350] Alternatively, the assisting deacon or priest can remain at the altar following benediction and immediately proceed with reposition. Immediately after benediction or after the conclusion of the Divine Praises, an acclamation of praise of some kind is sung or said while the act of reposition in the tabernacle takes place.[351] In many churches, all begin singing a hymn, such as "Holy God We Praise Thy Name," at this point. The assisting deacon or priest turns the monstrance perpendicular to the front of the altar toward the left, though still on the corporal. He moves the custodia onto the corporal and opens it. He then removes the lunette from the monstrance and places it in the custodia and closes it. He moves the monstrance off the corporal to his left, still perpendicular to the front of the altar. He then takes the custodia in both hands and places it into the tabernacle in the sanctuary, genuflecting before closing the door and locking it. All stand when the Blessed Sacrament is reposed in the tabernacle or when the hymn or acclamation at reposition concludes. In some churches, all begin singing a Marian antiphon at this point. The assisting deacon or priest may return briefly to the altar to veil the monstrance and place it perpendicular to the left side of the altar. He may then fold the corporal and place it in its burse. The burse remains flat at the center of the altar with the opening facing away from the assembly. All genuflect at their places before the lowest step of the sanctuary. Those standing two by two before the altar turn toward each other to face the opposite direction. Three or

[348] Elliott, *Ceremonies of the Modern Roman Rite*, 253.
[349] Elliott, *Ceremonies of the Modern Roman Rite*, 253.
[350] Elliott, *Ceremonies of the Modern Roman Rite*, 253–254.
[351] *HCWEOM*, 100.

more standing together before the altar turn to their right to face the opposite direction. All return to the sacristy in the same order in which they entered.

If the Blessed Sacrament will be reserved in a location outside the sanctuary where benediction has taken place, additional accommodations are needed. In that case, the two servers holding torches kneel in the sanctuary at the time of benediction. These torch bearers carry the torches in their outside hands, with their other hands resting on their chests. After the benediction, or perhaps after the Divine Praises, the assistant deacon or priest receives the humeral veil from a kneeling position either at the altar or on the lowest step of the sanctuary. He goes up to the altar, genuflects before the Blessed Sacrament, and removes the lunette from the monstrance as described above. With the custodia containing the lunette and both hands covered by the ends of the humeral veil, he returns to the place of reservation, flanked by two torch bearers. During this time, all sing a hymn or an acclamation of praise. After placing the Blessed Sacrament in the tabernacle, the assisting minister gives up the humeral veil from a kneeling position. One server may hold both torches momentarily while the second server removes the humeral veil and places it aside. The celebrant and those with him return to the sanctuary. Then, all stand and bow to the altar, and return to the sacristy in the same order by which they entered. The procession can be accompanied by instrumental music or a hymn.

Exposition following Vespers or Morning Prayer

At times, exposition and benediction of the Blessed Sacrament follow the celebration of Vespers or Morning Prayer. The celebrant and deacon wear the cope and dalmatic, respectively, of the color of the celebration. After the concluding Collect of the hour being celebrated, the celebrant omits the blessing and dismissal and proceeds to exposition of the Blessed Sacrament in the usual manner, as described above. A period of adoration follows, concluding with benediction.

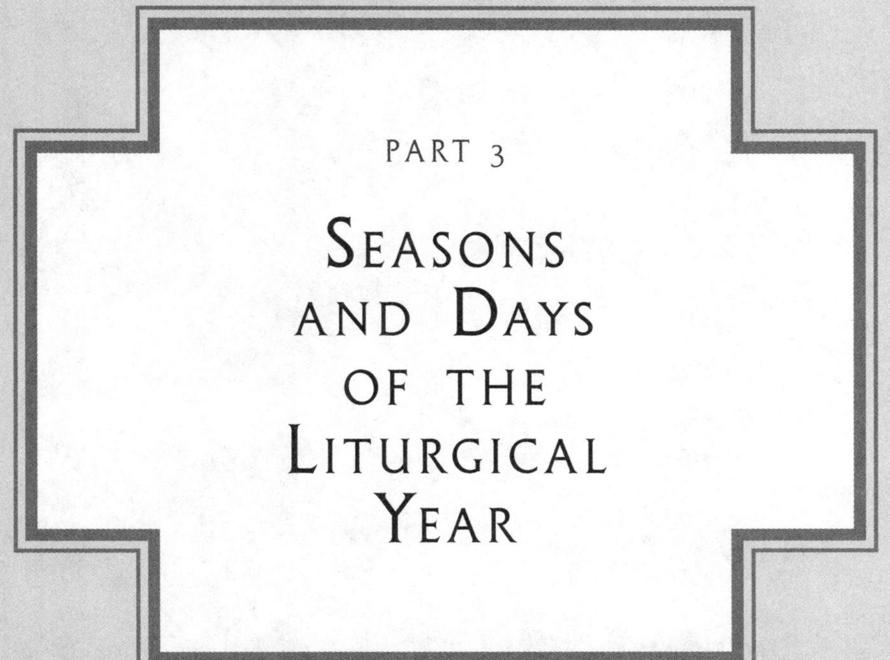

PART 3

Seasons and Days of the Liturgical Year

14

The Nativity Cycle

Annunciation (March 25) and Christmas (December 25)

On March 25 and on December 25, all kneel on both knees when one says, "and by the Holy Spirit was incarnate of the Virgin Mary and became man," in the Nicene Creed or when one says, "and was conceived by the Holy Spirit, born of the Virgin Mary," in the Apostles' Creed.[352] There is some confusion in the English translation of the *Order for Mass* on this point. At the Mass for Christmas Eve and at the three Masses for Christmas Day, the rubrics indicate that all kneel on two knees at this point. In contrast, at the Mass for the Annunciation of the Lord and in no. 137 of the *General Instruction,* the text indicates that all genuflect on one knee. In the rubrics for the Masses on Christmas and on the Annunciation, the Latin original uses the same word in all five cases, *genuflectitur*. The Latin text for no. 137 of the *General Instruction* uses the comparable term "*genua flectunt*." In Latin, these terms can refer either to kneeling or to genuflecting, hence the confusion if taken out of context.

The context for understanding the rubric should be the traditional practice of the Roman Rite. Historically, all have knelt on both knees, not merely genuflected, on those same occasions.[353] The 1982 translation of the same paragraph in the previous edition of the *General Instruction* (1975) thus rendered "*genua*

[352] André Philippe M. Mutel and Peter Freeman, *Cérémonial de la sainte messe à l'usage ordinaire des paroisses suivant le missel romain de 2002 et la pratique léguée du rit romain,* 2nd ed. (Perpignan, France: Éditions Artège, 2012), 106.

[353] Adrian Fortescue, J. B. O'Connell, and Alcuin Reid, eds., *The Ceremonies of the Roman Rite Described,* 15th ed. (New York: Bloomsbury, 2009), 310.

flectunt" as "kneel."[354] Seen in this light, the celebrant, standing at the chair to begin the Creed, kneels in his place on March 25 and December 25 at the point in the Creed when he would otherwise bow during the rest of the year. Historically, the ministers also bowed at the waist while kneeling, before standing once again to continue the rest of the Creed.

Appendix 1 of the missal contains the excerpt of the *Roman Martyrology* known as the announcement of the Nativity of the Lord. This is not strictly speaking part of the celebration of Mass on Christmas Eve or Christmas Day, nor can it replace any part of the Mass, such as the penitential act, for example. The proclamation may be recited or sung on December 24, immediately prior to the beginning of Mass on Christmas Eve or during the night. In some locations, it is sung in the context of the Office of Readings prior to midnight Mass. A deacon or a priest sings the proclamation from the ambo or a lectern wearing a cope. It may also be sung at the ambo or at a lectern by a lay cantor wearing an alb. In any event, the one singing the proclamation does not seek the blessing of the priest before doing so. All stand while it is sung.[355]

Epiphany

In contrast to the proclamation of the Nativity sung at Christmas, the announcement of the moveable feasts of the year can be included in the principal Mass celebrated on Epiphany, or indeed at any Mass on Epiphany. That announcement may be proclaimed after the Gospel and before the homily on Epiphany according to the chant found in appendix 1 of the Roman Missal. This is done at standing at the ambo or lectern. The minister singing this proclamation, whether a concelebrant or another priest in attendance, a deacon, or a cantor, makes the customary reverences to the altar and the celebrant before and after.[356] The ordained minister of the proclamation who is not a concelebrant or a deacon of the Mass may wear a cope.[357] A layperson sings the announcement wearing the alb. The minister of the announcement, whether ordained or lay, does not seek the blessing of the celebrant. All stand during the announcement.

The same announcement might also be done without any solemnity in the following manner. After the Post-Communion prayer and before the final blessing of

[354] *DOL*, 208, no. 1488.

[355] Peter J. Elliott, *Ceremonies of the Liturgical Year According to the Modern Roman Rite: A Manual for Clergy and All Involved in Liturgical Ministries* (San Francisco: Ignatius Press, 2002), 53.

[356] Fortescue, O'Connell, and Reid, *The Ceremonies of the Roman Rite Described*, 311.

[357] *CB*, 240.

Mass, the deacon (or the priest celebrant himself if he prefers) simply reads the text found in the appendix while standing at his chair and facing the people.[358]

Presentation of the Lord (February 2)

In addition to what is usually needed for Mass, the following need to be prepared:

At the entrance of the church:

- Candles for all present as they arrive

In the sacristy:

- A white cope for the celebrant for the procession or the solemn entrance, unless he prefers to use the chasuble for the procession; white stole and dalmatic for the deacon
- Gospel book for the deacon to carry[359]
- Thurible and incense boat, carried by a server to the place where the procession will begin[360]
- The missal, carried by a server to the place where the procession will begin
- Holy water and aspergillum, carried by a server to the place where the procession will begin[361]

At the place where the procession will begin:

- Candles for the sacred ministers and servers on a tray and covered with a white cloth, placed on a table covered in white

At the chair:

- The white chasuble draped over the presidential chair, if the celebrant wears the white cope for the procession

The Mass on February 2 can begin either with a procession properly speaking or with the solemn entrance. Contrary to the provision for the simple entrance on

358 *GIRM*, 184.

359 *CB*, 246

360 Mutel and Freeman, *Cérémonial de la sainte messe*, 234.

361 Elliott, *Ceremonies of the Liturgical Year*, 46.

Palm Sunday, it appears that there is no possibility for beginning Mass for the Presentation of the Lord without the blessing of candles and without either the procession or solemn entrance which follows. The celebrant may wear a white cope for the procession, properly speaking, if he wishes. Otherwise, the celebrant may wear a white chasuble for the procession, just as he necessarily does for the solemn entrance. The censer is not charged in the sacristy as usual, but only prior to the beginning of the procession or solemn entrance.[362]

In the case of the procession, all or most of the faithful gather in a location outside the body of the church, either in another chapel, or hall, or narthex, or even outdoors, weather permitting. In the case of the solemn entrance, the assembly gathers inside the body of the church. A representative group of the faithful joins the celebrant and ministers just inside the door of the church or just outside it. All hold unlit candles. The practice of extinguishing the lights of the church for the procession is without foundation.

If there is an altar in the location where the procession will begin, all the ministers bow to it or genuflect if the Blessed Sacrament is reserved upon arriving there from the sacristy. To conduct the blessing, the celebrant stands either on the epistle side of the altar[363] or before the table prepared for the candles, facing the assembly. If there is no altar where the procession will begin, a station is created whereby the processional cross itself and its candles become the focal point of the liturgical assembly.[364] The celebrant stands facing both the processional cross and candles and the table prepared with candles to be blessed. Therefore, as the cross bearer and candle bearers arrive in a location where there is no altar, they position themselves in a row in such a way that the celebrant and deacon face the cross, and the candles, as well as all those gathered. Other ministers can stand facing each other in two rows between the cross and candles and the celebrant and deacon.

Upon arriving at the place where the procession will begin, the celebrant, the deacon, and the ministers bow to the altar or to the processional cross. The candles for the celebrant and other servers are placed on a tray covered in a white cloth, on a table on the epistle side of the secondary altar, or in the front of the location where the celebrant will stand. A server removes the veil and holds the

[362] Mutel and Freeman, *Cérémonial de la sainte messe*, 234.

[363] Fortescue, O'Connell, and Reid, *The Ceremonies of the Roman Rite Described*, 312.

[364] Mutel and Freeman, *Cérémonial de la sainte messe*, 235.

tray directly before the celebrant[365] or leaves them on the table.[366] Upon arrival, servers immediately light the candles of all present, perhaps from the processional candles, as the proper chant is sung.[367] The deacon stands at the celebrant's right, as usual. A server, standing to the celebrant and deacon's right, holds the lit candles of the celebrant and perhaps of the deacon until both are free to take a candle. The servers holding the holy water and the censer and incense also stand slightly to the right of the celebrant. The book bearer stands slightly to the left of the celebrant. The celebrant begins with the Sign of the Cross and the greeting. The deacon or a concelebrant may direct the faithful to raise their candles in their hands for the blessing. After the invitation, the celebrant says the prayer of blessing with hands outstretched, palms down, over the candles. The celebrant makes the Sign of the Cross over the candles in the form of a Greek cross with the right hand during the prayer in the first case, or at the end of the prayer in the second case, the left hand resting on his chest. The deacon or the server assisting with the holy water, using the right hand, offers the celebrant the aspergillum. The celebrant then sprinkles the candles, saying nothing. He can do so standing in the same location, sprinkling the center, left, and then right of the assembly, or by walking through the assembly as described in chapter 5. The sprinkling concluded, the celebrant returns the aspergillum to the deacon or the server assisting with the holy water. The thurifer now comes before the celebrant at his right side. The celebrant imposes incense in the usual way. With his right hand, the deacon presents to the celebrant the spoon, then transfers the incense boat from his left hand to his right hand. Using his right hand, the celebrant imposes incense three times and returns the spoon. With his left hand on his chest, the celebrant blesses the incense in the form of a Greek cross with his right hand, saying nothing. The thurifer stands behind the processional cross, ready to turn on his right to the lead the procession into the church. The celebrant then receives his burning candle in his right hand from the deacon. The deacon invites the procession to begin. All bow to the altar, or to the cross in its absence, and the procession to the sanctuary begins.

If the deacon is to carry the book of the Gospels in the procession into the church, as indicated in the *Ceremonial of Bishops,* he takes the Gospel book in both hands at this time. Until this time, he has needed both hands free to assist the

[365] Mutel and Freeman, *Cérémonial de la sainte messe,* 235.

[366] Elliott, *Ceremonies of the Liturgical Year,* 46.

[367] Elliott, *Ceremonies of the Liturgical Year,* 47, n. 3.

celebrant. The deacon may initially carry the Gospel book from the sacristy to the place where the procession begins, and place it on the altar located there upon arriving. If there is no altar in the location where the procession into the church begins, another minister, perhaps a vested instituted lector or even a reader, might hold the Gospel book for the deacon during the entire time he is assisting with the holy water, incense, and celebrant's candle.[368] This minister returns the Gospel book to the deacon just as the procession is about to depart. If the deacon does not carry the Gospel book at all, he carries a burning candle in his right hand instead.

In the procession, all the ministers follow the thurifer and the cross and candles, and precede the celebrant. One server carries the missal, closed. Concelebrants immediately precede the celebrant. If the deacon is carrying the Gospel book, he follows the ministers and precedes the concelebrants and celebrant. If the deacon is not carrying the Gospel book, he walks to the right of the celebrant, holding a candle in his right hand. If the celebrant is wearing a cope, the deacon, the master of ceremonies, or two servers walk on either side of him, holding the edge of cope in their inside hands and a candle in their outside hands. The faithful follow behind the celebrant.[369] Often the choir are among the first of the faithful immediately behind the celebrant. All in the procession carry a burning candle in their outside hands.

Upon arriving at the sanctuary, the celebrant may extinguish his candle and hand it to the deacon or to a server. All then make the usual reverence to the altar, or to the Blessed Sacrament, if it is reserved there.[370] The celebrant is now free to remove the cope, if he is wearing it, and to take the chasuble. Normally, this is done at the chair, rather than in the nave or the entrance to the sanctuary.[371] Vested for Mass, he proceeds to the altar, kisses it, and incenses it. Alternatively, he may relinquish his candle upon arriving at the altar, make the required reverence, kiss the altar, incense it, and then go to the chair, where he removes the cope, if he is wearing it, and takes the chasuble for the opening rites of Mass. Immediately upon the celebrant's arrival at the chair, a server stands before him carrying the missal open to the Gloria. At the conclusion of the Introit, the schola immediately begins the Gloria. The penitential act is entirely omitted.[372] Then, the celebrant says, "Let us

368 Elliott, *Ceremonies of the Liturgical Year*, 47.

369 *CB*, 246.

370 Mutel and Freeman, *Cérémonial de la sainte messe*, 240.

371 Mutel and Freeman, *Cérémonial de la sainte messe*, 240, n. 33.

372 *RM*, February 2, no. 8. Even the *Kyrie* is omitted. See *Graduale Romanum*, proprium de sanctis, die 2 februarii, ad missam: "Omittịtur Kyrie Eleison, cantatur Gloria in excelsis." See also Mutel and Freeman, *Cérémonial de la sainte messe*, 241.

pray," with hands joined. After a moment of silence, he prays the Collect with hands extended. Then all sit for the Liturgy of the Word.

As the procession enters the church and the sanctuary, the other ministers and the faithful may extinguish their candles upon arriving at their seats.[373] Or, as an alternative, one commentator suggests that all keep their candles lit until the conclusion of the Collect, since one can argue that the Collect marks the end of the procession.[374] This is somewhat analogous to the directive at the Easter Vigil to extinguish candles just before the readings begin.[375] In that case, the deacon or a server will need to take the celebrant's candle from him whenever he is using his hands, for example, when removing the cope, when incensing the altar, and whenever he gestures with his hands for the Sign of the Cross, the greeting, the invitation to prayer, and the Collect itself. In practice following this approach, the celebrant holds his candle during the Gloria, and not during the rest of the opening rites, although everyone else simply holds them in their left hands throughout the opening rites, since they make the Sign of the Cross with their right hands. If Mass began with the solemn entrance rather than the procession, it may be better to keep the candles lit for this longer period. The faithful may need some indication by way of word or gesture in order to know when they should extinguish their candles.

Formerly, the candles were lit once again for the proclamation of the Gospel and from the *Sanctus* to the conclusion of the Eucharistic Prayer, or even until the conclusion of Communion, but these indications are not found in the Roman Missal of Paul VI.[376]

[373] Mutel and Freeman, *Cérémonial de la sainte messe,* 240.

[374] Elliott, *Ceremonies of the Liturgical Year,* 81.

[375] *RM 2002,* Order for Mass, Easter Vigil, no. 22.

[376] Mutel and Freeman, *Cérémonial de la sainte messe,* 241.

15

Ash Wednesday, the Days of Lent, and Palm Sunday

Ash Wednesday

THE IMPOSITION OF ashes is the distinctive mark of the Mass celebrated on the Wednesday prior to the first Sunday of Lent. The blessing and imposition of ashes on the ministers and faithful take place after the homily and before the Prayer of the Faithful. Prior to the celebration, in addition to everything needed for the celebration of Mass, the following items will also need to be prepared:

At the credence table:

- A tray with vessels of ashes, covered or veiled in violet[377]; cards with the formula for the imposition of ashes, if needed, on this tray also
- The vessel of holy water and aspergillum
- Pitcher, bowl, soap, and towel for washing the hands after the distribution of the ashes
- A gremial, if the celebrant is seated when washing his hands

Mass begins in the usual manner. The penitential act, however, is omitted, since the imposition of ashes will take its place. After the homily, the celebrant returns to the chair. If the chair is placed perpendicular to the altar, the server with the missal stands directly in front of the celebrant. A server holds the ashes slightly to the celebrant's left, standing to the book bearer's right. The vessels of ashes can

377 Peter J. Elliott, *Ceremonies of the Liturgical Year According to the Modern Roman Rite: A Manual for Clergy and All Involved in Liturgical Ministries* (San Francisco: Ignatius Press, 2002), 56.

be placed on a tray for this purpose. The covers for the vessels of ashes or the purple veils placed over them are removed before they are brought before the celebrant.[378] The server with the holy water stands to the celebrant's right, next to the deacon. The celebrant will turn to his right to face the assembly when addressing them, keeping his eyes on the missal to his left as needed. The celebrant faces the missal for the prayer of blessing. If the celebrant is standing at a chair oriented to face the assembly, the book bearer can stand at his left, and the server holding the ashes and the server holding the holy water together, side by side, on his right. The servers thus leave space between them so that they do not come between the celebrant and the assembly.

All stand. The celebrant addresses the assembly with hands joined. He pauses for a moment of silent prayer. He may close his eyes and bow his head during this time. He prays the blessing of the ashes with hands extended, making the Sign of the Cross at the point indicated in the prayer of blessing. His left hand rests on his chest when making the Sign of the Cross with his extended right hand; he then joins his hands. Then the deacon places the aspergillum in the celebrant's right hand. The celebrant sprinkles the ashes three times, center, left, and right, saying nothing. He returns the aspergillum to the deacon, who receives it in his right hand. The servers with the holy water and missal leave the chair and return to the credence table.

Once the ashes are blessed, another priest or even the deacon imposes ashes on the celebrant. This priest or deacon may take ashes between his thumb and index finger of his right hand and sprinkle the ashes on the head of the celebrant in the form of a cross, who receives them standing and bowing slightly. Or, he may place ashes on the forehead of the celebrant using the thumb of his right hand. With his thumb separated from the joined fingers of his right hand, as when he traces the Sign of the Cross on his forehead before proclaiming the Gospel, this priest or deacon traces the Sign of the Cross with the ashes on the forehead of the celebrant, who receives them standing and bowing slightly. If there is no other priest or deacon present, the celebrant imposes ashes on himself using the thumb of his right hand, the rest of the fingers of the hand extended and joined. He makes the Sign of the Cross on his own forehead, saying nothing.[379] He does so standing at the chair, or even standing at the altar while facing

[378] Adrian Fortescue, J. B. O'Connell, and Alcuin Reid, eds., *The Ceremonies of the Roman Rite Described*, 15th ed. (New York: Bloomsbury, 2009), 319.

[379] Fortescue, O'Connell, and Reid, *The Ceremonies of the Roman Rite Described*, 320.

it.[380] The deacon or a server may hold the bowl of ashes as the celebrant imposes ashes on himself and others,[381] or it may be more convenient for the celebrant to hold the bowl of ashes in his left hand.[382]

Standing at his chair or before the altar, or at some other convenient location in the sanctuary, the celebrant then proceeds to imposes ashes on the ministers and servers, beginning with concelebrants and the deacon. They receive the ashes standing and bowing slightly. In some locations, the sacred ministers and servers kneel to receive the ashes.[383] The celebrant hands vessels of the ashes to the servers who will accompany the ministers distributing ashes to the faithful. A server holding the bowl of ashes in the right hand may hold a card with the formula for the imposition of ashes in the left hand. That server will stand to the left of any minister imposing ashes, facing that person. Or, the vessels with ashes may instead be held by the assisting ministers themselves. The celebrant and those who will assist him then go to the entrance of the sanctuary to impose ashes on the faithful. The faithful may approach in one or two lines in a kind of procession. Or they may stand, bowing slightly, or kneel across the front of the sanctuary to receive ashes.[384] The celebrant and any assistant impose ashes on them moving from left to right.

When the imposition of ashes is completed, the vessels of ashes are returned to the credence table once again and covered. The celebrant goes to the chair[385] or some other convenient location to wash his hands, bowing to the altar whenever he passes before it. Once the celebrant arrives at the chair, a server comes before the celebrant to present a pitcher of water and bow with a towel over his left arm and another server presents a plate with soap on it. The celebrant may stand to wash and dry and his hands. If the celebrant prefers to wash his hands while seated at the chair, a gremial is placed on his lap by the deacon, and then removed by the deacon.[386] Those who imposed ashes with the celebrant wash their hands at the credence table or at a station near it.[387] If he prefers, the celebrant may wash his hands at this location rather than at the chair.

[380] Fortescue, O'Connell, and Reid, *The Ceremonies of the Roman Rite Described,* 320.
[381] Fortescue, O'Connell, and Reid, *The Ceremonies of the Roman Rite Described,* 320.
[382] Elliott, *Ceremonies of the Liturgical Year,* 57, n. 12.
[383] Fortescue, O'Connell, and Reid, *The Ceremonies of the Roman Rite Described,* 320.
[384] Elliott, *Ceremonies of the Liturgical Year,* 57–58; Fortescue, O'Connell, and Reid, *The Ceremonies of the Roman Rite Described,* 321.
[385] Elliott, *Ceremonies of the Liturgical Year,* 58.
[386] Elliott, *Ceremonies of the Liturgical Year,* 58.
[387] Fortescue, O'Connell, and Reid, *The Ceremonies of the Roman Rite Described,* 319.

After washing and drying his hands, the celebrant stands at the chair with hands joined, facing the assembly, to introduce the Prayer of the Faithful. A server holds the missal in both hands before the celebrant open to the Prayer of the Faithful, or the server holds the text of the Universal Prayer alone before the celebrant. Mass then continues in the usual way. At the end of Mass, the celebrant offers the prayer over the people as described below.

Sundays and Weekdays of Lent

On Ash Wednesday, and on the Sundays of Lent, including Palm Sunday, the prayer over the people is obligatory for the blessing at the end of Mass. It is optional on the weekdays of Lent. In the editions of the Roman Missal prior to 1969, in contrast, the prayer over the people was a distinctive feature of the ferial days of Lent. It was absent from Mass on the Sundays of Lent.

The celebrant may offer the prayer over the people either standing at the chair or at the altar following the Post-Communion prayer. It is perhaps easiest for the celebrant to impart this blessing over the people at the altar, facing the assembly, since the missal will likewise be resting on the altar directly in front of him. However, if the celebrant remains at the chair, he will have to turn his head slightly to left to read the proper Collect from the missal while at the same time keeping his arms directed forward toward the assembly. The server remains in the same position throughout the Post-Communion prayer and blessing; he does not change position based on the movements of the celebrant at the chair. If the celebrant is standing at the altar, his left hand rests on the altar while he gives the blessing with his right hand. If he is standing at the chair, his left hand rests on his chest while he gives the blessing with his right hand.

After the Post-Communion prayer, if the celebrant remains at the chair, he turns toward the people, looks at them, and extends and joins his hands to say, "The Lord be with you." The deacon, with hands joined and facing the assembly, invites them to bow their heads. Afterward, he bows toward the celebrant as well. All bow their heads slightly for the duration of the Collect and the blessing itself. The priest extends his arms with the palms of his hands held facing downward in the direction of the people, fingers joined, for the prayer over the people prior to the blessing. Standing at the chair, he may have to turn his glance to the left in order to read the text of the prayer over the people, since the server will have been holding the missal directly in front of him for the Post-Communion prayer. The celebrant imparts the blessing using the alternative formula noted in the missal. The deacon once again faces the assembly and dismisses them with hands joined.

The missal suggests that the Apostles' Creed may fittingly replace the Nicene Creed on the Sundays and Solemnities of Lent.[388]

Fifth Sunday of Lent

Prior to the celebration of first Vespers on the fifth Sunday of Lent, all the cross and crucifixes of the church and sacristies may be veiled in purple.[389] This includes the crucifix over the vesting case, the altar cross, the processional cross, and any freestanding crosses at the Stations of the Cross or elsewhere in the church. It does not include crosses which are part of the architecture of the building, like dedication crosses or crosses and crucifixes outside the church or sacristy. Crosses remain covered until the end of the Celebration of the Lord's Passion on Good Friday. Any statues of the saints may also be veiled in purple beginning with first Vespers on the fifth Sunday of Lent. Mosaics or paintings of the saints and the depictions of the Stations of the Cross are not veiled.[390] Images remain covered until the beginning of the Easter Vigil.

Palm Sunday: The Three Forms of the Entrance

The celebration of Mass on Palm Sunday of the Passion of the Lord can begin in one of three different ways, either with a procession of the entire assembly, or with the solemn entrance of the ministers and a representative group of the faithful, or with the simple entrance of the ministers of the Mass alone as usual.

In addition to all the usual items needed for Mass, the sacristan will need to prepare the following on Palm Sunday:

In the sacristy:

- A tray or a basket with palms for the faithful, servers, and clergy, and palms to attach to the processional cross, even if the cross is veiled in purple from the previous Sunday; the palm designated for the celebrant is often decorated or larger than others. The entire tray or basket is covered in a red veil.
- Two torches instead of candlesticks, if the procession begins outdoors

[388] *RM*, Order for Mass, no. 19.

[389] "In the Dioceses of the United States, the practice of covering crosses and images through the church from this Sunday may be observed." *RM*, rubric for the Fifth Sunday of Lent.

[390] Mutel and Freeman, *Cérémonial de la sainte messe*, 245, n. 46.

- Holy water in its vessel with aspergillum
- The missal
- A red cope, if the celebrant chooses to wear it for the procession instead of the chasuble, as for the solemn entrance

At the place where the procession will begin:

- A second set of pitcher, bowl, and towel on a table covered with a white cloth, if the celebrant washes his hands after distributing the blessed palms
- A lectern, covered in a red antependium, for the proclamation of the Gospel

In the sanctuary:

- Two bare lecterns for the reading of the Passion next to the ambo of the church
- Books for the reading or singing of the Passion

At the chair:

- A red chasuble draped over the presidential chair nearby, if the celebrant wore the red cope for the procession

In the case of the procession, all or most of the faithful gather in a location outside the body of the church, either in another chapel, or a hall, or the narthex. The procession may also begin outdoors, weather permitting. In the case of the solemn entrance, the assembly gathers inside the body of the church. A representative group gathers with the celebrant and ministers just inside or just outside the door of the church for the entrance rite. When the procession begins outside of the church, the celebrant may wear the chasuble for Mass or a red cope. When the solemn entrance begins just inside or just outside the door of the church, he wears the chasuble. All hold palm branches in their hands unless these will be distributed after the blessing.

The sacred ministers and servers make their way from the sacristy to the place where the palms will be blessed in the usual order. The schola sings the antiphon "Hosanna to the Son of David." The thurifer with the smoking censer leads the procession. The processional cross, perhaps veiled in purple from the previous Sunday, is carried between two candle bearers. A server carries the holy water. Another server carries the missal. Yet another server carries a platter or basket, covered with the red veil, holding the palms for the celebrant, the ministers of the Mass, and the servers. Alternatively, the holy water and palms can be placed on a credence table in the location where the palms will be blessed, along with everything needed to wash the celebrant's hands. The deacon carries the Gospel book.

If there is an altar in the location where the procession begins, all the ministers bow to it, or they genuflect if the Blessed Sacrament is reserved upon arriving there. The celebrant stands on the epistle side of the altar to conduct the blessing, or at the chair if there is one, facing the assembly. If there is no altar where the procession will begin, a station is created whereby the processional cross itself and its candles become the focal point of the liturgical assembly. The celebrant stands facing both the processional cross and the faithful in this case. Therefore, as the cross and candles arrive, they position themselves in a row in such as a way that the celebrant and deacon bow to the cross and then face the cross and candles as well as those gathered. Other servers stand facing each other in two rows between the cross and candles and the sacred ministers.

Upon arriving at the location where the procession begins, the book bearer stands directly in front of the celebrant, or perhaps slightly to his left, as circumstances require. The deacon stands to the right of the celebrant as usual. The server with holy water stands to the right of the celebrant and deacon. Another server holds the tray or basket of palms before the celebrant, slightly to the celebrant's left. The deacon or a server removes the red veil covering the palms on the tray or in the basket.[391] The celebrant begins with the Sign of the Cross, the liturgical greeting, and an address to the assembly, "Dear brethren." Then, the deacon or a concelebrant may invite the faithful to raise their palms in their hands for the blessing and sprinkling. After saying, "Let us pray," and a moment of silence, the celebrant says the prayer of blessing with arms extended in the *orans* position. The celebrant makes the Sign of the Cross in the form of a Greek cross over the palms during the prayer in the first case, or at the end of the prayer in the second case, the left hand resting on his chest. With the right hand, the deacon hands the celebrant the aspergillum. The celebrant then sprinkles the palms, center, left, and right, saying nothing. He can do so standing in the same

[391] Mutel and Freeman, *Cérémonial de la sainte messe,* 247; Fortescue, O'Connell, and Reid, *The Ceremonies of the Roman Rite Described,* 324.

location, sprinkling the center, the left, and then the right of the assembly, or by walking through the assembly, with the server holding the holy water walking on his left as described in chapter 5.[392] After the sprinkling, the celebrant returns the aspergillum to the deacon. The server puts the holy water aside in a convenience place. Another server takes some of the palms and attaches them to the processional cross with ribbons.[393] At this point, the celebrant may now stand in the center and distribute the palm branches to any who need to receive them. After distributing the palms, the celebrant may want to wash his hands before proceeding. Although the current liturgical books are silent on this practice, this washing of the hands after the distribution of the palms is part of the historical practice on Palm Sunday.[394] One server may approach the celebrant with the pitcher of water in the right hand. A second server approaches, holding the basin in both hands, with a towel draped over the left arm. If there is a credence table nearby, the celebrant may wash his hands there instead.

The sprinkling with holy water and the distribution of the palms concluded, the thurifer stands before the celebrant, who imposes incense in the usual way in preparation for the reading of the Gospel of the Lord's entry into Jerusalem. With his right hand, the deacon presents to the celebrant the spoon, then transfers the incense boat from his left hand to his right hand. Using his right hand, the celebrant imposes incense three times and returns the spoon. With his left hand on his chest, the celebrant blesses the incense in the form of a Greek cross with his right hand, saying nothing, and then joining his hands. The deacon bows low to ask for the celebrant's blessing. The celebrant begins with hands joined and concludes by blessing the deacon with his right hand, his left hand resting on his chest. The celebrant then receives from a server the blessed palm prepared for him. The celebrant holds it in his right hand during the reading of the Gospel, with his left hand resting on his chest.

As mentioned in the *Ceremonial of Bishops*, the deacon may carry the Gospel book from the sacristy to the place where the procession begins. The deacon places it on the altar upon arriving there,[395] or it may have been placed on the altar prior to the arrival of the celebrant, the deacon, and the ministers. If there is no altar in the location where the procession will begin, another minister, per-

[392] Mutel and Freeman, *Cérémonial de la sainte messe*, 248.

[393] *CB*, 270; *RM*, Palm Sunday, no. 9; Mutel and Freeman, *Cérémonial de la sainte messe*, 248.

[394] Mutel and Freeman, *Cérémonial de la sainte messe*, 249.

[395] *CB*, 270.

haps a vested instituted lector or even a reader, can hold the Gospel book for the deacon while he is assisting the celebrant with the holy water and incense. The deacon, with hands joined, bows profoundly before the celebrant to ask for his blessing. Standing upright, the deacon receives the Gospel book in his hands from the reader. Then, then there may be a procession to the place where the Gospel will be proclaimed that includes the thurifer, candle bearers, and the deacon carrying the Gospel book.

A lectern covered with a red antependium can be placed on the Gospel side of the altar for the proclamation of the Lord's entry into Jerusalem.[396] If there is no altar and no lectern, the reader can accompany the thurifer, candle bearers, and deacon in the Gospel procession. They make their way at some distance from the celebrant. The reader receives the Gospel book from the deacon and holds it open with both hands at the bottom for the deacon to read. The candle bearers stand on either side of the reader, facing each other, as they do at the Gospel during Mass. The deacon incenses the book in the usual way and proclaims the appointed Gospel passage in the usual way. In the absence of the deacon, a concelebrant, or even the celebrant himself, proclaims the Gospel. He greets the faithful with hands joined. He signs the book and himself with the thumb of his right hand, the left hand resting on his chest. He proclaims the Gospel and announces its conclusion with hands joined. The reading concluded, the deacon picks up the Gospel book to kiss it and places it down on the lectern or returns it to the reader to hold until the procession begins. After the proclamation of the Gospel, the celebrant may preach standing at the chair, or before the altar, or at the lectern. A server holds the celebrant's palm during the homily.

Then, the preparations for the beginning of the procession take place. If necessary, the celebrant may impose incense again as described above, assisted by the thurifer and the deacon. During this time, the celebrant momentarily hands his palm over to a server so that he has both hands free. After imposing and blessing the incense, the celebrant takes the blessed palm prepared for him in his right hand once again, his left hand resting on his chest. All carry palms in their right hands. The deacon invites the procession to begin, and then takes the Gospel book in both hands, either from a reader or from the lectern, and carries it in the usual way. All genuflect to the Blessed Sacrament or bow to the altar, or to the processional cross in its absence, and the procession to the sanctuary begins.

[396] Elliott, *Ceremonies of the Liturgical Year*, 71–72; Fortescue, O'Connell, and Reid, *The Ceremonies of the Roman Rite Described*, 376.

In the procession, the thurifer goes first, followed by the cross and candles walking together in a line. The other servers, the deacon carrying the Gospel book, the concelebrants, and the celebrant walk behind the cross and candles. Finally, the faithful follow the behind the celebrant.[397] Often the members of the choir are among the first of the faithful immediately behind the celebrant. If the deacon is carrying the Gospel book, he walks after all the servers and before the concelebrants and celebrant. If the deacon is not carrying the Gospel book, he walks to the right of the celebrant with a palm branch in his right hand, his left hand resting on his chest. If the celebrant is wearing a cope, the deacon, the master of ceremonies, or two servers walk on either side of him, holding the edge of cope in their inside hands and a palm in their outside hands.

Upon arriving at the sanctuary, the celebrant hands his palm branch to the deacon or to another server first. Then he makes the usual reverence to the altar, or to the Blessed Sacrament if it is reserved there.[398] The celebrant is now free to remove the cope, if he is wearing it, and to take the chasuble. Normally, this is done at the chair, rather than in nave or the entrance to the sanctuary.[399] Vested for Mass, he proceeds to the altar, kisses it, and incenses it. Alternatively, he may relinquish his palm branch upon arriving at the sanctuary, then go to kiss the altar and incense it, and then go to the chair, where removes the cope if he is wearing it and takes the chasuble. The other ministers may set aside their palm branches upon arriving at their seats.[400] The palm branches are not used again during the course of Mass. Upon arrival in the sanctuary, the server with the missal immediately stands directly in front of the celebrant, or slightly to his left depending on the disposition of the chair. The opening Collect follows the conclusion of the entrance chant immediately, unless the *Kyrie* follows the entrance chant, as circumstances suggest.[401]

The third form of the beginning of Mass on Palm Sunday is the simple entrance.[402] It is perhaps less well known. This form is designed for the situation where neither the procession nor the solemn entrance can take place. According to the simple entrance, Mass on Palm Sunday begins in exactly the same manner as Mass on any other day. In this case, the schola sings the entrance antiphon

397 *CB*, 270.

398 Mutel and Freeman, *Cérémonial de la sainte messe*, 252.

399 Mutel and Freeman, *Cérémonial de la sainte messe*, 240, n. 33.

400 Mutel and Freeman *Cérémonial de la sainte messe*, 240.

401 *RM*, Palm Sunday, no. 15.

402 *RM*, Palm Sunday, nos. 16–17.

with its psalm verses as the celebrant approaches the altar from the sacristy.[403] The entrance antiphon on Palm Sunday is particularly important, since it recalls Christ's triumphal entry into Jerusalem.

The simple entrance does not include the blessing of palms. The blessing of palms takes place in the other two forms because there will be a procession of some kind where those in procession carry blessed palms, recalling those who welcomed Christ to the Jerusalem. When no procession takes place, there is no blessing of the palms either. However, for the sake of fostering the devotion of the faithful, pastors will want to have palms blessed at a previous Mass available at the entrance of the church whenever Mass begins with the simple entrance.

Palm Sunday: The Proclamation of the Passion

The Passion can be read by the deacon alone, or in his absence by the celebrant alone. The Passion can also be read by three readers, preferably three readers in Holy Orders, but one or two laypersons can substitute for missing clergy. Since the Gospel book was used to proclaim the Gospel of the Lord's entry into Jerusalem, it is best to use it again for the proclamation of the Passion as well. Two other matching books containing the Passion are needed if three readers are used. If for some reason the Gospel book was not used at the entrance, it is preferable to use three identical books for the three readers. Two matching lecterns are set up on either side of the ambo for the three readers of the Passion. These bare, uncovered lecterns with microphones may be placed there prior to the beginning of Mass, or moved into position by servers after the second reading and before the Gospel Acclamation.

The three deacons who are to read the Passion come before the celebrant and bow to ask his blessing. Two of them hold the books of the Passion in their hands. After the blessing, the third goes to get the Gospel book from the altar. Neither incense nor candles accompany the readings of the Passion. However, two servers, side by side, do accompany the readers of the Passion if they are in Holy Orders, and stand on either side of the ambo and lecterns with hands joined, facing each other.

Once at the ambo, the deacon serving as narrator and reading from the Gospel book stands in the center. The deacon reading the part of Christ stands at the lectern to the right of the ambo. The deacon reading the other voices and perhaps even the part assigned to the crowd, unless this is done by the choir, stands to the left of the

403 *RM*, Palm Sunday, no. 17a.

ambo.[404] The Passion begins without any greeting and without signing oneself. During the reading of the Passion, all turn in their places to face the readers.

When three ordained ministers are lacking, many other alternative scenarios are possible. These scenarios should respect the hierarchical nature of the various ministries. Therefore, if three deacons are not possible, another priest, or even the celebrant himself in the absence of any other priest, normally reads the part of Christ. In that case, he stands at the ambo between two lecterns using the Gospel book which he carried from the altar to the ambo. The narrator, the deacon for example, stands to his right, and the other reader, perhaps another deacon or even an instituted lector or a reader, to his left.[405] Any deacon involved first seeks the blessing of the celebrant while holding the book of the Passion from which he will read. Any concelebrant or other priest who reads the part of Christ goes to the altar first and bows before the altar to say the prayer of preparation and take up the Gospel book; such a priest does not seek the blessing of the celebrant. Lay readers who substitute for absent priests or deacons do not seek the blessing of the celebrant. The book of the Passion which a lay reader will use should already be placed on the specific lectern beforehand.

The Passion is read with hands joined by all three readers, whether clerical or lay. At the mention of the death of the Lord, all kneel. The celebrant kneels at his chair, facing in the direction of the readers. The readers kneel in their places, facing the lecterns.[406] All rise for the final section of the Passion. The Passion concludes with the usual acclamation, but without kissing the book. The deacon may then carry the Gospel book back to the credence table or to some other suitable location, where it remains for the rest of Mass. The deacon holds the closed Gospel book with both hands at the bottom, with the top of the book resting on his chest. The other two deacons hold their books of the Passion in the same way, ahead of the deacon holding the Gospel book. The three deacons then follow the candle bearers and thurifer back to the credence table, and eventually to their seats. If they pass before the altar, they reverence it as a group with at least a bow of the head if they are carrying anything.[407] All return to their places. The two additional bare lecterns next to the ambo as well as their microphones may be removed by servers at this point.

[404] Mutel and Freeman, *Cérémonial de la sainte messe*, 254.
[405] Mutel and Freeman, *Cérémonial de la sainte messe*, 255.
[406] Mutel and Freeman, *Cérémonial de la sainte messe*, 256.
[407] Elliott, *Ceremonies Explained for Servers*, 92.

16

Holy Thursday

ALL MASSES WITHOUT a congregation are forbidden on Holy Thursday. Therefore, it is common for the evening Mass of the Lord's Supper to be concelebrated. For the details related to Mass concelebrated by several priests, see chapter 8. In addition, there are distinct features to the opening rites for Mass on Holy Thursday. Also, Mass that evening may include the washing of feet. Finally, Mass customarily ends with a procession to the place of reposition of the Blessed Sacrament for a period of adoration before midnight.

The Requisites for Mass

In the sacristy:

- Six torches, or least four

At the credence table:

- Everything usually needed for Mass
- A ciborium with hosts that are to be consecrated for Communion on Good Friday
- A white veil for the ciborium
- A wooden clapper or rattle (the crotalus)
- A white humeral veil

At the altar:

- Six candles

- The altar cross may be veiled in white rather than purple[408]

At the place for the foot washing in the nave or in the sanctuary:

- A gremial, or in its absence an amice, for the celebrant
- Benches or seats for those having their feet washed
- A pitcher of water and basin
- A basket with towels for drying the feet, one for each person; a second empty basket to receive them afterward
- A cushion for the celebrant to kneel upon if necessary

In a convenient place in the sanctuary:

- A second set of pitcher, bowel, towel, and soap to wash the celebrant's hands after the foot washing
- Candles for all those in the sanctuary
- Two censers with burning charcoals, incense boat, and stands

In the narthex:

- Candles for all those in the church
- The baldachin or the umbrellino, if the closing procession to the place of reposition proceeds at least partly outside the church

In the chapel where the Blessed Sacrament will be kept:

- The repository for the Blessed Sacrament
- Candles, flowers, and other suitable decorations

The Opening Rites

Mass on Holy Thursday begins with the tabernacle of the church completely empty and therefore unveiled. The sanctuary lamp is not lit and is often removed. The door to the tabernacle is left open. Well prior to the beginning of the evening Mass,

[408] André Philippe M. Mutel and Peter Freeman, *Cérémonial de la sainte messe à l'usage ordinaire des paroisses suivant le missel romain de 2002 et la pratique léguée du rit romain*, 2nd ed. (Perpignan, France: Éditions Artège, 2012), 259; Adrian Fortescue, J. B. O'Connell, and Alcuin Reid, eds., *The Ceremonies of the Roman Rite Described* (New York: Bloomsbury, 2009), 337.

the Hosts which were reserved there are transferred to a repository outside the church, distinct from the repository which will serve for adoration following Mass.[409] Often this secret repository is located in the sacristy. Since the tabernacle is empty at the beginning of Mass, there are no genuflections to be made as the procession arrives at the sanctuary. Servers and concelebrants will need to be reminded of this.

The thurifer leads the procession as usual. Upon arriving at the sanctuary, the servers carrying the censer, the cross, perhaps veiled in purple, and the candles bow their heads to the altar. The deacon carrying the Gospel book omits all signs of reverence and makes his way directly to the altar to place the Gospel book face-down in the center, slightly away from the edge of the altar. All others, servers, readers, other deacons, concelebrants, and the principal celebrant, make a profound bow from the waist to the altar upon arriving at the sanctuary. Then the concelebrants go up to the altar and kiss the altar, with both hands resting on the altar. The celebrant and the deacon kiss the altar, the deacon standing to the celebrant's right. Historically, the deacon does not place his hands on the altar when he kisses it. The celebrant may incense the altar with the assistance of the deacon. See chapter 4. Then the celebrant and the deacon go to their seats by the most direct route.

During the Gloria, the bells of the church are rung. According to custom, servers also ring one or more sets of handbells during this time. While liturgical actions properly speaking are done with the right hand, this function can be done with either the right hand or the left hand, depending on the ability of the servers. From that point on, the ringing of any bells is suspended until the Gloria of the Easter Vigil. In place of the bells, some locations instead use a wooden clapper or rattle (the crotalus) at the usual points of Mass.[410] Similarly, the use of the pipe organ is suspended until the Gloria of the Easter Vigil.[411]

The Washing of the Feet

The washing of the feet is optional on Holy Thursday during the celebration of the Mass of the Lord's Supper. In those locations where it takes place, the following indications describe the various actions of the celebrant, ministers, and servers.

Immediately following the homily, the celebrant returns to the chair. There he removes the chasuble and places it face down on the back of his chair. A server brings him a gremial, holding it by its two corners. The celebrant receives the

[409] Mutel and Freeman, *Cérémonial de la sainte messe*, 258.
[410] Fortescue, O'Connell, and Reid, *The Ceremonies of the Roman Rite Described*, 337.
[411] Mutel and Freeman, *Cérémonial de la sainte messe*, 257.

gremial. He passes its ribbons behind his back and draws them to his waist where he ties them with the slipknot at the front.

The missal does not indicate the number of persons, men or women, who are selected to have their feet washed. Historically, they have numbered eleven, twelve, or even thirteen.[412] A greater or lesser number is always possible. While the missal indicates that these persons are chosen from among the lay faithful, historically the clergy were selected for the washing of the feet in cathedral churches. In monasteries, members of the monastic community were chosen. If those chosen are clergy, they are seated in the sanctuary as usual. If those chosen are among the lay faithful, they are seated for Mass in the nave, perhaps together in one group in a designated section. After the homily, a master of ceremonies or a server goes to them to lead them from the nave to their places in the sanctuary. Long benches, or individual stools or seats if necessary, are prepared in the sanctuary for them. Ideally, these would be placed in such a way that two rows face each other across the sanctuary in the manner of a choir. However, it is often easier for the celebrant to wash the feet of those chosen if he kneels on a step in front of those seated. That may require the seats to be placed across the front of the sanctuary. Unless the benches or seats can be placed in the proper location before Mass begins in such a way that they do not hinder the opening rites and the Liturgy of the Word, servers will need to bring out the benches or seats after the homily. Upon arriving at their places, those chosen to have their feet washed remove the shoes and socks from their right feet.

Once those selected are in their places, the celebrant leaves the chair and goes to them. If they face each other in two rows in the sanctuary, the celebrant normally begins with those on the left side of the sanctuary as one faces it, starting with the person seated closest to the altar. Then the celebrant goes to those on the right side of the sanctuary as one faces it, beginning with the one closest to the altar. If those chosen are seated in a straight line before him across the entire sanctuary, the celebrant generally moves from left to right.

The deacon stands and kneels to the celebrant's immediate right with the basin. To the deacon's right stands a server with the pitcher of water. To the celebrant's left stands the master of ceremonies or the most experienced server. To that person's left stands one server with a basket of clean towels, one for each person, and another server with a basket to receive each towel after the celebrant has wiped the foot dry. The celebrant kneels to wash and dry the foot of each

[412] Mutel and Freeman, *Cérémonial de la sainte messe*, 263.

person. The deacon kneels to the celebrant's right whenever the celebrant kneels.[413] The deacon receives the pitcher from a server and presents it to the celebrant and takes it back from him when the celebrant wipes each foot. The deacon returns the pitcher each time to the server to his right. Kneeling to the celebrant's right, the deacon is responsible for placing the basin beneath the foot of each person. The deacon takes care to pick up the basin, stand, and then move the basin from person to person, before setting it down. The deacon does not slide the basin from one person to another. The master of ceremonies or a more experienced server standing to the celebrant's left is responsible for passing the celebrant a clean towel for each person, and then for immediately retrieving that same towel from the person whose foot the celebrant has just dried. The celebrant and deacon rise each time after washing and drying a foot, and kneel again to repeat the process with the next person.[414] If the celebrant will kneel on a hard surface, it may be helpful for the master of ceremonies to move a cushion to each successive person for the celebrant to kneel upon. The rubrics no longer obligate the celebrant to kiss each foot after washing and drying it.

After washing and drying the foot of the last person, the celebrant washes his hands at a second credence table set up for that purpose.[415] Such a table is more conveniently located near the last person to have his or her feet washed. The celebrant may also remove the gremial there. Meanwhile, the master of ceremonies leads those designated back to their places either in the sanctuary or in the nave, as the case may be. The celebrant returns to the chair, bowing when he passes in front of the altar, and puts on the chasuble once again. With the help of the deacon, he takes the chasuble from the back of his chair, and facing the chair puts it on once again. The deacon assists by adjusting the chasuble as needed. Or the celebrant may prefer to wash his hands at the chair, either standing, or while seated with the gremial. After washing his hands, he stands if he was seated, he removes the gremial, and he takes the chasuble one again.[416] Mass continues immediately with the Prayer of the Faithful.

413 Peter J. Elliott, *Ceremonies of the Liturgical Year According to the Modern Roman Rite: A Manual for Clergy and All Involved in Liturgical Ministries* (San Francisco: Ignatius Press, 2002), 102; Fortescue, O'Connell, and Reid, *The Ceremonies of the Roman Rite*, 338, 344, n. 41.

414 Fortescue, O'Connell, and Reid, *The Ceremonies of the Roman Rite Described*, 344, n. 41.

415 Mutel and Freeman, *Cérémonial de la sainte messe*, 265; Fortescue, O'Connell, and Reid, *The Ceremonies of the Roman Rite Described*, 339, 344.

416 Elliott, *Ceremonies of the Liturgical Year*, 102.

The Preparation of the Gifts

On Holy Thursday, sufficient hosts need to be prepared for the Communion of the faithful both on Holy Thursday evening itself and on Good Friday at the Celebration of the Lord's Passion. After the Communion of the faithful on Holy Thursday, it is best if the number of Hosts which remain can be contained in one large ciborium, rather than two. It is easiest if the Hosts for the Communion on Good Friday are placed in the single ciborium to be used for reposition, provided that ciborium will have enough room to receive the Hosts which remain after the Communion of the faithful on Holy Thursday.

The Eucharistic Prayer

According to the traditional practice, bells are not rung during the Triduum from the Gloria on Holy Thursday until the Gloria at the Easter Vigil on Holy Saturday. In place of the bells, some churches use a wooden clapper or rattle (the crotalus).[417] These are struck during the Eucharistic Prayer and even prior to Communion at the same points one would ring handbells. As in other actions which are not strictly liturgical, servers may strike this clapper with either the left hand or the right hand, whichever is easiest for them.

The Sign of Peace

Historically, the sign of peace was not exchanged on Holy Thursday, since the Lord was betrayed on that day by a kiss. Some churches continue this practice even today.[418] The Order for Mass provides for this on any occasion when it indicates, "Then, if appropriate, the Deacon or the Priest, adds: Let us offer each other the sign of peace."[419]

The Procession to the Repository

During the distribution of Holy Communion, a server brings the ciborium cover with its veil to the altar, placing it outside the corporal. A second server approaches the altar, genuflects, removes the missal and its stand, and genuflects again. This server places the missal near the celebrant's chair. Since the Blessed Sacrament in the ciborium for Good Friday is reposing on the altar during this time, servers

[417] Mutel and Freeman, *Cérémonial de la sainte messe*, 266; Elliott, *Ceremonies of the Liturgical Year*, 103, n. 24.

[418] Mutel and Freeman, *Cérémonial de la sainte messe*, 266.

[419] *RM*, Order for Mass, no. 128.

genuflect to the Blessed Sacrament upon approaching and departing from the altar each time. Once the distribution of Holy Communion is completed, the Precious Blood that remains is consumed at the altar, facing any side of the altar. The celebrant or the deacon places the Hosts that remain in the ciborium in the center of the corporal, and then covers and veils it. He genuflects and returns to his chair. All genuflect when passing in front of the altar, or whether approaching or departing from it on the sides. Any vessels used in the distribution of Communion are brought to the credence table to be purified over corporals.[420] Meanwhile, all in the sanctuary and in the nave take candles in hand. Servers assist in lighting everyone's candles in the sanctuary and in the nave.

The celebrant, standing at his chair, says the Post-Communion prayer. It is not permitted to say the Post-Communion prayer standing at the altar on Holy Thursday.[421] The concluding rites are completely omitted. At this point, the master of ceremonies directs the servers to take their positions in the center aisle, facing the altar. In practice, however, it may be more helpful to have the cross bearer, candle bearers, and additional servers stand in their places in the center aisle *before* the Post-Communion prayer, while the purifications are taking place, so that they will be in the proper position for the procession in advance of the Post-Communion prayer. The torch bearers could be positioned at the same time, either across the front of the sanctuary as they usually are, or ideally, in two rows facing each other on either side of the sanctuary, provided they do not impede access to the altar. In that position, they can easily flank the celebrant carrying the Blessed Sacrament when he departs from the altar.[422] Finally, it may be better for concelebrants to remain in the sanctuary so that each of them can kneel at a prie-dieu.

Then, the celebrant, the deacon, the master of ceremonies, and the two thurifers go before the altar steps, genuflect, and rise. Depending on the disposition of the sanctuary, they may face liturgical east or may face the assembly. All in the sanctuary and in the church, except the cross bearer and candle bearers, kneel. The celebrant turns to his right to face the two thurifers. The first thurifer gives the deacon the incense boat and spoon. Then the first thurifer faces the celebrant and presents him the open censer. The thurifers elevate the bowl of the censer in their right hands so that the celebrant can stand erect to impose incense. The deacon offers the celebrant the spoon in his right hand while holding the incense boat in

[420] Elliott, *Ceremonies of the Liturgical Year*, 104.

[421] *RM*, Mass of the Lord's Supper, no. 35.

[422] Elliott, *Ceremonies of the Liturgical Year*, 104.

his left. He then transfers the incense boat to his right hand and holds it close to the bowl of the censer. The celebrant imposes incense three times on the burning coals, using his right hand. The celebrant blesses the incense in the right hand in the form of a Greek cross, saying nothing, with his left hand resting on his chest. The celebrant does the same for the second censer. The celebrant returns the spoon to the deacon, who receives it in his right hand. The deacon returns the incense boat and spoon to the second thurifer, who receives it in his left hand.

The celebrant then turns to his left in order to face the altar once again and kneels on the lowest step, as do the deacon, master of ceremonies, and two thurifers. From a kneeling position, the first thurifer gives the censer to the deacon. The deacon places the rings of the chain in the left hand of the celebrant by using his own right hand. The deacon places the chains near the bowl of the censer into the right hand of the celebrant with his own left hand. The deacon may then hold back the edge of the celebrant's chasuble with his left hand, his right hand resting on his chest. The celebrant elevates the bowl of the censer to a position slightly below eye level. The celebrant incenses the Blessed Sacrament in silence with three double swings, bowing before and after from a kneeling position.[423] All those kneeling with the celebrant bow from a kneeling position at the same time he does. The celebrant then returns the censer to the deacon, who returns it to the first thurifer. When all are in the proper position to begin the procession, the master of ceremonies stands behind the kneeling celebrant and places the humeral veil on his shoulders and departs. The celebrant and deacon go up to the altar and genuflect there. The celebrant covers the ciborium and his hands with the humeral veil. If it is more convenient, the deacon may take the ciborium from the altar and hand it to the celebrant. Depending on which side of the altar the celebrant and the deacon stand, the deacon may now have to switch sides in order to be on the celebrant's right during the procession. The concelebrants and ministers stand from the kneeling position and then genuflect, as a eucharistic chant, for example "Pange Lingua" (excluding the last two verses), begins.[424] The procession is now ready to set off.

In the procession, the deacon walks to the celebrant's right. A server or a concelebrant may assist the celebrant, walking at his left, or a master of ceremonies may walk to his left. The torch bearers walk in two rows alongside the celebrant. They hold four or six torches in their outside hands, their inside hands resting on their chest. The two thurifers walk immediately in front of the celebrant, always

[423] *CB*, 306; Roman Missal, Holy Thursday, no. 37; Elliott, *Ceremonies of the Liturgical Year*, 105.

[424] Mutel and Freeman, *Cérémonial de la sainte messe*, 272.

facing forward.[425] Each holds the chain of the censer in his inside hand, his outside hand resting on his chest. The second thurifer holds the incense boat against the chest. The two thurifers walk in line with the two rows of concelebrants and servers ahead of them; they avoid walking directly in front of the Blessed Sacrament.

Thus, behind the cross and candles at the head of the procession walk the servers and then the concelebrants in two rows, then the two thurifers, the celebrant with the deacon flanked by torch bearers on either side. The faithful, or at least a representative group of the faithful, walk behind the celebrant. The choir may be the first among them. All hold lighted candles in their outside hands. Those who do not join the procession remain kneeling until the Blessed Sacrament has left the church or until it has been reposed in a chapel within view of the nave.[426]

If the procession to the repository passes outdoors, some churches maintain the use of the umbrellino, held over the celebrant by one server walking behind him, or even the use of the baldachin, held by four servers or four laypersons or even four concelebrants, with the celebrant walking beneath it and the torch bearers on either side.[427] In many locations, the baldachin or the umbrellino is used only for the portion of the procession that takes place outdoors. If a baldachin is used, those carrying it wait just outside the doors of the church.[428] The celebrant and those assisting him walk under it as they emerge from the church. The torch bearers walk on either side of those supporting the baldachin. Upon arriving at the location of the repository, those supporting the baldachin or umbrellino while the procession has passed outdoors allow the torch bearers and the celebrant with his assisting ministers to enter the church or chapel, while they remain outside.

The altar of repose is ornamented with altar cloths, candles, and flowers. Traditionally, the altar of repose does not include an altar cross or a sanctuary lamp, nor is the repository veiled, as a tabernacle usually is.[429] If the ciborium with the Blessed Sacrament will rest upon the altar of repose before being placed in the repository, a corporal is unfolded on that altar.

Arriving at the altar of repose, the cross bearer and candle bearers move together as a group to one side of the entrance to the temporary sanctuary and remain standing as they face the altar in a row. The other servers and concelebrants pass the cross and candles and part in order to face each other in two rows. The

[425] Mutel and Freeman, *Cérémonial de la sainte messe*, 273, n. 133.

[426] Elliott, *Ceremonies of the Liturgical Year*, 213.

[427] Mutel and Freeman, *Cérémonial de la sainte messe*, 268, n. 122.

[428] The use of the baldachin is optional according to no. 388 of the *Ceremonial of Bishops*.

[429] Elliott, *Ceremonies of the Liturgical Year*, 97–98.

torch bearers take their usual position either on either side of the entrance of the sanctuary in a single row, or in two rows facing each in the sanctuary in front of the servers and concelebrants. The torch bearers kneel. The thurifers, celebrant, and deacon enter the sanctuary. The thurifers kneel side by side to the celebrant's and deacon's right. The celebrant, or if it is more convenient, the deacon, places the veiled ciborium in the repository, keeping its door open, or he places the ciborium on the corporal on the table of the altar of reposition. Then the celebrant and the deacon genuflect together before the altar and kneel on the lowest step. The master of ceremonies, standing behind the kneeling celebrant, removes the humeral veil.

The celebrant allows time for all those who participated in the procession to arrive at the place of its conclusion and kneel. Once all have arrived in place, the schola can begin singing the last two verses of the "Pange Lingua." This will be the signal to the celebrant to begin the incensation of the Blessed Sacrament. Customarily, the Blessed Sacrament is incensed during the final verse of the hymn "Pange Lingua,"[430] that is at *Genitori genitoque*. Thus, during the verse which precedes it, *Tantum ergo*, it is customary to bow together from a kneeling position at the words *veneremur cernui*, after which the celebrant, the deacon, and the second thurifer rise in order to prepare the incense from a standing position.[431] After the incense is prepared, the deacon hands the incense boat back to the second thurifer. All kneel once again. The second thurifer may put the incense boat down momentarily on the altar step in order to have both hands free. The second thurifer passes the censer to the deacon. Using the right hand, the deacon places the chains of the censer in the celebrant's left hand. With the left hand, the deacon places the bowl of the censer in the celebrant's right hand. The celebrant elevates the bowl of the censer with the right hand to a position near eye level. The Blessed Sacrament is incensed with three double swings from a kneeling position, bowing before and after incensing. The celebrant returns the censer to the deacon, who returns it to the second thurifer.

After the incensation, the deacon goes up to the altar. He places the ciborium in the repository if necessary, genuflects, and closes and locks the door. He returns to the right side of the celebrant. After a period of prayer, all in the sanctuary rise with the celebrant and genuflect. They extinguish the candles they are holding. They return in silence to the sacristy in the usual order, led by the thurifers and cross and candle bearers.[432]

[430] *CB*, 308; *RM*, Holy Thursday, no. 39.

[431] Fortescue, O'Connell, and Reid, *The Ceremonies of the Roman Rite Described*, 299.

[432] Elliott, *Ceremonies of the Liturgical Year*, 108.

After Reposition

Holy water is removed from the stoups and the font.[433] Flowers are removed from the altar in the church. Carpets in the sanctuary are likewise removed.[434] Any candles burning in the church at altars or shrines are extinguished. Any crosses in the church are removed, if at all possible, or are entirely veiled in purple, unless this already took place on the Saturday prior to the fifth Sunday of Lent. Customarily, the celebrant, concelebrants, and the deacon remove their white Mass vestments in the sacristy and don purple stoles. Assisted by servers, they return to the church to remove the altar cloths from each altar. Usually, they begin by bringing the edges of the cloth toward the middle of the altar, and then again once or twice as needed. What remains is folded one final time from front to back. During this time, Psalm 22 is recited with its antiphon "They divided my garments among them, and for my vesture they cast lots." The clergy reciting the psalm stand on either side of the altar in two choirs, facing each other, while the celebrant, deacon, and servers remove the altar cloths, candles, and cross. This is done at each altar in the church. Psalm 22 is repeated as necessary to complete the actions. Some churches maintain the custom of washing the *mensa* of the altar or altars with water and wine after the altar has been stripped.[435]

Adoration on Holy Thursday never takes place before the Blessed Sacrament in a monstrance, and solemn adoration in common concludes before midnight.[436] At midnight, all flowers are removed from the place of reposition. All candles and lamps located there, except one, are extinguished.[437]

When the Passion Service Does Not Take Place in the Same Church on the Following Day

When no Celebration of the Lord's Passion takes place in the same church the following day, Good Friday, the small number of Hosts which remain after Communion on Holy Thursday are reserved in the tabernacle without any additional ceremony.[438] There is no reservation at the repository apart from the church, since the purpose of the repository is to provide for the Communion of the faithful

433 Elliott, *Ceremonies of the Liturgical Year*, 110; Fortescue, O'Connell, and Reid, *The Ceremonies of the Roman Rite Described*, 342, n. 28.

434 Mutel and Freeman, *Cérémonial de la sainte messe*, 276.

435 Elliott, *Ceremonies of the Liturgical Year*, 217, n. 38.

436 *RM*, Holy Thursday, no. 43; Congregation for Divine Worship, Circular Letter *Paschalis sollemnitatis* (January 16, 1988), no. 55, *Notitae* 24 (1988): 94.

437 Elliott, *Ceremonies of the Liturgical Year*, 217.

438 Congregation for Divine Worship, *Paschalis sollemnitatis*, no. 54, *Notitiae* 24 (1988): 94.

during the service on Good Friday. Reservation in the tabernacle in the church, rather than in a repository set up in a separate location, means that the procession to the repository does not take place at the end of Holy Thursday Mass either. But the other rubrics concerning the conclusion of Mass remain. The elimination of the rite of transfer does not mean that adoration itself is eliminated.

Thus, at the conclusion of Communion, for example, the Hosts which remain could be left in one ciborium, veiled in white, on a corporal on the altar. The celebrant offers the Post-Communion at the chair. After the Post-Communion prayer, the celebrant goes to the altar, genuflects, and takes the veiled ciborium in both hands to take it to the tabernacle. If he does not leave the sanctuary to bring the Blessed Sacrament to the tabernacle, the celebrant does not wear the humeral veil. At the tabernacle, he places the ciborium inside the tabernacle with the door open or on a corporal directly in front of the open tabernacle. The celebrant can incense the Blessed Sacrament in the usual way from a kneeling position, bowing before and after. Then the deacon, or in his absence, the celebrant himself rises, genuflects, and closes the door. A server lights the sanctuary lamp. The concluding rites are entirely omitted. All in the sanctuary spend some time in adoration, or they depart to remove vestments and return for some time in adoration.[439]

What happens at the conclusion of the period of adoration, however brief, depends on whether the church will be open the next day, Good Friday, for devotional prayers like the Stations of the Cross or for portions of the Liturgy of the Hours instead of the Celebration of the Lord's Passion. If any of these take place in the church, the Blessed Sacrament should not remain reserved in the tabernacle in the main body of the church on Good Friday. This is the long-standing practice of the Church to mark the day when the Bridegroom has been taken away. Thus, at the conclusion of even a brief period of adoration on Holy Thursday night, the Hosts from the Mass of the Lord's Supper are intended to be transferred without any ceremony from the tabernacle in the church to the secret repository established outside the church, most likely in the sacristy. The celebrant, wearing the humeral veil and holding the ciborium with both hands through the veil, is accompanied by two (or at least one) acolytes bearing candles. This action can take place at the same time as the removal or veiling of the crosses in the church, and the removal of the altar cloths and candles as described above.

[439] *RM*, Holy Thursday, no. 43.

17

Good Friday
The Celebration of the Lord's Passion

The Celebration of the Lord's Passion on Good Friday is comprised of three principal parts: the Liturgy of the Word, the adoration of the cross, and Holy Communion. Together they form a service whose origins are found in the liturgies of the presanctified gifts in the East and in the liturgies on certain penitential days in the West. In the Roman Missal of Paul VI, the structure of this service is greatly simplified compared to the past. And yet, since it is unique in the entire liturgical year, the gestures and postures associated with it may not always be clear, especially since the indications in the missal are minimal. The traditional practice of the Roman Rite can help to illuminate these cursory indications and provide a fuller description of the manner in which this service can be carried out.

The Blessed Sacrament is not reserved in the tabernacle of the church on Good Friday. It is reserved in the repository used for adoration the previous night, provided that this repository is not seen from the main body of the church and that access is limited only to those who are bringing Communion on Good Friday to the sick and the dying. Or, after the conclusion of adoration no later than midnight, the Blessed Sacrament may have been transferred from the chapel of reposition to the secret repository, most likely located in the sacristy, along with the Hosts which remained prior to the celebration of Mass on Holy Thursday. The tabernacle in the church is therefore completely empty, unveiled, and the door is left open. The sanctuary candle has been removed. The main altar of the church is completely bare, without altar cross, candles, or altar cloth, as are any other altars in the church. Any crosses which could not be removed are veiled in purple.

Before the Service

The following items need to be prepared in advance. Although the Celebration of the Lord's Passion is marked by great simplicity, it nevertheless demands a wide range of items in order to be carried out with dignity.

In the sacristy:

- Red Mass vestments for the priest celebrant and the deacon

In a convenient place, or in the sacristy itself:

- The cross, veiled in purple if the first form of veneration is used
- A stand for the cross, or a pillow on which it rests
- One or two purificators to wipe the cross
- Two candlesticks

In the chapel of reposition:

- A corporal, unfolded in front of the repository
- A red or white humeral veil[440]
- Two candlesticks
- An umbrellino, if used when the procession goes outdoors

In the sanctuary:

- The credence table is covered with a cloth which extends only to the edges of its top without falling on either side.
- The chairs for the celebrant and deacon are bare, without cushions.
- The lecterns for reading the Passion should be bare.
- Red cushions for the celebrant and deacon can be placed at the steps at the entrance of the sanctuary.
- Red stoles for the priests and deacons reading the Passion and receiving Communion are also prepared at their places.
- The missal is placed near the celebrant's chair.

[440] *CB*, 315.

- The lectionary is placed open at the bare ambo.
- The proper text for the Universal Prayer or a second missal is placed near the ambo.

On the credence table:

- An altar cloth of a size which covers only the table (*mensa*) of the altar
- A bare stand for the missal
- A red burse with a corporal or several corporals as needed
- Empty ciboria or patens as needed
- An ablution bowl and finger towel
- A purificator
- A cruet of water, if needed to purify the vessels
- A wooden rattle or clapper (the crotalus)
- The stand to receive the cross after veneration
- The books for reading the Passion

All except the celebrant and the deacon, and perhaps one other server or two other servers in the absence of the deacon, take their places prior to the start of the service. The clergy in attendance and additional servers are seated in the sanctuary prior to the beginning of the service. The holy water has been removed from all stoups from the previous evening, therefore no one takes holy water upon entering the church or departing from the sacristy. On Good Friday, the service does not begin with any kind of procession. The celebrant and the deacon, wearing the usual Mass vestments, simply approach the sanctuary from the sacristy in silence by the most direct route possible while passing through the church. As the celebrant and the deacon make their way from the sacristy to the sanctuary with hands joined, all stand. A server may sound a clapper (the crotalus) to alert the ministers and the faithful to stand as the celebrant and the deacon enter the church.

The Introduction to the Liturgy of the Word

Upon arriving at the sanctuary, the celebrant, the deacon, and server bow profoundly to the altar from the waist. After bowing profoundly to the altar, the celebrant and the deacon prostrate before the altar. They may prostrate entirely on the floor of the sanctuary,[441] or they may rest their head and forearms on the second step of the predella of the altar,[442] or they may prostrate on the floor of the nave if necessary. They prostrate by going down first on the right knee, and then the left knee. Using both hands in front of them, they then prostrate themselves fully, folding their forearms under their head. With one hand resting on the other, and with the forearms perpendicular to their body, they rest their foreheads on the back of the hand. Or, with one hand over the other below the chin, their foreheads may rest on two red pillows placed on the floor or the step of the altar ahead of time. The celebrant prostrates directly in the middle in front of the altar; the deacon prostrates three feet or so to his right. The server kneels to the left of the celebrant, without any pillow. If unable to prostrate himself, the celebrant may kneel on a bare prie-dieu instead; in that case those accompanying him kneel as well. All in the nave and in the sanctuary kneel as the celebrant and deacon prostrate themselves. After a time, the celebrant and deacon rise, first by using both arms to raise themselves to a kneeling position, and then by drawing first the left foot, and then the right foot to a standing position. All stand. Immediately, they proceed by the most direct route to the chair in silence, without kissing the altar. On Good Friday, the liturgical kiss is reserved for the veneration of the Cross.

At the chair, without making the Sign of the Cross, without the usual greeting of the people, and without the invitation "Let us pray," the celebrant immediately prays one or the other of the two prayers proposed in the missal. He faces the assembly with hands extended to do so.[443] At the conclusion, he joins his hands, and all sit to listen to the Scripture readings.

The Liturgy of the Word

The designated readers and cantor proclaim the readings and chants before the Passion in the usual manner. As is customary when the Passion is proclaimed, incense is not used and candles are not carried. Nevertheless, two servers with hands joined lead those who will read the Passion to their lecterns. Unlike the Mass on Palm Sunday, the *Ceremonial of Bishops* makes no mention of the Gospel book on Good Friday. The Passion can be read by the deacon alone, or in his

[441] André Philippe M. Mutel and Peter Freeman, *Cérémonial de la sainte messe à l'usage ordinaire des paroisses suivant le missel romain de 2002 et la pratique léguée du rit romain*, 2nd ed. (Perpignan, France: Éditions Artège, 2012), 285.

[442] Adrian Fortescue, J. B. O'Connell, and Alcuin Reid, eds., *The Ceremonies of the Roman Rite Described*, 15th ed. (New York: Bloomsbury, 2009), 348.

[443] *CB*, 317.

absence by the celebrant alone. In that case, he reads the Passion from the lectionary already resting on the ambo. The Passion can also be read by three readers, preferably three readers in Holy Orders, but one or two laypersons can substitute for missing clergy. Historically, the three readers of the Passion have used three distinct and matching books from which to read the Passion. Two matching bare lecterns and their microphones can be placed on either side of the ambo for the reading of the Passion. Those can be placed there before the beginning of the service, or they can be moved into position by servers after the second reading and before the Gospel Acclamation.

The three deacons who are to read the Passion come before the celebrant and bow to ask his blessing. They hold the books of the Passion in their hands. Two servers, side by side with hands joined, walk ahead of the ordained readers of the Passion. They stand on either side of the ambo or lecterns with hands joined, facing each other. No bow is made to the altar while in procession to the ambo.

Once at the lecterns, the deacon serving as narrator stands in the center at the ambo, and the deacon reading the part of Christ stands to his right. The deacon reading the other voices, and perhaps even the part assigned to the crowd, unless this is done by the choir, stands to the left of center.[444] When three deacons are lacking, many other alternative scenarios are possible. These scenarios should respect the hierarchical nature of the various ministries. Therefore, if three deacons are not possible, another priest, wearing an alb and a red stole, or even the celebrant himself in the absence of any other priest or deacon, normally reads the part of Christ. In that case, he stands in the center. The narrator, the deacon for example, stands to his right. The voice, perhaps another deacon or an instituted lector or even a lay reader, stands to the priest's left.[445] Any deacon involved first seeks the blessing of the celebrant. Any priest who reads any part of the Passion goes to the altar first and bows before the altar to say the prayer of preparation. He does not seek the blessing of the celebrant, nor do lay readers who substitute for absent deacons.

The Passion begins without any greeting and without signing oneself. During the reading of the Passion, all turn in their places to face the readers. The Passion is read with hands joined. At the mention of the death of the Lord, all kneel. The celebrant kneels at his chair, facing in the direction of the readers. The readers

444 Mutel and Freeman, *Cérémonial de la sainte messe*, 254.

445 Mutel and Freeman, *Cérémonial de la sainte messe*, 255.

kneel in their places, facing the lecterns.[446] All rise for the final section of the Passion. The Passion concludes with the usual acclamation but without kissing the book. All return to their places in the most direct manner possible, holding the book of the Passion in their hands and bowing to the altar if passing in front of it. Servers may remove the two additional lecterns and their microphones at the conclusion of the Passion.

After a brief homily, the solemn intercessions take place. The celebrant stands at the chair with a server holding the missal directly in front of him or slightly to his left according to the circumstances. The celebrant may also stand at the altar with the missal on its stand at the center of the altar before him.[447] Historically, the missal would not lay on the altar unless it was adorned with cloth, candles, and crucifix.[448] Perhaps in this case, it is better for a server to hold the missal before the celebrant standing at the altar just as he would hold the missal before the celebrant standing at the chair. Normally, the deacon stands at the ambo to offer the introduction to each intention. Another more convenient location for the deacon, as at the chair for example, is not entirely excluded.[449] In that case, the server holding the missal can stand between the celebrant and deacon, slightly on the celebrant's right, to serve for both. A layperson who replaces an absent deacon or even another priest stands at the ambo to offer the invitation to each intention.[450] In this scenario, two missals are needed, one at the chair and one at the ambo. In any event, the one announcing each intention faces the assembly to do so. The deacon, or the priest, or the lay minister offers the invitation with hands joined. The celebrant prays each Collect with hands extended, facing the altar if at all possible.

After announcing each intention, the deacon says, "Let us kneel." All kneel in their places for a brief period. The deacon kneels, at his place, facing the ambo if he is there. The celebrant kneels at the chair or at the altar. After a period of silent prayer, the deacon stands and says, "Let us stand." Alternatively, the people may kneel or stand through the entire period of the solemn intercessions. If a deacon or another priest is lacking, and a lay minister offers the invitation to each prayer, it is more fitting for the celebrant himself to invite the people to kneel and stand, since directions such as these are not offered by lay ministers to the assembled

[446] Mutel and Freeman, *Cérémonial de la sainte messe*, 256.

[447] *RM*, Good Friday, no. 11.

[448] Fortescue, O'Connell, and Reid, *The Ceremonies of the Roman Rite Described*, 356.

[449] *CB*, 319; Mutel and Freeman, *Cérémonial de la sainte messe*, 287.

[450] *RM*, Good Friday, no. 11.

faithful. The server holding the missal in front of the celebrant at the chair or at the altar remains standing throughout. When the faithful kneel, this server can bow his or her head and close his or her eyes to join them in silent prayer. Once the solemn intercessions are concluded, all sit while the preparations are made for the veneration of the cross. In some churches, this is the time when ushers take up the collection, if one is taken up at all on Good Friday.

The First Form of the Showing of the Cross

The altar cross, or one which replaces it, is venerated by the ministers and faithful on the day which recalls the Lord's sacrifice on the Cross of Calvary. That which the sacrifice of the Mass recalls on other days of the year is recalled by the action of adoring and venerating the cross, which reminds all those present of the same sacrifice. The portion of the service called the Adoration of the Holy Cross is made up of two parts: first, the showing of the holy cross, and second, the Adoration of the Holy Cross properly speaking. The showing of the cross can take place in two different ways.

The first form of the showing of the cross begins in the sacristy. There, the altar cross and candles, removed the previous evening on Holy Thursday, are found. On Good Friday, that cross is veiled in purple. At times, a larger cross may substitute for the normal altar cross on Good Friday in order to allow for more than one person to venerate it at the same time. Like the altar cross which it replaces, this cross for veneration also bears the image of the Crucified according to the consistent traditional practice, although this is not specified in the revised liturgical books.[451] Again, like the altar cross which it replaces, this substitute cross for veneration should not be so large that one person, in this case the deacon, cannot carry it unassisted. One commentator has suggested that this substitute cross should be sized between three feet tall and five feet tall.[452] The cross for veneration on Good Friday is a specific liturgical item. It is not a dramatic prop for some kind of theatrical re-enactment of the Crucifixion of the Lord. Therefore, life-sized crosses seem excluded from use on Good Friday. Two candles are also prepared. These should match the two candles which will eventually accompany the Blessed Sacrament from the place of reposition to the altar. These four candlesticks will eventually be placed together either on or near the altar in the course of the service.

[451] Mutel and Freeman, *Cérémonial de la sainte messe*, 288–289.

[452] Mutel and Freeman, *Cérémonial de la sainte messe*, 280.

The deacon, or another priest, or even another server in the absence of a deacon or second priest, goes to the sacristy with two servers to receive the cross. The deacon carries the cross, facing forward, from the sacristy to the altar through the church in silence, by means of the most direct route. Two servers holding candles walk on either side of the cross in the usual way. If sufficient space is lacking, the two candle bearers walk ahead of the cross. When the deacon enters the church, all stand in their places. A server may sound a wooden clapper or rattle (the crotalus) to indicate that all should stand. The celebrant goes from his chair to the altar, facing the people.

Upon arriving at the altar, the servers stand to either side, facing each other, holding their candles. The deacon hands the veiled cross to the celebrant standing before the altar so that the cross with the image of the Crucified faces the assembly. The celebrant begins by uncovering the upper part of the cross, but leaves the head of the Crucified covered.[453] He elevates the cross as he sings in a low tone, "Behold the wood of the Cross," and the people respond. A server may stand to the celebrant's left with the missal or a card with the musical notation. The celebrant may be assisted by others near him to sing the invitation. The celebrant may be assisted by the deacon or a master of ceremonies in unveiling the cross. After the response, all kneel for a brief moment to adore in silence. The celebrant remains standing and holds the cross raised. This is repeated a second time with the right arm of the cross, and then a third time with the left arm of the cross. The invitation "Behold the wood of the Cross" is sung each time in successively higher tones. After the third unveiling, the deacon or a master of ceremonies assists the celebrant to completely remove the purple veil. He sets it aside on the credence table.

The Second Form of the Showing of the Cross

The second manner of showing the cross has its origins in the presentation of the relic of the True Cross for the veneration of the faithful.[454] In this case, the celebrant himself, or the deacon, or another priest, or some other suitable minister carries the unveiled cross from the door of the church to the sanctuary. The unveiled cross, in a stand or resting flat on a pillow, and its candles are prepared in some location near the door of the church, perhaps a vesting sacristy. On the way from the door of the church to the sanctuary, there are three stations, first at the door

[453] Fortescue, O'Connell, and Reid, *The Ceremonies of the Roman Rite Described*, 350.

[454] Mutel and Freeman, *Cérémonial de la sainte messe*, 290, n. 181.

of the church, then in the middle of the church, and finally, at the entrance to the sanctuary. The two servers with candles accompany the cross, walking on either side of the cross as usual, if circumstances permit.[455] Otherwise, they walk ahead of the cross to light the way. All stand and perhaps turn to face the cross at the back of the church. The celebrant or the deacon carrying the cross holds it in both hands with the image of the Crucified facing forward. The minister himself faces forward at the first two stops, and then turns to face the assembly at the entrance to the sanctuary. The two servers holding candles turn to face the cross and each other at each stop. At each stop, the sacred minister, assisted by a cantor or cantors if necessary, elevates the cross and sings the acclamation, and the people respond. All kneel for a brief moment of silent adoration while the minister holding the cross and the servers holding candles remain standing.

The Veneration of the Cross

Whether the showing of the cross was accomplished by the unveiling in the sanctuary or by the procession through the nave, the adoration of the cross begins in the sanctuary with the act of adoration by the ministers. The celebrant, or the deacon as the case may be, hands the cross over to two servers to hold. The two servers stand on either side, nearly shoulder to shoulder behind the cross, supporting the arms of the cross by their inside hands, facing the assembly.[456] The servers holding the cross upright can rest the foot of the cross on one of the steps of the altar or on the floor of the sanctuary itself. Or, they can hold the cross elevated somewhat to make it easier to venerate from a standing position. With their outside hands, they wipe the cross with a purificator after each person has venerated it with a kiss, or this may be entrusted to another minister if both servers must use both hands to hold the cross securely. The candle bearers can hold their candles on either side, facing each other. Or, they can put them down on either side of the cross at some distance, and remain standing with hands joined, facing each other, unless these servers are holding the cross themselves out of necessity.

Those in the sanctuary venerate the cross there, beginning with the celebrant. At the chair, he may first remove his chasuble and lay it face down on the back of the chair. He may then sit and remove his shoes as well. The deacon does

[455] Peter J. Elliott, *Ceremonies of the Liturgical Year According to the Modern Roman Rite: A Manual for Clergy and All Involved in Liturgical Ministries* (San Francisco: Ignatius Press, 2002), 239.

[456] Mutel and Freeman, *Cérémonial de la sainte messe*, 293.

not remove his dalmatic.[457] Then the celebrant goes to the cross and makes some gesture of reverence. Historically, this gesture of reverence has included one or more genuflections, according to local custom. Customarily, all kiss the cross as well, often at the feet of the Crucified, either while genuflecting or standing.[458] The celebrant returns to the chair. First, he sits and puts on his shoes. Then, standing, and perhaps with his back to the assembly, puts on the chasuble and sits. The deacon of the service follows the celebrant to venerate the cross. Then, the priests in the sanctuary come forward and do the same, followed by any other deacons in attendance, and then the other ministers. If these are numerous, they can approach two by two and venerate the cross simultaneously if the cross is large enough for them to do so with ease. According to no. 69 of the *Ceremonial of Bishops*, all genuflect to the cross from the time that solemn adoration has begun until the beginning of the Easter Vigil whenever they pass before it.

Individual veneration of the cross by all those in the nave takes place after the veneration of those in the sanctuary. The two servers holding the cross before the altar take the cross to the entrance of the sanctuary for the veneration of the faithful. They hold the cross upright as before, resting its foot on the altar rail, or on the bottom step of the sanctuary, or on the floor of the nave. Depending on the design of the cross, they can also hold it elevated so that the faithful may venerate it more easily from a standing position. The two candle bearers move their candles to the first step of the sanctuary at the same time, on either side of the cross. After putting down their candles, they can remain standing facing each other with hands joined, unless the period of veneration will be too long for them to do so. In that case, they return to their seats. All come forward to venerate the cross like those in the sanctuary did. In some churches, a basket is placed next to the cross to receive the offerings of the faithful once they have venerated the cross.

When the veneration of the cross by the faithful is completed, all stand. The deacon, or the minister who carried the cross to the sanctuary in his absence, goes and receives the cross from the two servers holding it. They make their acts of adoration. The deacon carries the cross into the sanctuary and places it in its stand on or near the altar. The two candle bearers take up their candles and accompany the deacon on either side, and place them on or near the altar as well. Then all sit.

If the number of the faithful is too great to allow for individual veneration of the cross, after some of the clergy, servers, and faithful have adored, the celebrant

457 Mutel and Freeman, *Cérémonial de la sainte messe*, 295.

458 Mutel and Freeman, *Cérémonial de la sainte messe*, 294–295.

goes to the altar and instructs all present to adore the cross simultaneously in silence. The deacon may invite all to kneel for this period of veneration. The celebrant takes the cross in both hands and raises it for a brief time. Then all stand at the invitation of the deacon. The celebrant places the cross in its stand on or near the altar, and he returns to the chair. All sit. Ministers then prepare the altar for the rite of Holy Communion.

The Rite of Holy Communion

The deacon and the two candle bearers, after genuflecting together to the cross at the altar, and with hands joined, now leave the sanctuary to go to the place of reposition of the Blessed Sacrament, whether that be in the sacristy or elsewhere. In the absence of a deacon or another priest, the celebrant himself goes to the repository. These ministers may be preceded by a master of ceremonies. If the procession to the repository passes outdoors, some churches maintain the use of the ombrellino, held by one server over the deacon, walking behind him on the return from the place of reposition to the church.[459] In these churches, the ombrellino is often used only for the portion of the procession which takes place outdoors.

Since the altar of the church will be used for the distribution of Holy Communion, it must be prepared to do so. That means it must be vested with an altar cloth and receive altar candles, and that an altar cross, bearing the image of the Crucified,[460] must be arranged on or near it. After the Evening Mass of the Lord's Supper on Holy Thursday, the altar was stripped of its cloth, candles, and cross, in preparation for Good Friday. Throughout the day of Good Friday, whether during the celebration of the Office of Readings and Morning Prayer, or during devotions such as the Stations of the Cross, or for most the Service of the Lord's Passion, the altar stands completely bare. However, for the rite of Holy Communion, it is vested and adorned in the usual way. It is in view of the eventual use of the altar as the place for the rite of Holy Communion that the altar cloth, altar candles, and an altar cross are reintroduced on Good Friday.

Thus, while the celebrant or the deacon and servers go to the place of reservation of the Blessed Sacrament, servers place a folded or rolled altar cloth on the top of the altar. Usually, they begin by unfolding it from back to front. Then, they open it from the middle, and then to each side. Or, an altar cloth rolled on a tube can be unrolled from left to right. The cloth need only cover the top of the altar

[459] Mutel and Freeman, *Cérémonial de la sainte messe*, 299, n. 203.

[460] *GIRM*, 308.

itself. If the cross and its stand, as well as its candles, are intended to be placed directly *on* the altar after veneration, it is best for the servers to spread the altar cloth *before* the cross arrives at the altar at the conclusion of veneration. In some churches, the cross and its candles are placed along the back of the altar such that the Communion rite is carried out facing the crucifix.[461] This allows for the eventual transfer of the Hosts from the single ciborium of reservation into multiple patens in a more discrete way. Servers also bring the corporal(s) in a red burse and the missal and wooden stand, along with any extra patens or ciboria for the distribution of Communion if needed.

Once at the place of reposition, all genuflect and then kneel. The master of ceremonies, standing behind the deacon, places a red or white humeral veil on his shoulders. The deacon goes up to the repository, opens the door, genuflects, and takes the ciborium in his veiled hands. The servers stand, and then light the two candlesticks prepared there. Led by the master of ceremonies, the deacon, with the two candle bearers walking on either side, returns to the sanctuary by the most direct route.[462] If there is not enough room for the three to walk side by side, the candle bearers precede the Blessed Sacrament.[463]

When the Blessed Sacrament arrives in the body of the church, all stand in silence.[464] A server may strike the wooden clapper or rattle (the crotalus) to indicate this.[465] There is nothing to prevent those present in the nave and in the sanctuary from genuflecting in their places as the Blessed Sacrament passes by.[466] The deacon goes directly to the altar and places the ciborium down on the corporal. He stands to free his hands and removes the cover and veil from the ciborium. Meanwhile, the two candle bearers place their candlesticks down on or near the altar on either side. Standing at the center of the altar and at its sides, the deacon and the two servers genuflect together. The servers return to their places while the master of ceremonies removes the humeral veil from the shoulders of the kneeling deacon. If necessary, the deacon can now divide the Hosts in the ciborium into one or more patens or ciboria, depending on the number of Communion stations foreseen. The celebrant leaves the chair and goes to the altar,

461 Elliott, *Ceremonies of the Liturgical Year*, 243, n. 31.

462 Fortescue, O'Connell, and Reid, *The Ceremonies of the Roman Rite Described*, 352.

463 Mutel and Freeman, *Cérémonial de la sainte messe*, 300.

464 *RM*, Good Friday, no. 22.

465 Fortescue, O'Connell, and Reid, *The Ceremonies of the Roman Rite Described*, 352.

466 Fortescue, O'Connell, and Reid, *The Ceremonies of the Roman Rite Described*, 352.

ascending the steps from the middle. He genuflects upon arriving, with both hands placed on the altar outside the corporal.

With hands joined, the celebrant introduces the Our Father. He prays the Our Father and its embolism with hands extended in the *orans* position. He looks at the Hosts while praying the Our Father. He looks at the missal if he is singing the Our Father. At the end of the embolism, he joins his hands for the acclamation. The prayer for peace, sign of peace, and *Agnus Dei* are omitted on Good Friday. In those locations where the faithful are accustomed to kneel at the conclusion of the *Agnus Dei*, they may need some indication from the deacon to kneel after the acclamation "For the kingdom, the power, and the glory are yours," instead. Following that acclamation, the celebrant, bowing slightly, with hands joined and resting on the altar, prays, "May the receiving of your Body and Blood," silently. After genuflecting with both hands on the altar outside the corporal, he takes a Host between the index finger and thumb of his right hand, and holding it slightly raised over the ciborium, faces people to say, "Behold the Lamb of God." He responds with the people, then puts the ciborium down on the altar and says silently, "May the Body of Christ keep me safe for eternal life," and communicates himself with his right hand.

The celebrant, holding the ciborium in his left hand, then gives Communion to the deacon on his right, saying, "The Body of Christ." Then all in the sanctuary receive Communion there, beginning with the priests in attendance, wearing red stoles, followed by the deacons in attendance, also wearing red stoles, and then the servers. The priests in attendance receive Communion rather than communicate themselves, since they are not concelebrants. The celebrant says, "The Body of Christ," to each of the priests who receive Communion and to all others who will communicate. They respond, "Amen." The clergy and servers receive Communion in the sanctuary, in a straight line before the altar or in two rows facing each other on either side. The celebrant administers Communion from left to right. If the sanctuary is large enough, they also may approach the altar in a kind of procession, two by two, to receive Communion from the celebrant standing at the altar.

Then, the Communion of the faithful takes place in the usual way. Servers assist the celebrant and any other minister of Communion with the Communion paten. Other servers may hold a torch at each station.[467] After the Communion

[467] Mutel and Freeman, *Cérémonial de la sainte messe*, 301, n. 209.

of the faithful, the Hosts which remain can be consumed at the altar. Or, if a larger number remain, they are gathered into the original ciborium.

Any other ciboria or patens used for Communion are purified at the altar or, preferably, at a credence table over a corporal. At the altar, the extra ciboria or patens can be purified by wiping the particles with a purificator or the right thumb into the ciborium used for reservation. Then these vessels are brought to the credence table. Or, at the credence table itself, a server can pour water from a cruet into the first vessel to be purified. Then the minister who is purifying can pour this ablution from one vessel to another, until all the vessels are purified. The ablution is then poured into a bowl. Finally, the Communion patens used can also be purified at the credence table by wiping the particles from the vessels used into this ablution bowl using the right thumb. The ministers of Communion will then purify their fingers in this ablution bowl as well. Later, that ablution will be poured into the sacrarium or into the ground as usual.[468]

The deacon goes to the altar, genuflects, and covers and veils the ciborium. Meanwhile, two servers likewise go to the altar, and standing at each side, genuflect when he does. Then, they take up their candles. While the deacon kneels, the master of ceremonies places the humeral veil on his shoulders from behind.[469] Veiling his hands, the deacon then takes the ciborium in both hands. With the candle bearers on either side, the deacon leaves the sanctuary to return the Blessed Sacrament to the repository by the same route through the nave he took to arrive at the sanctuary. If the procession passes outdoors, some churches maintain the use of the ombrellino, held over the deacon by a server walking behind him.

If necessary, the Blessed Sacrament can be reserved temporarily in the tabernacle in the sanctuary of the church.[470] In that case, a server lights the sanctuary lamp and veils the tabernacle in red after the deacon has reserved the Blessed Sacrament there rather than at the repository. A server folds and removes the corporal from the altar. The Post-Communion prayer and prayer over the people can take place either at the chair or at the altar. If the Post-Communion prayer will take place at the altar, the server places the missal straight, in the center of

[468] Mutel and Freeman, *Cérémonial de la sainte messe*, 303; Fortescue, O'Connell, and Reid, *The Ceremonies of the Roman Rite Described*, 353.

[469] *CB*, 328.

[470] *RM*, Good Friday, no. 29.

the altar, with the bottom of the missal parallel to the edge of the altar.[471] Otherwise, the missal and its stand are removed to the credence table near the chair.

The celebrant does not continue with the service until the deacon and servers have returned to the sanctuary from the repository, unless the repository is at some great distance from the church. Then, standing at the chair or at the altar, the celebrant prays the Post-Communion prayer. The celebrant says, "Let us pray," facing the assembly with hands joined.[472] He prays the Post-Communion prayer with arms extended in the *orans* position, facing the missal. The celebrant does not say, "The Lord be with you." Rather, with hands joined and facing the people, the deacon, or in his absence the priest himself, may say immediately, "Bow down for the blessing."[473] The celebrant then prays the prayer over the people with hands outstretched over the assembly, palms open and facing down. There is no actual blessing with the Sign of the Cross at the conclusion of the Service of the Lord's Passion on Good Friday. Both the blessing with the Sign of the Cross and the dismissal are omitted.

The celebrant and the deacon, and any server who accompanied them at the beginning of the service, leave their places. All others remain in their places. The celebrant, the deacon, and the server stand before the cross and genuflect. Then they return to the sacristy by the most direct route as at the beginning of the service, passing through the church in silence with hands joined.

After the Service of the Lord's Passion

Afterwards, all those in the sanctuary remain for a time in silent prayer. As they depart, they make sure to genuflect to the cross, and to the Blessed Sacrament if reserved there. They do the same whenever passing in front of both. The cross remains at the altar with two candles burning for as long as the faithful remain in the church in silent prayer. The servers extinguish any other candles, and all the crosses in the church and in the sacristy are unveiled. The cross and its candles remain in the sanctuary until the beginning of the Easter Vigil.[474]

If the Blessed Sacrament has been reserved in the tabernacle of the sanctuary, it is now transferred to the repository, either in the place of reposition for Holy

471 Mutel and Freeman, *Cérémonial de la sainte messe*, 303, n. 217; Fortescue, O'Connell, and Reid, *The Ceremonies of the Roman Rite Described*, 353, 358.

472 *RM*, Good Friday, no. 30.

473 *RM*, Good Friday, no. 31. The greeting "The Lord be with you" is not said at any time during the Service of the Lord's Passion. See Mutel and Freeman, *Cérémonial de la sainte messe*, 303.

474 *GIRM*, 274.

Thursday, if this remains out of sight from those in the nave, or at the secret repository, usually in the sacristy. This takes place without ceremony. The priest or deacon wears the humeral veil. He is accompanied by at least one server with a torch.[475] The veil is removed from the tabernacle and the sanctuary lamp is extinguished.

Servers return to the church to remove the altar cloth without ceremony. Usually, they begin by bringing the edges of the cloth toward the middle of the altar, and then again once or twice as needed. What remains is folded one final time from front to back. They may roll the altar cloth on a tube, from right to left. Any veils over other crosses in the church or in the sacristy are removed. The veils over statues remain until the beginning of the Easter Vigil.[476]

[475] Mutel and Freeman, *Cérémonial de la sainte messe*, 302.

[476] Mutel and Freeman, *Cérémonial de la sainte messe*, 303, 303, n. 221.

18

The Easter Vigil

The Easter Vigil is comprised of four parts: the service of light, the Liturgy of the Word, in some cases the rites of Christian initiation as well as the renewal of baptismal promises, and the Liturgy of the Eucharist. While these parts of the Vigil have undergone a series of modifications over the twentieth century, the traditional practice of the Roman Rite can help today in celebrating them according to the Roman Missal of Paul VI.

Requisites for the Celebration

For the blessing of the fire:

- Everything needed to light and extinguish the fire
- A tray with the five grains of incense, stylus, charcoals, tongs, a follower for the Easter candle, and a candle for the celebrant
- Some means of lighting the Easter candle from the new fire
- Candles for those taking part, unless these are distributed elsewhere
- A table covered with a white cloth for all the items above

In the sacristy:

- The Easter candle
- Censer without charcoals and incense boat
- The missal to be carried by a server

In the sanctuary:

- Everything usually needed for Mass
- The processional cross and candles for the recessional
- The text of the Exsultet
- The Gospel book, laying flat, face down on the altar
- A stand for the Easter candle, to the right of the ambo or in the center of the sanctuary
- A lectern, veiled in white, near the stand for the Easter candle if this cannot be placed near the ambo
- Chrism, unless it remains in the ambry in the baptistry
- White veil for the tabernacle
- Some means of lighting the sanctuary lamp after Communion
- Cotton balls, bread, or lemons to cleanse the celebrant's hands after the Confirmations, along with a pitcher of water, bowl, and towel
- Gremial, if the celebrant will wash his hands seated

At the baptismal font or in the baptistry:

- A means of pouring water for the Baptisms, towels
- White garments for the newly baptized, if used in the case of adults
- Baptismal candles for the newly baptized adults
- Chrism, unless it is placed beforehand where the Confirmations will take place
- The rituals for the Christian initiation of adults or children as needed
- A vessel to receive the blessed water, aspergillum
- A table covered with a white cloth for all the items above

At the place of reservation of the Blessed Sacrament:

- White humeral veil
- Two processional candles

Prior to the beginning of the Easter Vigil, the veils on any statues have been removed. The holy water stoups remain empty. The tabernacle of the church is completely empty and unveiled; the door is left open. A sanctuary candle is prepared but remains unlit. The Presence of the Lord would require a burning sanctuary lamp in the church and this is contrary to the instruction that all the lights of the church are extinguished.[477] The Blessed Sacrament which remains from Mass on Holy Thursday and from the Celebration of the Lord's Passion on Friday is reserved outside the main body of the church, usually in the sacristy, where a light can burn next to it, or even in the repository set up on Holy Thursday, provided this is outside the view of those assembled in the nave. All who enter the sanctuary or pass before the altar bow to the altar. The lighting of the fire for the *lucernarium* will take place outside the church, either entirely outdoors or in the narthex, depending on the circumstances. The entire assembly may gather outdoors, or a representative portion of the faithful may gather just inside or just outside the doors of the church. Each person, except the catechumens, is given an unlit candle to hold. The catechumens will receive a candle immediately after their Baptism. The celebrant and deacon wear the vestments for Mass from the beginning of the Easter Vigil. The Vigil begins no sooner than nightfall.

Prior to the beginning of the Easter Vigil, the church may be illuminated in low light. The lights in the sacristy can remain on for as long as it is occupied. All the lights in the sacristy and the church are extinguished just before the Vigil begins. If the blessing of the new fire takes place outdoors, the light from the new fire may be sufficient for the celebrant to read by even without any exterior lighting. If the blessing of the new fire and the preparation and lighting of the Easter candle take place in the narthex of the church rather than outside, the lights in the narthex alone can remain on, so that the celebrant will have sufficient light to read from the missal and to prepare the Easter candle. The lights in the narthex can be extinguished once the Easter candle is lit and the celebrant has read the formula "May the light of Christ rising in glory."[478] At that point, the lights are no longer needed, since there are no further texts to read. The celebrant will prepare the incense by the light of the new fire and of the Easter candle alone.

At the appointed time, the ministers make their way from the sacristy to the place where the new fire will be blessed by means of a secondary door, rather than the main door of the church. The processional cross and candles are not carried; they are placed in the sanctuary for use at the end of Mass. The Gospel

[477] *RM*, Easter Vigil, no. 7.

[478] Adrian Fortescue, J. B. O'Connell, and Alcuin Reid, eds., *The Ceremonies of the Roman Rite Described*, 15th ed. (New York: Bloomsbury, 2009), 371.

book is not carried. If used for Mass, the Gospel book can be placed face down at the center of the altar prior to the beginning of the Easter Vigil. The thurifer carries the empty censer without lighted coals, as well as the incense boat. An instituted acolyte or another server carries the Easter candle. All follow the server carrying the Easter candle.[479] A server carries the missal. The ministers make their way from the sacristy to the new fire in an orderly way, but not in procession. The procession properly speaking will begin from the new fire rather than from the sacristy.

The Service of Light

The ministers gather at the place where the new fire will be blessed. If outdoors, the celebrant stands with his back to the door of the church, with the new fire between him and the assembled faithful. If in the narthex with most people inside the church, he stands facing the faithful with the new fire between them.[480] Normally, the deacon stands to the celebrant's right. In addition, the server holding the tray with the items needed to light the incense and the candle stands to the celebrant's right. The server with the missal stands to the celebrant's left. The minister with the candle also stands to the celebrant's left. Concelebrants can stand in two rows facing each other across the fire. Upon arrival, the thurifer uses tongs to place the unlit coals into the new fire, unless this has already been done by the sacristan. Once everyone has gathered outside, the main doors of the church are now opened.

The celebrant begins with the Sign of the Cross. He extends his hands for the greeting, and joins his hands for the instruction "Dear brethren, on this most sacred night." He extends both hands in the *orans* position to bless the fire, eventually joining his hands briefly, and then making the Sign of the Cross with his right hand over it at the point indicated in the text, his left hand resting on his chest. He then joining both hands before continuing with hands extended as before. He joins his hands once again at the conclusion, "Through Christ Our Lord."

The celebrant then prepares the Easter candle. From the tray on his right, the deacon places a stylus in the celebrant's right hand. The celebrant traces the cross, the alpha and the omega, and the date on the Easter candle, which the server on his

[479] *CB*, 338.

[480] André Philippe M. Mutel and Peter Freeman, *Cérémonial de la sainte messe à l'usage ordinaire des paroisses suivant le missel romain de 2002 et la pratique léguée du rit romain*, 2nd ed. (Perpignan, France: Éditions Artège, 2012), 318.

left holds upright for him. The server with the missal stands immediately next to the acolyte holding the Easter candle so that the celebrant can easily read the texts which accompany the preparation of the candle. Once finished, the celebrant returns the stylus to the deacon. The deacon holds before the celebrant a vessel containing five grains of incense. The celebrant places the each of the grains of incense into the candle in the shape of a cross, fixing each one in place with a nail. In many churches these acts of preparation are carried out ahead of time in the sacristy.[481] If so, the celebrant, holding the stylus in the right hand, simply traces the stylus over the figures already in place on the candle while saying the required formulas. He can touch the nails previously affixed with the joined fingers of his right hand while saying the required formulas. The deacon or a master of ceremonies takes a taper and lights it from the new fire.[482] He hands the taper to the celebrant. The celebrant lights the Easter candle with his right hand, saying the formula "May the light of Christ," and then returns the taper to the deacon. The celebrant may grasp the candle with his left hand, or may rest his left hand on his chest while doing so. In some churches, during the day of Saturday, the sacristan often lights the candle briefly ahead of time, so that the wick will burn more easily at the Vigil itself. In many churches, the deacon or the master of ceremonies now places a brass or glass follower over the Easter candle. The instituted acolyte or server holding the Easter candle goes to stand in the doorway of the church. A server may retain the taper lit until the Easter candle is shielded from the wind. If at any time the wind blows out the Easter candle, it is relit by the celebrant from the taper or from the blessed fire itself while repeating the required formula. Conversely, if all are gathered in the narthex, those lights are now extinguished. In the narthex, it will not be necessary to retain a lit taper.

Meanwhile, the thurifer retrieves the burning coals from the new fire with tongs and places them in the censer. Assisted by the deacon, the thurifer goes to the celebrant so that he may impose incense in the usual manner. After the imposition and blessing of incense, the deacon goes and takes the Easter candle from the minister. In the absence of a deacon, another suitable minister, such as a concelebrant, or an instituted acolyte, or even a server, may take the candle in both hands.[483] The celebrant receives an unlit candle from a server in his right

481 Mutel and Freeman, *Cérémonial de la sainte messe*, 319, n. 263.

482 Mutel and Freeman, *Cérémonial de la sainte messe*, 320.

483 *RM*, Easter Vigil, no. 15.

hand. An usher remains behind to make sure the Easter fire is extinguished once all have entered the church.

The thurifer leads the procession, followed by the deacon bearing the Easter candle and the celebrant. Concelebrants follow behind him, along with any deacons in attendance and servers. The faithful follow behind the liturgical ministers; the choir may be the first among them. At the door of the church or even just inside, the deacon stops. Facing forward into the church, he raises the candle and sings in a low tone, "The light of Christ," and all respond.[484] The celebrant alone lights his candle from the Easter candle at this point. If there is no deacon, and the celebrant himself is carrying the Easter candle, a server lights the celebrant's candle for him and carries it into the church before handing it over to the celebrant once the celebrant reaches the chair.

After the first acclamation of "The light of Christ," and the lighting of the celebrant's candle, the procession continues into the church. At the middle of the church, the deacon stops, still facing forward, raises the candle, and sings in a higher tone, "The light of Christ," a second time. The entire assembly lights their candles at this point. Historically, the clergy and servers alone lit their candles at this point. In order not to delay the procession, the procession may resume once these the clergy and servers *begin* to light the candles of the assembly behind them and next to them in procession.[485]

Finally, at the steps of the sanctuary, the deacon turns to face the assembly and sings in a higher tone, "The light of Christ," one final time.[486] At this point, any and all candles in the church itself may be lit. These would include the candles in the dedication crosses, candles at any minor altars, candles and lamps located in various shrines, and any other candles set up in the sanctuary. However, the candles at the main altar itself and the sanctuary lamp itself are not lit at this point. The candles at the main altar will be lit at the Gloria. The sanctuary lamp will be lit only once reservation in the tabernacle resumes, after the conclusion of Communion. In addition, the few electric lights needed for the Exsultet, the readings, the chants, and the Collects can be turned on at this point. Any lights turned on due to necessity remain lit throughout the Vigil. Electric lights are not turned on and turned off in succession throughout the Vigil. It may be better to delay turning on all or most the lights of the church until after the Exsultet, or even until the Gloria, as is the

[484] Mutel and Freeman, *Cérémonial de la sainte messe,* 322.

[485] Mutel and Freeman, *Cérémonial de la sainte* messe, 322, n. 269.

[486] *RM,* Easter Vigil, no. 17.

custom currently in some churches.[487] Otherwise, the words of the Exsultet, "This is the night," contradict the truth of the circumstances when the interior of the church is already as bright as day when this is sung! It may even be possible for servers holding lit candles to stand around the lectern, ambo, and chair in turn such that no electric lighting may be needed until later.

The deacon goes and places the Easter candle in its stand with the inscriptions on the candle facing forward. The stand for the Easter candle is placed near the ambo,[488] normally to its right, unless the circumstances dictate otherwise. If it is not possible for the Easter candle to be placed next to the ambo for some reason, the Easter candle and its stand can alternatively be located in the center of the sanctuary. In that case, a lectern covered in white, from which the deacon will sing the Exsultet, stands turned toward the assembly slightly to the left of the Easter candle as one faces the assembly.[489] All who enter the sanctuary bow profoundly to the altar. The deacon carrying the Easter candle and the thurifer carrying the censer bow their heads instead. There is no mention in any of the revised books of the celebrant, concelebrants, and deacon kissing the altar upon entering the sanctuary. The deacon goes to stand at his place to the right of the celebrant's chair, along with the thurifer and a server ready to hold the celebrant's candle. The book bearer stands at the celebrant's left at the chair.

Once all have their candles lit and have taken their places, the thurifer comes before the celebrant for the imposition of incense. The celebrant hands his candle to the master of ceremonies. The celebrant imposes and blesses incense in the usual way, assisted by the deacon. A server presents the deacon with the book containing the text of the Exsultet.[490] Then the deacon, holding the book with the text of the Exsultet, bows profoundly and asks for the celebrant's blessing to announce the Easter proclamation. With hands joined, the celebrant, standing at the chair, blesses the deacon with his right hand, his left hand resting on his chest, joining his hands once again. The book bearer holds the missal slightly to the celebrant's left for him to read the formula of blessing. The celebrant receives his burning candle in his right

487 Peter J. Elliott, *Ceremonies of the Liturgical Year According to the Modern Roman Rite: A Manual for Clergy and All Involved in Liturgical Ministries* (San Francisco: Ignatius Press, 2002), 280; Mutel and Freeman, *Cérémonial de la sainte messe*, 325, n. 278.

488 *CB*, 336.

489 *RM*, Easter Vigil, no. 19; Fortescue, O'Connell, and Reid, *The Ceremonies of the Roman Rite Described*, 364.

490 Mutel and Freeman, *Cérémonial de la sainte messe*, 281; Fortescue, O'Connell, and Reid, *The Ceremonies of the Roman Rite Described*, 364.

hand from the master of ceremonies. In the absence of a deacon, a concelebrant or a cantor may sing the proclamation, without asking for the celebrant's blessing beforehand. In case of necessity, the celebrant himself may sing the Exsultet. The celebrant or a concelebrant bows profoundly before the altar to pray the prayer of preparation in a low voice before proceeding to sing the Exsultet.

The deacon, following the thurifer, goes to the ambo or to the temporary lectern where he will sing the Exsultet. The deacon puts down the book from which he will sing. He receives the censer from the thurifer and incenses the book with three swings, center, left, and right, bowing before and after and saying nothing. He then incenses the Easter candle by walking around it in a counterclockwise direction, bowing before and after.[491] If the placement of the Easter candle makes it impossible to walk around it while incensing it, the deacon may simply incense the Easter candle from a standing position with three swings, bowing before and after. The deacon sings the Easter proclamation with hands joined. A layperson replacing the deacon does not incense the book or the candle. The layperson sings a modified form of the Exsultet compared to a cleric. In the case where a layperson sings the Exsultet, a concelebrant or even the celebrant himself may incense the Easter candle before the Exsultet is sung. The book containing the Exsultet is illuminated by the light of the Easter candle and by the candles of those standing near the deacon; in addition, some electric lights may be needed.

After singing the Exsultet, the deacon returns to his seat. A server removes the lectern, if one is used. The deacon or master of ceremonies signals everyone to extinguish their candles, and all are seated, as described in the missal.[492] On the other hand, following the custom in some churches, all may retain their candles lit until the Gloria, keeping their lamps lit, so to speak, for the coming of the Bridegroom. In that case, a server will need to take the candle from the celebrant each time he prays a Collect.[493] The lights of the church, or a significant portion of them, can be turned on at this point, if they were already not turned on before the Exsultet.[494] The celebrant, standing at the chair, faces the assembly to invite them to listen to the reading. A server holds the missal before him for this invitation.

491 Mutel and Freeman, *Cérémonial de la sainte messe*, 326.

492 *RM*, Easter Vigil no. 22.

493 Mutel and Freeman, *Cérémonial de la sainte messe*, 327.

494 Formerly, the lamps of the church were lit *during* the Exsultet. See Léon-Michael Le Vavasseur, *Cérémonial à l'usage des petites églises de paroisse selon the rite romain*, 2nd ed. (Paris: Éditions Lecoffre, 1864), 253, no. 250. The rubrics of the revised Easter Vigil in 1951 indicated that the lights of the church were turned on before the *beginning* of the Exsultet so that there would

The Liturgy of the Word

The Liturgy of the Word at the Easter Vigil comprises up to seven readings from the Law and the Prophets, an epistle, an extended Gospel Acclamation, and a Gospel passage. Each of the Old Testament readings is followed by a responsorial psalm and Collect. It is possible to replace each responsorial psalm with silence, concluding with the Collect nonetheless. After the conclusion of the first of the readings and its psalm, the celebrant stands at the chair and turns to the faithful to say, "Let us pray," with hands joined. Then facing the missal held directly in front of him by a server, he prays the Collect with hands extended in the *orans* position. The celebrant then sits for the next reading. The celebrant prays a Collect in the same way after each of the Old Testament readings. After the Collect that concludes the final Old Testament reading, he remains standing for the Gloria and the Collect of the Mass.

At the Gloria, the organ sounds once again for the first time since the Gloria on Holy Thursday evening. Servers light the altar candles from the Easter candle. In some churches, once the altar candles are lit, the celebrant and deacon come from their chairs, bow before the altar, and kiss it, before returning immediately to their places, in order to mark the beginning of the Vigil Mass properly speaking. Any additional electric lights which may be needed, especially in the sanctuary, are turned on at this point. The bells of the church are rung, and servers ring handbells with either their right or left hands.

After the Gloria, the celebrant, standing at the chair, prays the Collect of the Mass in the usual way. The celebrant is seated for the epistle which follows. Immediately after the epistle, an extended Gospel Acclamation, one with a triple introduction of the Alleluia and three verses, precedes the Gospel. Historically, the Alleluia is sung three times in successively higher tones. This Alleluia is intoned by the celebrant, with the people responding. A cantor may assist the celebrant in intoning the triple Alleluia or intone them himself or herself if the celebrant is unable to do so. The celebrant stands when the Alleluia is begun. The Roman Gradual provides only one verse for this acclamation. This single verse from the Roman Gradual can be sung as an alternative to the three verses

be sufficient light to sing the text. See Fortescue, O'Connell, and Reid, *The Ceremonies of the Roman Rite Described*, 364. This coincided with moving the time of the Easter Vigil from the morning, when additional lighting would not be necessary in order to sing the Exsultet, to the evening, when it would be needed. Thus, the timing for lighting the lamps of the church at the Easter Vigil has varied somewhat over the last century.

found in the Lectionary for Mass. While the schola sings the verse or verses to the Alleluia, the celebrant imposes incense standing and blesses the deacon who bows before him. Candles are not carried at the Gospel. The thurifer leads the Gospel procession, followed by the servers walking side by side with hands joined. The deacon goes to the altar to take up the Gospel book, if it was placed there prior to the beginning of the Vigil. Otherwise, he walks with hands joined to the ambo, where he proclaims the Gospel from the lectionary placed there. All in the Gospel procession proceed without any sign of reverence to the altar. At the ambo, the two servers stand facing each other on either side of the ambo, with hands joined. The deacon incenses the Gospel book and proclaims the Gospel in the usual manner. After the proclamation of the Gospel, all return to their places, bowing to the altar when passing in front of it. The homily follows, either at the chair, or at the ambo, or at another suitable place, depending on the circumstances.

The Baptismal Liturgy

The Easter Vigil can present a daunting challenge to many celebrants because its form can vary greatly from year to year, depending on which of the Sacraments of Initiation, if any, are celebrated. Six different scenarios are possible: 1) the Baptism and Confirmation of adult catechumens, 2) the Baptism of infants alone, 3) the Baptism of adults and infants and the Confirmation of adult catechumens, 4) the Baptism of adult catechumens and the Confirmation of both neophytes and candidates for full communion, 5) the renewal of baptismal promises without any Baptisms or Confirmations at all, 6) the reception and Confirmation of candidates for full communion alone joined to the renewal of baptismal promises. This last scenario is not foreseen by any of the liturgical books but nevertheless does take place in some churches from time to time. The postures and gestures of each of these scenarios will be described in turn.

1) The Baptism and Confirmation of Adult Catechumens

In the case of the initiation of adult catechumens, the baptismal liturgy can take place either in the baptistry, if this can be seen by the faithful, or in the sanctuary, at a temporary font erected there. The rite of Confirmation normally takes place in the sanctuary,[495] regardless of whether the Baptisms took place there or in the

[495] *CB*, 367; Mutel and Freeman, *Cérémonial de la sainte messe*, 338.

baptistry. However, the ritual also provides for Confirmation at the font in the baptistry, depending on local circumstances.[496] For a more detailed description of the rites of Baptism and Confirmation of adults on occasions apart from the Easter Vigil, see chapter 23.

At the Easter Vigil, as on other occasions, the Baptism of adults follows the homily. Those to be baptized are called forward before the celebrant with their godparents. An indication is given for all to stand. The Easter candle will be needed during the course of the Baptisms to light the candles of the neophytes. Therefore, an instituted acolyte or another server carries the Easter candle at the head of the procession to the font. The server holding the Easter candle is followed by the catechumens and godparents and other family members, servers, concelebrants, and finally the celebrant and deacon.[497] One server carries the *Rite of Christian Initiation of Adults*, unless it has already been placed at the font.

All who will take part in the procession to the font take their places in proper order, facing the altar. Once all is ready for the procession, two cantors in alternation begin the litany at the saints. At the invocation "Holy Mary, Mother of God," all bow to the altar, except the server carrying the Easter candle.[498] All then turn and make their way to the font in the baptistry. If the Baptisms take place in the sanctuary, the litany of the saints begins once all are gathered at the temporary font there and the celebrant introduces the blessing of the water.

Once at the font, the acolyte or server sets down the Easter candle, even on the edge of the font, or places it in a stand. All in the nave are invited to face the font. The celebrant first faces and addresses those present with hands joined. A server holds the ritual for adult initiation slightly to his left. Then, facing the font, the celebrant proceeds to bless the water. Even if the font is large enough to accommodate the immersion of an adult, the celebrant stands outside the font to bless the water and baptize the elect. According to the first form of the blessing,[499] the celebrant stands with hands extended in the *orans* position.[500] At the point indicated, he may receive the Easter candle from the deacon and lower it into the water with both hands. He may lower the candle once or three times. According to the historical practice, if he lowers the candle three times,

496 *RCIA*, 232.

497 *CB*, 358; *RM*, Easter Vigil, no. 39; Mutel and Freeman, *Cérémonial de la sainte messe*, 335, n. 308.

498 Mutel and Freeman, *Cérémonial de la sainte messe*, 335.

499 *RCIA*, 222A.

500 *CB*, 360; Mutel and Freeman, *Cérémonial de la sainte messe*, 336.

he repeats each time in a successively higher tone the line "We ask you Father, with Your Son to send the Holy Spirit upon the waters of this font." He lowers the candle progressively lower into the font each of the three times.[501] The third time, he holds the candle in the font until the conclusion of the blessing. Then, he lifts the candle out of the font and hands it to the deacon. A server wipes the Easter candle. Meanwhile, all sing a baptismal acclamation.[502]

If the second form of the blessing is used,[503] the celebrant prays with hands joined. At the point indicated, the celebrant touches the water with the open palm of his right hand, his left hand resting on his chest.[504] At the conclusion of the second form, celebrants in many locations make the Sign of the Cross with the right hand over the water, the left hand resting on the chest. In the third form of the blessing,[505] the celebrant prays with hands joined. At the place indicated, he makes the Sign of the Cross with the right hand, the left hand resting on the chest, and joins his hands to conclude. At the conclusion of the blessing of the water, the master of ceremonies or the deacon takes some of the baptismal water in a pitcher and pours it into a vessel with its aspergillum for the sprinkling eventually following the renewal of baptismal promises.

With hands joined, the celebrant stands near the font, facing the catechumens and godparents, and leads them in the renunciation of sin. They respond as a group.[506] He then asks for the profession of faith from each catechumen individually. Each candidate is baptized immediately after his or her profession of faith. The celebrant baptizes each catechumen by pouring water three times on the head, using the right hand, and saying the sacramental formula in the manner indicated in the ritual.[507] The water poured must flow over the bare skin. Historically, the celebrant pours the water over the head in the form of a cross each of the three times.[508] He may also baptize by immersing either the whole body, or the head only, with godparents supporting the catechumen. After all have been baptized, the celebrant then may say the formula pertaining to the white garment with hands joined

[501] Mutel and Freeman, *Cérémonial de la sainte messe*, 336.

[502] *RM*, Easter Vigil, no. 45.

[503] *RCIA*, 222B.

[504] Fortescue, O'Connell, and Reid, *The Ceremonies of the Roman Rite Described*, 365.

[505] *RCIA*, 222C.

[506] The anointing of adult catechumens with the oil of catechumens at this point is always anticipated during the period of the catechumenate in the United States. See the general introduction to the *Rite of Christian Initiation of Adults*, no. 33, §7.

[507] *RCIA*, 226B.

[508] Fortescue, O'Connell, and Reid, *The Ceremonies of the Roman Rite Described*, 425.

while godparents place the garments on the neophytes. The conferral of the white garment is optional, however, in the case of adults.[509] The deacon then takes the Easter candle from its stand or from a server. The celebrant receives the Easter candle in both hands from the deacon and invites a godparent for each of the neophytes forward to light a baptismal candle from the Easter candle. Alternatively, the celebrant, grasping the Easter candle in his left hand, could light a candle with his right and present it to each godparent if this is more convenient.[510] The godparents immediately give the lighted candles to their godchildren as the celebrant, now with hands joined, says the formula once for the entire group. If the Easter candle is too heavy or too tall for either of these options, the celebrant may simply take a long taper, receive the flame from the Easter candle, and light the baptismal candles held by the godparents with the taper.

Normally, the Sacrament of Confirmation is conferred in the sanctuary. Therefore, all return to the sanctuary from the baptistry in procession. The neophytes carry their lighted candles in their right hands. They and their godparents immediately follow the server with the Easter candle. Behind them process the servers and clergy, and finally the celebrant with the deacon walking to his right. One server still carries the ritual, another carries the holy water, and a third carries the chrism for Confirmation taken from the ambry in the baptistry, unless the chrism is already located in the sanctuary. Upon arriving at the sanctuary, the Easter candle is returned to its stand near the ambo. If for some reason the stand for the Easter candle had been placed in the center of the sanctuary instead during the service of light and the Liturgy of the Word, the conclusion of the baptismal liturgy may be the time for the servers to move the candle and its stand to the ambo, or if this is not possible, to the left or Gospel side of the altar as one faces it from the nave.[511] Meanwhile, the neophytes with the godparents stand in a row before the celebrant at the entrance of the sanctuary, facing the altar. Each godparent has his or her right hand on the shoulder of his or her godchild. They may take their godchild's baptismal candle in their left hands for the duration of the Confirmation ceremony.

Once all are standing in their places, the celebrant proceeds with the Confirmation of the newly baptized. The celebrant offers the invitation to prayer with hands

[509] *RCIA*, 229.

[510] Mutel and Freeman, *Cérémonial de la sainte messe*, 337, n. 316; Fortescue, O'Connell, and Reid, *The Ceremonies of the Roman Rite Described*, 426.

[511] Mutel and Freeman, *Cérémonial de la sainte messe*, 313, n. 248; Elliott, *Ceremonies of the Liturgical Year*, 131.

joined. He may close his eyes and bow his head for a moment. Then, with hands outstretched, palms open and facing downward over the entire group to be confirmed, he says the prayer "All-powerful God, Father of Our Lord Jesus Christ."[512] If there will be a large number of Confirmations, the assembly may receive an indication to sit. The celebrant then anoints each of the neophytes on the forehead with the thumb of his right hand, making the Sign of the Cross. Although this gesture is no longer indicated in the revised books, the minister of Confirmation historically placed the joined fingers of his right hand on the crown of each person's head while anointing them on the forehead with the thumb.[513] The candidates for Confirmation may go to the celebrant individually, or he may go to them. If they are standing side-by-side in a line before him, the celebrant begins on his left and concludes on his right. A server with the ritual stands to the celebrant's left. The deacon holding the chrism stands to his right.[514]

After each Confirmation, the godparents return the baptismal candles to their godchildren. The newly confirmed and their godparents return to their places as each is confirmed, or after the entire group has been confirmed. Having confirmed all the neophytes, the celebrant, still standing at the entrance to the sanctuary, cleanses his thumb with crusts of bread or with cotton presented to him on a tray by a server.[515] In this way, the celebrant can proceed to the renewal of baptismal promises of the entire assembly without delay. Or, two other servers may approach him with pitcher, basin, and towel to cleanse the thumb more thoroughly.[516]

While the celebrant is washing and drying his hands, servers with tapers light the candles of everyone in the sanctuary and in the nave from the Easter candle in preparation for the renewal of baptismal promises. If they are seated, all stand to receive the blessed light. Alternatively, this may take place instead as the procession initially made its way from the font to the sanctuary after the Baptisms

512 *RCIA*, 234.

513 Fortescue, O'Connell, and Reid, *The Ceremonies of the Roman Rite Described*, 419.

514 Peter J. Elliott, *Ceremonies Explained for Servers According to the Roman Rite: A Manual for Altar Servers, Acolytes, Sacristans, and Masters of Ceremonies* (San Francisco: Ignatius Press, 2019), 260. This approach seems much more convenient than the traditional practice, where a minister held the chrism to the bishop's *left* during Confirmation. See Fortescue, O'Connell, and Reid, *The Ceremonies of the Roman Rite Described*, 418–419.

515 Mutel and Freeman, *Cérémonial de la sainte messe*, 338.

516 After Mass, the bread, lemons, and cotton are burned. The ashes are poured into the sacrarium in the sacristy, along with the water used to wash the hands. See Elliott, *Ceremonies Explained for Servers*, 262, and Fortescue, O'Connell, and Reid, *The Ceremonies of the Roman Rite Described*, 421.

and prior to the Confirmations, the servers sharing the light from the Easter candle with those standing at the ends of each row as they move from the font to the sanctuary. All have their candles burning during the Confirmation rite, just like the candidates for Confirmation themselves have.

The celebrant stands before the people with hands joined to lead the renunciation of sin and renewal of baptismal promises with hands joined.[517] This may be at the entrance of the sanctuary where he just celebrated Confirmation, or before the altar,[518] or it may be at the chair.[519] Following the renunciation of sins and renewal of baptismal promises, the celebrant sprinkles all present with baptismal water, as described in chapter 5. During this time, or even after the sprinkling is completed if necessary, the deacon or other servers brings the remainder of the blessed water to the font in the baptistry, if Baptism took place in the sanctuary rather than the baptistry, and to the holy water stoups at the doors.

As a second possibility, the Confirmation of the neophytes could take place in the baptistry where they were baptized. In that case, after the presentation of the lighted candle, the celebrant immediately begins the rite of Confirmation as described above. Once the celebrant has confirmed all the neophytes in the baptistry, servers with tapers light the assembly's candles from the Easter candle near the font. Or, this may have already taken place as the procession *first* made its way from the sanctuary to the baptistry after the homily, the servers sharing the light from the Easter candle with those standing at the ends of each row as they move from the sanctuary to the font. In this case, all have candles lit during the entire baptismal rite, during the course of which the neophytes likewise receive a burning candle, and during the entire Confirmation rite. Once all the candles are lit, the celebrant stands before the people with hands joined to lead the renunciation of sin and renewal of baptismal promises for the assembly.[520] He does so while still standing next to the font in the baptistry, presuming this is in sight of the assembly. The celebrant then sprinkles all present, as described in chapter 5, beginning at the font in the baptistry and concluding at the sanctuary.

As a third possibility, when Confirmation has taken place at the font in the sanctuary, the renunciation of sin and renewal of baptismal promises can also take place there. In that case, after the presentation of the lighted candle, the

517 *CB*, 368.

518 Elliott, *Ceremonies of the Liturgical Year*, 149.

519 Mutel and Freeman, *Cérémonial de la sainte messe*, 339.

520 *CB*, 368.

celebrant immediately begins the rite of Confirmation as described above. Once the celebrant has confirmed all the neophytes, servers with tapers light the assembly's candles from the Easter candle near the font. Once all the candles are lit, the celebrant stands at the font in the sanctuary,[521] or before the altar, or at the chair, facing the people with hands joined, to lead the renunciation of sin and renewal of baptismal promises.[522] The celebrant then sprinkles all present as described in chapter 5, beginning at the sanctuary and concluding at the rear of the church. During this time, or even after the sprinkling is completed if necessary, the deacon or other servers brings the remainder of the blessed water to the font in the baptistry and to the holy water stoups at the doors. All bow to the altar whenever passing in front of it, or when departing or entering the sanctuary. The neophytes and their godparents are led to their places from the font in the sanctuary whenever the celebrant himself departs from the font at any given point.

The celebrant offers the concluding prayer to the sprinkling at the chair with hands joined.[523] The deacon instructs the assembly to extinguish their candles. The Creed is omitted. All remain standing for the general intercessions. A server holds the missal before the celebrant at the chair. The celebrant introduces the general intercessions with hands joined. He prays the final Collect with hands extended in the *orans* position, and then all are seated for the preparation of the gifts and the altar. Some of the neophytes may bring forward the gifts, either to the entrance of the sanctuary, or to the chair, or even to the altar itself. A master of ceremonies may accompany them to their left to guide them. All bow from the waist when passing before the altar, or when entering or departing the sanctuary. All make a bow of the head to the celebrant when approaching or departing from him.

2) *The Baptism of Infants Alone*

There may be pastoral reasons why infants might be baptized at the Easter Vigil instead of adults. For example, there may be no adults to baptize at Easter in a given year in a particular parish. Celebrating the Baptism of children at the Easter Vigil that year helps to maintain the fundamentally baptismal nature of the celebration. The provisions for the Baptism of infants at the Easter Vigil are found at number 28 of the introduction to the *Order of Baptism of Children*. That paragraph

[521] Elliott, *Ceremonies of the Liturgical Year*, 149.

[522] *CB*, 368.

[523] This Collect is found in no. 240 of the *Rite of Christian Initiation of Adults*. It is not found in form of the sprinkling rite indicated in the Roman Missal, Easter Vigil, nos. 56–58.

indicates that the usual rite of receiving the children, the prayer of exorcism, and the anointing with the oil of catechumens all take place on a separate occasion, prior to the Easter Vigil itself. The parts of the usual Liturgy of the Word from the Baptism rite are omitted, as are the assent of the celebrant and community after the profession of faith, the handing on of the lighted candle, and the ephphetha rite. Thus, the rite of Baptism for children at the Easter Vigil begins after the homily with the procession to the font.

As in the case of the Baptism of adults, the Easter candle itself leads the procession to the font located in the baptistry outside the sanctuary. The candle is carried by an instituted acolyte or server. In the procession, the families *follow* the celebrant and the deacon, according to historical practice.[524] One server carries the *Order of Baptism of Children*, unless it is already in place near the font. Another server carries the Roman Missal. Meanwhile, the litany of the saints is sung. All bow from the waist to the altar when passing before it, or when departing from the sanctuary as described above.

Once at the font, the acolyte or the server sets down the Easter candle, even on the edge of the font, or places it in a stand. All are invited to face the font. The celebrant first faces and addresses those present with hands joined. A server holds the ritual slightly to his left. Another server, holding the missal, also stands to the celebrant's left. Then, facing the font, the celebrant proceeds to bless the water according to the form proper to the Easter Vigil, as found in the missal.[525] See the description above for the first form of the blessing of the water. The master of ceremonies or the deacon fills a container with holy water for the sprinkling rite following the renewal of baptismal promises.

With hands joined, the celebrant faces the parents and godparents and leads them in the renunciation of sin, the profession of faith, and the request for Baptism. The celebrant baptizes each child by pouring water three times on the head, using the right hand, and saying the sacramental formula in the manner indicated in the ritual.[526] Historically, the celebrant pours the water over the head of the child in the form of the cross each time, making sure that the water flows across the bare skin.[527] The celebrant may also baptize by immersing the body of the child including the head, or at least only the head, three times, supporting the

524 *CB*, 440; Fortescue, O'Connell, and Reid, *The Ceremonies of the Roman Rite Described*, 425.

525 *RM*, Easter Vigil, no. 44–46.

526 *OBC*, 285.

527 Fortescue, O'Connell, and Reid, *The Ceremonies of the Roman Rite Described*, 425.

child with his right hand. In either case, the child is held by a parent.[528] The deacon stands to the celebrant's right holding the chrism taken from the ambry in the baptistry. The celebrant anoints each child on the crown of the head with chrism, using the thumb of the right hand with the fingers of the open right hand joined together but separated from the thumb. The celebrant cleanses his thumb with cotton balls before proceeding. The celebrant then says the formula pertaining to the white garment with hands joined while parents and godparents place the garments on the children. The presentation of the lighted candle and the ephphetha rite, normally part of the Baptism of infants on other occasions, are omitted when such a Baptism takes place at the Easter Vigil.[529]

All now return from the baptistry to the sanctuary and to their places as a processional chant is sung.[530] The ritual of infant Baptism can now remain in the baptistry; it will not be needed again during the course of the Easter Vigil. A server carries the missal from the baptistry to the sanctuary. Another server carries the holy water with its aspergillum. Servers and clergy follow the server with the Easter candle. Behind them process the celebrant with the deacon walking to his right, and finally the baptized children, their parents, and their godparents.[531] The servers and clergy take their places in the sanctuary, and the families of the newly baptized children return to their places in the nave.

Upon arriving at the sanctuary, the Easter candle is returned to its stand near the ambo. Meanwhile, servers with tapers begin to light the candles of everyone in the sanctuary and in the nave from the Easter candle in preparation for the renewal of baptismal promises. If they are seated, all stand to receive the blessed light. Alternatively, as the procession makes its way from the font to the sanctuary, the servers may share the blessed light from the Easter candle to those standing at the ends of each row as they move from the font to the sanctuary.

The celebrant stands before the people with hands joined to lead the renunciation of sin and renewal of baptismal promises.[532] A server holding the missal stands to his left. The server with the holy water also stands to the celebrant's left. As usual, the deacon stands to the celebrant's right. The celebrant may stand either the

[528] *OBC*, 285.
[529] *CB*, 365.
[530] *CB*, 366.
[531] *CB*, 445.
[532] *CB*, 368.

entrance of the sanctuary or before the altar,[533] or at the chair.[534] Following the renunciation of sins and renewal of baptismal promises, the celebrant sprinkles all present with baptismal water as described in chapter 5. During this time, or even after the sprinkling is completed if necessary, the deacon or other servers brings the remainder of the blessed water to the holy water stoups at the doors. Having completed the sprinkling of the assembly, the celebrant stands at the chair. The deacon directs all present to extinguish their candles. The Creed is omitted. All remain standing for the general intercessions. A server holds the missal once again before the celebrant at the chair. The celebrant introduces the general intercessions with hands joined. He prays the final Collect with hands extended in the *orans* position, and then all are seated for the preparation of the gifts and the altar.

The Baptism of children at the Easter Vigil may also take place at a font erected in the sanctuary. In that case, the children and their parents and godparents are called forward to the font after the homily. The litany of the saints is sung once all are gathered at the font rather than during a procession to the font in the baptistry. The Baptisms and explanatory rites are carried out as indicated above. The celebrant then continues immediately with the renewal of baptismal promises of all present. Servers light the candles of all present from the Easter candle in the sanctuary. Standing before the blessed water with the families of the newly baptized children,[535] the celebrant introduces the renewal of baptismal promises with hands joined. He then asks everyone to reject sin and profess their faith. He says the concluding prayer with hands joined as well. The deacon takes the vessel with newly blessed water for the sprinkling and hands the celebrant the aspergillum in his right hand. The celebrant then sprinkles all present as described in chapter 5, beginning at the font, or even at the altar if it is nearby, and standing at the entrance of the sanctuary or passing through the church, concluding at the rear of the church. All bow to the altar whenever passing in front of it, or when departing or entering the sanctuary. Once the sprinkling has begun, the newly baptized children, their parents, and their godparents are finally led to their places from the font.[536] During this time, or even after the sprinkling is completed if necessary, the deacon or other servers brings the remainder of the blessed water to the font in the baptistry, and to the holy water stoups at the doors.

533 Elliott, *Ceremonies of the Liturgical Year,* 149.
534 Mutel and Freeman, *Cérémonial de la sainte messe,* 339.
535 Elliott, *Ceremonies of the Liturgical Year,* 149.
536 *RM,* Easter Vigil, no. 57.

After sprinkling the clergy and the faithful, the celebrant and deacon return to their chairs. The deacon instructs all present to extinguish their candles. The Creed is omitted. Standing at the chair, the celebrant, standing with hands joined and facing the people, introduces the Prayer of the Faithful. The deacon offers the intentions in the usual way, and the celebrant prays the concluding Collect with hands extended. All are seated for the preparation of the gifts and the altar.

Some of the parents and godparents may bring forward the gifts, either to the entrance of the sanctuary, or to the chair, or even to the altar itself. A master of ceremonies may accompany them to their left to guide them. All bow from the waist when passing before the altar, or when entering or departing the sanctuary. All make a bow of the head to the celebrant when approaching or departing from him.

3) *The Baptism of Adults and Infants, and the Confirmation of Adult Neophytes*

At times, the unbaptized children of adult catechumens are baptized at the Easter Vigil along with their parents. The adaptations to the Easter Vigil Mass when children are baptized were discussed above. In general, whenever the Baptisms of adults and children are joined in the same celebration of the Easter Vigil, the usual order of events remains unchanged. However, at each stage, the celebrant first addresses the adult catechumens or neophytes before addressing the parents, godparents, and children. Thus, when children are baptized along with adults at the Easter Vigil, the following adaptations are made.

Before beginning the procession to the font, the adult catechumens are called forward first, then the parents, godparents, and children are called.[537] As described in the previous section, the parents, godparents, and children have historically followed *behind* the celebrant in procession to the font. When children and adults are baptized at the same liturgy, modern commentators have generally joined the children and their families to the procession of catechumens and godparents who walk *after* the Easter candle and *ahead* of the celebrant as indicated in no. 358 of the *Ceremonial of Bishops*.[538]

At the font, one server holds the *Rite of Christian Initiation of Adults*. A second server holds the *Order of Baptism of Children*. Both stand to the celebrant's left, side by side. The celebrant blesses the water according to any one of the three forms

537 *CB*, 357.

538 Elliott, *Ceremonies of the Liturgical Year*, 144, 150; Mutel and Freeman, *Cérémonial de la sainte messe*, 335, 338.

available in the *Rite of Christian Initiation of Adults* as described above. The deacon or the master of ceremonies sets some of the blessed water aside in a container for the sprinkling rite, which concludes the renewal of baptismal promises. Regarding the renunciation of sin, the celebrant first faces the catechumens with hands joined and addresses them as a group according to the form found in the *Rite of Christian Initiation of Adults*. Then he does the same with the parents and godparents of the children as a group according to the form of the renunciation of sin found in the *Order of Baptism of Children*. He repeats this for the profession of faith of the two groups. In the case of adult catechumens, however, he asks for the profession of faith individually from each catechumen, looking at each one as he addresses him or her. Each catechumen is baptized immediately after his or her profession of faith. In the case of the children to be baptized, he asks for the profession of faith from the parents and godparents as a group. He then proceeds to baptize the children one after the other, receiving the parents' consent in each case. The celebrant baptizes each adult or child by pouring water three distinct times on the head using the right hand, and saying the sacramental formula in the manner indicated in the ritual.[539] Historically, the celebrant has poured the water in the form of a cross each time.[540] The water poured should flow over the bare skin of the head; it may be best to avoid water flowing over the features of the person being baptized.[541] The celebrant may also baptize by immersing the body of the adult or child, including a portion of the head, three times. In either case, a child is held by a parent.[542] The celebrant, or one of the godparents, may then wipe the head of the newly baptized with a towel.[543]

After the individual celebration of Baptism, the explanatory rites of Baptism follow, with the following adaptations. The celebrant faces the children, and says the formula for the anointing with chrism once over the entire group. The deacon presents the chrism on the celebrant's right. Then, in silence, the celebrant anoints each of the children on the crown of the head with chrism, using the thumb of his right hand. He may then cleanse his thumb with cotton balls before proceeding. Afterwards, adults may be presented with a white garment, or this explanatory rite may be omitted.[544] Each of the children are presented with a white garment, as indicated above. Finally, the godparents of the adult neophytes

539 *OBC*, 285.

540 Fortescue, O'Connell, and Reid, *The Ceremonies of the Roman Rite Described*, 425

541 Fortescue, O'Connell, and Reid, *The Ceremonies of the Roman Rite Describe*, 425.

542 *OBC*, 285.

543 Fortescue, O'Connell, and Reid, *The Ceremonies of the Roman Rite Described*, 425.

544 *RCIA*, 229

each receive a candle lit from the Easter candle. The presentation of the candle and the ephphetha rite are omitted for children. The Confirmation of the adult neophytes, the renewal of baptismal promises of all the faithful present, and the sprinkling rite then follow as described above, either in the baptistry or in the sanctuary. There are no further adaptations to the rites of the Easter Vigil due to the presence of children to be baptized.

4) The Baptism and Confirmation of Neophytes and Confirmation of Candidates for Full Communion

The reception of baptized non-Catholics into the communion of the Church is intended to take place normally at a solemnity or on a Sunday apart from the Easter Vigil.[545] That rite of reception is described more fully in chapter 23. However, there will be occasions when such candidates join the neophytes to receive Confirmation at the Easter Vigil nonetheless, especially when some of the candidates are related to those who will be baptized. The details of this combined rite can be found at nos. 562 to 594 of the *Rite of Christian Initiation of Adults*.

If the Baptisms of the catechumens take place in the baptistry and the celebrant leads the renewal of baptismal promises from the font there as well, the candidates for full communion may join in the procession to the baptistry, led by the Easter candle as usual. After Baptism of the catechumens and explanatory rites, all remain at the font for the renewal of baptismal promises, provided the assembly can easily see and hear the celebrant from their places. After the presentation of the baptismal candles to the neophytes, servers with tapers light the assembly's candles from the Easter candle. Alternatively, servers may have lit the assembly's candles as the procession first made its way from the sanctuary to the baptistry, for example, the servers sharing the light from the Easter candle to those standing at the ends of each row as they move from the sanctuary to the font. Once all the candles are lit, the celebrant stands at the font with hands joined to lead the renunciation of sin and the renewal of baptismal promises.[546] Those to be received into full communion join in this renewal of baptismal promises.

Normally, the Sacrament of Confirmation is conferred in the sanctuary. Therefore, all return to the sanctuary from the baptistry in procession. All carry lighted candles in their right hands. The neophytes and their godparents immediately follow the server with the Easter candle. Behind them process the candidates for full

[545] *RCIA*, 487; National Statutes for the Catechumenate (USA), no. 33.

[546] Elliott, *Ceremonies of the Liturgical Year*, 149.

communion and their sponsors, servers and clergy, and finally the celebrant with the deacon walking to his right. One server carries the ritual for adult initiation, another carries the holy water, and a third carries the chrism for Confirmation taken from the ambry in the baptistry, unless the chrism is already located in the sanctuary. The celebrant then sprinkles all present as described in chapter 5, beginning at the font in the baptistry and concluding at the sanctuary. Meanwhile, servers bring some of the blessed water to the holy water stoups at the doors.

Upon arriving at the sanctuary, the Easter candle is returned to its stand near the ambo. If the stand for the Easter candle had been placed in the center of the sanctuary instead during the service of light and the Liturgy of the Word for some reason, the conclusion of the baptismal liturgy may be the time for the servers to move the candle and its stand to the ambo, or if this is not possible, to the left or Gospel side of the altar as one faces it from the nave.[547] Meanwhile, the neophytes with the godparents and the candidates for full communion and their sponsors stand in a row before the celebrant at the entrance of the sanctuary, facing the altar. Each godparent and sponsor has his or her right hand on the shoulder of his or her godchild or candidate. The celebrant and deacon stand at the entrance to the sanctuary, facing the assembly and the neophytes and candidates. The godparents and sponsors may take the lit candles from the hands of those to be confirmed. The celebrant, with hands joined, asks the candidates for full communion to make the statement of profession as a group. Then, the candidates with their sponsors each go to the celebrant, who receives them into full communion individually.

The celebrant may also lead the renewal of baptismal promises from the sanctuary, rather than from the baptistry, especially if this will promote the participation of those in the assembly. In this case, the candidates for full communion will not have joined the procession to the baptistry but will have remained in their places in the nave during the baptismal liturgy. At the conclusion of the baptismal liturgy, servers will light the candles of the assembly once the newly baptized have received their candles, as the procession makes its way from the baptistry to the sanctuary. Once all the candles are lit, the celebrant stands before the altar or at the chair, facing the people with hands joined, to lead the renunciation of sin and renewal of baptismal promises.[548] The celebrant then sprinkles all present as de-

[547] Mutel and Freeman, *Cérémonial de la sainte messe*, 313, n. 248; Elliott, *Ceremonies of the Liturgical Year*, 131.

[548] *CB*, 368.

scribed in chapter 5, beginning at the sanctuary and concluding at the rear of the church. During this time, or even after the sprinkling is completed if necessary, servers bring the remainder of the blessed water to the holy water stoups at the doors. All bow to the altar whenever passing in front of it, or when departing or entering the sanctuary. The sprinkling concluded, the neophytes with the godparents and the candidates for full communion and their sponsors stand in a row before the celebrant at the entrance of the sanctuary, facing the altar. Each godparent and sponsor has his or her right hand on the shoulder of his or her godchild or candidate. The godparents and sponsors may take the lit candles from the hands of those to be confirmed. The celebrant and deacon stand at the entrance to the sanctuary, facing the assembly and the neophytes and candidates. The celebrant, with hands joined, asks the candidates for full communion to make the statement of profession as a group. Then, the candidates with their sponsors each go to the celebrant, who receives them into full communion individually.

Finally, the Baptisms and renewal of baptismal promises may also both take place at the font in the sanctuary. Servers light the candles of the assembly after the neophytes have received their baptismal candles. The celebrant stands at the font in the sanctuary,[549] or before the altar, or at the chair, facing the people with hands joined, to lead the renunciation of sin and renewal of baptismal promises.[550] The celebrant then sprinkles all present as described in chapter 5, beginning at the sanctuary and concluding at the rear of the church. During this time, or even after the sprinkling is completed if necessary, the deacon or servers bring the remainder of the blessed water to the font in the baptistry, and to the holy water stoups at the doors. All bow to the altar whenever passing in front of it, or when departing or entering the sanctuary. The sprinkling concluded, the neophytes with the godparents and the candidates for full communion and their sponsors stand in a row before the celebrant at the entrance of the sanctuary, facing the altar. Each godparent and sponsor has his or her right hand on the shoulder of his or her godchild or candidate. The godparents and sponsors may take the lit candles from the hands of those to be confirmed. The celebrant and deacon stand at the entrance to the sanctuary, facing the assembly and the neophytes and candidates. The celebrant, with hands joined, asks the candidates for full communion to make the statement of profession as a group. Then, the candidates with their sponsors each go to the celebrant, who receives them into full communion individually.

549 Elliott, *Ceremonies of the Liturgical Year*, 149.

550 *CB*, 368.

Having received the candidates into full communion according to any one of the scenarios described above, the celebrant proceeds with the Confirmation of both the neophytes and the newly received while standing at the entrance to the sanctuary. A server with the ritual for adult initiation stands to the celebrant's left. The deacon holding the chrism stands to his right. Godparents and sponsors may hold their godchild's candle or candidate's candle in their own left hands for the duration of the ceremony. Each godparent and sponsor continues to have his or her right hand on the shoulder of his or her godchild or candidate. The celebrant offers the invitation to prayer with hands joined. He may close his eyes and bow his head for a moment. Then, with hands outstretched, palms open and facing downward over the entire group to be confirmed, he says the prayer "All-powerful God, Father of Our Lord Jesus Christ."[551] Then, if the Confirmations are numerous, the assembly may receive an indication to sit. The celebrant first begins with the Confirmation of the neophytes, and then the Confirmation of the candidates for full communion. The candidates for Confirmation may go to the celebrant individually, or he may go to them. If they are standing side-by-side in a line before him, the celebrant begins on his left and concludes on his right. He then anoints each of the neophytes on the forehead with the thumb of his right hand, making the Sign of the Cross. Historically, the minister of Confirmation placed the joined fingers of his right hand on the crown of each person's head while anointing the forehead with the thumb. After each Confirmation, the godparents or sponsors return the candle to their godchildren or candidates. The newly confirmed and their godparents and sponsors return to their places as each is confirmed, or after the entire group has been confirmed. All throughout the church then extinguish their candles.

Having finished confirming, the celebrant cleanses his hands. He may do so either standing at a credence table,[552] or at some other suitable place,[553] or standing at the chair,[554] or even seated at the chair with a gremial on his lap.[555] He may simply cleanse his thumb with lemons and bread or with cotton. Or he may more thoroughly wash and dry his hands as described above. The celebrant stands at the chair to introduce the general intercessions, with a server holding the missal standing before him. After the general intercessions, all are seated, and the Easter Vigil continues in the usual way.

551 *RCIA*, 234.

552 Elliott, *Ceremonies Explained for Servers*, 262.

553 Mutel and Freeman, *Cérémonial de la sainte messe*, 338; Fortescue, O'Connell, and Reid, *The Ceremonies of the Roman Rite Described*, 313.

554 Elliott, *Ceremonies Explained for Servers*, 202.

555 Elliott, *Ceremonies of the Liturgical Year*, 58.

5) The Renewal of Baptismal Promises Alone

If there are no Baptisms or Confirmations at all to celebrate, the baptismal liturgy is carried out in the following manner. As soon as the homily is concluded, servers can begin to light the candles of those in the sanctuary and those in the nave. The Easter candle remains in its stand; servers bring the blessed light to all by means of tapers. Once all have their candles lit, the celebrant and the deacon go to the location in the sanctuary where water has been prepared to be blessed. All bow to the altar from the waist when passing in front of it. Or, the lighting of the candles can be postponed until after the blessing of the water and just prior to the renewal of baptismal promises.[556] A server accompanies the celebrant and deacon with the missal. Another server holds the vessel to receive the blessed water and aspergillum. These items, along with a small pitcher to draw the water for the sprinkling, can also be placed on a credence table nearby.

A server holds the missal to the celebrant's left as he stands before the water to be blessed. The deacon stands to his right. The server holding the vessel for the sprinkling and the aspergillum stands to the deacon's right. Facing the assembly, the celebrant invites all to pray, with hands joined. All stand in their places, perhaps already holding a lighted candle at this point. The celebrant can close his eyes and bow his head for a time in silence. Then, with hands extended, he says the prayer of blessing found in the Roman Missal. In this case, the Easter candle is not lowered into the water, nor does he touch the water with his right hand. At the word "bless," he makes the Sign of the Cross with his right hand, his left hand resting on his chest, before continuing with hands extended once again.[557] The deacon or the master of ceremonies fills a vessel with the blessed water. If they have not already done so, servers now light the candles of all those present from the Easter candle.

Standing before the blessed water,[558] or in some other suitable place, such as the chair,[559] or before the altar,[560] or even at a lectern or at the ambo if necessary, the celebrant introduces the renewal of baptismal promises with hands joined. He then asks everyone to reject sin and profess their faith. He says the conclud-

556 Elliott, *Ceremonies of the Liturgical Year*, 149.

557 The indication to make the Sign of the Cross is missing in the text at no. 54 of the Roman Missal, the Easter Vigil. However, the Sign of the Cross is indicated at no. 2 of appendix 2 of the Roman Missal, where the same prayer of blessing can be found. No. 2 in appendix 2 also indicates that the prayer is said with hands joined. The order for the Easter Vigil at no. 54 indicates, rather, that the prayer is said with hands extended.

558 Elliott, *Ceremonies of the Liturgical Year*, 149.

559 Mutel and Freeman, *Cérémonial de la sainte messe*, 339.

560 Elliott, *Ceremonies of the Liturgical Year*, 149.

ing prayer with hands joined as well. A server holds the vessel with blessed water for the sprinkling. The deacon hands the celebrant the aspergillum in his right hand. The sprinkling takes place according to the description in chapter 5. During this time, or even after the sprinkling is completed if necessary, the deacon or other server brings the remainder of the blessed water to the font in the baptistry, and to the holy water stoups at the doors.

After sprinkling the clergy and faithful, the celebrant and deacon return to the chair. All extinguish their candles. The Creed is omitted because of the renewal of baptismal promises. At the chair, the celebrant, standing with hands joined and facing the people, introduces the Prayer of the Faithful. The deacon offers the intentions in the usual way, and the celebrant prays the concluding Collect with hands extended. All are seated for the preparation of the gifts and the altar.

6) The Reception and Confirmation of Candidates for Full Communion

The reception of baptized non-Catholics into the communion of the Church is intended to take place normally on a solemnity or on a Sunday apart from the Easter Vigil.[561] At times, however, when there are no adults or infants to baptize in given year, some parishes choose to celebrate the reception of baptized non-Catholic candidates into the full communion of the Catholic Church at the Easter Vigil by a profession of faith and Confirmation. This is a circumstance which is not described in any of the liturgical books. However, its outline can be deduced from the previous scenarios which are in fact described in the ritual.

Since there are no adults or children to baptize, the blessing of water takes place in the sanctuary after the homily as described above, according to the prayer of blessing found in the missal. Servers with tapers light the candles of the assembly from the Easter candle in the sanctuary, either immediately after the homily and before the blessing of water, or immediately after the blessing of water and before the renewal of baptismal promises. A server with the missal stands to the celebrant's left for the blessing and what follows. After the blessing of the water, the candidates are called forward and stand with their sponsors across the front of the sanctuary in order to make the renunciation of sin and profession of faith with all those assembled. The celebrant leads all in making the renunciation of sin and the profession of faith according to the formula found in the missal for the Easter Vigil. He may stand at the chair, or at the font, or at the center of the sanctuary before the

[561] *RCIA*, 487–98; National Statutes for the Catechumenate (USA), no. 33.

altar, or even at the ambo to do so. Their sponsors place their right hands on the shoulders of the candidates. All are standing with lighted candles in their hands. Following the renewal of baptismal promises, the celebrant moves through the church, sprinkling all with blessed water as described in chapter 5. He may begin at the font in the sanctuary, or even before the altar.

Upon returning to the entrance of the sanctuary, the celebrant stands before the candidates. The sponsors may now take their candidates' candles into their left hands for the duration of the act of reception and rite of Confirmation. A server now holds the *Rite of Christian Initiation of Adults* before the celebrant, slightly to his left. With hands joined, the celebrant reads the words of invitation and invites the candidates to make their profession as a group. Then the candidates and sponsors each go to the celebrant, who receives them individually, reciting the required formula. They return to their places before the sanctuary.

The deacon now holds the chrism while standing at the celebrant's right. A server holds the ritual for adult initiation to the celebrant's left. After the invitation to prayer for Confirmation, the celebrant, with hands outstretched over the entire group of the newly received, says the prayer "All-powerful God, Father of Our Lord Jesus Christ."[562] If the number of Confirmations will be numerous, the assembly may be seated. The celebrant then anoints each of the candidates on the forehead with the thumb of his right hand, making the Sign of the Cross. Afterwards, they and their sponsors return to their seats in the nave, either individually or as a group. All extinguish their candles and are seated.

Standing at a credence table, or standing at the chair, or even seated at the chair with a gremial on his lap, the celebrant washes his hands, or cleanses the thumb with lemon and bread or with cotton. After washing and drying his hands, the celebrant, standing at the chair, introduces the general intercessions, with a server holding the ritual for adult initiation standing before him. He prays the concluding Collect with hands extended. Then all are seated, and the Easter Vigil continues in the usual way.

The Liturgy of the Eucharist

After the celebration of Confirmation, or after the sprinkling rite if there are no Baptisms and Confirmations, Mass continues with the preparation of the gifts and the altar. All bow from the waist to the altar when passing in front of it or

[562] *RCIA*, 590.

when entering the sanctuary. Some of the neophytes, newly received, parents, godparents, and sponsors may bring forward the gifts, either to the entrance of the sanctuary, or to the chair, or even to the altar itself. A master of ceremonies may accompany them to their left to guide them. All make a bow of the head to the celebrant when approaching or departing from him. The priests of the parish will often concelebrate together. See chapter 8 for the details regarding the concelebration of the Eucharistic Prayer.

At the conclusion of the Communion of the faithful, the Hosts that remain from the celebration of the Easter Vigil Mass are gathered into one ciborium at the altar and brought, covered and veiled, to the tabernacle which has been empty since the beginning of the Paschal Triduum. A server lights the sanctuary lamp and veils the tabernacle. Meanwhile, or even after Mass if necessary, the Hosts which have been reserved in the sacristy or other repository since Holy Thursday or Good Friday are brought to the tabernacle in the church without ceremony. A concelebrant or the deacon of the Mass, wearing a white humeral veil, and accompanied by two servers with torches on either side or by at least one server with a candle, brings the ciborium from the secret repository to the tabernacle in the sanctuary.[563] The vessels used for Communion are then purified as usual.

Alternatively, an ordinary minister may bring the ciborium from the secret repository to the altar first in the manner described above, just as Communion is concluding, to receive any Hosts which remain from Communion at the Easter Vigil Mass, thus eliminating the need for a second ciborium. At the altar, he genuflects. While kneeling, a master of ceremonies removes the humeral veil. The concelebrant or deacon then uncovers the ciborium and transfers any Hosts which remain from the conclusion of Communion of the Vigil Mass. He covers and veils the ciborium once again. Taking the ciborium in both hands, he brings the ciborium to the tabernacle. After placing the ciborium in the tabernacle, he genuflects and then closes and locks the door. A server lights the sanctuary lamp and veils the tabernacle. The vessels are then purified as usual.

Concluding Rites

Mass concludes with a solemn blessing, as indicated in the missal; the solemn blessing is obligatory on this day. The celebrant offers the proper solemn blessing either at the altar or at the chair. At the altar, he stands facing the assembly with the missal

[563] Mutel and Freeman, *Cérémonial de la sainte messe*, 340.

placed directly before him, at the center, with its bottom edge parallel to the edge of the altar. He extends and then joins his hands when greeting the faithful with "The Lord be with you." The deacon, with hands joined, invites those present to bow their heads. The deacon also bows his head and orients himself slightly toward the celebrant. Then, with hands outstretched over the people, palms facing down, the celebrant prays the invocations of the solemn blessing. All respond, "Amen," to each invocation. He joins his hands and gives the blessing with his right hand, his left hand resting on the altar, before joining his hands once again.

If the celebrant gives the solemn blessing standing at the chair instead, a server holds the missal directly before him or slightly to his left. If the chair is perpendicular to the altar, the celebrant will turn toward the assembly to greet them and extend his hands over them. He will look to his left to read the invocations from the missal. The server holding the missal remains in the same position throughout the entire time the celebrant prays the Post-Communion prayer and the solemn blessing. He does not change position as the celebrant does. At the chair, when imparting the blessing with his right hand, the celebrant's left hand rests on his chest.

After the final blessing of the faithful, the deacon sings the dismissal. Every effort should be made for the deacon, or one of the concelebrants, or the celebrant himself to sing the proper dismissal formula, provided that those present are capable of responding in song. A server may hold the missal or a card with the musical notation before the deacon so that the dismissal can more easily be sung. All depart in the usual way. In this procession, the processional cross and the processional candles lead the way. As usual, the censer and the Gospel book are not carried out in procession.[564]

After all have departed, the Blessed Sacrament that remained in the secret repository since the end of the Triduum can be brought to the tabernacle in the sanctuary without ceremony if this was not done earlier. The Easter candle is extinguished last among all the candles to be extinguished. On successive days of the Easter season, the Easter candle is always lit first at any significant liturgical celebration.

[564] Mutel and Freeman, *Cérémonial de la sainte messe*, 181, 209, n. 80.

19

Easter Sunday and the Sundays of the Easter Season

Easter Sunday and Its Octave

If water blessed the night before at the Easter Vigil is available, the celebrant should use this water for the sprinkling rite on Easter Sunday.[565] In that case, the prayer of blessing of the water is omitted, since it is superfluous. In his invitation to the sprinkling rite for this instance, the celebrant will modify the text in order to refer to giving thanks for the water which has already been blessed rather than directing the faithful to ask God to bless the water. If for some reason the Easter Vigil was not celebrated in the same church the night prior to Easter Sunday, the celebrant will want to bless enough water at the beginning of Mass for both the sprinkling rite and the devotion of the faithful, using the special form of the blessing designated for the Easter season. For a description of the sprinkling rite, see chapter 5.

On Easter Sunday, all remain seated after the second reading while the sequence is sung. Then all stand for the Alleluia. In the same manner, the sequence "Victimae Paschale Laudes" can be sung every day of the octave, including the following Sunday, prior to the Gospel Acclamation.

On Easter Sunday alone, those present can profess their faith in one of three ways. After the homily, they can stand to recite or sing the Nicene Creed as usual. Or, they can profess the Apostles' Creed, as the Roman Missal suggests: "Instead of the Niceno-Constantinopolitan Creed, especially during Lent and Easter Time, the baptismal Symbol of the Roman Church, known as the Apostles' Creed, may

[565] Congregation for Divine Worship, Circular Letter *Paschalis sollemnitatis* (January 16, 1988), no. 97, *Notitiae* 24 (1988): 104.

be used."[566] Or, in the United States, they can respond to the same renewal of baptismal promises as the one found in no. 55 of the missal for the Easter Vigil. In that case, the celebrant stands at the chair, facing the people, with hands joined to conduct the renewal of baptismal promises. A server stands before him with the missal. If the sprinkling with water did not already take place at the beginning of Mass, it may follow the renewal of baptismal promises.[567] Otherwise, after the prayer which concludes the renewal of baptismal promises, the celebrant immediately introduces the Prayer of the Faithful from the chair, with hands joined. A server holds the missal before his eyes. From this point on, Mass continues in the usual way.

On Easter Sunday, and on every day of the Easter Octave, concluding the following Sunday, every effort should be made for the deacon, or one of the concelebrants, or the celebrant himself to sing the proper dismissal formula, provided that those present are capable of responding in song. A server may hold before the deacon the missal, or a card with the musical notation, so that the dismissal can more easily be sung.

The Sundays of Easter

As the missal points out, "On Sundays, especially of Easter Time, the blessing and sprinkling of water as a memorial of Baptism may take place from time to time in all churches and chapels, even in Masses anticipated on Saturday evenings."[568] See chapter 5 for the description of the sprinkling rite. Likewise, the missal suggests that the Sundays and solemnities of the Easter season are appropriate occasions to use the Apostles' Creed instead of the Nicene Creed.

The Extended Vigil of Pentecost

In the editions of the Roman Missal prior to 1962, the eve of Pentecost included a full baptismal vigil very similar to, but not identical to, the Easter Vigil. Since the publication of the third edition of the missal in 2002, it is possible to celebrate the Liturgy of the Word either in the usual manner or in an extended vigil once again. The extended Liturgy of the Word at the Vigil of Pentecost comprises a

[566] *RM*, Order of Mass, no. 19.

[567] Peter J. Elliott, *Ceremonies of the Liturgical Year According to the Modern Roman Rite: A Manual for Clergy and All Involved in Liturgical Ministries* (San Francisco: Ignatius Press, 2002), 156; Peter J. Elliott, *Ceremonies Explained for Servers According to the Roman Rite: A Manual for Altar Servers, Acolytes, Sacristans, and Masters of Ceremonies* (San Francisco: Ignatius Press, 2019), 245.

[568] *RM*, appendix 2, no. 1.

series of four readings from the Law and the Prophets, along with four corresponding psalms, an epistle, a Gospel Acclamation, and a Gospel passage. The four readings and four psalms are found in a published supplement to the current edition of the lectionary, which includes only the four readings and one psalm. In the extended form of the Vigil of Pentecost, the four Old Testament readings are preceded by the usual entrance chant for Mass, the opening rites, the penitential act, and a Collect, as well as an invitation to the readings, much like the invitation which introduces the readings at the Easter Vigil. Each of the four readings is followed by a responsorial psalm and Collect, similar to the pattern of the Old Testament readings at the Easter Vigil. It is possible to replace each responsorial psalm with silence, concluding with the Collect nonetheless. Then, as at the Easter Vigil, after the Gloria and the Collect of the Mass, the epistle follows without any responsorial psalm. The Alleluia and its verse immediately introduce the Gospel reading.

After the initial Collect of the extended vigil, the celebrant, standing at the chair with the missal held directly before him, faces the assembly, and with hands joined reads the invitation to listen to the readings which follow. After the conclusion of the first of the readings, and perhaps its psalm, the celebrant stands at the chair and turns to the faithful to say, "Let us pray," with hands joined. Then facing the missal held directly in front of him by a server, he prays the Collect. The celebrant then sits for the next reading. The celebrant prays a Collect in the same way after the second and third readings. After the Collect that concludes the fourth Old Testament reading, he remains standing for the Gloria and the Collect of the Mass. The celebrant is seated for the epistle which follows, but stands once again when all begin to sing the Alleluia. Then Mass continues in the usual way.

If Baptisms and Confirmations of neophytes or the Baptisms of infants are celebrated at the Vigil Mass of Pentecost, those rites are described in chapter 22, "Baptism of Children," and chapter 23, "Christian Initiation of Adults." After the celebration of Baptism and Confirmation of adults, or after the celebration of the Baptism of infants, the Creed is omitted, and Mass continues with the Prayer of the Faithful. In both cases, Mass then continues with the preparation of the gifts and the altar.

Unlike the Mass on Pentecost Day, the Mass for the Vigil of Pentecost does not include the sequence after the second reading.

Pentecost Day

As for the Mass of Easter Day, all remain seated for the sequence which follows the second reading on Pentecost. After the conclusion of the sequence, all stand as the Alleluia is sung.

On Pentecost Sunday, every effort should be made for the deacon, or one of the concelebrants, or the celebrant himself to sing the proper dismissal formula, provided that those present are capable of responding in song. A server may hold before the deacon the missal, or a card with the musical notation, so that the dismissal can more easily be sung.

20

The Solemnity of the Body and Blood of the Lord

THE PROCESSION WITH the Blessed Sacrament exposed in the monstrance often begins immediately following Mass on Corpus Christi. In that case, in addition to everything usually needed for the celebration of Mass, the following items must also be prepared:[569]

On the credence table:

- On the paten, a second host to be consecrated for the procession, unless this second host will be consecrated directly in the lunette
- The empty lunette to receive the consecrated Host
- The monstrance for the procession, veiled in white
- Two censers with burning coals, stands, incense boat
- A white humeral veil

In a convenient place:

- Four or six torches
- Hand candles for all those present
- A white cope for the procession, if the celebrant so chooses
- Copes for the priests in the procession who are not concelebrants
- The baldachin (optional)

[569] *CB*, 388, 390.

At the place where the final benediction is given:

- The custodia to receive the lunette
- A veil for the monstrance
- A burse for the corporal on the right-hand side of the altar
- *Holy Communion and Worship of the Eucharist Outside Mass,* or at least a card with the necessary prayers
- Handbells, if necessary

On the solemnity of Corpus Christi, the sequence "Lauda Sion" may follow the second reading and precede the Alleluia, according to the indications in the Lectionary for Mass. The sequence may be sung in its shorter form, or in its entirety, or omitted altogether. All remain seated while it is sung.

During the course of Mass, the host to be used for the procession is consecrated along with the hosts for the Communion of the faithful. Normally, it is placed in the lunette to be consecrated and brought to the altar with the other gifts at the preparation of the altar.[570] If the host to be consecrated is placed in the lunette from the beginning of the preparation of the gifts, the lunette is opened and closed by the deacon or the celebrant at the same time as the covers to the ciboria are removed and replaced. Alternatively, at the fraction rite, the Host consecrated at that Mass, on a paten along with the principal Host for that Mass, is placed in the lunette brought to the altar by a server.[571] In either case, the lunette containing the Host consecrated for the procession is left on the corporal during the entire time of Communion.[572] During this time, all genuflect whenever approaching the altar or departing from it, even at the side, as if the Blessed Sacrament were already exposed in the monstrance.[573] Naturally, those carrying the Blessed Sacrament in their hands during the time of Communion omit this sign of reverence.

During the time of Communion, a server brings the empty monstrance to the altar and places it off the corporal to the left, perpendicular to the front of the

570 Adrian Fortescue, J. B. O'Connell and Alcuin Reid, eds., *The Ceremonies of the Roman Rite Described*, 15th ed. (New York: Bloomsbury, 2009), 389.

571 Peter J. Elliott, *Ceremonies of the Modern Roman Rite: The Eucharist and the Liturgy of the Hours*, rev. ed. (San Francisco: Ignatius Press, 1995), 258.

572 Elliott, *Ceremonies of the Modern Roman Rite*, 258.

573 André Philippe M. Mutel and Peter Freeman, *Cérémonial de la sainte messe à l'usage ordinaire des paroisses suivant le missel romain de 2002 et la pratique léguée du rit romain*, 2nd ed. (Perpignan, France: Éditions Artège, 2012), 268.

altar. In many churches, the monstrance is brought to the altar veiled. The server genuflects and departs. A second server approaches the altar, genuflects, removes the missal and its stand, genuflects again, and departs. This server places the missal near the celebrant's chair. After the distribution of Holy Communion, any remaining Precious Blood is consumed at the altar. Any Hosts remaining after Communion are gathered into one ciborium at the altar and placed in the tabernacle. Any vessels used in the distribution of Communion are brought to the credence table to be purified over corporals.[574] Meanwhile, all in the sanctuary and in the nave take candles in hand. Servers assist in lighting everyone's candles in the sanctuary and in the nave while the purification of the vessels takes place. After the purifications have been completed, preferably at the credence table, the deacon, or the celebrant in his absence, goes to the altar and genuflects. First, he removes the veil from the monstrance and hands it to a server, who places it on the credence table. Next, he moves the monstrance onto the corporal, oriented perpendicular to the front of the altar, and opens the door to the monstrance. Then, he reverently places the lunette with his right hand into the monstrance and closes the door. He then reverently places the monstrance at the center of the corporal, facing the assembly, and genuflects and returns to his chair. If he is a priest, he genuflects with both hands resting on the altar outside the corporal. He if is a deacon, he genuflects with hands joined off of the altar.

The celebrant, standing at his chair, says the Post-Communion prayer there. It is not permitted to say the Post-Communion prayer standing at the altar on Corpus Christi.[575] The concluding rites are completely omitted. At this point, the master of ceremonies directs the servers to take their positions in the center aisle, facing the altar. In practice, however, it may be more helpful to have the cross bearer, candle bearers, and additional servers stand in their places in the center aisle *before* the Post-Communion prayer, while the purifications are taking place, so that they will be in the proper position for the procession in advance of the Post-Communion prayer. The torch bearers could be positioned at the same time, either across the front of the sanctuary, as they usually are, or, ideally, in two rows facing each other on either side of the sanctuary, provided they do not impede access to the altar. In that position, they can easily flank the celebrant carrying the Blessed Sacrament when he departs

574 Elliott, *Ceremonies of the Liturgical Year*, 104.
575 *CB*, 389.

from the altar.[576] Finally, it may be better for concelebrants to remain in the sanctuary so that each of them can kneel at a prie-dieu.

Still standing at the chair, the celebrant may set aside the chasuble and put on the cope for the procession. Then, the celebrant, the deacon, the master of ceremonies, and the two thurifers go before the altar steps, genuflect, and rise. Depending on the disposition of the sanctuary, they may face liturgical east or may face the assembly. All in the sanctuary and in the church, except the cross bearer and candle bearers, kneel. The celebrant turns to his right to face the two thurifers. The first thurifer gives the deacon the incense boat and spoon. Then the first thurifer faces the celebrant and presents him with the open censer. The thurifers elevate the bowl of the censer in their right hands so that the celebrant can stand erect to impose incense. The deacon offers the celebrant the spoon in his right hand while holding the incense boat in his left. He then transfers the incense boat to his right hand and holds it close to the bowl of the censer. The celebrant imposes incense three times on the burning coals, using his right hand. The celebrant blesses the incense in the right hand in the form of a Greek cross, saying nothing, with his left hand resting on his chest. The celebrant does the same for the second censer. The celebrant returns the spoon to the deacon, who receives it in his right hand. The deacon returns the incense boat and spoon to the second thurifer, who receives it in his left hand.

The celebrant then turns to his left in order to face the altar once again and kneels on the lowest step, as do the deacon, master of ceremonies, and two thurifers. From a kneeling position, the first thurifer gives the censer over to the deacon. The deacon places the rings of the chain in the left hand of the celebrant by using his own right hand. The deacon places the chains near the bowl of the censer into the right hand of the celebrant with his own left hand. The deacon may then hold back the edge of the celebrant's chasuble or cope with his left hand, his right hand resting on his chest. The celebrant elevates the bowl of the censer to a position slightly below eye level. The celebrant incenses the Blessed Sacrament in silence with three double swings, bowing before and after from a kneeling position.[577] All those kneeling with the celebrant bow from a kneeling position at the same time he does. The celebrant then returns the censer to the deacon, who returns it to the first thurifer. When all are in the proper position to begin the procession, the master of ceremonies stands behind the kneeling celebrant, places the humeral veil on

[576] Elliott, *Ceremonies of the Liturgical Year*, 104.

[577] *CB*, 91, 94..

his shoulders, and departs. The celebrant and deacon go up to the altar and genuflect there. The celebrant takes the monstrance in his veiled hands. If it is more convenient, the deacon may take the monstrance from the altar and hand it to the celebrant. Depending on which side of the altar the celebrant and the deacon stand, the deacon may now have to switch sides in order to be on the celebrant's right during the procession. The concelebrants and ministers stand from the kneeling position and then genuflect, as a eucharistic chant, for example "Pange Lingua" (excluding the last two verses), begins.[578] The procession is now ready to set off.

In the procession, the deacon walks to the celebrant's right. A server or a concelebrant may assist the celebrant, walking to his left, or a master of ceremonies may walk to his left. The torch bearers walk in two rows alongside the celebrant. They hold four or six torches in their outside hands, their inside hands resting on their chests. The two thurifers walk immediately in front of the celebrant, always facing forward.[579] Each holds the chain of the censer in his inside hand, his outside hand resting on his chest. The second thurifer holds the incense boat against his chest. The two thurifers walk in line with the two rows of concelebrants and servers ahead of them; they avoid walking directly in front of the Blessed Sacrament.

Thus, behind the cross and candles at the head of the procession walk the servers and then the concelebrants in two rows, then the two thurifers, with the celebrant with the deacon flanked by torch bearers on either side. The faithful, or at least a representative group of the faithful, walk behind the celebrant. The choir may be the first among them. All hold lighted candles in their outside hands. Those who do not join the procession remain kneeling until the Blessed Sacrament has left the church.[580]

If the procession to the repository passes outdoors, some churches maintain the use of the umbrellino, held over the celebrant by one server walking behind him, or even the use of the baldachin, held by four servers or four laypersons or even four concelebrants, with the celebrant walking beneath it and the torch bearers on either side.[581] In many locations, the baldachin or the umbrellino is used only for the portion of the procession that takes place outdoors. If a baldachin is used, those carrying it wait just outside the doors of the church.[582] The

578 Mutel and Freeman, *Cérémonial de la sainte messe*, 272.

579 Mutel and Freeman, *Cérémonial de la sainte messe*, 273, n. 133.

580 Elliott, *Ceremonies of the Liturgical Year*, 213.

581 Mutel and Freeman, *Cérémonial de la sainte messe*, 268, n. 122.

582 The use of the baldachin is optional according to no. 388 of the *Ceremonial of Bishops*.

celebrant and those assisting him walk under it as they emerge from the church. The torch bearers walk on either side of those supporting the baldachin. For the order of procession, see figure 8.

Normally, the procession on Corpus Christi begins in the sanctuary of one church and concludes in the sanctuary of a second church or a distinct chapel of the original church.[583] In some cases, it may only be possible for the procession to proceed outdoors for some distance before returning to the sanctuary of the same church. The procession is not intended to take place entirely within the walls of a single church. A eucharistic procession on public streets requires the permission of the diocesan bishop.[584] The procession may be arranged with stations at which the Blessed Sacrament rests on an altar and hymns and prayers can be offered. At these altars, the *Tantum Ergo* or some other eucharistic song is sung, the Blessed Sacrament is incensed from a kneeling position as usual, and the Collect is offered, perhaps preceded by the usual versicle and response. Strictly speaking, benediction should not be given. In the past, benediction at the stations was in fact tolerated if such was the custom, and it took place no more than twice during the procession.[585] Upon arriving at the location where the procession will conclude, those supporting the baldachin or the umbrellino allow the torch bearers and the celebrant with his assisting ministers to enter the church or chapel, while they remain outside.

Arriving at the sanctuary, cross bearer and candle bearers move together as a group to one side of the sanctuary and remain standing to face the altar in a row. The other servers and concelebrants part and remain facing each other on either side of the sanctuary. The torch bearers take their usual positions on either side of the entrance of the sanctuary in a single row, or in two rows facing each other in the sanctuary in front of the servers and concelebrants. The torch bearers kneel. The thurifers, celebrant, and deacon enter the sanctuary. The thurifers kneel side by side, to the celebrant's and the deacon's right. The celebrant places the monstrance on the corporal on the altar with its front facing the assembly. If it is more convenient, the deacon may receive the monstrance from the celebrant and position it on the altar with its front facing the assembly. Then the celebrant and the deacon genuflect together before the altar and kneel on the lowest step,

[583] *CB*, 393; *HCWEOM*, 107.

[584] *HCWEOM*, 101–102.

[585] Fortescue, O'Connell, and Reid, *The Ceremonies of the Roman Rite Described*, 387–388, 391.

as they did prior to the procession. The master of ceremonies, standing behind the celebrant, removes the humeral veil for the time being.

The celebrant allows time for all those who participated in the procession to arrive at the place of its conclusion and kneel. Once all have arrived in place, the schola can begin singing the last two verses of the "Pange Lingua." This will be the signal to the celebrant to begin the incensation of the Blessed Sacrament. Customarily, the Blessed Sacrament is incensed during the final verse of the hymn "Pange Lingua,"[586] that is at *Genitori genitoque*. Thus, during the preceding verse, *Tantum ergo,* it is customary to bow together from a kneeling position at the words *veneremur cernui*, after which the celebrant, the deacon, and the second thurifer rise in order to prepare the incense from a standing position.[587] After the incense is prepared and blessed as described above, the deacon hands the incense boat to the second thurifer. All kneel once again. The second thurifer can momentarily place the incense boat down on the altar step. The second thurifer hands the censer to the deacon. Using the right hand, the deacon places the chains of the censer in the celebrant's left hand. With the left hand, the deacon places the bowl of the censer in the celebrant's right hand. The celebrant elevates the bowl of the censer with the right hand to a position slightly below eye level. The Blessed Sacrament is incensed with three double swings from a kneeling position, bowing before and after incensing. The celebrant hands the censer to the deacon, who hands it to the second thurifer.

The hymn and the incensation concluded, the celebrant alone rises, without bowing. The ritual, *Holy Communion and Worship of the Eucharist Outside Mass,* or at least a card with the necessary prayers, can be placed near the center of the altar steps where the celebrant will kneel and stand. One of the servers, standing, holds the ritual or a card for him in both hands, preferably to his left, unless the celebrant knows the Collect from memory. With hands joined and bowing his head, he intones the Collect with "Let us pray." Then, with hands extended, he sings the Collect.[588] After the Collect, the celebrant kneels, and the master of ceremonies returns with the humeral veil and comes behind him to place it over his shoulders once again. The celebrant secures it in the front and stands to go up directly to the altar without any further reverence. It is often more convenient to give the blessing from the side of the altar closest to the assembly. The celebrant may also go around the

586 *CB*, 308; *RM*, Holy Thursday, no. 39.

587 Fortescue, O'Connell, and Reid, *The Ceremonies of the Roman Rite Described*, 299.

588 *CB*, 1113.

altar to face the assembly and give the blessing from there as well. As he approaches the altar, the celebrant may enfold his joined hands in the humeral veil in order to lift its edges and avoid tripping on it.

Once at the altar, the celebrant frees his hands, places them flat on the altar outside the corporal, and genuflects. The celebrant then covers his hands with the humeral veil once again to take the monstrance. Or, if it is more convenient, the deacon may accompany the celebrant to the altar, genuflecting simultaneously with him, and place the monstrance in the celebrant's veiled hands such that the front of the monstrance will be facing the assembly as the celebrant holds it. The celebrant can hold the monstrance facing forward, with the right hand at the node, and the left hand steadying its base, or he can take it at the node with both hands.

The celebrant turns to his right if he is not already facing the assembly. He makes the Sign of the Cross once over the people, saying nothing. Normally, the deacon kneels facing the celebrant to receive the blessing, whether at the altar or at his place at the foot of the altar, unless it is impossible to do so. The celebrant keeps his eyes fixed on the Blessed Sacrament throughout this action. He begins by raising the monstrance slightly above eye level.[589] He lowers the monstrance, with its base no lower than the table of the altar, and raises it again halfway, at about eye level. Turning to the left, not beyond his left shoulder, he makes a straight line to the right, again not beyond his right shoulder and not moving his feet.

During the time of the blessing, the thurifer may incense the Blessed Sacrament with three double swings, bowing from a kneeling position before and after. He may do so either at the center of the sanctuary steps, or from his place at the right-hand side of the altar.[590] If it is the custom, a server may ring the handbells three separate times during the course of the blessing. Historically, it was usual to ring the bells once as the celebrant turned to the people, once at the middle of the blessing, and once as he turned back to the altar.[591] If the celebrant is already facing the assembly when he imparts the blessing, perhaps this custom could be adapted. The server could first ring the handbells to accompany the raising of the monstrance for the blessing. The server could ring them a second time when the monstrance moves from the center to the left, and a third time when the monstrance moves from the center to the right. The thurifer incensing

[589] Elliott, *Ceremonies of the Modern Roman Rite*, 252.

[590] Elliott, *Ceremonies of the Modern Roman Rite*, 253.

[591] Fortescue, O'Connell, and Reid, *The Ceremonies of the Roman Rite Described*, 300.

the Blessed Sacrament could coordinate the swings of the censers with the three rings of the handbells during the blessing.[592] In some locations, all those present bow while kneeling at their places in order to receive the blessing. They may also sign themselves once with the Sign of the Cross.

Having completed the blessing, the celebrant returns the monstrance to the center and pauses, before turning to his right to the altar if necessary, completing the circle, lowering the monstrance to place it on the corporal, its front facing the assembly. Alternatively, the celebrant may hand the monstrance to the deacon now standing next to him at his right. The deacon repositions the monstrance on the corporal so that the front of the monstrance is once again facing the assembly.

After genuflecting at the altar, the celebrant and the deacon return to their places at the center of the sanctuary steps and kneel. The master of ceremonies removes the humeral veil from the kneeling celebrant. In some locations, the Divine Praises are said at this point before proceeding with reposition.[593] If not, the deacon can remain at the altar while the celebrant returns to the center of the sanctuary and proceed directly with reposition. Meanwhile, all begin singing a hymn, such as "Holy God We Praise Thy Name," or an acclamation as reposition is taking place.[594]

The deacon, or in his absence the celebrant, no longer wearing the humeral veil, begins reposition by placing the monstrance perpendicular to the front of the altar toward the left, yet still on the corporal. He moves the custodia which will receive the lunette onto the corporal and opens it. He then removes the lunette from the monstrance, places it in the custodia, and closes its cover. He closes the door to the monstrance and moves the monstrance off of the corporal to his left, still perpendicular to the front of the altar. He then takes the custodia in both hands and places it in the tabernacle in the sanctuary, genuflecting before closing the door and locking it. When the door to the tabernacle is closed or when the singing which accompanied reposition ends, all stand. In some churches, all begin singing a Marian antiphon at this point. The deacon may then return briefly to the altar, bowing when he approaches it and departs from it, to veil the monstrance, and to fold the corporal and place it in its burse. The burse is now placed at the center of the altar with its closed edge

592 Elliott, *Ceremonies of the Modern Roman Rite*, 253.

593 Elliott, *Ceremonies of the Modern Roman Rite*, 253–254.

594 *CB*, 1114; *HCWEOM*, 100; Elliott, *Ceremonies of the Modern Roman Rite*, 254.

facing the assembly. All genuflect in their places before the lowest step of the sanctuary before departing and return to the sacristy in the usual order.

Additional accommodations must be made if the Blessed Sacrament is normally reserved in a location outside the sanctuary where benediction just took place. After the blessing, or perhaps after the Divine Praises, the assistant deacon or the assistant priest receives the humeral veil from a kneeling position either at the altar or on the lowest step of the sanctuary. He goes up to the altar, genuflects before the Blessed Sacrament, and removes the lunette from the monstrance as described above. With the custodia containing the lunette and his hands covered by the ends of the humeral veil, he returns to the place of reservation, preceded by two of the torch bearers who served in the procession.[595] Upon returning to the sanctuary, the assisting minister gives up the humeral veil from a kneeling position. He may return to the altar to veil the monstrance and fold the corporal and place it in its burse. Then, all stand and bow to the altar and return to the sacristy in the usual way.

595 Elliott, *Ceremonies of the Modern Roman Rite*, 248.

21

All Souls Day (November 2)

MANY OF THE postures and gestures which were associated specifically with Masses for the dead in the editions of the missal prior to 1969 are now customarily incorporated into every celebration of Mass according to the Roman Missal of Paul VI. Thus, Masses for the dead have relatively few distinctive elements left when it comes to postures and gestures. However, a few such gestures still remain possible, and could be incorporated in the celebration of Mass on All Souls Day, November 2.

Mass for the Dead in General

According to the traditional practice of the Roman Rite, incense was not used during the entrance procession or to venerate the altar or at the Gospel.[596] If there is a Gospel procession at Masses for the dead, the deacon carries the Gospel book as usual, but the thurifer does not carry the incense, and the servers do not carry candles. Two servers accompany the deacon for the proclamation of the Gospel with hands joined and stand at the ambo facing each other during the proclamation of the Gospel.

At the Offertory, the gifts themselves, the altar cross, and the altar are incensed, in that order. First, the celebrant and then any concelebrants as well are honored with incense. Otherwise, the ministers and the faithful are not honored with incense. Two or four torches may be used at the Eucharistic Prayer, but not six.[597] At the elevations, the minister with the censer has customarily knelt at the

[596] Formerly, the use of incense at Masses for the dead was limited to the Offertory and to the two elevations. See Adrian Fortescue, J. B. O'Connell, and Alcuin Reid, eds., *The Ceremonies of the Roman Rite Described*, 15th ed. (New York: Bloomsbury, 2009), 157–159.

[597] Fortescue, O'Connell, and Reid, *The Ceremonies of the Roman Rite Described*, 158.

right-hand side of the altar, facing its opposite end, to incense both species at each elevation.[598]

As on other penitential occasions, the kiss of peace is not exchanged, according to the traditional practice of the Roman Rite.

All Souls Day

Apart from the variations mentioned above which are common to all Masses for the dead, there are no distinctive features to the celebration of Mass on All Souls Day. However, the *Ceremonial of Bishops* does mention the possibility of concluding Mass on All Souls Day with a procession to bless graves.[599] Obviously, this will only be possible if the cemetery in question is in close proximity to the church where Mass is celebrated. The following items need to be prepared in addition to everything usually needed for the celebration of Mass:

At the credence table:

- The vessel with holy water, and aspergillum
- The censer and incense boat
- A copy of the funeral ritual

In the sacristy or a suitable place:

- A cope in the color of the vestments of Mass on a stand

When the procession to the cemetery follows immediately, Mass ends with the prayer after Communion. The concluding rites are entirely omitted. The celebrant may offer the Post-Communion prayer at the chair or at the altar. He may join the procession vested in the chasuble, following the general rule that liturgical actions which immediately follow upon Mass permit the use of the chasuble. Or he may change from the chasuble into the cope, according to the general rule that the celebrant wears the cope for processions, especially those which take place outdoors.

When the celebrant prays the Post-Communion prayer at the chair, he may then change into the cope there if he wishes, leaving the chasuble draped over the chair. The deacon assists him. Remaining in the chasuble, or having assumed the cope, the celebrant then imposes incense for the procession while standing

[598] Fortescue, O'Connell, and Reid, *The Ceremonies of the Roman Rite Described*, 159.

[599] *CB*, 399–403.

at the chair. Having imposed and blessed the incense, the celebrant goes with the deacon to the altar, kisses it in the usual manner, makes the required reverence upon leaving the sanctuary, and then takes his place in the procession.

The celebrant may pray the Post-Communion prayer at the altar instead. Presuming he intends to remain in the chasuble, he imposes incense there, at the center of the altar, placing his left hand on the altar as he blesses it. Then, he and the deacon immediately kiss the altar as usual, and descend from the altar to make the required reverence either to the Blessed Sacrament reserved there or to the altar. Then they take their place in the procession.

Finally, the celebrant may pray the Post-Communion prayer at the altar, but may prefer to change from the chasuble to the cope. In that case, after praying the Post-Communion prayer, the celebrant and the deacon both kiss the altar in the usual way and go to the chair. There, the deacon assists the celebrant to change from the chasuble to the cope. Standing at the chair, the celebrant imposes and blesses incense, assisted by the deacon.[600] Then, the celebrant and the deacon go to the edge of the sanctuary to make the required reverence either to the Blessed Sacrament reserved there or to the altar, and join the procession.

The procession from the church then forms. It is led by the thurifer, followed by the cross and candle bearers walking together in a line. Then follow the server with holy water and the other servers and concelebrants, walking two-by-two. One server carries the funeral ritual closed, with both hands at the bottom. The celebrant, with the deacon walking to his right, follows the concelebrants. All the faithful follow the celebrant. The choir may be the first among them in order to lead the singing. The choir may sing various psalms indicated in the *Order of Christian Funerals*,[601] or the antiphons "May the angels lead you into paradise," "May the choirs of angels welcome you," or "Whoever believes in me."[602]

Upon arriving at the cemetery, if there is an altar there, those in procession make the usual reverence before it. If there is no altar in the cemetery, the depiction of Calvary sometimes found in cemeteries can serve as the focal point for the station which will take place. Lacking even this, the cross and candles of the procession can stand together in such a way that the celebrant can face them and those assembled in order to begin the station.

600 Peter J. Elliott, *Ceremonies of the Liturgical Year According to the Modern Roman Rite: A Manual for Clergy and All Involved in Liturgical Ministries* (San Francisco: Ignatius Press, 2002), 189.

601 *OCF*, 176D.

602 *OCF*, 176A, B, C.

Servers, ministers, and the celebrant bow to the altar or the Calvary or the processional cross upon arrival. The deacon, thurifer, and server with holy water stand to the celebrant's right. A server with the funeral ritual stands to his left. The celebrant begins by sprinkling the graves. The deacon hands him the aspergillum with his right hand. The celebrant receives the aspergillum in his right hand and sprinkles the grave, standing in one location and sprinkling three times, center, left, and right. Alternatively, he and the deacon may walk through a portion of the cemetery sprinkling the graves to the right and to the left as they go. In that case, the server with the holy water walks with the celebrant on his left, and the deacon walks on his right.

Then the celebrant incenses the graves. Depending on the length of the procession from the church to the cemetery, the celebrant may need to impose incense in the usual manner again upon arriving at the cemetery. The thurifer stands before him; the deacon assists him at his right as usual. The celebrant may incense the graves from a standing position, center, left, and then right. Or, he may walk through a portion of the cemetery, incensing as he goes with the deacon at his right. Another server may walk to his left.

After incensing the graves, the celebrant stands at the epistle side of the altar or before the Calvary. Lacking these, he may stand facing the processional cross as well as those present, and says, "Let us pray," with hands joined. Then, with the server holding the ritual before him, he prays one of the prayers from the *Order of Christian Funerals* with arms extended in the *orans* position. He blesses the assembly, facing them, in the usual way, and the deacon dismisses them, also while facing them. All in the procession bow to the altar, or the Calvary, or the processional cross, and return to the church in the same order in which they came.

Selected Sacraments and Sacramentals

22

Baptism of Children

The Baptism of children can take place either apart from Mass or during the celebration of Mass. The manner of joining the rite of infant Baptism to Mass is described in nos. 29 and 30 of the *Order of Baptism of Children*. A more detailed description is found in the appendix to the same rite, addressing the particulars of the Baptism of one child or several children. When infant Baptism is joined to the celebration of the Easter Vigil, additional adaptations must take place. Those are described in number 28 of the general introduction to the *Order of Baptism of Children*, and in chapter 18 of this work, "The Easter Vigil." The introduction to the *Order of Baptism of Children* itself says, however, that joining Baptism to Mass "should not happen too often."[603] This chapter will describe both contexts when Baptism can be celebrated, drawing on the traditional practice of the Roman Rite.

Prior to the celebration, the following items need to be prepared:

In the sacristy:

- White cope (optional) and stole for the priest if Baptism takes place apart from Mass[604]
- White dalmatic (optional) and stole for the deacon if Baptism takes place apart from Mass
- A copy of the *Order of Baptism of Children*

[603] *OBC*, 9.
[604] *OBC*, 35.

On a table near the font covered with a white cloth:

- The oil of catechumens, unless it is used in the sanctuary or omitted
- The chrism
- Cotton wool on a platter
- Baptismal candles
- White garments for the newly baptized, unless they are provided by the families
- A vessel for pouring the baptismal water
- Towels to wipe the heads of the children

In the baptistry:

- A lectern with a white antependium if the readings apart from Mass takes place at the font
- The Easter candle and stand, unless the Easter candle will be borne in procession from the sanctuary to the baptistry

Baptism apart from Mass

When Baptism is celebrated apart from Mass, the priest celebrant, the deacon, and the ministers may wait for the families at the door of the church. The rite of Baptism will begin there. Once all are in place at the door of the church, the celebrant begins with the Sign of the Cross and the liturgical greeting, followed by the particular greeting of the families indicated in the ritual. A server holds the ritual in both hands, slightly to the left of the celebrant. The celebrant faces them for this greeting and the questions which follow. After the questions and the reception of the children in the name of the Church, the celebrant traces the Sign of the Cross on the forehead of each child with his right thumb, the extended fingers of the right hand held together and separated from the thumb, his left hand resting on his chest. He then invites the parents, and perhaps the godparents, to do the same. If the number of children is very large, the celebrant makes the Sign of the Cross with his right hand once over all the children, his left hand resting on his chest. Then the parents or godparents trace the Sign of the Cross on the forehead of each child.[605] Following this, all process from the door of the church

[605] *OBC*, 111.

to their places in the nave or the sanctuary for the Liturgy of the Word. This procession may go directly to the baptistry for what follows instead. In that case, a brief Liturgy of the Word takes place at a lectern set up near the font.

The procession from the door of the church forms in the following order. The families with children take their place in the procession last of all, following the celebrant and the deacon.[606] Meanwhile the processional chant is sung or recited. The celebrant himself can read the texts indicated in the ritual for the processions from the door of the church to the ambo,[607] from the ambo to the font,[608] and from the font to the altar,[609] in the event there is no one to lead the singing. Eventually, all take their places in the church as the celebrant, deacon, and servers enter the sanctuary. The ministers make the usual reverence to the altar or to the Blessed Sacrament reserved in the sanctuary. Whenever passing in front of the Blessed Sacrament reserved in the sanctuary during the course of the rite, all genuflect before proceeding.[610] Otherwise, all bow to the altar whenever passing before it.

The readings are proclaimed from the ambo in the sanctuary. All sit to listen to the readings and to the homily. All stand for the Gospel passage, if one is chosen, for the intercessions, for the invocation of the saints, and for the prayer of exorcism. The celebrant introduces the proper Prayer of the Faithful, with hands joined, standing at the chair. Or, he may even have introduced the Prayer of the Faithful standing near the children and may remain there for what follows. The deacon offers the intercessions. After the proper intercessions, the invocation of the saints follows. For the prayer of exorcism and the anointing or imposition of the right hand which follows, the celebrant, if he had been standing at the chair until this point, now goes to the children for this portion of the liturgy, or they may be brought to him. A server stands to the celebrant's left, holding the ritual open to the proper page. The celebrant prays the exorcism with hands joined.[611]

Following the prayer of exorcism, the celebrant either anoints the children with the oil of catechumens or simply imposes his right hand on them. If he chooses to anoint the children, he first says the formula for the anointing once.

[606] Adrian Fortescue, J. B. O'Connell, and Alcuin Reid, eds., *The Ceremonies of the Roman Rite Described*, 15th ed. (New York: Bloomsbury, 2009), 425.

[607] Ps. 85:7–9ab, *OBC*, 42.

[608] Ps. 23, *OBC*, 52.

[609] *OBC*, 67, 225–245.

[610] The prescription to bow to the altar rather than genuflect to the Blessed Sacrament in the tabernacle whenever passing before both pertains specifically to the celebration of Mass. See *GIRM*, 274. This rubric is not found in any other liturgical book.

[611] Fortescue, O'Connell, and Reid, *Ceremonies of the Roman Rite Described*, 428.

A server holds the oil of catechumens to the celebrant's right if necessary. Another server stands to the celebrant's right with cotton wool on a tray for him to wipe his thumb. The celebrant dips the thumb of his right hand in the oil of catechumens. Using the thumb of the right hand with the fingers of the open right hand joined together but separated from the thumb, he anoints each child on the bare skin of the chest in the shape of a Greek cross, saying nothing. His left hand rests on his chest. He wipes his thumb on cotton to cleanse it. If there are many infants to baptize, the deacon may assist the priest in anointing them with the oil of catechumens. Instead of the anointing, the celebrant may impose his right hand on each child. In this case, he first says the corresponding formula once. Then he holds the fingers of his right hand together and imposes the open palm of his right hand on the head of each child in silence.[612] His left hand rests on his chest. Following the anointing or the imposition of the hand, the procession to the font begins.

During the Easter season when the Easter candle stands in the sanctuary, the candle itself leads the procession to the font, whether located in the sanctuary or in the baptistry. The candle is carried by an instituted acolyte or server. At other times of the year, the Easter candle already burns near the font. If a suitable server is lacking to carry the Easter candle from the sanctuary to the font during the Easter season, it may be necessary to locate the burning Easter candle at the font prior to the beginning of the Baptism, as is the case during the rest of the year.[613] Apart from the Easter season, two servers lead the procession to the font. Like the procession from the door of the church to the ambo at the beginning of the Baptism, the families with children take their places in the procession last of all, following the celebrant and the deacon once again.[614] Meanwhile, the processional chant is sung.[615] All bow from the waist to the altar when departing from the sanctuary. Once at the font, the acolyte or server sets down the Easter candle, even on the edge of the font, or places it in a stand.

If only one reading is to be proclaimed, for example, all might process directly to the font from the door of the church. The reading could be proclaimed from a lectern placed near the font while everyone stands to listen. In that case, the

[612] *OBC*, 51.

[613] Peter J. Elliott, *Ceremonies Explained for Servers According to the Roman Rite: A Manual for Altar Servers, Acolytes, Sacristans, and Masters of Ceremonies* (San Francisco: Ignatius Press, 2019), 124.

[614] *CB*, 440; Fortescue, O'Connell, and Reid, *The Ceremonies of the Roman Rite Described*, 425.

[615] *OBC*, 277.

reading and brief homily are followed by the intercessions, the invocation of the saints, and the prayer of exorcism, as does either the anointing or the imposition of the hand. All stand around the lectern and the font during this entire time. The Easter candle burns nearby.

Once at the font, after the anointing or the imposition of the hand, the celebrant first faces and addresses those present with hands joined. A server holds the ritual slightly to his left. Then, facing the font, the celebrant proceeds to bless the water or give thanks to water already blessed. According to the first form of the blessing,[616] the celebrant stands with hands extended.[617] At the point indicated, he touches the water with the open palm of his right hand, his left hand resting on his chest.[618] At the conclusion of the first form, celebrants in many locations make the Sign of the Cross with the right hand over the water, the left hand resting on the chest. If the second form of the blessing is used,[619] the celebrant prays with hands joined. Again, if using this form as a blessing, and not as a thanksgiving over the water, celebrants in many locations conclude the formula with the Sign of the Cross while saying nothing. In the third form of the blessing, the celebrant prays with hands joined.[620] At the place indicated, he makes the Sign of the Cross with the right hand, the left hand resting on the chest, and joins his hands to conclude. During the Easter season when using the second or third forms as prayers of thanksgiving over water already blessed at the Easter Vigil, the celebrant prays with hands joined throughout.

With hands joined, the celebrant faces the parents and godparents and leads them in the renunciation of sin, the profession of faith, and the request for Baptism. The celebrant baptizes each child by pouring water three distinct times on the head, using the right hand, and saying the sacramental formula in the manner indicated in the ritual.[621] Historically, the celebrant has poured the water in the form of a cross each time.[622] The water poured should flow over the bare skin of the head; it may be best to avoid water flowing over the features of the child.[623]

[616] *OBC*, 54.

[617] André Philippe M. Mutel and Peter Freeman, *Cérémonial de la sainte messe à l'usage ordinaire des paroisses suivant le missel romain de 2002 et la pratique léguée du rit romain*, 2nd ed. (Perpignan, France: Éditions Artège, 2012), 336.

[618] Fortescue, O'Connell, and Reid, *The Ceremonies of the Roman Rite Described*, 365.

[619] *OBC*, 223.

[620] *OBC*, 224.

[621] *OBC*, 285.

[622] Fortescue, O'Connell, and Reid, *The Ceremonies of the Roman Rite Described*, 425

[623] Fortescue, O'Connell, and Reid, *The Ceremonies of the Roman Rite Described*, 425.

The celebrant may also baptize by immersing the child, including a portion of the head, three times, supporting the child with his right hand. In either case, the child is held by a parent.[624] The celebrant, or one of the godparents, may then wipe each child's head with a towel.[625]

With hands joined, the celebrant says the prayer "Almighty God, the Father of Our Lord Jesus Christ," once. Then in silence, he anoints each child on the bare skin of the crown of the head with chrism, using the thumb of the right hand with the fingers of the open right hand joined together but separated from the thumb. His left hand rests on his chest. The deacon stands to the celebrant's right, holding the chrism. The celebrant then wipes his thumb with cotton to cleanse it. If the children are numerous, the deacon may assist the celebrant in anointing them. With hands joined, the celebrant then says the formula pertaining to the white garment while parents and godparents place the garment on the children.

The deacon then takes the Easter candle from its stand or from a server. The celebrant receives the Easter candle in both hands from the deacon and invites a member of each family forward to light a baptismal candle from the Easter candle. Alternatively, if this is more convenient, the deacon holds the Easter candle in his own hands so that the celebrant can light the baptismal candles from it and present them to each family.[626] If the Easter candle is too heavy or too tall for either of these options, the celebrant may simply take a long taper, receive the flame from the Easter candle, and light the baptismal candles held by the family members with the taper. Once all the families have received a lighted candle, the celebrant addresses the parents and godparents with hands joined. If he celebrates the ephphetha rite, the celebrant uses the thumb of his right hand to touch the ears and mouth of each child while saying the formula, his left hand resting on his chest.[627] Or, if the children are numerous, he may say the formula once, omitting the touching of the ears and mouth.[628] If there are a very large number of children, the ephphetha rite is omitted entirely.[629]

During the Easter season, the Easter candle, held by an instituted acolyte or server, leads the way from the baptistry to the sanctuary, and then is placed in its

[624] *OBC*, 285.

[625] Fortescue, O'Connell, and Reid, *The Ceremonies of the Roman Rite Described*, 425.

[626] Mutel and Freeman, *Cérémonial de la sainte messe*, 337, n. 316; Fortescue, O'Connell, and Reid, *The Ceremonies of the Roman Rite Described*, 426.

[627] *OBC*, 65.

[628] *OBC*, 66.

[629] *OBC*, 127.

stand in the sanctuary. Otherwise, servers, two by two, lead the way. The lighted candles are carried for the baptized children. Once again, the families follow the celebrant, with the deacon to his right, back to the sanctuary. Upon arrival there, the families stand facing the altar for the Our Father and the solemn blessing. The celebrant may stand before the altar or at his chair in order to face the families for the conclusion to the rite of Baptism. All genuflect to the Blessed Sacrament reserved in the sanctuary whenever passing before it. At the end of the rite of Baptism, the celebrant imparts the solemn blessing. A server stands before him or to his left, depending on the circumstances, holding the ritual in both hands. The celebrant extends and then immediately joins his hands to greet those present, saying, "The Lord be with you." With hands joined, the deacon invites them to bow their heads. Then the celebrant extends and then joins his hands when greeting the faithful with "The Lord be with you." The deacon, with hands joined, invites those present to bow their heads. Then, with hands outstretched over the parents of the children, palms facing down, the celebrant prays the first invocation of the solemn blessing over the mothers, the second invocation over the fathers, and the third invocation over the entire assembly.[630] The manner in which the celebrant extends his hands to bestow the final blessing should reflect this. Depending on the disposition of the parents and the assembly before him, he should direct his hands toward those to whom each particular invocation refers. Then to impart the blessing itself, the celebrant first joins his hands, and gives the blessing as usual with his right hand, his left hand resting on his chest. The deacon, with hands joined, dismisses those present. After the dismissal by the deacon, the priest celebrant and ministers depart from the sanctuary, bowing to the altar or genuflecting to the Blessed Sacrament reserved in the sanctuary, depending on the circumstances.

Baptism Joined to Mass

Whenever Baptism is celebrated during the course of the celebration of the Eucharist, the proper ritual Mass "For the Conferral of Baptism," provided in the Roman Missal, should be used. White vestments are worn. This will only be possible on days when ritual Masses in general are permitted, however. The ritual Mass for Baptism is permitted on Sundays in Ordinary Time and on the Sundays of Christmas (except Epiphany, when this is observed on a Sunday). The ritual

[630] *OBC*, 70.

Mass for Baptism is not permitted on the Sundays of Advent, Lent, or Easter, or on solemnities which may fall on a Sunday. Even when the ritual Mass for Baptism is not permitted, the rite of Baptism itself can still be carried out during the course of Mass, without using the texts for the Mass "For the Conferral of Baptism."[631] This poses no problem when the vestments for the Mass in question are white, as would normally be the case for the celebration of Baptism. A problem arises when the vestments of the Mass in question, as on a Sunday of Advent or on Pentecost for example, are not white. Although the preparatory rites for Baptism were historically celebrated in violet vestments, Baptism itself was always celebrated in white or festive vestments. Nothing in the *Order of Baptism of Infants* describes what should be done when the proper Mass of the day prescribes vestments of a color other than white. The traditional practice of the Roman Rite can help provide some guidance on this question.

There is ample historical precedent for celebrating the preparatory rites of Baptism up to and including the blessing of the water and renunciation of sin in purple vestments.[632] White vestments were worn beginning with the profession of faith through the conclusion of the baptismal ceremony. Thus, if Mass is being offered in purple vestments, the celebrant might remove the chasuble at the chair before introducing the intercessions for Baptism. Then, at the font, he would remove the purple stole after the renunciation of sin and put on a white stole for the profession of faith and everything that follows. After the conferral of the baptismal candle, he could replace the white stole with a purple stole once again, and resume the chasuble upon arriving at the chair and before beginning the preparation of the gifts and the altar. When offering Mass in red vestments, it may be simplest to remove both the chasuble and the stole prior to introducing the proper intercessions for Baptism, and taking the white stole at that point. After handing over the baptismal candle to the parents and godparents, and before proceeding with the preparation of the gifts and the altar, the celebrant replaces the white stole with the stole and chasuble of the color of the Mass of the day.

It must be noted that the Roman Missal of Paul VI consistently avoids frequent change of vestments during the celebration of Mass.[633] A celebrant might exchange a cope for a chasuble or vice versa at the beginning or conclusion of a Mass

631 *OBC*, 252.

632 Fortescue, O'Connell, and Reid, *The Ceremonies of the Roman Rite Described*, 368, 425.

633 When the Baptism of infants takes place during Mass celebrated in white vestments, there is no need to remove the chasuble at any point, according to the principle in the revised rites that the chasuble can be worn for those sacraments which take place during Mass.

involving a procession, as on the Presentation of the Lord, Palm Sunday, and Corpus Christi. At the dedication of an altar, the bishop removes the chasuble for the anointings of the altar and the walls. On Holy Thursday, the celebrant removes the chasuble for the washing of the feet. Otherwise, the missal does not indicate any change of vestments on any other occasions. Given this consistent bias again changing vestments during the course of the celebration of the Eucharist, pastors may want to celebrate the Baptism of infants apart from Mass on the days when the ritual Mass "For the Conferral of Baptism" is not permitted or when white vestments are not worn. Otherwise, there are many liturgical and practical reasons to commend the celebration of infant Baptism during Mass only on those Sundays when white vestments are worn or when the ritual Mass "For the Conferral of Baptism" can be celebrated in white vestments.

When Baptism is joined to the celebration of Mass, while the proper entrance chant from the missal or the Roman Gradual is sung, the celebrant, deacon, and servers make their way in the usual manner from the sacristy to the door of the church where the families with infants are waiting.[634] The procession may make its way to the main door of the church, or even a side door of the church, if this will promote the participation of the faithful. Once all are in place at the door of the church, the celebrant begins with the Sign of the Cross and the liturgical greeting, followed by the particular greeting of the families indicated in the ritual. A server holds the ritual in both hands, slightly to the left of the celebrant. The celebrant faces the families for this greeting and the questions which follow. After the questions and the reception of the children in the name of the Church, the celebrant traces the Sign of the Cross on the forehead of each child with his right thumb, the extended fingers of the right hand held together and separated from the thumb, his left hand resting on his chest. He then invites the parents, and perhaps the godparents, to do the same. If the number of children is very large, the celebrant makes the Sign of the Cross with his right hand over all the children, his left hand resting on his chest. Then the parents or godparents trace the Sign of the Cross on the forehead of each child.[635]

Following this, all process from the door of the church to their places either in the nave or the sanctuary for the Liturgy of the Word. The procession from the door of the church forms in the following order. The families with children take

[634] *OBC*, 257.

[635] *OBC*, 111.

their places in the procession last of all, following the celebrant and the deacon.[636] Meanwhile, the processional chant from the *Order of Baptism of Children* is sung. Eventually, all take their places in the church as the celebrant, deacon, and servers enter the sanctuary. The ministers make the usual reverence to the altar, or to the Blessed Sacrament reserved in the sanctuary. The celebrant and the deacon kiss the altar. The celebrant may incense the altar. On this occasion, the penitential act is omitted. Therefore, the Gloria, when required, follows the conclusion of the processional chant immediately, and then the celebrant prays the Collect.

The Liturgy of the Word takes place as usual. On days when the ritual Mass is permitted, as on the Sundays of Christmas or Ordinary Time, the Mass texts can be taken from the ritual Mass for Baptism and the readings can be taken entirely from the corresponding section of the Lectionary for Mass (nos. 756–760).[637] Or, during the Sundays of Ordinary Time or of the Christmas season, the proper Mass of the day with its readings can be retained. In that case, it is possible to substitute a reading from the lectionary for Baptisms for one of these appointed readings.[638] On solemnities and on the Sundays of Advent, Lent, and Easter when the ritual Mass for Baptism is not permitted, all the proper readings are required.[639] All sit to listen to the readings. After the homily, all stand. The celebrant introduces the proper Prayer of the Faithful from the ritual for Baptism standing at the chair, with hands joined. Or, he may even have introduced the Prayer of the Faithful standing near the children and may remain there for what follows. After the proper ritual intercessions, local intercessions may be added to these, especially at Sunday Mass. The deacon offers the intercessions. The invocation of the saints follows. The procession to the font and what follows take place as described above.

After the explanatory rites following the Baptism, the families once again follow the celebrant, with the deacon to his right, back to their places in the nave. During the Easter season, the Easter candle, held by an instituted acolyte or server, leads the way and then is placed in its stand in the sanctuary. Otherwise, servers, two by two, lead the way. The lighted candles are carried for the baptized children. Once the families arrive at their places in the nave, they extinguish the baptismal candles and sit.

636 Fortescue, O'Connell, and Reid, *The Ceremonies of the Roman Rite Described*, 425.

637 OBC, 29.

638 *CB*, 434.

639 *CB*, 434.

The profession of faith and general intercessions of Mass are omitted. Mass continues instead with the preparation of the gifts and the altar. All bow from the waist to the altar when passing in front of it or when entering the sanctuary. Some of the parents and godparents may bring forward the gifts, either to the entrance of the sanctuary, or to the chair, or even to the altar itself. A master of ceremonies may accompany them to their left to guide them. All make a bow of the head to the celebrant when approaching or departing from him. During the Eucharistic Prayer, there are proper inserts for the occasion for each Eucharistic Prayer. (See ritual Masses, "For the Conferral of Baptism.")

At the end of Mass, the celebrant may impart the solemn blessing from the *Order of Baptism of Children*. The celebrant offers both the Post-Communion prayer and the proper solemn blessing either at the altar or at the chair. In preparation for the solemn blessing, depending on the disposition of the seats in the nave, a master of ceremonies may direct the families of the newly baptized to come forward from their places in order to stand before the celebrant.[640] At the altar, the celebrant stands facing the assembly with the missal placed directly before him, at the center, with its bottom edge parallel to the edge of the altar. He prays the Post-Communion prayer with hands extended. Then, the master of ceremonies places the rite of Baptism of children before him, open to the solemn blessing. The celebrant extends and then joins his hands when greeting the faithful with "The Lord be with you." The deacon, with hands joined, invites those present to bow their heads. Then, with hands outstretched over the parents of the children, palms facing down, the celebrant prays the first invocation of the solemn blessing over the mothers, the second invocation over the fathers, and the third invocation over the entire assembly.[641] If the circumstances warrant it, the manner in which the celebrant extends his hands to bestow the final blessing should reflect this. Depending on the disposition of the parents and the assembly before him, he should direct his hands toward those to whom each particular invocation refers. All respond, "Amen," to each invocation. After the last invocation, the celebrant briefly joins his hands and then blesses those present in the usual way with his right hand, his left hand resting on the altar, before joining his hands once again. If the celebrant offers the Post-Communion prayer standing at the chair instead, a server stands before him, holding the missal in both hands. Another server stands next to the first, holding the Baptism ritual slightly to the

640 *CB*, 447.
641 *OBC*, 70.

celebrant's left. At the chair, when imparting the blessing with his right hand, the celebrant's left hand rests on his chest.

Having given the blessing, he joins his hands once again. The deacon, with hands joined, dismisses those present. After the dismissal by the deacon, all depart from the sanctuary in the usual order, having first bowed to the altar or genuflected to the Blessed Sacrament reserved in the sanctuary as the case may be.

23

Christian Initiation of Adults

The full initiation of adults by the reception of the Sacraments of Baptism, Confirmation, and First Communion is preceded by the period of catechesis known as the *catechumenate*. This period is marked by any number of liturgical celebrations. Some of these take place during Mass and others take place apart from Mass. This chapter will treat only two such rites. The first, the rite of acceptance into the catechumenate, generally takes place during Mass in most parishes, although it may take place apart from Mass.[642] Secondly, the three scrutinies of those elected for Baptism must take place during the course of Mass with their proper readings.[643]

Admission to the Catechumenate

The admission of the catechumenate takes place on a Sunday or a weekday when the inquirers are prepared to take this step. The Mass of the day with its readings can be used. Historically, the priest wore purple vestments for the rites connected with making catechumens.[644] Pastors may want to schedule the rite of admission to the catechumenate on a day during Advent or Lent. Or, outside of Advent or Lent, on the days when it is permitted, the celebrant might choose to offer the Mass for various needs and occasions entitled "For the Forgiveness of Sins," and might celebrate the rite of acceptance into the catechumenate then. The current ritual, on the contrary, directs the celebrant to wear a stole, and even a cope, "of

642 *RCIA*, 44.

643 *RCIA*, 146.

644 Adrian Fortescue, J. B. O'Connell, and Alcuin Reid, eds., *The Ceremonies of the Roman Rite Described*, 15th ed. (New York: Bloomsbury, 2009), 424–425, 428–429.

a festive color,"[645] when the admission to the catechumenate takes place apart from Mass. This indication suggests that the Easter or Christmas seasons are also appropriate times to celebrate the rite of admission to the catechumenate during Mass. Finally, on days when they are permitted, the pastor could arrange to offer the Masses for various needs and occasions entitled "For the Church," or "For Evangelization," and celebrate the admission to the catechumenate then, wearing vestments of a color which corresponds to the season in question.[646] The following description refers to the celebration of the rite of admission to the catechumenate during the celebration of Mass.

While the entrance chant is sung, the celebrant, deacon, and servers make their way in the usual manner from the sacristy to the location where the inquirers, their sponsors, and a group of the faithful are waiting.[647] This may be outside the church, or just inside or outside the doors to the church, unless some other location is more suitable. Thus, the procession may make its way to the main door of the church, or even a side door of the church, if this will promote the participation of the faithful. Once at the door and once the chant ends, the celebrant begins with the Sign of the Cross and the liturgical greeting as usual for Mass, followed by the particular greeting of the inquirers indicated in the ritual. The celebrant faces the assembly and those to be admitted with hands joined for this greeting and the questions which follow. A server stands to the celebrant's left, holding the ritual. After the questions and the reception of the inquirers in the name of the Church, the celebrant traces the Sign of the Cross on the forehead of each catechumen with his right thumb, the extended fingers of the right hand held together and separated from the thumb. He then invites the sponsor to do the same. If the number of catechumens is very large, the celebrant makes the Sign of the Cross with his right hand over all of them at once, his left hand resting on his chest. Then, the sponsors trace the Sign of the Cross on the forehead of each catechumen.[648] The signing of the senses by the sponsor, if observed, takes place in the same way. The celebrant then prays the concluding prayer with hands extended. Following this, the processional chant from the door to the nave and to the sanctuary begins.

The procession forms in the usual order. The catechumens and sponsors take their places in the procession last of all, following the celebrant and the deacon.[649]

645 *RCIA*, 48.
646 *GIRM*, 347.
647 *RCIA*, 48.
648 *RCIA*, 54B.
649 Fortescue, O'Connell, and Reid, *The Ceremonies of the Roman Rite Described*, 425.

Eventually, they take their places in the church as the celebrant, deacon, and servers enter the sanctuary. The ministers make the usual reverence to the altar or to the Blessed Sacrament reserved in the sanctuary. The celebrant and the deacon kiss the altar; the celebrant may incense the altar. They then take their places. The penitential act being omitted, Mass continues immediately with the Gloria, when required, and the Collect.

After the homily, the deacon offers the proper intercessions of the new catechumens with hands joined. The celebrant offers the prayer over them with hands outstretched, palms down, over the catechumens. The catechumens may remain in their places, or may stand before him, facing the celebrant and the altar. Then, looking at them, the celebrant dismisses them, with hands joined. Mass continues with the general intercessions and the Creed, unless it continues immediately with the preparation of the gifts instead for pastoral reasons.[650]

The Scrutinies

In exceptional circumstances there may be one scrutiny of those preparing for Baptism,[651] but normally there are three. These take place on the third, fourth, and fifth Sundays of Lent, with the readings from cycle A of the Lectionary for Mass appointed for those days and with the corresponding Mass texts from the ritual Masses "For the Conferral of the Scrutinies." Even when the scrutinies, for some necessity, take place outside of Lent on a day when ritual Masses are permitted, the proper readings and Mass texts are used. Violet vestments are worn, and the three scrutinies take place roughly one week apart from each other. Regardless of the circumstances or time of the year, all three scrutinies follow the same format, with the same gestures on the part of the celebrant.

After the homily, the elect with their godparents stand before the celebrant. They stand facing the celebrant and the altar. The celebrant stands either at the entrance of the sanctuary, or at the chair, or at the altar. With hands joined, the celebrant invites the elect to kneel or bow their heads. The deacon offers the intercessions for the elect with hands joined. Then, the celebrant prays the proper exorcism prayer with hands joined.[652] If it can conveniently be done, he lays both hands, palms open and flat, on the heads of each of the elect. Then, he prays with hands outstretched over them, palms open. With hand joined, he dismisses them. Mass

650 *RCIA*, 68.
651 *RCIA*, 34
652 *RCIA*, 154, 168, 178.

continues with the Universal Prayer and Creed if required, unless, for pastoral reasons, it continues immediately with the preparation of the gifts instead.

Baptism, Confirmation, and First Communion of Adults

The Christian initiation of adults at the Easter Vigil is described in chapter 18. This chapter will describe the occasion when, for some serious reason, the Baptism, Confirmation, and First Communion of adults takes place apart from the Easter Vigil. The celebration may take place on Easter Sunday, or during the octave of Easter, or on some Sunday of the Easter season, some other day in the Easter season, or some Sunday during the year.[653] According to tradition, white vestments are worn for the celebration of Baptism. There are many liturgical and practical reasons to limit the celebration of adult initiation to those Sundays when white vestments are worn, or when the ritual Mass "For the Conferral of Baptism" can be celebrated. On the Sundays of Christmas or Ordinary Time, for example, the Mass texts can be taken from the ritual Mass for Baptism and the readings can be taken entirely from the corresponding section of the Lectionary for Mass (nos. 756–760).[654] Or, during the Sundays of Ordinary Time or of the Christmas season, the proper Mass of the day with its readings can be retained. In that case, it is possible to substitute a reading from the lectionary for Baptisms for one of these appointed readings.[655] On solemnities and on the Sundays of Advent, Lent, and Easter when the ritual Mass for Baptism is not permitted, all the proper readings are required.[656]

Historically, Pentecost was also a time for the celebration of the Sacraments of Initiation of adults. On Pentecost, like on the other Sundays of the Easter season, the ritual Mass "For the Conferral of Baptism" is not permitted. The proper readings either for Pentecost Vigil or for Pentecost Day are required. If the Baptism of adults takes place on either day, the celebrant removes both the red chasuble and the red stole at the chair. Before making his way to the font, he takes a white stole. If the Confirmations take place at the font immediately following the Baptisms, the celebrant can retain the white stole until after the Confirmations are completed. At the chair, he removes the white stole before assuming the red stole and chasuble once again for the Prayer of the Faithful and the preparation of the gifts and the altar. If Confirmation takes place in the sanctuary, he can remove the white stole

653 *RCIA*, 23, 26–27, 208.

654 *RCIA*, 338.

655 *CB*, 434.

656 *CB*, 434.

upon first arriving at the chair from the baptistry, and can assume the red stole and chasuble at once before proceeding with the Confirmations at the entrance to the sanctuary. While these directions are not indicated in any of the revised liturgical books, they attempt to take into account the traditional association of white vestments with the celebration of Baptism. According to the revised books, Confirmation can be celebrated either in white or red vestments.

Prior to the celebration, in addition to the various vestments needed, the following items must also be prepared:

In the sanctuary:

- The chrism, unless this is prepared in the baptistry
- Cotton balls, lemon, bread to cleanse the celebrant's hands after the Confirmations, along with a pitcher of water, bowl, and towel
- Gremial, if the celebrant will wash his hands seated
- A white stole for the celebrant, if needed

On a covered table at the font:

- The chrism, unless this is prepared in the sanctuary
- Baptismal candles
- Baptismal garments, if used
- A vessel for pouring the baptismal water
- Towel
- The ritual for Baptism of adults

In the baptistry or near the font:

- The Easter candle and stand, unless the Easter candle will be carried from the sanctuary to the font during the Easter season

Like at the Easter Vigil, all the preliminary rites preparatory to Baptism normally take place at some earlier occasion. In this case, the opening rites of Mass include the penitential act and *Kyrie* as usual, followed by the Gloria. The Christian initiation of adults on some other suitable occasion follows the homily with the blessing of the water or the thanksgiving over the water.

During the Easter season, unless the font is located in the sanctuary, there is a procession to the font, led by a minister bearing the Easter candle in both hands, as all sing the litany of the saints.[657] The candidates, their families, and their sponsors follow immediately behind the Easter candle,[658] then the servers and celebrant with the deacon walking to his right. Outside the Easter season, when the Easter candle is already at the font, whether in the sanctuary or in the baptistry, the traditional practice whereby the catechumens and their godparents follow the servers and ministers of the Mass can be followed.[659]

At the font, the celebrant blesses the water using forms A, B, or C.[660] During the Easter season, the celebrant gives thanks over water already blessed at the Easter Vigil by using forms D or E. A server stands slightly to his left, holding the ritual in both hands. The celebrant says form A of the blessing with hands outstretched; he says the other four forms (B, C, D, and E) with hands joined. Outside of the Easter Vigil, the Easter candle is not lowered into the baptismal water by the celebrant. According to Form B, where the rubrics say that the celebrant "touches the water with his right hand," this is done with the open palm of the right hand. In many locations, celebrants conclude form A and form B by making the Sign of the Cross over the water with the right hand, the left hand resting on the chest. In Form C, he makes the Sign of the Cross with his right hand, his left hand resting on his chest, at the point indicated. No Sign of the Cross is made during forms D or E, which both give thanks over water previously blessed. Even if the font is large enough to accommodate the Baptism of adults by immersion, the celebrant stands outside the font for the blessing of the water and the Baptisms of the elect.

With hands joined, the celebrant stands near the font, facing the catechumens, and leads them in the renunciation of sin. They respond as a group to the renunciation of sin.[661] He then asks for the profession of faith from each catechumen individually. Each candidate is baptized immediately after his or her profession of faith. The celebrant baptizes each catechumen by pouring water three times on the head, using the right hand, and saying the sacramental

[657] *RCIA*, 219.

[658] *RCIA* 219B; *CB*, 358.

[659] Fortescue, O'Connell, and Reid, *The Ceremonies of the Roman Rite Described*, 425.

[660] *RCIA*, 222.

[661] The anointing of adult catechumens with the oil of catechumens at this point is always anticipated during the period of the catechumenate in the United States. See the general introduction to the *Rite of Christian Initiation of Adults*, no. 33, §7.

formula in the manner indicated in the ritual.[662] The water should flow over the bare skin of the head. Historically, the celebrant has poured the water in the form of a cross each time.[663] The celebrant may also baptize by immersing three times either the whole body, or the head only, with godparents supporting the catechumen.

After all have been baptized, the celebrant then may say the formula pertaining to the white garment with hands joined while godparents place the garments on the neophytes. However, this clothing of the neophytes with the white garment after Baptism is always optional.[664] Conversely, the presentation of the lighted candle to each of the neophytes is obligatory.[665] The deacon then takes the Easter candle from its stand or from a server. The celebrant receives the Easter candle in both hands from the deacon and invites a godparent for each of the neophytes forward to light a baptismal candle from the Easter candle. Alternatively, the celebrant, grasping the Easter candle in his left hand, could light a candle with his right and present it to each godparent if this is more convenient.[666] The godparents immediately give the lighted candles to their godchildren as the celebrant, now with hands joined, says the formula once for the entire group. If the Easter candle is too heavy or too tall for either of these options, the celebrant may simply take a long taper, receive the flame from the Easter candle, and light the baptismal candles held by the godparents with the taper.

The rite of Confirmation then follows immediately in the sanctuary or at the font in the baptistry.[667] Normally, the Sacrament of Confirmation is conferred in the sanctuary. Therefore, all return there in procession. The neophytes carry their lighted candles in their right hand. During the Easter season, they and their godparents immediately follow the server with the Easter candle. Behind them process the servers and clergy, and finally the celebrant with the deacon walking to his right. Outside the Easter season, the neophytes and their godparents follow the servers and clergy. One server carries the ritual for adult initiation, and another carries the chrism for Confirmation, unless this has already been prepared in the sanctuary. Upon arriving at the sanctuary, the Easter candle is returned to

662 *RCIA*, 226B.

663 Fortescue, O'Connell, and Reid, *The Ceremonies of the Roman Rite Described*, 425.

664 *RCIA*, 229.

665 *RCIA*, 230.

666 Mutel and Freeman, *Cérémonial de la sainte messe*, 337, n. 316; Fortescue, O'Connell, and Reid, *The Ceremonies of the Roman Rite Described*, 426.

667 *RCIA*, 231.

its stand near the ambo. Meanwhile, the neophytes with the godparents stand in a row before the celebrant at the entrance of the sanctuary, facing the altar. Each godparent has his or her right hand on the shoulder of his or her godchild. They may take their godchild's baptismal candle in their left hands for the duration of the Confirmation ceremony.

Alternatively, the Confirmation of the neophytes could take place in the baptistry or near a font erected in the sanctuary. In that case, after the presentation of the lighted candle, each godparent places his or her right hand on the shoulder of his or her godchild. They may take their godchild's baptismal candle in their left hand for the duration of the Confirmation ceremony. The celebrant immediately begins the rite of Confirmation, as described below.

Once all are in their places, the celebrant proceeds with the Confirmation of the newly baptized. A server with the ritual stands to the celebrant's left. The deacon holding the chrism stands to his right.[668] The celebrant offers the invitation to prayer with hands joined. He may close his eyes and bow his head for a moment. Then, with hands outstretched over the entire group to be confirmed, he says the prayer "All-powerful God, Father of Our Lord Jesus Christ."[669] If there will be many Confirmations, the assembly may receive an indication to sit at this point.

The celebrant then anoints each of the neophytes on the forehead with the thumb of his right hand, making the Sign of the Cross. Although the current rubrics do not indicate the gesture, the minister of Confirmation historically placed the joined fingers of his right hand on the crown of each person's head while anointing the forehead with the thumb.[670] The candidates for Confirmation may go to the celebrant individually, or he may go to them.[671] If they are standing side-by-side in a line before him, the celebrant begins on his left and concludes on his right. After each Confirmation, the godparents return the baptismal candle to their godchildren. The newly confirmed and their godparents return to their places either individually or after the entire group has been confirmed.[672] If the Confirmation took place in the baptistry, they return in procession to their places

668 Peter J. Elliott, *Ceremonies Explained for Servers According to the Roman Rite: A Manual for Altar Servers, Acolytes, Sacristans, and Masters of Ceremonies* (San Francisco: Ignatius Press, 2019), 260. This approach seems much more convenient than the traditional practice, where a minister held the chrism to the bishop's *left* during Confirmation. See Fortescue, O'Connell, and Reid, *The Ceremonies of the Roman Rite Described*, 418–419.

669 *RCIA*, 234.

670 Fortescue, O'Connell, and Reid, *The Ceremonies of the Roman Rite Described*, 419.

671 *CB*, 466.

672 *RCIA*, 236.

in the nave. During the Easter season, they follow the Easter candle. The servers and clergy follow the newly confirmed. Outside the Easter season, the newly confirmed follow the servers and clergy.

The celebrant now washes his hands or cleanses the thumb standing at the chair or at a credence table, or even seated at the chair with a gremial on his lap.[673] He may likewise cleanse his thumb with lemon and crusts of bread, or with cotton, presented to him on a tray by a server. There is no renewal of baptismal promises of the assembly or sprinkling of the assembly apart from the Easter Vigil.[674] The profession of faith is not said.[675] Mass continues with the Prayer of the Faithful in the usual way. After washing and drying his hands, the celebrant, now standing at the chair, introduces the general intercessions with a server holding the ritual before him. He prays the concluding Collect with hands extended. Then all are seated, and Mass continues with the preparation of the gifts in the usual way.

During the Eucharistic Prayer, there are proper inserts for the occasion for each Eucharistic Prayer. (See ritual Masses, "For the Conferral of Baptism.") Prior to "Behold the Lamb of God," the celebrant may address the neophytes directly about the Eucharist, which they will receive for the first time.[676]

Reception of Adults into Full Communion by Confirmation and First Communion

The reception of baptized non-Catholics into the communion of the Church is intended to take place normally at a solemnity or on a Sunday, apart from the Easter Vigil.[677] Except in the case of Orthodox Christians,[678] the rite of reception into full communion of baptized non-Catholics is joined to the celebration of Confirmation. The celebration of Confirmation takes place in white or red vestments.[679] Therefore, the rite of reception and celebration of Confirmation should

673 According to custom, this water is poured into the sacrarium in the sacristy. Any cotton balls used are burned and the ashes are likewise poured into the sacrarium. See Elliott, *Ceremonies Explained for Servers*, 262, and Fortescue, O'Connell, and Reid, *The Ceremonies of the Roman Rite Described*, 421.

674 *RCIA*, 237–240.

675 *RCIA*, 241.

676 *RCIA*, 243.

677 *RCIA*, 487; *National Statutes for the Catechumenate* (USA), no. 33.

678 *RCIA*, 474.

679 *CB*, 459.

take place on a Sunday or a solemnity when white or red vestments are worn.[680] Or, the rite of reception and Confirmation could take place on a Sunday of Ordinary Time or Christmas, for example, when the ritual Mass "For the Conferral of Confirmation" is permitted. Finally, the rite of reception and Confirmation could take place, wearing white vestments, on a day during Ordinary Time or the Christmas and Easter seasons when the Mass for various needs and occasions entitled "For the Unity of Christians" is permitted.[681]

The reception of baptized Christians into full communion takes place after the homily. The celebrant may stand at the chair to conduct the rite, or at the entrance to the sanctuary, or at the altar. A server, holding the ritual in both hands, stand slightly to his left. The deacon, holding the chrism, stands to his right. Those to be received into full communion come before the celebrant, facing him and the altar. Their sponsors place their right hands on the shoulders of the candidates. With hands joined, the celebrant asks the candidates to recite the Creed with the assembly. Afterward, he invites each of the candidates to make his or her profession individually. Then, the same candidate and sponsor immediately go to the celebrant, who receives the candidate into full communion, reciting the required formula. The process is repeated for each candidate.

When the candidates for Confirmation are numerous, the celebrant first addresses the candidates and the faithful with hands joined.[682] He then holds his hands outstretched, palms open, over the entire group, while saying the prayer of invocation.[683] The celebrant anoints each candidate with the thumb of his right hand, making the Sign of the Cross on the forehead. Historically, the joined fingers of the hand have rested on the head of each candidate as the celebrant anoints the forehead with the thumb. The candidates may go individually to the celebrant, or he may go to them.[684] If they are standing in a line before him, the celebrant begins by confirming the first candidate on his left and concludes with the last candidate on his right. The newly confirmed and their sponsors return to their places in the nave individually after the anointing or as a group once all the Confirmations are completed.[685] Both the celebrant and the newly confirmed return to their seats. Standing at the chair or at a credence table or even seated at

680 *RCIA*, 487.
681 *RCIA*, 487.
682 *RCIA*, 589.
683 *RCIA*, 590.
684 *CB*, 466.
685 *RCIA*, 591.

the chair with a gremial on his lap, the celebrant washes his hands, or cleanses the thumb with lemon and bread or with cotton. After washing and drying his hands, the celebrant, standing at the chair, introduces the general intercessions with a server holding the ritual before him. He prays the concluding Collect with hands extended. Then all are seated. Mass continues with the preparation of the gifts.

If there is only one person to receive into full communion and to confirm, the celebrant, immediately after the formula of reception, lays both hands, palms open, on the head of the candidate in silence, then says the prayer of invocation for Confirmation with hands outstretched, palms down, over the candidate.[686] He then anoints the candidate with the thumb of his right hand, making the Sign of the Cross on the forehead. Historically, the joined fingers of the hand have rested on the head of each candidate as the celebrant anoints the forehead with the thumb. The celebrant momentarily turns to his right and cleanses his thumb with lemon and bread or with cotton held before him by the server. The celebrant then briefly takes both hands, joined palm-to-palm, of the newly-received person into his own two hands.[687] The single candidate remains standing in the same location for the general intercessions. The deacon offers the intentions for the candidate and for the world with hands joined. At the conclusion of the Universal Prayer, the celebrant prays the Collect from the ritual with hands extended. After this, the sponsor and even the entire assembly may greet the newly received with the sign of peace in the customary way. In that case, the sign of peace before Communion may be omitted.[688] Then the newly confirmed and the sponsor return to their seats.

During the Eucharistic Prayer, there are proper inserts for the occasion for each Eucharistic Prayer. (See ritual Masses, "For the Conferral of Confirmation.") Prior to "Behold the Lamb of God," the celebrant may address directly those admitted to full communion about the Eucharist which they will receive for the first time.[689]

At the end of Mass, the celebrant may impart the solemn blessing from the Mass "For the Conferral of Confirmation." The celebrant offers both the Post-Communion prayer and the proper solemn blessing either at the altar or at the chair. In preparation for the solemn blessing, depending on the disposition of the seats in the nave, a master of ceremonies, may direct the newly confirmed to

686 *RCIA*, 493.
687 *RCIA*, 495.
688 *RCIA*, 497.
689 *RCIA*, 243.

come forward from their places in order to stand before the celebrant.[690] At the altar, the celebrant stands facing the assembly, with the missal placed directly before him, at the center, with its bottom edge parallel to the edge of the altar. After praying the Post-Communion prayer with hands extended, the celebrant extends and then joins his hands to greet the faithful with "The Lord be with you." The deacon, with hands joined, invites those present to bow their heads. Then, with hands outstretched over the newly confirmed, palms facing down, the celebrant prays the three invocations of the solemn blessing. All respond, "Amen," to each invocation. After the last invocation, the celebrant briefly joins his hands and then blesses those present in the usual way with his right hand, his left hand resting on the altar, before joining his hands once again. If the celebrant gives the solemn blessing standing at the chair instead, a server holding the missal slightly to his left stands before him. At the chair, when imparting the blessing with his right hand, the celebrant's left hand rests on his chest.

Having given the blessing, he joins his hands once again. The deacon, with hands joined, dismisses those present. After the dismissal by the deacon, all depart from the sanctuary in the usual order, having first bowed to the altar or genuflected to the Blessed Sacrament reserved in the sanctuary, as the case may be.

[690] *CB*, 471.

24 Matrimony

The Marriage of a Catholic can take place in the course of Mass or apart from Mass. In addition, the Marriage of a Catholic to an unbaptized person takes place apart from Mass in a distinctive form. This chapter will examine each of these scenarios. The following items are needed whether the Marriage is celebrated during Mass or apart from Mass:

In a convenient place:

- Rings for the bridegroom and bride on a platter
- A vessel of holy water with aspergillum
- The *Order of Celebrating Matrimony*

In the sanctuary (or in the nave, as circumstances suggest):

- Chairs (and kneelers or cushions) for the bride and groom
- Chairs (and kneelers or cushions) for the witnesses
- Microphones, as required

The Wedding Mass

The wedding Mass is celebrated in white vestments with the proper texts for this ritual Mass from the Roman Missal and the Lectionary for Mass. Ritual Masses such as the nuptial Mass are not permitted on the Sundays of Advent, Lent, and Easter, and on solemnities. On solemnities and the Sundays of Easter, the rite of Marriage can nevertheless take place in the context of Mass prayers and readings proper to the day. The ritual Mass "For the Celebration of Marriage" is permitted on the Sundays of Christmas and Ordinary Time. However, whenever the celebration of Matrimony on those days takes place during a parish Mass, the Mass of that Sunday must nevertheless be used.[691] In any event, whenever the ritual Mass for Marriage is not permitted, one of the readings from the *Order of Celebrating Matrimony* can substitute for a proper reading on those occasions.[692]

The celebration of Matrimony modifies four specific moments of the nuptial Mass: the introductory rites, the Liturgy of the Word, during which the Marriage rite itself takes place, the Communion Rite, which includes the nuptial blessing, and the solemn blessing during the concluding rite.

1) The Introductory Rites

The introductory rites of the nuptial Mass include one of two forms of the greeting of the couple by the celebrant. In the first case, the celebrant, deacon, and servers await the arrival of the wedding party at the door of the church. When the bride and groom arrive, the celebrant "warmly greets them."[693] The entrance procession then forms in the usual way, namely, candle bearers alone, or candle bearers with the cross bearer, lead the way, followed by any other servers, the deacon carrying the Gospel book or walking to the celebrant's right, and finally the celebrant. The bridal party follows the celebrant according to the form which corresponds to local custom. All approach the sanctuary while the entrance chant is sung. The servers and ministers enter, venerate the altar, and go to their places as usual. The wedding party takes their seats outside the sanctuary. The celebrant directs the bride and groom to their seats.

In many locations, the celebrant awaits the bridal couple at his chair, or at the chairs prepared for the couple. When the couple has arrived at their places, the celebrant greets them there instead of greeting them at the door of the church. In the United States, the celebrant and servers can lead the groom to his seat while the bride enters the church and takes her place. There, the celebrant greets both parties. In some locations, the father of the bride places her right hand into the right hand of the groom once they have reached their places and before they take their seats.

The celebrant and the deacon bow to the altar or genuflect to the Blessed Sacrament reserved in the sanctuary. They both venerate the altar with a kiss,

[691] *OCM*, 34, 54.
[692] *OCM*, 34, 54.
[693] *OCM*, 45.

and then go to their seats while the entrance chant is sung. The Mass begins with the Sign of the Cross and greeting in the usual manner. Still facing the assembly, the celebrant, with hands joined, then continues with one of the two formulas of address indicated in the ritual. A server holds the ritual before him. The Penitential Act is omitted. All sing the Gloria. The ministers and servers sing with hands joined. All bow their heads at the name of Jesus. Then, the celebrant prays the desired Collect in the usual way.

2) *The Rite of Marriage during the Liturgy of the Word of Mass*

After the homily, the celebrant, deacon, and servers go to the couple. The celebrant may meet the couple at the entrance of the sanctuary or invite them to stand with him in the sanctuary itself. The couple, the witnesses, and all present stand.[694] The celebrant stands with his back to the altar at the entrance of the sanctuary. A server holds the ritual before the celebrant to his left. The celebrant, with hands joined, addresses the couple, asking them to state their intentions. He then leads them in the exchange of consent.

Unless the couple has memorized the formula of the vows, the bride and groom may read their vows from the ritual or from a card held before them by a server. Or, the celebrant may prompt the couple with short phrases to repeat the vows after him or ask them to respond, "I do," to the vows posed to the bride and groom in the form of a question. The bride and groom join their right hands during this time. They may both put their left hands together under their joined right hands. Traditionally, the groom took the bride's right hand into his right hand while he declared his consent. Then the bride took the groom's right hand into her right hand while she declared her consent.[695] While the couple's hands are still joined, the celebrant declares the Church's reception of their consent.

After the reception of consent, one server brings the holy water and aspergillum to the celebrant and a second server takes a silver platter from the credence table to the celebrant, unless both servers already did so when the celebrant first approached the couple for the exchange of consent. The server holds the platter before the celebrant on his right, bearing one or two rings to be blessed. The ring or rings may be placed on the plate at that moment by the husband or best man, or they may have been placed on it from the beginning of Mass. The celebrant

[694] *OCM*, 59.

[695] Adrian Fortescue, J. B. O'Connell, and Alcuin Reid, eds., *The Ceremonies of the Roman Rite Described*, 15th ed. (New York: Bloomsbury, 2009), 443.

blesses them with his right hand, his left resting on his chest. The deacon, standing at the celebrant's right, hands the celebrant the aspergillum. The celebrant, using the right hand with his left hand resting on his chest, sprinkles the rings once with holy water.[696] The celebrant returns the aspergillum to the deacon. Then, holding the plate with the rings on it himself, the celebrant first offers the bride's ring to the groom. The groom takes the ring off the plate and prepares to place it on the fourth finger of the bride's left hand. Repeating after the priest, the groom says the formula as he places the ring on the bride's finger. Then the celebrant, holding the plate once again, offers the groom's ring to the bride. She takes it and places it on the fourth finger of the groom's left hand while repeating the required formula after the celebrant. In many locations, the kiss of peace between the couple is anticipated at this point in the ceremony rather than after the nuptial blessing. A hymn of praise may accompany this gesture. When the bride and groom have already exchanged the sign of peace during the Marriage rite, the exchange of the sign of peace in preparation for Communion is often omitted.

The Prayer of the Faithful follows, as does the Creed, if required by the rubrics. The bride and groom may present the bread and wine at the entrance of the sanctuary, or at some other suitable place, even at the altar itself.

3) *The Nuptial Blessing during the Communion Rite*

After the Our Father, the embolism "Deliver us" is omitted. The celebrant standing at the altar prepares to invoke the nuptial blessing. If he is already facing the couple, he remains in place. If he is celebrating *ad orientem*, he genuflects and goes to the epistle side of the altar to face the couple. A server holds the ritual before him. The couple kneels in their places.[697] If they are at some distance from the altar, they also may approach the altar, genuflect, and kneel on its lowest step to receive the blessing. The celebrant introduces the blessing with hands joined. He may bow his head and close his eyes to pray in silence for a moment. Then, he imparts the blessing with hands outstretched over the couple. Historically, the nuptial blessing was imparted by the celebrant of the Mass, even if he was not the priest who assisted at the exchange of consent.[698]

After the nuptial blessing, the couple genuflects and returns to their places if they have been kneeling elsewhere. The celebrant returns to the center of the altar

[696] Fortescue, O'Connell, and Reid, *The Ceremonies of the Roman Rite Described*, 443.
[697] *OCM*, 73.
[698] Fortescue, O'Connell, and Reid, *The Ceremonies of the Roman Rite Described*, 441.

and genuflects if he has been standing at the epistle side. The prayer "Lord Jesus Christ, You said to Your apostles" is omitted. The celebrant immediately faces the assembly to say, "The peace of the Lord be with you always." The deacon invites all to share some sign of peace. If the bride and groom have already exchanged the kiss of peace at the conclusion of the rite of Matrimony, the kiss of peace is often omitted at this point in many churches. The celebrant ministers Communion to the Catholic spouse or spouses first, before ministering Communion to others.

4) *The Concluding Rites of the Nuptial Mass*

The celebrant prays the Post-Communion prayer at the altar or at the chair, with hands extended. After the Post-Communion prayer, the celebrant offers the solemn blessing for the couple either at the altar or at the chair. At the altar, he stands facing the assembly with the missal placed directly before him, at the center, with its bottom edge parallel to the edge of the altar. He extends and then joins his hands when greeting the faithful with "The Lord be with you." The deacon, with hands joined, invites those present to bow their heads. Then with hands outstretched over the people, palms facing down, the celebrant prays the invocations of the solemn blessing. All respond, "Amen," to each invocation. The celebrant joins his hands and gives the blessing with his right hand, his left hand resting on the altar, before joining his hands once again. If the celebrant gives the solemn blessing standing at the chair instead, a server holds the ritual directly before the celebrant or slightly to his left, as the circumstances suggest. At the chair, when imparting the blessing with his right hand, the celebrant's left hand rests on his chest. If the celebrant has offered Mass *ad orientem* and imparts the solemn blessing from the altar, he turns to his right at the center of the altar to face the couple.[699] A server holds the ritual before him for the solemn blessing. Historically, the couple has knelt at their places for this blessing as well; this is not currently indicated in the revised books.

Once the celebrant has blessed the faithful, the deacon, with hands joined, says the dismissal. Following the dismissal, the minister and servers may lead the wedding party to the doors of the church as at the beginning of the wedding, or the wedding party may go there unaccompanied. In that case, the ministers and servers return to the sacristy by the most direct route. Before departing, the celebrant and deacon kiss the altar. Likewise, all bow to the altar or genuflect to the Blessed Sacrament reserved in the tabernacle of the sanctuary as usual before departing.

[699] Fortescue, O'Connell, and Reid, *The Ceremonies of the Roman Rite Described*, 445.

Marriage apart from Mass

When a wedding is celebrated apart from Mass, the priest celebrant wears a white stole and may even wear a white cope. The deacon who assists him wears the white stole and white dalmatic. Whenever passing in front of the Blessed Sacrament reserved in the sanctuary, all genuflect before proceeding.[700] During the introductory rites, the Gloria is not sung. Otherwise, all the indications given above apply until the introduction to the Prayer of the Faithful following the exchange of consent and exchange of rings.

If Holy Communion is not distributed during this wedding ceremony, the bride and bridegroom remain in their places. The priest, still standing in the same location with them, begins by introducing the Prayer of the Faithful with hands joined, and the deacon offers the intentions. After the last intention, the celebrant immediately begins to pray the Our Father with all present. He holds his hands in the *orans* position. Then, with hands joined, he invites those present to pray for the couple. While the couple kneels in their places,[701] the celebrant offers the nuptial blessing. With hands extended over the couple, palms down, he prays the nuptial blessing itself. He joins his hands at "Through Christ Our Lord. Amen." The blessing of those present immediately follows. The celebrant holds his left hand on his chest while he blesses those present with his raised right hand.

If Holy Communion is distributed during the wedding ceremony, following the introduction to the Prayer of the Faithful and its intentions, the invitation to pray for the couple and the nuptial blessing take place as described above, omitting for the time being the Our Father, which will be prayed during the course of the Communion rite instead. Once the nuptial blessing has been imparted, the priest or deacon brings the Blessed Sacrament from the place of reservation, places it on a corporal on the altar, and genuflects.[702] As usual, the celebrant introduces the Our Father with hands joined, but prays the Our Father with hands in the *orans* position. Immediately after concluding the Our Father, if appropriate, the deacon may invite those present to offer a sign of peace.[703] In those churches where the couple customarily exchanges the kiss of peace after exchanging vows and rings, the sign of peace is often omitted at this point. The celebrant genuflects, takes up a Host,

[700] The prescription to bow to the altar rather than genuflect to the Blessed Sacrament in the tabernacle whenever passing before both pertains specifically to the celebration of Mass. See *GIRM*, 274. This rubric is not found in any other liturgical book.

[701] *OCM*, 104.

[702] *OCM*, 108.

[703] *OCM*, 109.

and invites the assembly to Communion with the words "Behold the Lamb of God."[704] After the distribution of Communion and the Post-Communion prayer prayed at the altar, the Marriage ceremony ends with the blessing of the bride, bridegroom, and assembly as described above.

When a deacon presides at a wedding apart from Mass in the place of a priest, he does so from his own chair in the sanctuary. Normally, the deacon prays the Our Father with hands joined. Otherwise, the postures and gestures of the deacon are the same as those of a priest celebrant.

The Marriage of a Catholic to a Non-baptized Person apart from Mass

The marriage of a Catholic to a non-baptized person always takes place apart from Mass, but it differs in some ways from a sacramental Marriage between two baptized persons, which also may take place apart from Mass. According to this form of the rite of Matrimony, the priest celebrant wears a white stole and may even wear a white cope.[705] The deacon who assists him wears the white stole and white dalmatic. Whenever passing in front of the Blessed Sacrament reserved in the sanctuary, all genuflect before proceeding.

The rite of reception takes place without the Sign of the Cross or the liturgical greeting, "The Lord be with you." A Liturgy of the Word, even the briefest one, follows. The celebration of matrimony itself takes place as described above. The blessing and giving of rings may be omitted. Otherwise, the blessing and exchange of rings takes place as described above, with the proper texts. Remaining before the couple, the priest introduces the Prayer of the Faithful; the deacon offers the intentions. The Our Father follows. With hands joined, the priest or deacon invites those present to pray for the couple. They couple may kneel or remain standing. The priest or deacon offers the nuptial blessing with hands extended over the couple, palms down. Or, he offers the alternate prayer for them, with hands joined instead. The ceremony ends with a simple blessing of the assembly. The celebrant blesses those present with his right hand, while the left hand rests on his chest.

[704] *OCM*, 111.
[705] *OCM*, 119.

25

Penance and Reconciliation

From time to time, the parish priests will celebrate the rite of Reconciliation of several penitents with individual Confession and absolution.[706] In addition, in order to foster the virtue of penance among the faithful, they may also periodically preside at penitential services which do not include sacramental Reconciliation.[707] These services are also useful in helping children gradually form their consciences and in assisting catechumens to strengthen their resolve for conversion of life. This chapter will describe both forms of celebration.

Rite of Reconciliation with Individual Confession and Absolution

The priest celebrant wears a purple stole over his cassock and surplice or alb, as do the other priests present to hear Confessions. In addition, the presiding priest may also wear a purple cope. A deacon wears a purple stole over the alb. If the presiding priest wears the cope, the deacon may also wear the dalmatic.[708] A psalm or other appropriate song is sung as the priests and ministers enter the church.[709] Unless the ministers take their places in the sanctuary before the rite begins, all may make their way from the sacristy to the sanctuary led by the cross and candles as at Mass. (See chapter 5, "The Introductory Rites.") All make the necessary reverence either to the altar or to the Blessed Sacrament reserved in the sanctuary. During the course of

706 *Order of Penance,* nos. 48–59.

707 See *Order of Penance,* nos. 36–37 and appendix 2.

708 Peter J. Elliott, *Ceremonies Explained for Servers According to the Roman Rite: A Manual for Altar Servers, Acolytes, Sacristans, and Masters of Ceremonies* (San Francisco: Ignatius Press, 2019), 153.

709 *CB,* 623, *Order of Penance,* no. 48.

the celebration, all genuflect to the tabernacle whenever passing in front of it.[710] Otherwise, all bow to the altar whenever passing before it.

At the chair, the priest who is presiding begins with the Sign of the Cross and the liturgical greeting. If necessary, the book bearer holds the *Order of Penance* in both hands before him. The presiding priest may instruct the people briefly about the purpose of the rite. The deacon, standing to the presider's right, may do the same. Or, one of the other priests, standing at his seat in the sanctuary or at some other suitable place, may give the introduction. Then, with hands joined, the presiding priest invites the faithful to pray. He pauses for a moment of silence. He may close his eyes during this period or lower his gaze. He then prays the Collect with hands extended, joining them once again at its conclusion. Then, all are seated.

The Liturgy of the Word may include one or more readings. If there is only one reading, it is preferably taken from the Gospels.[711] The Liturgy of the Word may be conducted in the same manner as at Mass, including the use of candles and incense at the proclamation of the Gospel. (See chapter 6, "The Liturgy of the Word.") After the homily and a period of silence, one of the priests, or the deacon, or the presiding priest leads the faithful in an examination of conscience. This may take place from the chair or from some other suitable place, rather than from the ambo.

After the communal examination of conscience, the rite of Reconciliation begins. Apart from the Easter season or a Sunday, the deacon invites all present to kneel, unless all bow instead for the general confession. Some form of general confession, like the *Confiteor,* is used. In that case, all strike their breast three times as at Mass.[712] At the conclusion of the general confession, all stand. The presiding priest, with hands joined, introduces the litany or song of contrition. The deacon or cantor may lead the litany from his place or from some other suitable location. At the end of the litany or song, the presiding priest, with hands joined, invites all the pray the Our Father. The Our Father is never omitted. The presiding priest extends his hands for the Our Father and for the concluding Collect. A server holds the ritual open with both hands in front of the presiding priest as needed.

[710] The prescription to bow to the altar rather than genuflect to the Blessed Sacrament in the tabernacle whenever passing before both pertains specifically to the celebration of Mass. See *GIRM,* 274. This rubric is not found in any other liturgical book.

[711] *Order of Penance,* no. 51.

[712] Peter J. Elliott, *Ceremonies of the Modern Roman Rite: The Eucharist and the Liturgy of the Hours,* rev. ed. (San Francisco: Ignatius Press, 1995), 93, n. 14.

Then the confessors go to their seats or confessionals in order to hear the individual Confessions of the penitents.[713] The confessors hear the Confessions of the penitents individually, offer guidance, impose a penance, and grant absolution. All present who expressed their contrition communally omit the individual act of contrition during Confession itself.

When the individual Confessions are completed, the presiding priest returns to the chair. All stand. The other confessors stand around the presiding priest.[714] A server stands before the presiding priest holding the *Order of Penance* open in both hands. With hands joined, the presider invites all present to sing a hymn or litany or song of thanksgiving for God's mercy. Then, with hands extended, the presiding priest offers the final prayer of thanksgiving. He then blesses those present according to the usual form, or with the solemn blessing or the prayer over the people. (See chapter 9, "The Communion Rite and the Concluding Rites.") The deacon offers the dismissal with hands joined, facing the faithful, according to the proper formula. After the usual reverence to the Blessed Sacrament reserved in the sanctuary or to the altar, all return to the sacristy in the same manner as they approached the sanctuary.

Penitential Services without Confession and Absolution

The purpose of such services is to provide the faithful with an opportunity to hear the Word of God, which invites them to deeper conversion. Such penitential services can serve to properly dispose the faithful to future sacramental celebrations of Penance and Reconciliation. These services take place in the same way as the rite of Reconciliation described above. After the Collect which follows the Our Father, the presiding priest offers the final blessing, and the deacon dismisses those present. The individual Confession of penitents, the imposition of a penance, and the conferral of absolution are omitted.[715]

[713] Adrian Fortescue, J. B. O'Connell, and Alcuin Reid, *The Ceremonies of the Roman Rite Described*, 15th ed. (New York: Bloomsbury, 2009), 432. Penance and Reconciliation is the only sacrament administered sitting by a priest.

[714] *CB*, 630; *Order of Penance*, no. 56.

[715] *CB*, 643.

26

The Anointing of the Sick

From time to time, the Sacrament of the Anointing of the Sick may be celebrated for several seriously sick persons simultaneously during the course of Mass. At other times, the Anointing of the Sick is celebrated in the church apart from Mass, with or without the opportunity for the sick to receive Holy Communion. The indications for each of these scenarios can be found in *Pastoral Care of the Sick*, the *Ceremonial of Bishops*, and in contemporary commentaries on that portion of the *Roman Ritual*.[716] This chapter will first describe the Anointing of the Sick during Mass and then note the modifications necessary when the Anointing of the Sick takes place apart from Mass. The following items need to be prepared:

At the credence table:

- Oil stocks with the oil of the sick on a silver platter
- Bread, ewer with water, bowl, lemon, and towel to cleanse the hands after the Anointings
- Cards with the form of Anointing, if needed
- White humeral veil, if needed to transfer the Blessed Sacrament from a location outside the sanctuary to the altar for Communion

[716] *PCS*, 131–148; Peter J. Elliott, *Ceremonies of the Modern Roman Rite: The Eucharist and the Liturgy of the Hours*, rev. ed. (San Francisco: Ignatius Press, 1995), 207–209; Peter J. Elliott, *Ceremonies Explained for Servers According to the Roman Rite: A Manual for Altar Servers, Acolytes, Sacristans, and Masters of Ceremonies* (San Francisco: Ignatius Press, 2019), 161–167.

At the chair:

- The *Pastoral Care of the Sick*

Suitable seating for those to be anointed should be arranged in advance. It is always possible for those to be anointed to approach the priest in a kind of procession for the laying on of hands and for the Anointing. In most cases however, the condition of the sick may require that they remain seated in their places for the laying on of hands and the Anointing. The several priests present will need to go to the sick rather than have the sick come to them. In that case, the arrangement of the seating for the sick must allow for the priests to have direct physical access to the sick for the laying on the hands and the Anointing. It is best to seat the sick at the ends of each pew or in every other pew so that the priests will be able to approach them individually without difficulty. Prior to the celebration, the pastor will want to provide an opportunity and a location for those who wish to celebrate the Sacrament of Penance and Reconciliation.[717]

Anointing of the Sick during Mass

When the Anointing of the Sick is celebrated during Mass, the ritual Mass is used on days when it is permitted, as on the Sundays of Ordinary Time and the Christmas season. The ritual Mass for the sick is taken from the "Mass for the Sick" in the section of the Roman Missal for Masses for various needs and occasions (no. 45). Whenever the ritual Mass is permitted, the priest wears white vestments.[718] The readings are taken from the corresponding section of volume 4 of the Lectionary for Mass or from the readings found in *Pastoral Care of the Sick*.[719] The ritual Mass for the sick is not permitted on solemnities or on the Sundays of Advent, Lent, or the Easter season. In that case, the priest wears the color of vestments proper to the day and the Mass texts and readings are also proper to the day. Unless the day is a solemnity, one of the readings appointed for the day can be replaced by one reading referring to the Anointing of the Sick from either volume 4 of the Lectionary for Mass or from *Pastoral Care of the Sick*.[720]

Historically, the Anointing of the Sick was celebrated with violet vestments;[721] currently, white vestments are prescribed. Thus, whenever the Anointing of the

717 *PCS*, 113, 133.

718 *CB*, 648; *PCS*, 133.

719 *CB*, 648; *PCS*, 134.

720 *CB*, 648; *PCS*, 134.

721 Adrian Fortescue, J. B. O'Connell, and Alcuin Reid, eds., *The Ceremonies of the Roman Rite Described*, 15th ed. (New York: Bloomsbury, 2009), 455–457.

Sick is celebrated during Mass on a Sunday in Advent or Lent, for example, when the ritual Mass for the Anointing is not permitted, the celebrant will retain the violet stole and chasuble until after the homily. At the chair, he removes the violet stole and chasuble, and dons a white stole. Just prior to the preparation of the altar and gifts, he removes the white stole at the chair and takes the violet stole and chasuble once again.[722] The same could be done if the Anointing of the Sick is celebrated on solemnities which require red vestments.

The opening rites of Mass are celebrated as usual. After the Sign of the Cross and the liturgical greeting, the celebrant addresses the sick according to one or the other of two forms indicated in *Pastoral Care of the Sick*.[723] A server holds the ritual in both hands slightly to the left of the celebrant. The Gloria, if required, is said or sung. A second server holds the open missal in both hands, once again slightly to the left of the celebrant. The celebrant offers the Collect with hands extended. After the homily, the liturgy of Anointing properly speaking begins with the litany. The celebrant may lead the litany from the chair or standing before the altar closer to the sick who are present.[724] A server stands to the left of the celebrant holding the ritual. Other priests who may be assisting with the Anointing stand on either side. The deacon offers the intentions of the litany with hands joined, unless these are sung by the cantor. In some locations, the litany is deferred until after the Anointings are completed.[725]

Then the priests go and lay hands in silence on the sick persons each of them will eventually anoint.[726] Normally, the minister of the Sacrament places the open palms of both hands, fingers joined, on the head of each person in silence. There is nothing to prevent those who are capable from coming forward to receive the laying on of the hands, if the circumstances suggest it.[727]

Returning to the position where he stood, either at the chair or at the entrance to the sanctuary, the celebrant then offers the prayer of thanksgiving over the

[722] When the Anointing of the Sick takes place during Mass celebrated in white vestments, there is no need to remove the chasuble for the rite of Anointing, according to the principle in the revised rites that the chasuble can be worn for those sacraments which take place during Mass.

[723] *PCS*, 135.

[724] Elliott, *Ceremonies Explained for Servers*, 164.

[725] This possibility is mentioned in Elliott, *Ceremonies Explained for Servers*, 164, 166 and Elliott, *Ceremonies of the Modern Roman Rite*, 209, following the indication given in *CB*, 652. No such indication in given anywhere in *Pastoral Care of the Sick* itself.

[726] *CB*, 653; *PCS*, 139.

[727] Elliott, *Ceremonies Explained for Servers*, 165.

blessed oil with hands joined. A server holds the vessels or vessels of blessed oil of the sick before him, perhaps on a tray.[728] If no oil of the sick blessed by the bishop is available, the celebrant has the faculty in the universal law to bless oil made from plants for this single occasion during the course of the celebration of the Sacrament.[729] If the celebrant uses form A of the blessing,[730] he joins his hands to say, "Let us pray." Then he says the prayer of blessing with hands extended in the *orans* position. At the point indicated, he makes the Sign of the Cross with the right hand over the oil, the left hand resting on his chest. After momentarily joining his hands, he extends them again in the *orans* position until the conclusion of the prayer. If the celebrant uses form B of the blessing,[731] he joins his hands for the three invocations of the Persons of the Trinity. He extends his hands in the *orans* position for the concluding Collect, joining his hands once again at its conclusion. He may add the Sign of the Cross at the conclusion, according to the general principle that when blessing prayers do not indicate the Sign of the Cross, the celebrant may add the Sign of the Cross at the conclusion of the prayer.

Then the priests each take an oil stock and go to the designated sick persons each of them is intended to anoint. The priests anoint each person on the forehead and heads, saying the entire sacramental formula once for every person. A server may accompany each priest, holding a card with the sacramental formula if necessary. Each priest generally carries his own vessel of oil in his left hand. Using his right hand, he dips his thumb into the blessed oil and anoints the sick person on the forehead first, tracing a Greek cross on the forehead and saying the first part of the sacramental formula. Then, he anoints the open palms of both hands of each sick person, tracing a Greek cross on each palm, beginning with the right hand, while saying the second portion of the sacramental formula once during the Anointing of both hands.[732]

Once all the sick are anointed, the celebrant and other priests return to the sanctuary.[733] The vessels with oil are returned to the credence table or the ambry. The

[728] Elliott, *Ceremonies Explained for Servers*, 165.

[729] *PCS*, 21; *CIC*, 999, §2. After the celebration for which it was needed, this oil is discarded. The celebrant is instructed to absorb what is left in cotton and burn the cotton balls. See *PCS*, 22. Traditionally, the ashes and any water used to cleanse the priests' hands after the Anointings were then poured down the sacrarium. See Elliott, *Ceremonies Explained for Servers*, 122 and Fortescue, O'Connell, and Reid, *The Ceremonies of the Roman Rite Described*, 456.

[730] *PCS*, 140A.

[731] *PCS*, 140B.

[732] *PCS*, 23, 124; Fortescue, O'Connell, and Reid, *The Ceremonies of the Roman Rite Described*, 456.

[733] The historic practice included wiping off the oil with cotton balls after each Anointing. See Fortescue, O'Connell, and Reid, *The Ceremonies of the Roman Rite Described*, 455. The current rite discourages this practice. See *PCS*, 107.

celebrant and other priests may wash and dry their hands at the credence table set up for this purpose in the sanctuary with all the items indicated above.[734] Alternatively, the celebrant may wash his hands standing at the chair. In this case, servers bring a bowl and a pitcher of water, lemons or bread, and a towel for him to wash and dry his hands. If the celebrant washes his hands seated, the deacon or server spreads a gremial on his lap before he washes and dries his hands and removes it afterward.

Standing at the chair, the celebrant may now offer the prayer after the Anointing with hands extended. A server stands with the ritual in both hands slightly to his left. Or, if the litany was not prayed earlier, the celebrant introduces it now instead, with hands joined.[735] With hands joined, the deacon offers the intentions of the litany, unless these are sung by the cantor. Then the celebrant extends his hands in the *orans* position for the concluding prayer until its conclusion, when he joins his hands once again.

The Prayer of the Faithful of Mass is omitted, having been replaced by the litany. On Sundays and solemnities, the Creed is said. Then, the celebrant sits, and Mass continues in the usual way with the preparation of the gifts. At the conclusion of Mass, the celebrant offers the Post-Communion prayer at the altar or at the chair. He may also offer the solemn blessing found in the proper ritual Mass for the Anointing of the Sick. At the altar, he stands facing the assembly with the missal placed directly before him, at the center, with its bottom edge parallel to the edge of the altar. He prays the Post-Communion prayer with hands extended. The celebrant then extends and then joins his hands when greeting the faithful with "The Lord be with you." The deacon, with hands joined, invites those present to bow their heads. Then, with hands outstretched over the people, palms facing down, the celebrant prayers the invocations of the solemn blessing. All respond, "Amen," to each invocation. He joins his hands and gives the blessing with his right hand, his left hand resting on the altar, before joining his hands once again. If the celebrant offers the Post-Communion prayer and the solemn blessing standing at the chair instead, a server holding the missal slightly to his left stands before him. At the chair, when imparting the blessing with his right hand, the celebrant's left hand rests on his chest.

Once the celebrant has blessed the faithful, the deacon, with hands joined, says the dismissal. All depart from the sanctuary in the usual order, having first

734 Elliott, *Ceremonies Explained for Servers*, 165.

735 *CB*, 652; Elliott, *Ceremonies Explained for Servers*, 164, 166; Elliott, *Ceremonies of the Modern Roman Rite*, 209.

bowed to the altar or genuflected to the Blessed Sacrament reserved in the sanctuary, as the case may be.

Anointing apart from Mass

The Anointing of the Sick can also be celebrated in the church apart from Mass for a few persons or for a larger number of persons.[736] The priest celebrant wears a white stole. As in other cases where sacraments are celebrated apart from Mass, he may also wear a white cope.[737] He can be assisted by a deacon wearing a white stole and a white dalmatic. All genuflect to the Blessed Sacrament reserved in the sanctuary whenever passing before it.[738] Otherwise, they bow to the altar whenever crossing the sanctuary. The introductory rites begin with the Sign of the Cross and liturgical greeting, as usual. It may include a brief instruction, as at Mass, and will always include the penitential act, but never the Gloria. There is no Collect. The Liturgy of the Word might be simplified to one reading. The litany (unless it is deferred until after the Anointings), laying of the hands, thanksgiving over the blessed oil or its blessing, the Anointing, and the prayer after Anointing all take place as described above. When Holy Communion is not distributed, all then pray the Lord's Prayer together. The liturgy of the Anointing of the Sick ends with the proper blessing and dismissal, as described above. Or, after the Anointings, the liturgy may instead end with the litany, the Our Father, the prayer after Anointing, and the proper blessing and dismissal, in that order.[739] A server holds the ritual in both hands slightly to the left of the celebrant.

If Holy Communion is to be distributed, the priest or the deacon brings the Blessed Sacrament from the place of reservation after the litany and post-Anointing prayer. First, a server brings a corporal in a burse from the credence table to the altar. The server holds the burse open in both hands, at eye level. The deacon removes the corporal from the burse and opens it flat upon the altar at the center. The deacon then goes to the tabernacle and opens the door. He genuflects and takes the ciborium in hand. If no other vessels with the Blessed Sacrament remain in the tabernacle, he leaves the door open. If other vessels containing the Blessed Sacrament remain, he puts down the ciborium momentarily on a corporal open

[736] *PCS*, 111–130.

[737] *PCS*, 111; *CB*, 661.

[738] The prescription to bow to the altar rather than genuflect to the Blessed Sacrament in the tabernacle whenever passing before both pertains specifically to the celebration of Mass. See *GIRM*, 274. This rubric is not found in any other liturgical book.

[739] *CB*, 652, 665.

before the tabernacle. He genuflects and closes the door of the tabernacle before taking up the ciborium once again. If the place of reservation is outside the sanctuary, the priest or the deacon wears a white humeral veil to transfer the Blessed Sacrament. He is accompanied by two servers with lit candles, or at least by one.

Upon arriving at the altar, the priest or deacon places the ciborium on a corporal on the altar and genuflects. He places the cover and veil of the ciborium outside the corporal. The celebrant introduces the Our Father with hands joined and prays the Our Father with hands in the *orans* position. Holding a Host in his right hand and the vessel in his left hand at eye level, he invites those present with "Behold the Lamb of God." After the distribution of Communion, the Blessed Sacrament is returned to the place of reservation. The priest prays the Post-Communion prayer and offers the proper solemn blessing from *Pastoral Care of the Sick* in the manner described above. The deacon gives the dismissal with hands joined. All return to the sacristy in the usual manner after first reverencing the altar with a bow or genuflecting to the Blessed Sacrament reserved in the sanctuary.

27

Funerals and Burials

Funeral Masses are the most common form of Masses for the dead. Celebrants in some locations incorporate at funeral Masses some of the customs mentioned in chapter 21 that are characteristic of Masses for the dead in general, according to the traditional practice of the Roman Rite. Moreover, the funeral Mass is distinguished by two distinctive elements: the greeting of the body at the door of the church and the final commendation. In addition to what is usually prepared for Mass, the following items are needed:

- Funeral pall or other Christian symbols, if used
- Easter candle, if used, placed near the position the body will eventually occupy
- Incense and censer, if used
- Holy water and aspergillum
- White humeral veil, if Holy Communion will be distributed outside of Mass and the Blessed Sacrament is reserved outside the sanctuary
- Lectern outside the sanctuary, covered in an antependium in the color of the Mass, and a microphone for words of remembrance, if there are any

For the entire funeral Mass, ordained ministers wear either white, violet, or black Mass vestments. For the funeral apart from Mass, the priest may wear the cope over the stole and the deacon may wear the dalmatic over the stole.[740]

[740] *OCF*, 182.

The Funeral Mass

Just prior to the arrival of the body at the church, the celebrant and ministers make their way from the sacristy to the door of the church where the body will be received. They do so in an orderly way, but without ceremony. The procession at the beginning of the funeral Mass begins at the door where the body is received, not from the sacristy. Once the body arrives at the church, the cross and candles stand closest to the altar, since the procession will move toward the altar. The celebrant stands at the foot of the body, at the center, facing the coffin and the mourners standing behind it. The deacon stands to his right, with the server with holy water to his right. A server with the *Order of Christian Funerals* stands to the celebrant's left. The celebrant begins with the Sign of the Cross and the greeting. He receives the aspergillum in his right hand from the deacon and sprinkles the body three times, first in front of him, then to this left, and finally to his right.[741] The pall may be placed on the coffin at this time, if desired. Then all turn on their right and the procession to the sanctuary begins. The casket follows immediately behind the celebrant. The mourners follow the casket.

Once the procession has reached the sanctuary, the ministers make the usual reverence to the Blessed Sacrament if it is reserved there or to the altar. If desired, the celebrant and deacon may instead turn toward the assembly and face the body until it is finally in the proper position and any further symbols of the Christian life are placed upon it. The body of the deceased is oriented to the altar in the same position the person occupied in life. Thus, for a layperson, the body is oriented with the feet closest to the altar such that the body is facing the altar. For a cleric, that is, a bishop, a priest, or a deacon, the body is oriented with the head closest to the altar, such that the body is facing the assembly. Once the celebrant is assured that the body is in the proper position, and having offered the appropriate reverences to the Blessed Sacrament or to the altar, the celebrant and the deacon go up to the altar. They reverence it with a kiss. The celebrant may incense the altar in the usual way.[742] The celebrant, deacon, and servers go to their places. A server immediately stands at the chair before the celebrant with the missal or funeral ritual held open with the hands at the bottom of each page.

741 Adrian Fortescue, J. B. O'Connell, and Alcuin Reid, eds., *The Ceremonies of the Roman Rite Described*, 15th ed. (New York: Bloomsbury, 2009), 461.

742 Formerly, the use of incense at funeral Masses was limited to the Offertory, the two elevations, and the final absolution. See Fortescue, O'Connell, and Reid, *The Ceremonies of the Roman Rite Described*, 157–159, 465.

The penitential act is omitted entirely. The celebrant faces the assembly and immediately says, "Let us pray," with hands joined. The Collect follows with hands extended in the *orans* position. The Liturgy of the Word follows in the usual way, as do the preparation of the gifts and the altar, the Eucharistic Prayer, and the Communion rite.

If the sign of peace which prepares for the reception of Holy Communion might be confused in the minds of those present with the customary offering of sympathies to the bereaved family, it may be best to omit this gesture, as the Order for Mass suggests: "Then, if appropriate, the Deacon or the Priest, adds: Let us offer each other the sign of peace."[743] Historically, in the Roman Rite, the funeral rite did not include the exchange of the sign of peace.[744] Mass concludes with the Post-Communion prayer. The celebrant retains the chasuble for everything that follows the Post-Communion prayer.[745]

The celebrant may pray the Post-Communion prayer at the altar or at the chair. If the celebrant offers the Post-Communion prayer at the altar, he stands facing the assembly with the missal placed directly before him, at the center, with its bottom edge parallel to the edge of the altar. He prays the Post-Communion prayer with hands extended. If the celebrant offers the Post-Communion prayer standing at the chair instead, a server holds the missal standing before him or slightly to his left. After praying the Post-Communion prayer, the celebrant and deacon kiss the altar in the usual manner and proceed to the final commendation.

The servers with cross and candles stand together either in the sanctuary or at its entrance furthest away from the altar. They turn to face the altar. The servers with book, incense, and holy water (if needed) stand between the cross and candles bearers and the altar. The celebrant and deacon stand closest to the altar. All face the altar. Unless they are holding something in their hands, all genuflect together to the Blessed Sacrament reserved in the sanctuary or bow from the waist to the altar. Those carrying something in their hands do not genuflect or bow from the waist but bow their heads instead. All turn to their right and leave the sanctuary to take their places around the casket for the final commendation.

Words of remembrance may be offered by a relative or friend of these deceased. These form part of the final commendation, not the rite of Communion. Therefore, they take place after the Post-Communion prayer, not before. In addition,

743 *RM*, Order for Mass, no. 128.

744 Fortescue, O'Connell, and Reid, *The Ceremonies of the Roman Rite Described*, 159.

745 *CB*, 833.

they ideally take place after the priest and deacon have kissed the altar, signifying the end of the funeral Mass. The person offering the words of remembrance should stand at a lectern near the body or at some other suitable place outside the sanctuary. The ambo is not the proper place for the words of remembrance. If the words of remembrance will be brief, after the Post-Communion prayer, the celebrant and ministers might kiss the altar, and then bow to the altar or genuflect to the Blessed Sacrament upon leaving the sanctuary to stand near the coffin to listen to them, while the rest of the assembly remains seated.[746] Otherwise, if the words of remembrance are not expected to brief, after kissing the altar, the celebrant and the deacon may return to their places in the sanctuary and sit. At the conclusion of the words of remembrance, the celebrant, deacon, and ministers rise from their places. They bow to the altar or genuflect to the Blessed Sacrament reserved in the sanctuary and take their places around the casket for the final commendation.

For the final commendation, the servers with the cross and the candles stand furthest away from the altar, but facing it together in a straight line, with the casket before them. This is true whether the deceased is a layperson or a cleric.[747] If it is not possible for the three of them to stand side by side, the candle bearers stand behind the cross, so that they are then leading the cross when they turn around for the procession. These three servers will leave room between themselves and the casket for the celebrant to pass during the final commendation. The celebrant stands just outside the sanctuary, facing the casket. If the Blessed Sacrament is not reserved in the sanctuary, he may stand at the center.[748] If the Blessed Sacrament is reserved in the center of the sanctuary, it is customary for the celebrant to stand slightly to the left of center as he faces the nave (the epistle side) so as not to stand directly in front of the Blessed Sacrament.[749] The deacon, thurifer, and server with holy water stand to his right. The server with the funeral ritual stands to his left. All in the assembly stand.

The celebrant invites the assembly to pray, with hands joined. After bowing his head and closing his eyes in prayer for a time, he then turns to his right,

[746] *OCF*, 197.

[747] Peter J. Elliott, *Ceremonies Explained for Servers According to the Roman Rite: A Manual for Altar Servers, Acolytes, Sacristans, and Masters of Ceremonies* (San Francisco: Ignatius Press, 2019), 177.

[748] Elliott, *Ceremonies Explained for Servers*, 178; Fortescue, O'Connell, and Reid, *The Ceremonies of the Roman Rite Described*, 470.

[749] Fortescue, O'Connell, and Reid, *The Ceremonies of the Roman Rite Described*, 464, 470, n. 49.

imposes incense, and blesses it in the usual way, if incense is used.[750] If the deceased is a layperson, the celebrant begins to sprinkle the body at the foot of the casket, that is, facing the assembly. If the deceased is a cleric, namely a bishop, a priest, or a deacon, the celebrant and those ministers assisting him likewise position themselves at the foot of the casket, that is, facing the altar, in order to begin the sprinkling and the incensation.

Once in the proper position, the celebrant receives the aspergillum from the deacon in his right hand. The celebrant and the deacon assisting him with the holy water as necessary walk around the casket in a counterclockwise direction.[751] The celebrant sprinkles the right-hand side of the coffin three times, first at the feet, then at the center, then at the head, before passing to the left side of the coffin and doing the same at the head, the center, and the feet, as he moves toward the sanctuary. The sprinkling with holy water can take place before, during, or after the song of farewell.[752] If the body was sprinkled with holy water at the beginning of the funeral, this gesture is usually omitted at this point.[753] The celebrant returns the aspergillum to the deacon and the deacon returns the aspergillum and holy water to a server.

The celebrant immediately receives the censer from the deacon. Together they proceed to incense the body of the deceased in the same manner as the sprinkling of the body. They bow low to the body and then move in a counterclockwise direction. The celebrant incenses the right-hand side of the casket with three swings of the thurible and then does the same on the opposite side of the casket. Upon arriving where he began, the celebrant and the deacon bow low to the body, following the general rule that one bows before and after incensing an object or person. The celebrant hands the thurible to the deacon standing on his right, who hands it to the thurifer. The thurifer takes his place behind the processional cross and candles in the center aisle, so as to lead the closing procession to the place of burial or at least to the door of the church.

Facing the assembly once again, whether celebrating the commendation of a deceased layperson or a deceased cleric, the celebrant now prays the commendation with arms extended in the *orans* position. With hands joined, the deacon invites all to join in the procession to the cemetery. The celebrant, servers, and

750 Fortescue, O'Connell, and Reid, *The Ceremonies of the Roman Rite Described*, 464; *OCF*, 200.
751 Elliott, *Ceremonies Explained for Servers*, 178.
752 *OCF*, 200.
753 *OCF*, 200.

deacon bow to the altar or genuflect to the Blessed Sacrament reserved there one final time. They take their places between the cross and candles and the coffin in the same manner as they did before the altar at the end of the funeral Mass. All face the coffin while it is reoriented, if necessary, for the final procession. Perhaps it is best for the deacon to remain momentarily at the celebrant's left at this point. When the procession departs, the deacon will once again be standing at the celebrant's right side, without any additional movement. Once the body has been reoriented as needed for the procession, the ministers can turn to their right and set off in procession. The deacon and celebrant turn toward each other. The deacon is now walking at the celebrant's right. The casket follows the celebrant. The mourners follow the body.

If the place of burial is close by, the procession can continue all the way to the cemetery in that order. Otherwise, it can conclude just inside the door of the church, or even at the hearse outside the church, depending on the circumstances and the weather. At the door of the church, the cross and candles stand together in a row to the right with the other servers behind them. The priest and deacon might take their places to the left. All face the casket as it passed between them. At the hearse instead, the cross and candles stand together nearby, with the servers behind them. All face the door of the church. The priest and deacon stand opposite them. The celebrant may sprinkle the casket a final time before it is placed in the hearse, especially if this will not take place at the cemetery.[754]

At the door of the church, the celebrant may remove the chasuble and wear the cope for the procession to the cemetery and the prayers there.

The Funeral apart from Mass

There are times when the funeral liturgy takes place in the church apart from Mass. In that case, all genuflect to the Blessed Sacrament whenever passing before it.[755] Otherwise, all bow to altar whenever crossing the sanctuary. The indications described above are followed until the conclusion of the Prayer of the Faithful, which the priest prays at his chair with hands extended.

After the conclusion to the Prayer of the Faithful, the funeral outside of Mass continues either with the distribution of Holy Communion and final

[754] Elliott, *Ceremonies Explained for Servers*, 180.

[755] The prescription to bow to the altar rather than genuflect to the Blessed Sacrament in the tabernacle whenever passing before both pertains specifically to the celebration of Mass. See *GIRM*, 274. This rubric is not found in any other liturgical book.

commendation, or with the Our Father and final commendation. If Communion is not distributed, following the conclusion of the Prayer of the Faithful, the celebrant then immediately introduces the Our Father with hands joined. He prays the Our Father with hands extended in the *orans* position. Following the Our Father, the priest and ministers can take their places at the foot of the coffin, as described above, for the final commendation.

If Holy Communion will be distributed, the deacon or the server brings the corporal to the altar in a burse and unfolds it as described in chapter 7. (See figure 6.) A server places the *Order of Christian Funerals* on the altar to the left of the corporal at an angle, open to the proper page. The priest himself or the deacon assisting him brings the Blessed Sacrament from the place of reservation, places it on a corporal on the altar, and genuflects. If the place of reservation is located outside the sanctuary, the celebrant or the deacon wears the humeral veil and is accompanied by two servers with candles.

The priest celebrant introduces the Our Father with hands joined, but prays the Our Father with hands in the *orans* position. The celebrant genuflects, takes up a Host, and invites the assembly to Communion with the words "Behold the Lamb of God."[756] After the distribution of Communion, the celebrant or the deacon returns the ciborium to the tabernacle. Again, if the place of reservation is located outside the sanctuary, he wears the humeral veil and is accompanied by two servers with candles. The Post-Communion prayer is prayed at the altar. The ritual is open at the center of the altar with its edge parallel to the edge of the altar. The priest says, "Let us pray," with hands joined and prays the Post-Communion prayer with hands extended. The funeral apart from Mass continues with the words of remembrance, if any, and the final commendation.

If the words of remembrance will be brief, the celebrant and ministers might bow to the altar or genuflect to the Blessed Sacrament upon leaving the sanctuary to stand near the coffin to listen to them, while the rest of the assembly remains seated.[757] Otherwise, if the words of remembrance are not expected to brief, the celebrant and the deacon may return to their places from the altar and sit. At the conclusion of the words of remembrance, the celebrant, deacon, and ministers rise from their places. They bow to the altar or genuflect to the Blessed Sacrament reserved in the sanctuary and take their places at the coffin for the final commendation.

[756] *OCF*, 409.
[757] *OCF*, 197.

This form of the funeral is most likely to take place on Holy Thursday, Good Friday, and Holy Saturday, when funeral Masses themselves are forbidden. On Good Friday and Holy Saturday, the Blessed Sacrament is not reserved in the sanctuary, and cannot be distributed to those present for Communion, therefore all reverences are directed to the altar instead. All genuflect when passing before the cross reverenced during the Passion service on Good Friday. On Good Friday and Holy Saturday as well, funerals apart from Mass are celebrated without singing, music, or the tolling of bells, since the Paschal Triduum has begun the evening before.[758] If holy water was entirely removed from the church after the Evening Mass of the Lord's Supper on Holy Thursday,[759] then funerals apart from Mass on Good Friday and Holy Saturday will not include the sprinkling of the body. If holy water is not used, it would seem inappropriate to drape the coffin in the pall which, like the sprinkling with holy water, is also a reminder of Baptism. Other symbols of the Christian life could be placed on the coffin instead. On the contrary, some holy water was always retained in the sacristy on Holy Thursday according to the traditional practice of the Roman Rite for use as needed during the Triduum.[760] In that case, holy water would be available for use at a funeral outside of Mass on Good Friday and Holy Saturday, and the use of the baptismal pall would likewise be consistent. While none of the modern books mention it, it would also seem inappropriate to use the paschal candle at a funeral apart from Mass once the Paschal Triduum has begun. In any event, the use of the paschal candle at any funeral is always optional.[761]

When the deacon presides over the funeral outside of Mass in the place of the priest, he does so from his own chair in the sanctuary. Normally, the deacon prays the Our Father with hands joined. Otherwise, the postures and gestures of the deacon are the same as those of the priest.

The Rite of Committal

The rite of committal is very brief. Historically, the priest celebrant stood at the foot of the coffin, as during the final commendation.[762] Whenever possible, a cross bearer

[758] Congregation for Divine Worship, *Paschalis sollemnitatis*, no. 61, *Notitiae* 24 (1988): 95.

[759] Peter J. Elliott, *Ceremonies of the Liturgical Year According to the Modern Roman Rite: A Manual for Clergy and All Involved in Liturgical Ministries* (San Francisco: Ignatius Press, 2002), 110.

[760] Fortescue, O'Connell, and Reid, *The Ceremonies of the Roman Rite Described*, 342, n. 28.

[761] *OCF*, 133.

[762] Elliott, *Ceremonies Explained for Servers*, 181; Fortescue, O'Connell, and Reid, *The Ceremonies of the Roman Rite Described*, 465.

stood at the head of the coffin, facing the celebrant, with candle bearers on either side, as for the final commendation in the church. Another minister or one of the mourners can hold the *Order of Christian Funerals* in both hands, standing to the left of the priest. The invitation, Scripture verse, and the various forms of the prayer over the place of committal are said with hands joined. At the conclusion of form A of the prayer over the place of committal, which is used to bless the grave, the priest or deacon may add the Sign of the Cross, saying nothing. Likewise, since the grave is being blessed, incense and holy water are used. The celebrant imposes incense with the assistance of the deacon to his right and blesses it as usual. The server with incense can stand to the celebrant's right. The server with the holy water can also stand to the celebrant's right. The priest receives the aspergillum from the deacon. While standing stationary, the priest customarily sprinkles the grave and the coffin together three times, at the center, to the left, and to the right. The priest returns the aspergillum to the deacon. The deacon receives the censer from the thurifer and hands it to the priest. The priest then incenses both the grave and the body together in the same manner, bowing before and after.[763] The priest returns the censer to the deacon, who in turn returns the censer to the thurifer. The deacon may hold back the edge of the cope while the priest incenses the coffin and the grave. If the cemetery or the grave are already blessed, neither the coffin nor the grave itself are sprinkled with holy water or incensed.

After the prayer of committal, the celebrant then prays the introduction to the intercessions with hands joined. The deacon may offer the intentions. At their conclusion, the priest then immediately begins praying the Our Father. Historically, while praying the Our Father, the priest sprinkled the coffin (making the Sign of the Cross), not going around it.[764] The Our Father is said with the hands in the *orans* position. The prayer over the people is prayed with hands extended over the people, with palms down. At the verses which begin, "Eternal rest grant them O Lord," the priest historically made the Sign of the Cross over the coffin with the right hand, his left hand resting on his chest.[765] The deacon offers the dismissal with hands joined.

[763] *CB*, 836; Fortescue, O'Connell, and Reid, *The Ceremonies of the Roman Rite Described*, 465.

[764] Fortescue, O'Connell, and Reid, *The Ceremonies of the Roman Rite Described*, 465.

[765] Fortescue, O'Connell, and Reid, *The Ceremonies of the Roman Rite Described*, 465.

28

The Liturgy of the Hours

FROM TIME TO time, the parish priest may be called upon to officiate at public celebrations of the Liturgy of the Hours. These take place according to the provisions of the *General Instruction on the Liturgy of the Hours*. The *Ceremonial of Bishops* also provides guidance. As always, the traditional practice of the Roman Rite can provide details which these two sources may lack.[766]

Solemn Vespers

The primary parish celebration of the Liturgy of the Hours is Sunday Vespers. The following describes the solemn form of such a celebration. The requisites include:

In the sacristy:

- Alb, or the surplice over the cassock, for the priest celebrant.[767] In addition, he wears a stole in the color of the day. He may wear a cope of the same color over the stole.[768]
- Dalmatics without stoles for assisting deacons who attend the celebrant.[769] If such deacons carry out some other functions where they would normally wear a stole, for example, exposing and reposing the Blessed Sacrament or

[766] See Adrian Fortescue, J. B. O'Connell, and Alcuin Reid, *The Ceremonies of the Roman Rite Described*, 15th ed. (New York: Bloomsbury, 2009), 250–253.

[767] One commentator indicates that the celebrant wears the alb when assisted by one or two deacons. Otherwise, when the priest celebrant has no assistants, he wears the alb or the surplice. See Peter J. Elliott, *Ceremonies of the Modern Roman Rite*, rev. ed. (San Francisco: Ignatius Press, 1995), 266.

[768] *GILH*, 255.

[769] *GILH*, 255.

preaching, they would wear the stole under the dalmatic. In either case, the deacons wear (the stole and) dalmatic over the alb or surplice, depending on the choice of the celebrant for himself.[770]

- A cope without the stole for an assisting priest, in the absence of an assisting deacon.[771] They too wear the cope over the alb or surplice, depending on the choice of the celebrant.
- Processional cross and candles, or processional candles alone if servers are lacking

In the sanctuary:

- A lectern before the presidential chair, covered with an antependium in the color of the Office, if servers are lacking
- A second matching lectern in the middle of the sanctuary, covered with an antependium in the color of the Office, facing the altar for the cantors[772]
- Stools facing the altar on either side of the sanctuary for the cantors
- Censer and incense, and stand
- Two books containing the *Liturgy of the Hours* cover in material of the color of the day, one at the ambo for the reading and intercessions and another at the presidential chair for the prayers
- Six candles, or at least four, on or near the altar
- The dust cover is removed from the altar.

Once all is ready, all bow to the sacristy crucifix and proceed to the sanctuary. Organ music accompanies the procession. A hymn is not sung. The order of the procession is the same as at Mass. Assisting deacons or priests walk on either side of the celebrant and may hold back the sides of his cope.[773] Upon arriving before the altar, those who are not carrying anything bow to the altar or genuflect to the Blessed Sacrament if the tabernacle is located in the sanctuary. During the course of Vespers, all will genuflect to the Blessed Sacrament reserved in the sanctuary

770 *GILH*, 255. The deacon who presides in the absence of a priest wears only the stole over the alb or cassock and surplice.

771 *GILH*, 255.

772 Fortescue, O'Connell, and Reid, *The Ceremonies of the Roman Rite Described*, 251.

773 Elliott, *Ceremonies of the Modern Roman Rite*, 268.

whenever passing before it.[774] At Vespers, the servers place their candles on either side of the lowest step of the altar or, if necessary, on either side of the lowest step of the sanctuary.[775] If this is impractical, they can place their candles at the rear corners of the credence table as at Mass. The clergy in procession make their reverence to the altar or the tabernacle two by two as they arrive before the altar, taking care to do so together. Then they turn slightly to each other and greet each other with a moderate bow, before turning back to go to their places on either side.[776] The celebrant and assistants go up to the altar and kiss it. The celebrant goes to the chair; his assistants join him on either side. A master of ceremonies can sit on a stool near them.

All remain standing as the celebrant makes the Sign of the Cross and intones the introductory verse. All bow at the *Gloria Patri*. Historically, this bow is made in the direction of the altar. For this reason, in many locations where the Liturgy of the Hours is celebrated in choir, all begin the hour facing the altar for the Sign of the Cross, introductory verse, and *Gloria Patri*. Then, all face each other and, still standing, sing the hymn. If the final verse of the hymn is a doxology which mentions the three Divine Persons, all should bow once again in their places during that verse. Two cantors come to the lectern in the middle of the sanctuary, bow to each other, then bow to the altar or genuflect to the Blessed Sacrament, and stand together at the lectern in the center of the sanctuary facing the altar to intone the antiphon. All remain standing during the antiphon to the first psalm. Once the cantors have intoned the first line of the first psalm up to the asterisk, all sit.[777] The cantors bow to the altar or genuflect to the Blessed Sacrament, bow to each other, and return to their seats.

Local custom determines the manner of singing of the psalms. The stanzas of the psalm may be sung in alternation between the two sides of the choir or the two sides of the church. The entire assembly might also alternate the singing with the cantor alone or with the schola. The assembly may sing the antiphon alone between the stanzas of the psalm. Or the assembly may sing the entire psalm from

[774] The prescription to bow to the altar rather than genuflect to the Blessed Sacrament in the tabernacle whenever passing before both pertains specifically to the celebration of Mass. See *GIRM*, 274. This rubric is not found in any other liturgical book.

[775] Peter J. Elliott, *Ceremonies Explained for Servers According to the Roman Rite: A Manual for Altar Servers, Acolytes, Sacristans, and Masters of Ceremonies* (San Francisco: Ignatius Press, 2019), 188; Elliott, *Ceremonies of the Modern Roman Rite*, 268.

[776] Fortescue, O'Connell, and Reid, *The Ceremonies of the Roman Rite Described*, 52.

[777] If the asterisk is missing in the printed editions of the *Liturgy of the Hours* being used, all sit at the end of the first line of the psalm instead.

beginning to end without a break, without any antiphon, and without any alternation.[778] At the end of each psalm, all bow their heads at the *Gloria Patri.*

The psalm prayers after each psalm always remain optional. If a psalm prayer is said or sung after each psalm, all stand after the antiphon has been repeated. The celebrant says, "Let us pray," with hands joined, then offers the prayer with hands extended in the *orans* position.[779] A server holds an Office book before him, or the Office book rests on the lectern before his chair. The psalm prayer concludes with the short ending "Through Christ Our Lord," and all answer, "Amen." Then all sit for the singing of the next psalm or the New Testament canticle. The cantor follows the same procedure described above to intone the antiphon before each succeeding psalm and canticle.

After the New Testament canticle, a reader goes to the ambo to proclaim the reading. If the reader passes before the altar or enters the sanctuary on the way to the ambo, he or she bows to the altar or genuflects if the Blessed Sacrament is reserved there. Once at the ambo, the reader bows to the celebrant and proclaims the reading with both hands resting on the edges of the Office book.[780] Unlike Mass, the reading at the Liturgy of the Hours is proclaimed without introduction (e.g., "A reading from the Letter of St. Paul to the Galatians") and without conclusion, (e.g., "The Word of the Lord"). After the customary reverence to the celebrant and to the altar or to the Blessed Sacrament, the reader returns to his or her place. A homily may follow. The priest may preach at the chair or at the ambo, or at some other suitable place. The deacon may preach at the ambo or at some other suitable place. Then a short responsory or some other chant may be sung while all remain seated, or silence may be observed instead.[781]

Incense may be used during the Gospel canticle of Evening Prayer.[782] Therefore, when the antiphon to the Magnificat is intoned, the thurifer brings the incense to the chair. Another server or one of the celebrant's assistants may move the lectern temporarily to the side if one is used. The thurifer bows to the celebrant,

778 *GILH*, 121–123.

779 Elliott, *Ceremonies of the Modern Roman Rite*, 269. *CB* 198 does not indicate any specific position for the hands during the psalm prayer. However, *CB* 205 does indicate hands extended for the concluding Collect of the hour. Finally, *CB* 104 indicates hands extended for any prayer directed to God by the bishop or a priest while standing. Conversely, it appears that deacons, while standing, pray Collects addressed to God with hands joined, according to the traditional practice.

780 Elliott, *Ceremonies Explained for Servers*, 188.

781 *GILH*, 49.

782 *GILH*, 261.

then kneels. The celebrant imposes incense seated. The server kneels before the celebrant with the censer, and the assisting deacon or priest stands to the celebrant's right with the boat. After the celebrant imposes and blesses the incense, the assistant returns the incense boat to another server or to its stand. The thurifer stands and bows to the celebrant. The thurifer goes to the altar just to the right of where the priest celebrant will stand at the middle. As the Magnificat begins, all stand, including the celebrant, and make the Sign of the Cross at the first words.[783] The celebrant and his assistants come before the altar at its center and bow, but do not kiss the altar. The thurifer gives the censer to the assistant to the celebrant's right, who passes it to the celebrant. The altar cross and altar itself are incensed as described in chapter 4. The assistants may hold back the celebrant's cope on either side during the incensation. Having concluded the incensation of the altar at the right-hand corner (as the celebrant faces it), the celebrant returns the censer to the assistant at his right, who passes it to the thurifer. The celebrant and his assistants return directly to their places by the shortest route.

At the chair, the thurifer hands the censer to the first assistant, the one to the celebrant's right. Standing in front of the chair, the first assistant incenses the celebrant, bowing before and after, and returns the censer to the thurifer.[784] The thurifer then incenses both assistants separately, beginning with the assistant on the celebrant's right and then the one on the celebrant's left. Next, he goes to a convenient place where he can incense any clergy in choir, and then any servers in choir. He then goes to the front of the sanctuary, where he incenses the faithful. The thurifer bows before and after incensing each individual or group of individuals. If the incensation is not completed and the choir begins to sing the *Gloria Patri*, the thurifer stops in his place and turns to bow before the altar, facing it with the censer, until the doxology has been sung.[785] Then the server resumes the final incensations during the antiphon, reverences the altar, and returns the censer to the sacristy or to its stand in the sanctuary.

Meanwhile, one of the assistants or a server can return the lectern to its place before the celebrant. The two servers may take their candles from the lowest altar step and stand on either side of the lectern, facing each other.[786] A server may hold an Office book before the celebrant instead of the lectern. The celebrant introduces

783 *CB*, 203; Elliott, *Ceremonies of the Modern Roman Rite*, 270; Elliott, *Ceremonies Explained for Servers*, 189.

784 Fortescue, O'Connell, and Reid, *The Ceremonies of the Roman Rite Described*, 256.

785 Fortescue, O'Connell, and Reid, *The Ceremonies of the Roman Rite Described*, 256.

786 Elliott, *Ceremonies Explained for Servers*, 190.

the intercessions. A deacon offers the intentions from the ambo or from his place. The same is true for a lay reader. When reading the intentions from the ambo or a lectern, the deacon or reader places the hands on the edges of the book. The celebrant may introduce the Our Father with hands joined. He prays the Our Father with hands extended.[787] Without saying "Let us pray," he immediately offers the Collect with hands extended in the *orans* position with the longer ending, "Through Our Lord Jesus Christ Your Son." The servers with candles turn and bow to the celebrant. They then stand at the entrance to the sanctuary, facing the altar. The celebrant turns toward the people if necessary and extends his hands toward the assembly, saying, "The Lord be with you." He blesses them in the customary way or uses one of the solemn blessings or blessings over the people. An assisting deacon or priest, or even the celebrant himself, sings the dismissal, and all respond.

If circumstances suggest it, the celebrant and his assistants may go to the altar and kiss it. Then, they descend the altar steps and face the altar. The ministers and servers depart in the same order as in the opening procession. The candles, and perhaps the cross between them, lead the way. Then the clergy in choir file out. As the clergy leaves their places, they bow to each other when they reach the middle of the sanctuary, then turn to reverence the altar or the Blessed Sacrament. They turn toward each other in pairs, before falling into line. Lastly, the celebrant and his assistants make their reverence to the altar or the Blessed Sacrament and turn to their right to join the procession. The assistants may hold the edges of the celebrant's cope on either side as they walk in procession.

Whenever Morning Prayer is celebrated in a solemn way, the indications described above are also followed.

The Major Hours in the Presence of the Blessed Sacrament

At times, the major hours, that is, Morning Prayer and Evening Prayer, are celebrated in the presence of the Blessed Sacrament exposed. The Blessed Sacrament may have been exposed for some time already before the beginning of the hour in question. Or, exposition may take place just prior to the beginning of Morning Prayer or Evening Prayer. In either case, during the course of the Liturgy of the Hours, whenever anyone passes before the altar where the Blessed Sacrament is exposed or whenever anyone approaches the altar in order to carry out a function in the sanctuary, even from the side of the altar, that person always genuflects

[787] Contrary to Elliott, *Ceremonies of the Modern Roman Rite*, 272, *CB* 104 indicates hands extended whenever the bishop or the priest addresses a prayer to God while standing.

toward the Blessed Sacrament exposed before continuing. Whenever the Blessed Sacrament it is exposed, all signs of reverence are directed exclusively toward it.

Whenever Evening Prayer or Morning Prayer is celebrated in the presence of the Blessed Sacrament exposed, and the celebrant wishes to incense the altar at the Gospel canticle, he must take this circumstance into account. While both the *Ceremonial of Bishops* and the *Rite of Eucharistic Exposition and Benediction* mention the possibility of the celebration of one of the major hours in the presence of the Blessed Sacrament, neither provides any guidance on how this is to be done.[788] One commentator offers this description of the manner in which they could be accomplished at Vespers:

> At the Magnificat, having prepared incense at the chair, the celebrant and assistants come before the altar, genuflect, and kneel while the celebrant incenses the Eucharist. They rise, go up to the altar, genuflect and continue the incensation as usual, and they genuflect together whenever they pass before the monstrance.[789]

Again, this same commentator repeats: "Before incensing the altar itself, the celebrant and any assistants kneel on the edge of the footpace, and the celebrant incenses the Blessed Sacrament with three double swings, bowing before and after, his cope held back by assistants."[790] This advice reflects the long-standing practice of the Roman Rite: "At the Magnificat, the celebrant ... kneeling on the edge of the footpace incenses the Blessed Sacrament with three double swings, bowing low before and after. He incenses the altar, but not the cross."[791]

A Simple Form of the Liturgy of the Hours

It is not always possible to celebrate Evening Prayer or Morning Prayer publicly with all the ceremony indicated above. For example, the priest may preside without assistants at his side. He may simply wear the stole over the alb or cassock and surplice.[792] In the absence of a priest, the deacon presides from his own proper chair in the sanctuary. In the absence of a schola, there may only be a cantor to lead the singing. One server may assist with the book and incense, but the arrival and departure of the presider will take place without cross and candles. An even simpler form of

788 *CB*, 1111; *HCWEOM*, 95.

789 Elliott, *Ceremonies of the Modern Roman Rite*, 274.

790 Elliott, *Ceremonies Explained for Servers*, 192.

791 Fortescue, O'Connell, and Reid, *The Ceremonies of the Roman Rite Described*, 262–263.

792 *GILH*, 255.

Evening Prayer or Morning Prayer may not include the use of incense at all. The hymn might be sung in unison without a cantor, but the psalms and canticles may need to be recited. In that case, the recitation of the psalms and canticles can alternate between the two choirs, or the two sides of the church, or between the presider on the one hand and the entire assembly on the other. The same is true whenever the Office of Readings or any one of the daytime hours or Compline is celebrated.

The Office of Readings on Certain Days of the Year

According to the *Ceremonial of Bishops*, the Office of Readings is sometimes joined to the celebration of the Mass at Night on Christmas.[793] In that case, the priest celebrant can wear the chasuble instead of the cope for the Office of Readings. The Office of Readings can take place either in the extended form, with three additional canticles and the proclamation of the Gospel, or in its usual form. The indications given above for the solemn celebration of Vespers apply in both cases. If a Gospel passage is read, the priest imposes incense and the deacon seeks his blessing, as at Mass. A Gospel procession with Gospel book, incense, and candles takes place in the same way as at Mass. After the Gospel reading, or after the second responsory if the usual form is celebrated, the Gloria is sung in place of the *Te Deum*.[794] If not already standing, all stand to sing the Gloria. The opening Collect of the Mass is said immediately, the introductory rites and penitential act being omitted entirely.[795]

The Office of Readings is also often joined to the celebration of Morning Prayer on Good Friday and Holy Saturday. This practice is recommended by the *Ceremonial of Bishops*.[796] The indications given above for the solemn celebration of Vespers apply. The celebration of the Office of Readings and Morning Prayer may include a hymn at the beginning of each hour, or the hymn appointed for Morning Prayer alone may be sung after the invitatory at the beginning of the Office of Readings.[797] At the conclusion of the Office of Readings, the final Collect and verse are omitted. Morning Prayer begins immediately with the hymn or with the first antiphon and its psalm, as the case may be, omitting the introductory verse and *Gloria Patri* usually sung at the beginning of Morning Prayer.[798]

[793] *CB*, 238; *GILH*, 98, 215.
[794] *CB*, 238; *GILH*, 98.
[795] *GILH*, 98.
[796] *CB*, 296; *GILH*, 210.
[797] *GILH*, 99.
[798] *GILH*, 99.

PART 5

The Roles for Priests and Deacons at Parish Celebrations by a Bishop

29

The Parish Mass Celebrated by a Bishop

From time to time, a bishop may be the celebrant of a parish Mass. For the most part, the descriptions of the postures and gestures for such a Mass are not found in the *General Instruction of the Roman Missal*, but rather in the *Ceremonial of Bishops*.[799] Although the current *General Instruction* and *Ceremonial of Bishops* have largely eliminated the ritual differences which existed formerly between a Mass celebrated by a bishop and a Mass celebrated by a priest, a few such differences still remain. Where these differences still exist, the traditional practice of the Roman Rite can help clarify what is intended by the descriptions found in the *Ceremonial of Bishops*. In addition, the traditional practice of the Roman Rite can clarify what is expected from the priests and deacons who will assist the bishop during the celebration of Mass in the parish church. This chapter presumes all the indications given in Part 1 of this work, "The Mass." In addition, it addresses what is specific to the celebration of Mass by a bishop above and beyond what is required during the course of the celebration of Mass by a priest.

Preparations for Mass

In addition to everything usually prepared for the celebration of the Eucharist, the following items are also needed when Mass is celebrated by a bishop:[800]

- At the altar, six candles or at least four. If the diocesan bishop is the celebrant, seven candles are prepared.

[799] *CB*, 119–170.
[800] *CB*, 125–127.

- Seven processional candles, if the diocesan bishop is the celebrant, or at least two
- Two, four, six, or even eight torches[801]
- A brass or silver ewer and basin with towel in the sacristy and in the sanctuary
- Chasubles and stoles in the color of the Mass being celebrated or in white for the bishop and concelebrants
- Dalmatics and stoles for the two assisting deacons and for the deacon of the Mass in the color of the Mass being celebrated
- Vimpas (a specialized form of the humeral veil) for the miter and crozier bearers, if available
- Texts of the Eucharistic Prayer for the concelebrating priests
- A chair (the faldstool) for the bishop in the sacristy if he washes his hands seated, or receives the miter seated, or prays the prayers of preparation and thanksgiving seated
- A gremial or an amice if the bishop washes his hands seated, either in the sacristy prior to Mass or in the sanctuary during Mass

Historically, the bishop has been seated at Mass on the side of the sanctuary opposite to the side where a priest celebrant normally sits. Often, the placement of the ambo will make this position impractical for the bishop's chair. If the Blessed Sacrament is not reserved at the head of the apse, this is also a traditional position for the chair of the bishop in the sanctuary. This may mean moving the presidential chair from its usual position when a bishop is the celebrant. Customarily, the chair for the bishop is raised at least one step above the floor of the sanctuary.

Seats for the miter bearer, staff bearer, book bearer, and master of ceremonies are generally placed near the bishop, behind him or to his left if possible.[802] During the course of Mass, when required, the miter bearer holds the miter upright in both hands with the fanons, or tails of the miter, toward himself.[803] Customarily, the miter bearer veils his hands with each end of the vimpa to hold the miter.

[801] Adrian Fortescue, J. B. O'Connell, and Alcuin Reid, *The Ceremonies of the Roman Rite Described*, 15th ed. (New York: Bloomsbury, 2009), 219, n. 83.

[802] Peter J. Elliott, *Ceremonies of the Modern Roman Rite: The Eucharist and the Liturgy of the Hours*, rev. ed. (San Francisco: Ignatius Press, 1995), 174.

[803] Fortescue, O'Connell, and Reid, *Ceremonies of the Roman Rite Described*, 203.

The staff bearer always hands the pastoral staff to the bishop and takes it from him directly.[804] The staff bearer carries the crozier with the crook facing forward. When handing the staff to the bishop, the server hands the crozier to the bishop with the crook toward himself or herself so that the bishop receives the crozier with the crook facing forward.[805] Similarly, the staff bearer customarily veils his or her hands in the end of the vimpa whenever holding the crozier in both hands. When the miter and staff bearers are not holding anything in their hands, they keep their hands joined outside the vimpas.[806] Often, the master of ceremonies hands the miter and staff to the bishop and receives them from the bishop before handing them to the miter bearer and staff bearer.

The bishop wears the miter whenever he is seated. The bishop wears the miter to impart blessings, like the blessing of the deacon before the Gospel or the blessing at the end of Mass. He also wears the miter at certain specific points in the celebration of the various sacraments and sacramentals. The bishop holds the pastoral staff during the entrance procession, the proclamation of the Gospel, and the recessional. He also holds the staff during specific points of the celebration of various sacraments and sacramentals, like during the renunciation of sin and profession of faith at Baptism, for example. A master of ceremonies directs the miter and staff bearers as to when the bishop uses either item and when he sets them aside. Finally, the master of ceremonies will determine a place to stand the crozier if there are times when neither the bishop nor the staff bearer is holding it.

The two deacons assisting the bishop are seated immediately on either side of the bishop. The deacon sitting to the bishop's right at the chair, or standing to his right at the chair and at the altar, is often referred to as the first assistant deacon.[807] The first assistant deacon places the miter or zucchetto on the bishop's head when needed, unless a master of ceremonies does so.[808] To place the miter on the bishop, the first assistant deacon faces him, holding the miter in both hands, with the two fanons attached to the back of the miter neatly draped over his fingers. The first assistant deacon stands directly before the bishop, receives the miter from the miter bearer, and lowers the miter onto the bishop's head from

804 Fortescue, O'Connell, and Reid, *Ceremonies of the Roman Rite Described*, 203.

805 Fortescue, O'Connell, and Reid, *Ceremonies of the Roman Rite Described*, 203.

806 Peter J. Elliott, *Ceremonies Explained for Servers According to the Roman Rite: A Manual for Altar Servers, Acolytes, Sacristans, and Masters of Ceremonies* (San Francisco: Ignatius Press, 2019), 250.

807 Elliott, *Ceremonies of the Modern Roman Rite*, 173.

808 Fortescue, O'Connell, and Reid, *The Ceremonies of the Roman Rite Described*, 202.

behind, lowering it over the forehead first and then bringing it down at the back, quickly arranging the two fanons neatly, before returning to his place at the bishop's side.[809] Or, the bishop places the miter on his own head after receiving the miter from the first assistant deacon or master of ceremonies. The first assistant deacon will also assist with the preparation of the incense in the sacristy, at the chair, and at the altar, and with the washing of the bishop's hands in the sacristy, at the altar, and after Communion.[810] He will assist with the pall at the altar and elevate the chalice at the doxology. The second assistant deacon, who sits and stands to the bishop's left, stands directly before the bishop, removes the bishop's miter when needed, and then hands it to the miter bearer, before returning to his position at the bishop's side. He also removes the zucchetto at the altar. Again, a master of ceremonies may remove the miter and the zucchetto instead. To remove the miter, the second assistant deacon takes it off with a vertical and backward movement, so as not to disturb the zucchetto.[811] Or, the bishop takes the miter off himself and hands it to the second assistant deacon or master of ceremonies. The second assistant deacon turns the pages of the missal either at the chair or at the altar, and moves the missal into position at the altar as needed. When assistant deacons are lacking, concelebrants can fulfill these functions, unless a master of ceremonies assures all these duties instead.[812] The first and second assistant deacons have no speaking role during Mass.

The actual deacon of the Mass can be seated opposite the bishop, where the deacon would normally sit at a Mass celebrated by a priest when these seats are perpendicular to the altar. If the bishop is seated at the head of the apse instead, the deacon of the Mass may be seated to the right of the first assisting deacon unless some other location is more appropriate. It will be the duty of the deacon of the Mass to proclaim the Gospel, to announce the intentions to the Prayer of the Faithful, to prepare the gifts at the altar, to incense the bishop and concelebrants, and to incense the species at each elevation. He may offer the tropes to the penitential act if necessary, unless a cantor does so. He may also offer directions to the faithful during the course of the celebration, if necessary. A fourth deacon may "promote the active participation of the people,"[813] in the place of the deacon of the Mass. This fourth deacon can be seated with the deacon of the

809 Elliott, *Ceremonies of the Modern Roman Rite*, 180.
810 Elliott, *Ceremonies of the Modern Roman Rite*, 173.
811 Elliott, *Ceremonies of the Modern Roman Rite*, 180.
812 *CB*, 131.
813 *CB*, 122.

Mass on the opposite side of the sanctuary from the bishop or with the bishop and the other deacons in the apse of the sanctuary. He invites the faithful to sit, stand, or kneel, to offer the sign of peace, and to bow their heads when necessary. He dismisses them at the end of Mass. The master of ceremonies will need to instruct the deacons present carefully regarding their specific roles.

A concelebrant will assume the duties normally entrusted to the deacon of the Mass if no deacon at all is present to assist the bishop. In the presence of one deacon, two concelebrants can fulfill the functions of the two assisting deacons while the single deacon of the Mass retains his proper functions. In this case, the two concelebrants are seated immediately next to the bishop with the deacon seated to the right of the first assistant concelebrant. The description of the stational Mass of the bishop in this chapter will take into account the presence of three deacons, the normative practice.

Even when three deacons are ministering to the bishop, the pastor or the most senior concelebrating priest is also normally seated near the bishop. He can be considered the first among the concelebrants. Historically, the assisting priest sat next to one of the assisting deacons, perpendicular to him when the bishop was seated to one side of the sanctuary. It may be better to have the first among the concelebrants sit in this same position, but facing the assembly, rather than with his back to the assembly, as was historically the case.[814] Or, if the bishop is seated at the head of the apse, the assisting priest may simply sit to the right of the first assistant deacon, in a line with the seats of the bishop and the two deacons. The deacon of the Mass sits to the right of the first concelebrant in this case. Customarily, the first among the concelebrants may greet the bishop at the beginning of Mass or thank him at its conclusion. He might fittingly preach if the bishop does not. He would normally take the first concelebrant's portion of the Eucharistic Prayer, unless the bishop prefers to pray the entire prayer himself. He will assist in the fraction of the Eucharist if needed, in presenting the Body of the Lord to concelebrants, and in ministering Holy Communion to the servers and to the faithful. He might repose the Blessed Sacrament after Communion as well.

Ideally, any other concelebrants are also seated in the sanctuary for Mass. One or two concelebrants could be seated opposite the bishop in the sanctuary, especially if the bishop is seated to one side of the sanctuary. If possible, when concelebrants are more numerous, they should be seated in two choirs facing each other

[814] Fortescue, O'Connell, and Reid, *The Ceremonies of the Roman Rite Described*, 200, n. 13.

across the sanctuary, rather than in a long row at the back of the sanctuary facing the nave. At times, the number of the concelebrants and the size of the sanctuary may not make it possible for most or all of the concelebrants to be seated in the sanctuary. When seated in the nave instead, they are seated together as a group, with no other person seated in front of them between them and the sanctuary.

Prior to the beginning of Mass celebrated by the diocesan bishop, servers light four, six, or even seven candles at the altar.[815] Historically, the seventh candle is placed before, behind, or beneath the altar cross, in a row with the six other altar candles. If the altar candles are arranged in two rows on either side of the altar, the seventh candle should still be placed before, behind, or beneath the altar cross, if possible. If the altar cross is not centered on or above the altar, the seventh candle can be added to those on the right side of the altar. This practice is not followed for the Mass celebrated by a bishop who is not the diocesan bishop, such as an auxiliary bishop or a bishop emeritus.

Receiving the Bishop

The clergy of the parish await the arrival of the bishop at the main door of the church, unless they plan to escort him from his place of arrival in the territory of the parish to the church itself. A server carrying the holy water vessel and aspergillum also waits with them at the door. According to custom, another server, holding a cushion upon which rests a crucifix, also awaits the bishop at the door. Upon the bishop's arrival at the door of the church for Mass, the parish priest, wearing cassock and surplice, and even a white cope on more solemn occasions, welcomes him there. First, the parish priest offers the bishop the crucifix to kiss.[816] Using his right hand, the parish priest then hands the bishop the aspergillum, unless the blessing and sprinkling of water is to replace the penitential act.[817] With head uncovered, the bishop first takes the aspergillum and traces the Sign of the Cross on his own forehead, or applies holy water to his forehead with the thumb of the right hand in the manner described in chapter 5, "The Introductory Rites." The bishop then sprinkles those around him, before returning the aspergillum to the parish priest, who then returns it to the server.

Then, the bishop may be led in procession to the Blessed Sacrament chapel, where he will make a brief visit. He may simply be led there by the parish priest and

[815] *CB*, 128.
[816] Elliott, *Ceremonies Explained for Servers*, 248.
[817] *CB*, 79.

other clergy without ceremony. However, if that procession takes place in a solemn manner, the cross bearer, two servers with processional candles, and the thurifer with the censer and incense have also been awaiting the arrival of the bishop at the main door of the church.[818] The bishop imposes incense and blesses it in the usual way, assisted once again by the pastor. The procession proceeds into the church. The thurifer goes first, then the cross bearer between the two servers bearing candles. The clergy precede the bishop, who always processes last. He blesses the people as he goes. All kneel to receive the blessing as he passes. Traditionally, the antiphon *Sacerdos et pontifex*, or the responsory *Ecce sacerdos magnus* is sung.[819]

Upon arriving at the Blessed Sacrament chapel, or before the altar of the church if the Blessed Sacrament is reserved there instead, the bishop removes his zucchetto, genuflects, and then kneels on a kneeler prepared there. Historically, this kneeler has been covered in green cloth.[820] Six candles, or at least four, are lit on this altar for the duration of the time the bishop spends there.[821] He prays silently for a time, then rises, genuflects once again, and replaces his zucchetto. He is then escorted to the sacristy or vesting room to prepare for Mass.

Alternatively, upon arriving at the church, the bishop may go directly to the vesting room. In that case, the clergy wait to receive him there in the same manner as they would receiving him at the door of the church.[822] Deacons and servers should be vested prior to the vesting of the bishop himself. Historically, a bishop has vested at an altar. Therefore, if there is an altar in the sacristy, it would be fitting for the bishop to vest there, rather than at a vesting table or cabinet.[823] The candles on this altar are lit while the bishop vests. Servers present the bishop a silver or brass basin and ewer and towel with which to wash and dry his hands. This same set of silver or brass basin and ewer can be used for the washing of the hands at the preparation of the gifts, unless a second set is prepared at the credence table. The bishop may sit to wash his hands, in a faldstool or chair placed for him before the altar or facing the sacristy crucifix. In that case, the first assistant deacon places a gremial on his lap before the bishop begins to wash his hands. The first assistant deacon presents the hand towel for the bishop to dry

818 Fortescue, O'Connell, and Reid, *The Ceremonies of the Roman Rite Described*, 407; Elliott, *Ceremonies Explained for Servers*, 248.

819 Fortescue, O'Connell, and Reid, *The Ceremonies of the Roman Rite Described*, 407.

820 Fortescue, O'Connell, and Reid, *The Ceremonies of the Roman Rite Described*, 198.

821 Fortescue, O'Connell, and Reid, *The Ceremonies of the Roman Rite Described*, 198.

822 *CB*, 79.

823 Fortescue, O'Connell and Reid, *The Ceremonies of the Roman Rite Described*, 228.

his hands. The second assistant deacon removes the gremial from the bishop's lap after the bishop has dried his hands.

Then, the two assisting deacons present the vestments to the bishop for him to vest. The servers may bring each item from the altar or vesting cabinet to the bishop in a kind of procession if the space permits this. Or, if space and servers are lacking, the bishop may simply take the vestments himself from the vesting case, as in the manner of a priest. In this case, the two assisting deacons stand on either side of bishop to help him vest. All maintain an atmosphere of silence during this time.

Once vested, the bishop may sit for a time, in order to say the prayers of preparation in the missal. When Mass is ready to begin, the first assistant deacon places the miter on the bishop's head. The bishop imposes incense for the procession in the usual way, as the first assistant deacon ministers the spoon and holds the incense boat for him. Again, the bishop may prefer to sit to receive the miter and to impose and bless incense. In that case, the thurifer kneels before the bishop rather than stands before him. Standing, the bishop receives the crozier directly from the staff bearer or the master of ceremonies. The bishop and all with him bow to the cross in the sacristy and the procession makes its way to the sanctuary.

If seven processional candles are used, two candle bearers walk on either side of the processional cross in a straight line. The other five candle bearers walk behind the cross and candles. The seventh candle bearer walks behind and between the last pair. Other servers and any other deacons or priests in attendance walk behind the candle bearers two by two. As usual, the deacon of the Mass carries the Gospel book ahead of any other deacons with a role at Mass and concelebrants. The two assisting deacons walk together slightly behind the bishop. (See figure 9.) Also, the servers who will eventually attend to the miter, staff, and missal walk together side by side behind the assisting deacons.[824] The server who will hold the missal walks between the other two servers in a row with them. The staff-bearer walks to his left, since the bishop holds the staff in his left hand. The miter bearer walks to missal bearer's right. If space does not allow them to walk together in a row, the server carrying the missal can walk alone behind and between the staff bearer and miter bearer.[825]

[824] *CB*, 128.

[825] Elliott, *Ceremonies Explained for Servers*, 250.

The Introductory Rites and the Liturgy of the Word

The procession from the sacristy to the altar takes place as depicted in figure 9. Unless they are holding something in their hands, all reverence the altar with a bow or the Blessed Sacrament reserved in the sanctuary with a genuflection. Concelebrants go up to the altar two by two and kiss the altar, touching it briefly with their closed lips, with both hands resting on the altar. It is perhaps easiest for concelebrants to kiss the altar as they approach it, on the side closest to the nave. Then they go to their places. The deacon of the Mass enters the sanctuary without any sign of reverence,[826] places the Gospel book flat, face down, on the altar, and kisses the altar. He goes to his place immediately. Upon reaching the steps of the sanctuary, the bishop directly hands his crozier to the staff bearer or to the master of ceremonies. The second assistant deacon or the master of ceremonies removes the miter from the bishop's head, or the bishop removes it himself and hands it to the miter bearer or master of ceremonies. Then the bishop and the deacons assisting him either bow to the altar or genuflect to the Blessed Sacrament reserved in the sanctuary. The assistant deacons kiss the altar with the bishop. The bishop turns to his right at the center of the altar to prepare incense. The first assistant deacon ministers the spoon and the incense boat. (See chapter 4, "The Use of Incense at Mass.") The bishop incenses the altar cross and the altar, accompanied on either side by the two assistant deacons.[827] Then all three go to their places. The missal bearer stands before the bishop, holding the open missal in both hands at the bottom. The second assistant deacon turns the pages of the missal as needed. The bishop greets the faithful with the Sign of the Cross and the formula "Peace be with you." Otherwise, from the beginning of Mass to the Gospel Acclamation, there is no difference between the Mass celebrated by a priest or by a bishop. The first concelebrant may welcome the bishop after the Sign of the Cross and the liturgical greeting, "Peace be with you." The deacon of the Mass may offer the tropes of the penitential act if desired, unless a cantor does so. The assistant deacons serve the bishop and accompany him during the sprinkling rite if this takes place. (See chapter 5, "The Introductory Rites.")

During the course of Mass, the bishop is greeted by a deep bow from the waist whenever ministers or others approach him, depart from his immediate

[826] *GIRM*, 173.

[827] *CB*, 131.

presence, or pass in front of him.[828] A profound bow toward the bishop is made by each of the readers, the psalmist, and the homilist, immediately before and immediately after accomplishing their ministry. Normally, this is done at the ambo itself, standing in place, but turning in the direction of the bishop, if this is possible given the disposition of the sanctuary. The deacon proclaiming the Gospel omits this reverence, since he has already asked for and received the bishop's blessing to proclaim the Gospel.

Prior to the Gospel, the bishop always imposes and blesses incense while seated at the chair. At the Alleluia or Gospel Acclamation, both assistant deacons stand, even as the bishop remains seated to impose incense or bless the deacon or priest who will proclaim the Gospel. The miter and staff bearers approach the chair together. They may stand together to the bishop's left side, perpendicular to the bishop and deacons, or the miter bearer may stand to the bishop's right side and the staff bearer may stand to the bishop's left side, both facing him, if this position is more convenient in the end. The server or servers ministering the incense boat and the censer kneel before the bishop. The first assistant deacon, standing to his right, presents the spoon to the bishop and then holds the incense boat close to the bowl of the censer. The bishop continues to be seated while imparting the blessing to the deacon of the Mass or a concelebrant who will read the Gospel in his absence. The deacon or priest reading the Gospel seeks his blessing in the usual manner, that is, bowing profoundly before the bishop. Then the second assistant deacon, standing to the bishop's left, or the master of ceremonies, removes the miter and the bishop stands. The bishop may remove the miter himself and hand it to the second assistant deacon or master of ceremonies. After signing himself on the forehead, the lips, and the heart, the bishop receives the staff in his left hand from the crozier bearer or the master of ceremonies standing nearby. The bishop holds the staff in both hands directly before him for the entire proclamation of the Gospel.[829] After the proclamation of the Gospel, the bishop relinquishes the staff to the staff bearer or master of ceremonies, who has been standing nearby throughout the proclamation of the Gospel.

[828] *CB*, 76; André Philippe M. Mutel and Peter Freeman, *Cérémonial de la sainte messe à l'usage ordinaire des paroisses suivant le missel romain de 2002 et la pratique léguée du rit romain*, 2nd ed. (Perpignan, France: Éditions Artège, 2012), 40; Elliott, *Ceremonies of the Modern Roman Rite*, 74.

[829] Elliott, *Ceremonies of the Modern Roman Rite*, 180; Fortescue, O'Connell, and Reid, *The Ceremonies of the Roman Rite Described*, 213.

After the proclamation of the Gospel, the bishop may wish to kiss the Gospel book himself, rather than having the deacon kiss the Gospel book.[830] In that case, the deacon of the Mass, with the servers who accompanied him, carries the Gospel book open, with his hands at the bottom of each page, from the ambo to the bishop. He does so by the most direct route, without any sign of reverence to the altar.[831] The bishop takes the Gospel book in both hands to kiss it at the opening words of the day's passage. After kissing the Gospel book, the bishop may immediately bless the faithful with it.[832] Holding the closed Gospel book upright in both hands, the bishop makes a Greek cross over the people, saying nothing. Customarily, all bow slightly and make the Sign of Cross at the blessing. The bishop then returns the Gospel book into the hands of the deacon of the Mass, who closes the book and places it on the credence table or some suitable place. The deacon may also hand the Gospel book over to the master of ceremonies or to an instituted acolyte or the server who accompanied him to and from the ambo for disposition elsewhere. The deacon does not present a lectionary to the bishop to venerate, only a Gospel book. If the deacon proclaims the Gospel from a lectionary, he venerates it himself at the ambo after reading the appointed passage. He places it on the credence table, or hands it to the instituted acolyte or server assisting him to do so. (See chapter 6, "The Liturgy of the Word.")

If the bishop preaches seated, the first assistant deacon or the master of ceremonies places the miter on his head, unless the bishop does so himself. The bishop may also receive the staff from the crozier bearer or master of ceremonies, in order to hold it while he preaches while seated at the chair or standing at the pulpit. The first concelebrant fittingly preaches the homily if the bishop does not, bowing to the bishop before beginning and after concluding. After the homily, the second assistant deacon or master of ceremonies removes the miter from the bishop, who is seated. Or, the bishop may hand the miter to the assistant deacon or master of ceremonies himself. The missal bearer stands again before the bishop with the missal open to the Creed, when this is required. Then, the missal bearer holds the missal with both hands at the bottom of the pages, the missal resting on the chest. The bishop stands to lead the profession of faith and the Prayer of the Faithful. The deacon of the Mass offers the intentions to the

[830] *GIRM*, 175.

[831] Fortescue, O'Connell, and Reid, *The Ceremonies of the Roman Rite Described*, 130, 213; Elliot, *Ceremonies of the Modern Roman Rite*, 180.

[832] *GIRM*, 175.

Prayer of the Faithful, either from the ambo, or from his seat, or from some other suitable place. The bishop prays the concluding Collect from the missal or from a text held before him. After the conclusion to the Prayer of the Faithful, all sit. The first assisting deacon or the master of ceremonies receives the miter from the miter bearer and places it on the bishop's head, unless the bishop prefers to do so himself.

The Liturgy of the Eucharist

The deacon of the Mass prepares the altar while the bishop and the assisting deacons remain seated. The servers bring all the necessary items from the credence table to the altar for the deacon of the Mass to arrange. The bishop receives the gifts in a suitable place. Generally, he receives the gifts either seated at the chair or standing at the entrance to the sanctuary. As the gifts are presented to the bishop, the assistant deacons stand beside him, even if the bishop remains seated. They take the gifts from the bishop and give them to servers who bring them to the altar. The deacon of the Mass receives the gifts from the servers at the altar and arranges them on the corporals. Once all is prepared, the deacon of the Mass may turn toward the bishop and bow, signaling to him that the bishop and assistant deacons should now approach the altar. (See chapter 7, "The Preparation of the Gifts and the Altar.")

Upon arriving at the middle of the altar, the bishop and the two assistant deacons bow.[833] The assistant priest may also accompany the bishop to the altar if he is needed to remove the missal from the altar at the incensation and space allows him to fulfill this function. The second assistant deacon removes the miter and hands it to the miter bearer, unless the bishop does so himself. The two assistant deacons and the assistant priest stand at some distance from the altar to permit the deacon of the Mass to fulfill his duties. The deacon of the Mass presents the paten to the bishop using both hands. The deacon of the Mass then prepares the chalice at the right-hand corner of the altar, pouring wine and then water.[834] Once the chalice is prepared, the deacon offers the chalice to the bishop

[833] Mutel and Freeman, *Cérémoniale de la sainte messe*, 112.

[834] A fourth deacon, the deacon charged with directing the participation of the faithful, might approach the altar along with the bishop and the assistant deacons. At the preparation of the chalice, the deacon of the Mass might pour the wine while this fourth deacon adds the water. During the Eucharistic Prayer, he could stand and kneel behind the celebrant, between the two assistant deacons. He will step forward to one side and face the assembly to invite them to exchange a sign of peace.

with both hands. The deacon places his right hand on the node of the chalice and his left at its base. The deacon of the Mass then steps away from the far-right side of the altar. The first assistant deacon covers the chalice with the pall. The thurifer approaches with the censer and incense boat. The bishop turns to his right at the center of the altar to impose incense. The first assistant deacon to the bishop's right helps him prepare incense. The bishop proceeds to incense the gifts, the cross, and the altar, in that order. (See chapter 4.) The first assistant deacon may hold back the chasuble if necessary. Both assisting deacons accompany the bishop for the incensation of the altar. During the incensation of the altar, the assistant priest or the master of ceremonies removes the missal and its stand from the altar. He stands at the left-hand end of the altar, facing it. Once the top (*mensa*) of the altar has been incensed, the assistant priest returns the missal and its stand to its position slightly to the left of the corporal, at an angle. At the right-hand corner of the altar, the deacon of the Mass receives the censer from the bishop and incenses him first and then the concelebrants. The deacon of the Mass himself is incensed by the thurifer. The deacon of the Mass or the thurifer may also incense the assisting deacons, servers, and faithful. Servers approach the bishop to wash his hands. The first assistant deacon, to the bishop's right, offers him the towel to dry his hands. After the prayer over the gifts, the second assistant deacon, standing to the bishop's left, removes the zucchetto with his right hand, unless the bishop does so himself. In many cases, the master of ceremonies removes the zucchetto. A server holding a silver platter receives the zucchetto from the second assistant deacon and brings it to the credence table.[835]

After the prayer over the gifts and before the *Sanctus*, concelebrants approach the altar, or as many approach as possible. (See Chapter 8, "The Eucharistic Prayer.") The first concelebrant stands to the bishop's right at the altar. A second concelebrant can join him at the bishop's left at the altar. The two assisting deacons stand between the bishop and the concelebrants, slightly behind the bishop on either side of him.

At the *Sanctus*, eight torch bearers, instead of the customary two, four, or six, may accompany the thurifer and place themselves before the altar in their usual manner.[836] The deacon of the Mass accompanies them, following last, having added incense to the censer before leaving the sacristy. Upon arriving at the sanctuary, the deacon stands in the middle between the torch bearers with the

835 Elliott, *Ceremonies of the Modern Roman Rite*, 183.

836 Elliott, *Ceremonies Explained for Servers*, 253.

thurifer to his right. At the conclusion of the *Sanctus,* the deacon of the Mass kneels at the center of the sanctuary and receives the censer from the thurifer kneeling to his right. He incenses the Lord's Body and Blood at each elevation, bowing profoundly from a kneeling position before and after each time. After the second incensation, he returns the censer, while kneeling, to the thurifer kneeling to his right.

The second assistant deacon, to the bishop's left, assists with the missal throughout the Eucharistic Prayer. The first assistant deacon, to the bishop's right, places and removes the pall and elevates of the chalice at the doxology. After the prayer of preparation of the chalice, the deacon places the pall on the chalice. He removes the pall just before the epiclesis. He places the pall on the chalice again after the elevation following the consecration. He removes and replaces the pall for the elevation at the final doxology. He removes and places the pall for the comingling after the Lamb of God. Finally, he removes the pall prior to the Communion of the bishop from the chalice and replaces it afterward. The two assisting deacons kneel on either side of the bishop and behind him at the epiclesis of the Eucharistic Prayer until the chalice is placed on the altar again after its elevation.[837] In practice, it may be more graceful for them to rise as the bishop rises from the genuflection after the elevation of the chalice. During Eucharistic Prayer I, both assisting deacons have historically withdrawn from their places to the far edges of the altar and bowed during the duration of the time the bishop prays silently for the *memento* of the living and the *memento* of the dead. At the doxology, the first assistant deacon removes the pall with his right hand, his left hand resting on his chest. He elevates the chalice with the cup of the chalice at the same height as the paten held in the bishop's hands. He places his right hand on the node of the chalice and his left hand on the base of the chalice. After the conclusion of the doxology, he replaces the chalice in the same position it had on the corporal prior to the elevation. He covers it with the pall in his right hand, his left hand resting on his chest.

After the doxology of the Eucharistic Prayer, the deacon of the Mass, thurifer, and servers return to the sacristy and eventually to the sanctuary. The deacon of the Mass, standing near the altar or at his place, offers the invitation "Let us offer each other the sign of peace." The bishop begins by offering the sign of peace to two of the concelebrants closest to him, then to the assistant deacons.[838] The

[837] *CB,* 155.
[838] *CB,* 161.

concelebrants who received the peace from the bishop may then go to offer the peace to the other concelebrants. The assistant deacons in turn offer the sign of the peace to the deacon of the Mass and to the servers. All in the sanctuary may offer and receive the sign of peace in the traditional manner, as described in chapter 9, "The Communion Rite and the Concluding Rites."

During the Lamb of God, the first concelebrant may assist the bishop in the fraction of the Hosts and the distribution of those Hosts to the concelebrants at this time. Again, when the bishop receives each species in Holy Communion, the assistant deacons again withdraw from their places to the far edges of the altar and bow. After the bishop has received Communion under both species, he ministers Holy Communion to the three deacons who stand together in a line, the deacon of the Mass between the two assisting deacons. The first concelebrant, after receiving both species himself at the altar, may minister the chalice to the deacons, unless the bishop prefers to do so himself. The first concelebrant may also rightly bring Communion to the other concelebrants after his own Communion, unless the concelebrants will come to the altar to receive Communion there instead. One or more concelebrants, not deacons, may assist him as needed. First, they bring the Hosts to the concelebrants for their Communion.[839] Then, one or more deacons may present the chalice to the concelebrants for their Communion. Concelebrants may also receive both species at the altar as described in chapter 8, "The Eucharistic Prayer." After receiving Communion, the two assisting deacons sit at their places unless they will join in distributing Holy Communion to the faithful.

When the bishop returns to the chair after distributing Holy Communion, both assisting deacons stand to receive him, and then they sit when the bishop sits. The first concelebrant or the deacon of the Mass may repose in the tabernacle the Hosts which remain after Communion. After the Blessed Sacrament has been reposed in the tabernacle, a server holding a silver platter presents the zucchetto to the first assistant deacon, who takes it and places it on the bishop's head once again, unless the master of ceremonies does so.

The bishop may wash his hands after the distribution of Communion.[840] Two servers approach with ewer, basin, and towel once again and come before the bishop.[841] Both assistant deacons stand on either side of the bishop. Ordinar-

[839] *GIRM*, 242.

[840] *CB*, 166.

[841] Elliott, *Ceremonies of the Modern Roman Rite*, 184.

ily, the bishop washes his hands at the chair, either standing or sitting. If the bishop washes his hands while standing, the servers stand directly in front of him. If the bishop washes his hands while sitting, the first assistant deacon, standing, places a gremial across his lap before the servers approach with ewer and basin. The servers bow to the bishop, then kneel before him for the washing of the hands. The first assistant deacon, still standing, offers the towel to the bishop for him to dry his hands. Once the bishop has dried his hands and the first assistant deacon has returned the towel, the servers stand, bow once again, and depart. The second assistant deacon, also standing, removes the gremial from the bishop's lap if necessary.[842]

The bishop may pray the Post-Communion prayer at the chair or at the altar. At the chair, servers approach the bishop holding the miter, staff, and missal. The missal bearer stands immediately in front of the bishop, or slightly to his left, holding the missal open with both hands at the bottom of the pages. The miter and staff bearers stand side by side, perpendicular to the bishop and deacons. Or, the miter bearer may face the bishop on his right side and the staff bearer may face the bishop on his left side. In this case, the missal bearer stands between the miter and staff bearers. At the altar, the second assisting deacon repositions the missal directly in front of the bishop at the center, its edge parallel to the edge of the altar. The miter and staff bearers can stand directly behind the bishop side by side, the miter bearer to his right and the staff bearer to his left. In that way, the assisting deacons, or even the master of ceremonies, can take the miter and staff as needed.

Concluding Rite

Immediately following the Post-Communion prayer, the first assistant deacon or the master of ceremonies stands before the bishop and places the miter on the bishop's head, unless the bishop prefers to do so himself. At the chair, the bishop may prefer to sit to receive the miter. Once the bishop has received the miter, the first concelebrant may offer words of thanks to the bishop and may invite the faithful to any gathering which will follow Mass. The bishop may then offer the blessing over the people or the solemn blessing. In addition, he may bless the people using the form of blessing proper to a bishop, "Blessed be the Name of the Lord."[843] In each of these cases, he extends his hands to greeting

[842] Fortescue, O'Connell, and Reid, *The Ceremonies of the Roman Rite Described*, 202.
[843] *CB*, 1121.

the people first, saying, "The Lord be with you." The deacon of the Mass, or even the fourth deacon present, invites the faithful to bow their heads. For the blessing over the people or the solemn blessing, the bishop holds both hands directly outstretched before him over the people, palms down. For the pontifical blessing, he joins his hands. The bishop takes the staff directly from the crozier bearer or the master of ceremonies when imparting the blessing itself. He takes the staff in his left hand, his right hand resting on his chest. Then, he raises his right hand to impart the blessing. His right hand rests on his chest once again. The deacon of the Mass, or even the fourth deacon present, dismisses the people with hands joined, standing at his place or near the bishop. Then all take their positions for the recessional.

The bishop and assistant deacons go from the chair to the altar, unless the bishop has already prayed the Post-Communion prayer and blessing at the altar. At the altar, the bishop may relinquish the staff momentarily to the crozier bearer in order to be able to place both hands on the altar when kissing it.[844] Concelebrants are not expected to kiss the altar at the conclusion of Mass.[845] The cross and candles bearers, servers, and deacon of the Mass stand two by two in the center aisle, facing the altar in reverse order. The concelebrants may remain in their places in the sanctuary or stand facing the altar on either side of the center aisle across the front of the sanctuary. After kissing the altar, the bishop and the assistant deacons come before the altar to make the required reverence to it or to the Blessed Sacrament. Unless one is holding something in one's hands, each person bows to the altar or genuflects to the Blessed Sacrament simultaneously with the bishop. The bishop and assistant deacons turn to face the nave and the procession begins. If the concelebrants have remained in the sanctuary, they now leave their places and follow behind the servers and deacon of the Mass, while the bishop and assistant deacons wait before the altar, facing the nave. The deacon of the Mass precedes any other deacons and the concelebrants as usual. The procession returns to the sacristy in the same way in which it entered the church, except that neither the Gospel book nor the censer are carried out.[846]

844 Elliott, *Ceremonies Explained for Servers*, 254; Fortescue, O'Connell, and Reid, *The Ceremonies of the Roman Rite Described*, 222.

845 *CB*, 170; Elliot, *Ceremonies of the Modern Roman Rite*, 169.

846 Mutel and Freeman, *Cérémonial de la sainte messe*, 181, 209, n. 80.

In the Sacristy after Mass

Upon arriving in the sacristy, all bow to the crucifix there or to the processional cross held by the cross bearer, who faces everyone in this case. Then, the clergy and servers bow low to the bishop. All kneel as the bishop blesses those present.[847] The miter bearer and staff bearer receive the miter and staff. Before removing their own vestments, the two assistant deacons and the servers help the bishop remove his vestments first. The servers approach the bishop in a kind of procession, one after the other, to receive the vestments one by one from the assisting deacons. They lay these vestments on the altar in the sacristy or on the vesting cabinet. All make sure to maintain an atmosphere of silence and recollection during this time. Once the bishop has removed his vestments, he may sit at the chair in the sacristy to say the prayers of thanksgiving from the missal or he may do so seated in the first place in choir in the sanctuary instead. Those assisting the bishop may now remove their vestments to make their own thanksgiving as well.

[847] Elliott, *Ceremonies Explained for Servers*, 255.

30

The Parish Celebration of Confirmation with the Bishop

The celebration of Confirmation by a bishop can take place during Mass or apart from Mass. In either case, the following items are prepared for the celebration of Confirmation:[848]

- At the altar, six candles or at least four, all of the same design. If the diocesan bishop is the celebrant, seven matching candles are prepared.
- Seven matching processional candles, if the diocesan bishop is the celebrant, or at least two
- Two, four, six, or even eight matching torches if Mass is celebrated[849]
- A vessel containing the holy chrism; if other priests will assist the bishop in confirming, the multiple vessels of chrism are placed on a platter
- A brass or silver ewer and basin with towel for washing the hands after Confirmation, along with lemon wedges and crusts of bread on platters
- A chair (the faldstool if available) for the bishop, if he confirms seated
- A gremial for the bishop's lap, if he confirms and/or washes his hands while seated
- Vimpas (a specialized form of the humeral veil) for the miter and crozier bearers, if available
- The *Roman Pontifical*, or at least the *Rite of Confirmation*

[848] *CB*, 457.

[849] Adrian Fortescue, J. B. O'Connell, and Alcuin Reid, *The Ceremonies of the Roman Rite Described*, 15th ed. (New York: Bloomsbury, 2009), 219, n. 83.

Confirmation during Mass

If the ritual Mass of Confirmation is permitted, red or white vestments are worn.[850] On days when the ritual Mass of Confirmation is not permitted, the vestments are the color of the Mass which is required. The reception of the bishop, the entrance into the church, the introductory rites, and the Liturgy of the Word up to Gospel take place in the usual way as described in chapter 29.

After the Gospel reading, two servers place a chair before the altar and perhaps a cushion if the candidates for Confirmation will kneel before the bishop. The bishop may prefer to confirm at the usual presidential chair instead and remain there through the whole rite of Confirmation.[851] After the conclusion of the proclamation of the Gospel, the bishop hands the crozier directly to the staff bearer on his left in order to venerate the Gospel book and bless those present with it as circumstances suggest. The bishop then sits at the presidential chair. The first assistant deacon places the miter on the bishop's head, unless the master of ceremonies does so, or the bishop prefers to do so himself.[852] The bishop may remain at the presidential chair, seated and wearing the miter, or he may go to the chair prepared for him before the altar. In that case, the bishop may stand and go to the chair before the altar with the staff in his left hand or not as he prefers. Once seated in the chair before the altar, the staff bearer once again receives the crozier directly from the bishop if necessary. Whether the bishop is seated and wearing the miter either at the presidential chair or at the chair prepared at the altar, the designated cleric or catechist then presents the candidates to the bishop either individually by name or as a group.[853] It is best if this presentation does not take place at the ambo, but at some other location. The candidates and their sponsors come before the bishop as they are called, or they simply stand in their places instead. Then, the deacon of the Mass may invite all to sit to listen to the bishop's homily.

The bishop preaches seated or standing at the presidential chair or before the altar, or standing at the ambo, or at some other suitable place. The bishop may wear the miter and hold the crozier in his left hand while preaching. If the bishop does not preach at the chair where he will confirm, he goes to the presidential chair or the chair before the altar after the homily. The miter and crozier bearers should join the bishop there, standing together to his left, perpendicular to him.

850 *CB*, 459.
851 *CB*, 461.
852 *CB*, 461.
853 *CB*, 461.

The assisting deacons stand on either side of the bishop and remain standing throughout. At the end of the homily, the bishop sits if he is not already seated. The first assistant deacon places the miter on his head if he is not already wearing the miter. The staff bearer presents the crozier to the bishop, still seated, who receives it in his left hand if necessary.[854] The bishop, now seated with both miter and staff, addresses the candidates standing before him and leads them in the renewal of baptismal promises.[855] A server kneels to the bishop's left, holding the *Roman Pontifical* or the *Rite of Confirmation* open to the proper page. The server holding the ritual book will stand when the bishop prays standing and kneel when the bishop prays or speaks seated.

After the renewal of baptismal promises, the staff bearer receives the crozier directly from the hand of the bishop. The second assistant deacon removes the miter while the bishop remains seated and hands the miter to the miter bearer near him. The bishop then stands. The deacon of the Mass invites all present to stand. Any priests who will join the bishop in confirming some of the candidates come forward and stand with him. With hands joined and facing the assembly, the bishop gives the invitation to prayer. After a brief pause in silence, the bishop extends his hands simultaneously over all the candidates standing before him while saying the prayer "All-powerful God, Father of Our Lord Jesus Christ." If there is only one candidate, the bishop can impose his hands on that candidate's head prior to the prayer.[856]

The bishop then sits, and the first assistant deacon places the miter on his head, unless the master of ceremonies does so or the bishop does this himself.[857] The deacon of the Mass invites all except the candidates and sponsors to sit. The deacon of the Mass, or the pastor in his absence, brings vessel(s) of chrism to the bishop. Any priests who will assist the bishop in anointing a number of the candidates each receive a vessel of chrism directly from the bishop. If convenient, the bishop receives the crozier in his left hand directly from the staff bearer. Then, the deacon of the Mass, or even the pastor in his absence, stands to the bishop's right, holding the vessel of chrism for him.[858] The first assistant deacon or the master of

[854] *CB*, 463.

[855] *CB*, 463.

[856] *RCIA*, 365, 390, 493.

[857] *CB*, 465.

[858] Peter J. Elliott, *Ceremonies Explained for Servers According to the Roman Rite: A Manual for Altar Servers, Acolytes, Sacristans, and Masters of Ceremonies* (San Francisco: Ignatius Press, 2019), 260. This approach seems much more convenient than the traditional practice, where the second assistant held the chrism to the bishop's *left*. See Fortescue, O'Connell, and Reid, *The Ceremonies of the Roman Rite Described*, 418–419.

ceremonies or even a server places the gremial (or amice) on the bishop's lap, and ties each end securely to the chair if necessary.[859] The candidates approach the bishop individually. Each sponsor places his or her right hand on the candidate's shoulder and gives the candidate's Confirmation or baptismal name to the bishop as the case may be. Or, the candidate may even give his or her own name. Or the sponsor may present the first assisting deacon with a card on which is written the name of the candidate; the assisting deacon gives the candidate's name to the bishop. Depending on the age and size of the candidates, the candidates, but not the sponsors, kneel on a cushion before the bishop seated before the altar.

The celebration of Confirmation may take place in a number of other ways as well. For example, the candidates and their sponsors may approach the bishop in a proper procession. In that case, the bishop stands before the altar, with miter and crozier. The assisting deacons stand on either side of him, slightly behind him, and the deacon of the Mass or the pastor stands to his right with the vessel of chrism. Or, the bishop, with miter and staff, and with the deacon of the Mass or pastor assisting him, may rather go to the individual candidates. In that case, the candidates and their sponsors stand or kneel in a line before the bishop, side by side at the entrance to the sanctuary, and the bishop goes to them from left to right, beginning with the first candidate to his left and concluding with the last candidate on his right. Finally, the candidates and sponsors may be seated at the edge of each pew in the center aisle, and the bishop may go to them in the center aisle while they remain standing at their places instead.[860] He begins with those on his right, from front to back, before confirming those on his left, from front to back.

After the anointing, the candidates return to their places either individually or as a group. The bishop gives up the crozier to the staff bearer in order to wash his hands. He may wash his hands standing or sitting at the chair before the altar or at the presidential chair, or standing at the credence table, or at some other suitable place. The servers assisting him with the washing of the hands stand or kneel before him as circumstances suggest. The servers approach with basin, ewer, and towel, along with quartered lemons and crusts of bread on platters if desired, in order to cleanse the bishop's hands.[861] They bow

859 Elliott, *Ceremonies Explained for Servers*, 260.

860 Elliott, *Ceremonies Explained for Servers*, 261.

861 According to custom, any cotton, lemons, or bread used to cleanse the hands are burned. The ashes are poured into the sacrarium in the sacristy, along with the water used to wash the hands. See Elliott, *Ceremonies Explained for Servers*, 262, and Fortescue, O'Connell, and Reid, *The Ceremonies of the Roman Rite Described*, 421.

upon approaching him and upon departing from him. The first assistant deacon presents the towel to the bishop for him to dry his hands. If the bishop is seated, the second assistant deacon or the master of ceremonies or a server removes the gremial and folds it once the bishop has finished washing and drying his hands.[862] Meanwhile, priests who have also confirmed put down their vessels of chrism at a credence table, where they also wash their hands in the same way while standing. They may be assisted by servers if sufficient numbers are available. Two servers remove the chair (and cushion) placed before the altar for Confirmation.

Then, with the bishop seated at the presidential chair, the second assistant deacon removes the miter. The second assistant deacon hands it to the miter bearer standing next to him. A server stands before the bishop with the missal or the *Rite of Confirmation* in both hands open to the text of the Universal Prayer. The bishop stands and introduces the general intercessions with hands joined. The deacon of the Mass offers the intentions. The bishop says their concluding prayer with hands extended. The rest of Mass continues as described in chapter 29 from this point on. Often, the bishop will use the solemn blessing proper to Confirmation at the conclusion of Mass.

Confirmation apart from Mass

While the conferral of the Sacrament of Confirmation is normally joined to the celebration of Mass, it may on occasion take place apart from Mass. In that case, the bishop wears a white stole and cope. Priests who will confer Confirmation with the bishop wear a white stole over the cassock and surplice or alb. They may also wear a white cope. Deacons who assist the bishop wear a white stole over the alb.[863]

The reception of the bishop, the entrance into the church, the introductory rites, the Liturgy of the Word, and the rite of Confirmation take place as just described above. After the conclusion of the Prayer of the Faithful, the bishop, standing at the chair with hands joined, without miter or staff, leads everyone in the Lord's Prayer.[864] The bishop extends his hands during the Our Father. Or, the Lord's Prayer may precede the concluding prayer of the

[862] Fortescue, O'Connell, and Reid, *The Ceremonies of the Roman Rite Described*, 420.

[863] *CB*, 473; *Rite of Confirmation*, no. 19.

[864] *Rite of Confirmation*, no. 48.

general intercessions.[865] Then the bishop blesses the people using either the solemn blessing proper to Confirmation, the prayer over the people, or the pontifical blessing, as described in chapter 29. The deacon faces the assembly and dismisses them with hands joined.[866]

[865] *CB*, 474.
[866] *CB*, 477.

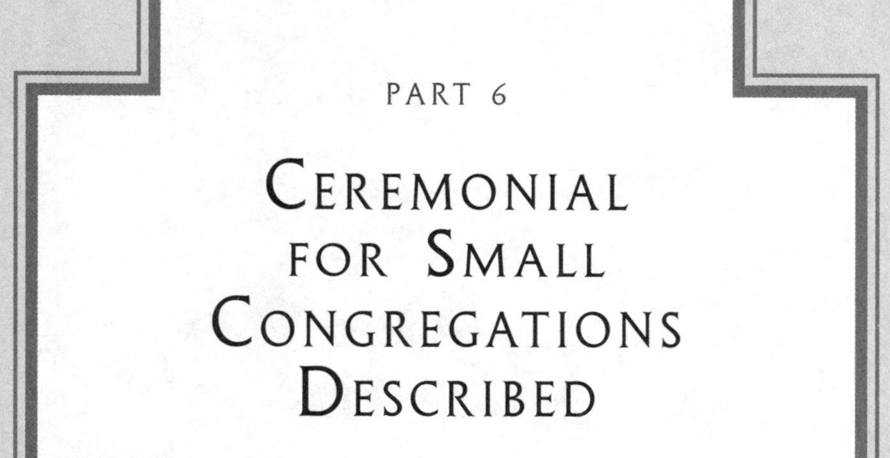

PART 6

Ceremonial for Small Congregations Described

Introduction

All the liturgical books of the Roman Rite begin with an introduction and include rubrical directions for the celebrant and ministers throughout. These describe the optimal circumstances for the celebration, namely, a full complement of ministers, singing by the assembly and a schola, and a fully participating assembly. For the Roman Missal, these indications are found in the *General Instruction to the Roman Missal*. Sadly, the building blocks of the liturgy described in all the liturgical books can often be lacking in many celebrations. This is likely to happen in churches with small congregations, whether they be in urban or rural settings. These may lack all the resources to implement the full description of the rites of the Church found in the liturgical books.

For this reason, at one time or another, the Holy See has provided guidance on how the rites of the Church might be carried out in more modest circumstances. For example, as early as 1725, Pope Benedict XIII published his *Memoriale rituum* with instructions on how Candlemas, Ash Wednesday, Palm Sunday, and the Paschal Triduum might be simplified due to necessity. In more recent times, the Sacred Congregation of Rites provided much the same guidance when it issued *Ordo Hebdomadae Sanctae Instauratus, Ritus Simplex*, on February 5, 1957. In addition, the various classic manuals for the celebration of the liturgy have always included simplified descriptions for various rites "in small churches."[867]

867 For example, see Léon-Michel Le Vavasseur, *Cérémonial à l'usage des petites églises de paroisse selon le rite romain*, 2nd ed. (Paris: Éditions Lecoffre, 1864); Léon-Michel Le Vavasseur, Joseph Haegy, and Louis Stercky, *Manuel de liturgie et cérémonial selon le rit romain*, 2 vols., 16th ed. (Paris: Éditions Gabalda, 1935); Adrian Fortescue, J. B. O'Connell, and Alcuin Reid, eds., *The Ceremonies of the Roman Rite Described*, 15th ed. (New York: Bloomsbury, 2009).

The following chapters are intended to serve the same purpose for the current Roman liturgical books. Contemporary descriptions of the rites have only addressed this need in part.[868] What is proposed here is a more comprehensive description of Mass, the Liturgy of the Hours, and selected sacraments as might be celebrated in a typical parish church with few ministers. For example, this ceremonial will assume the absence of a deacon and of concelebrants. It will take into account the ministry of one or two servers who may be inexperienced and largely untrained. It will offer guidance on alternatives when there is no one to lead the singing of the faithful. Finally, it will attempt to foster the participation of the gathered faithful in the simplest way possible.

The goal of these chapters is not to provide shortcuts to a minimalist celebration of the rites of the Church. Rather, it is intended to offer a vision of the *ars celebrandi* which is at the same time graceful, practical, and guided by the traditional practice of the Roman Rite. It does so taking into account less than ideal circumstances, which are often the case. Even in small churches, even in churches with few resources and small congregations, the sacred liturgy should be celebrated with as much dignity and decorum as one can muster. The adjustments and modifications described in this ceremonial are the result of necessity. They should not become the norm in those communities where greater solemnity is possible. But rather, the following chapters may help those celebrants who are perplexed as to what to do when the conditions seem to make it impossible for them to do all that the Church intends. It is meant to offer encouragement to those who despair at doing better, since they have so few resources at hand. Hopefully, the following descriptions may give some pastors the impetus to try to accomplish goals they thought were beyond their reach. Among these aspirational goals could be Sunday Mass celebrated each week with a measure of solemnity, greater dignity for the celebration of solemnities and feasts which occur during the week, sung Sunday Vespers with the faithful, and exposition and benediction without a full complement of servers.

[868] Peter J. Elliott, *Ceremonies of the Modern Roman Rite: The Eucharist and the Liturgy of the Hours*, rev. ed. (San Francisco: Ignatius Press, 1995).

31

Sunday Celebrated in Small Congregations

Sunday Mass with Solemnity

An early morning Sunday Mass or late Saturday evening Mass in a very small rural or urban community often lacks the full complement of ministers required by the *General Instruction of the Roman Missal.* The following description assumes that the celebrant will not be joined by one or more deacons or one or more concelebrants. He will nevertheless be joined by one reader and one server. There may be someone available to provide instrumental music but no one to lead the singing of the assembly. For a complete description of the ceremonial for Mass, see Part 1: The Celebration of Mass.

Requisites for the Celebration of Mass[869]

A complete description of everything needed for Mass is found in chapter 3. That list can be modified for a small congregation in the following ways.

In the sacristy:

- Vestments in the color of the Mass for the priest; cassock and surplice or alb for ministers and the server
- Censer and incense boat, charcoals, and incense, if used

[869] See *CB*, 125; André Philippe M. Mutel and Peter Freeman, *Cérémonial de la sainte messe à l'usage ordinaire des paroisses suivant le missel romain de 2002 et la pratique léguée du rit romain*, 2nd ed. (Perpignan, France: Éditions Artège, 2012), 48–68; Peter J. Elliott, *Ceremonies of the Modern Roman Rite*, rev. ed. (San Francisco: Ignatius Press, 1995), 88–90.

At the ambo:

- The Lectionary for Mass open to the proper page; the lectionary is covered in cloth the color the Mass
- The text of the Universal Prayer, unless it will be needed elsewhere in the sanctuary
- An antependium or fall in the color of the Mass

At the altar:

- One or more altar cloths, at least one of which reaches to the floor on both sides, the uppermost cloth being white
- Four or six matching candles, as the circumstances suggest
- Crucifix on or near the altar
- An antependium or frontal in the color of the Mass

At the tabernacle:

- Sanctuary lamp burning
- At least two candles burning during the course if Mass, if the tabernacle is not located on the altar
- A corporal, unfolded on the ledge in front of the tabernacle or folded in a burse nearby; the burse should be the same color as the color of the tabernacle veil
- The key to the tabernacle, unless placed at the credence table
- An ablution cup or bowl with finger towel, unless placed at the credence table
- A veil (white or the color of the Mass) over the tabernacle, or at least covering its doors

At the chair:

- The Roman Missal open to the proper page; the missal is covered in cloth the color of the Mass
- The text of the Universal Prayer for the celebrant, unless the missal is used
- The vessel(s) of water (and salt) to be blessed when used during the penitential act

- Cloth cover for the chair, or at least the seat, in the color of the Mass

At the credence table:

- A white cloth covering the top of the credence table and falling to the floor on both sides
- The chalice, purificator, paten with host covered by the pall and veil in the color of the Mass or white
- The burse containing the corporal(s) needed at the altar, placed on the chalice and veil, and of the same color as the veil
- Other ciboria (with or without covers) with hosts as needed; other cups with wine (with or without palls, or placed behind the chalice and covered with the veil) as needed; purificators as needed (in the burse or under the veil of the chalice, or unfolded over the chalice itself)
- The cruets of wine and water on their glass platter
- Finger towel
- Communion plate for the Communion of the faithful
- Missal stand covered in cloth the same color as the Mass or a cushion for the missal made of cloth of the same color as the Mass
- A set of handbells, unless needed elsewhere
- An ablution cup or bowel with finger towel, unless it is placed at the tabernacle
- Key to the tabernacle, unless it is placed in the tabernacle prior to the beginning of Mass

In a convenient place:

- Baskets for the offerings of the faithful
- Microphones in the locations where they will be needed
- Stand for the censer and boat, if needed

Regarding all the liturgical items listed above, it is important to keep in mind that what is not prepared is as significant as what is intended to be prepared. For example, no processional candles are indicated, since these are used as a pair and cannot be used when only one server is available. Likewise, the processional cross is not indicated. The processional cross is used to lead a procession of ministers. A single celebrant and a server do not constitute a procession; therefore the use of the processional cross is superfluous in this case. With only one server available, sufficient ministers are lacking in order to carry the censer and candles during the Gospel procession. Therefore, the Gospel book, and the Gospel procession which accompanies it, are omitted. The Gospel passage appointed for the day is simply read from lectionary. While the Roman Missal enumerates five different occasions during Mass when incense can be used *ad libitum*, historically there have been two degrees of solemnity in the use of incense. Either incense was used at all the possible occasions when servers with candles could accompany the entrance and gospel processions, or incense was simply used at the Offertory and at the elevations, without being used at any other point in Mass. Thus, it seems that if a choice has to be made as to when to use incense during Mass, priority should be given to the use of incense at the Offertory and the elevations above all.[870] This may be the only feasible option when there is one server.

The celebrant might sing all or some of the dialogues with the faithful throughout the course of Mass, or even the three Collects of Mass, with the faithful responding, "Amen." He could intone some of the more simple acclamations which are somewhat repetitive, such as "Lord have mercy," or "Lamb of God." Finally, many communities are able to sing very well the Our Father to the chant melody in the Roman Missal, even if they might not sing the doxology which accompanies it. If instrumental music is available, music could accompany the entrance of the priest and server, the preparation of the altar and the gifts, the Communion procession of the faithful, and finally the recessional of the celebrant and minister. If this is the case, it is best if the instrumentalist does not use familiar hymn melodies for this purpose. It can appear incongruous to those present to hear hymn tunes which no one will be singing. The celebrant will take note to read the entrance antiphon and the Communion antiphon at the proper times in place of sung chants.

The Entrance of the Celebrant and Ministers

If there is singing or instrumental music, the celebrant and server can make their way from the sacristy or from the back of the church to the sanctuary. If there is neither instrumental music nor any singing in common, it may be best for them

[870] Mutel and Freeman, *Cérémonial de la sainte messe*, 71.

to enter the sanctuary directly from the sacristy through doors on either side of the altar, as at a weekday Mass, for example. Normally, they approach through doors on the Gospel side of the altar (the left side of the altar as one faces it from the nave), and depart from the altar at the end of Mass through doors on the epistle side of the altar (the right side of the altar as one faces it from the nave).[871] However, when this is not possible, as when the sacristy is located at the back of the church rather than behind the sanctuary, the celebrant will have no choice but to make his way to the altar by the nave. Since there is neither music nor singing to accompany the movement of the celebrant, perhaps the celebrant could recite aloud the entrance antiphon on a card from the back of the church through the nave to the sanctuary. Or, a reader could read the antiphon from the ambo while the celebrant and server make their way to the sanctuary. If the antiphon itself is not long enough to accompany the celebrant's procession from the sacristy to the sanctuary, the celebrant could add a Glory Be, with everyone responding. He might even repeat the antiphon a second time if necessary. The priest, with hands folded, vested in stole and chasuble, walks alone behind the server. Everyone stands from the beginning of the entrance antiphon, or from the moment the priest leaves the sacristy, indicated by the ringing of the bell. All remain standing until the priest has concluded the opening Collect for Mass.

The Greeting and Penitential Act

Once the priest has arrived at his chair in the sanctuary, the server brings the missal, open to the first words of the introductory rites for Mass, to the celebrant. At an early morning Sunday Mass, when a server might not always be available, it seems that there is no alternative than to place a lectern in front of the celebrant's chair for the missal, since there is no provision in the *General Instruction* for beginning Mass with a congregation at the altar. The celebrant stands at the chair with hands joined. If there has been no singing at the entrance, and neither the celebrant nor the reader has proclaimed the entrance antiphon, the celebrant now reads the entrance antiphon from the missal. The celebrant then begins the introductory rites with the Sign of the Cross and greeting with the missal being held before his eyes. Alternatively, the celebrant may read the entrance antiphon after the Sign of the Cross and greeting and before the invitation to the penitential act.[872]

[871] Adrian Fortescue, J. B. O'Connell, and Alcuin Reid, eds., *The Ceremonies of the Roman Rite Described*, 15th ed. (New York: Bloomsbury, 2009), 65.

[872] *GIRM*, 31, 47.

The Sprinkling Rite

On Sundays, even at Masses on Saturday evening, the penitential act can be replaced by the sprinkling rite, found in appendix 2 of the missal. For a complete description of the rite of blessing and sprinkling with holy water, see chapter 5.

If only one server is available, a table will need to be placed immediately to the right of the celebrant's chair. The water to be blessed is located there prior to the beginning of Mass. The table should also be large enough to eventually accommodate the open missal as well.

At the beginning of Mass, immediately following the Sign of the Cross and the greeting of the assembly, the celebrant, standing at the chair with hands joined and still turned toward the assembly, invites all to join him in the prayer of blessing. A server holds the missal in both hands before him at the chair. After inviting the assembly to pray, the celebrant, closing his eyes and bowing his head, pauses for a brief moment of silence. He then begins the prayer of blessing of the water with hands joined. With his right hand, his left hand resting on his chest, he makes the Sign of the Cross in the shape of a Greek cross over the water at the point indicated in the text. The celebrant then reads one of the appointed antiphons, unless there will be singing during the action of sprinkling.

The server puts the open missal down on the table next to the celebrant's chair and picks up the vessel of holy water in the left hand. With the right hand, the server presents the aspergillum to the celebrant, who receives the aspergillum in his right hand. The celebrant, still standing at the chair, sprinkles himself by touching his forehead with the aspergillum, making the Sign of the Cross, in the manner described in chapter 5. Alternatively, transferring the aspergillum from his right hand to his left, the celebrant touches the thumb of his right hand to the top of the aspergillum and traces the Sign of the Cross on his forehead before returning the aspergillum to his right hand. While holding the aspergillum in his right hand, his left hand always rests on his chest.

Still standing at the chair, the celebrant can then extend the aspergillum to the server, who touches the top of the aspergillum with the closed fingers of his right hand and makes the Sign of the Cross. It is then perhaps best for the celebrant to proceed to the front of the altar to sprinkle the reader and any others in the sanctuary, unless, of course, the celebrant is already standing directly behind the altar when he is at the chair. Standing at the altar, the celebrant faces the sanctuary with his back to the assembly. The server stands to the celebrant's right, also facing the altar. After sprinkling the reader and anyone else in the sanctuary, the celebrant and the server bow to the altar and turn toward each other to sprinkle the people. Upon turning to face the people, the server with the vessel of water will now be on the celebrant's left.[873] This position makes it easier for the celebrant to dip the aspergillum in the vessel with water as he sprinkles the people.

As an alternative to beginning the sprinkling rite at the chair, the celebrant and the server holding the holy water may leave the chair immediately after the blessing of the water and after reciting the proper antiphon if there is no singing. They stand together facing the altar, as described above. The celebrant blesses himself with the holy water and the server next to him on his right. Then, the celebrant sprinkles those in the sanctuary. The celebrant and server now turn toward each other and toward the faithful; the server with the holy water is now on the celebrant's left. The celebrant can then proceed to sprinkle the assembly, center, left, and right, standing in the same position in front of the altar. Or, the celebrant may sprinkle the people while walking through the assembly.

Once the celebrant has concluded sprinkling the assembly, he and the server return to the chair. The server takes the holy water from the celebrant and places it down on the table next to the chair. The server picks up the open missal in both hands and holds it before the celebrant. The celebrant reads the concluding prayer to the sprinkling rite with hands joined, and proceeds with the Gloria, if required, and the Collect as usual.

The Liturgy of the Word

On Easter Sunday and on Pentecost Sunday, a sequence immediately follows the second reading and precedes the Alleluia. A sequence may be sung on Corpus Christi and Our Lady of Sorrows (September 15), according to the circumstances. All listen or join in singing the sequence while remaining seated.[874] If there is no singing, the sequence could be read in alternation between the reader at the ambo and the celebrant at the chair. The server, kneeling, will need to hold a second lectionary before the celebrant, who remains seated at the chair. Alternatively, the server can provide the celebrant with a card having the text of the sequence printed on it.

The high point of the Liturgy of the Word is the proclamation of the Gospel. As the Alleluia chant or Lenten acclamation begins, all stand. The celebrant goes immediately to the middle of the altar and prays, "Cleanse my heart." The priest then proceeds with hands joined to the ambo. If there is no singing, the celebrant can

[873] Mutel and Freeman, *Cérémonial de la sainte messe*, 88.

[874] Mutel and Freeman, *Cérémonial de la sainte messe*, 97, n. 87.

either intone or recite the Gospel Acclamation or Lenten acclamation upon arriving at the ambo before proceeding to proclaim the passage appointed for the day.

The Preparation of the Altar with the Gifts

After the conclusion to the Universal Prayer, the celebrant sits. A server brings the chalice from the credence table to the altar.[875] Then the celebrant goes to the right-hand side of the altar to prepare the chalice. If there is no server suitable for these tasks available, the priest himself should go to the credence table at the conclusion of the Universal Prayer to begin to prepare the gifts first and then to the altar in the manner described in chapter 7.

Incense may be used at the preparation of the gifts if two trained servers are available. One server might light the coals during the homily. During the preparation of the altar, after the celebrant rises from saying the prayer "With humble spirit and contrite heart," he turns to his right, without stepping away from the center of the altar. The server approaches the celebrant with both the censer and the incense boat, within an arm's length of the celebrant. Historically, a second server removed the missal from the altar at this time, so that the celebrant could more easily incense the entire top (*mensa*) of the altar on the left side. The server then replaces the missal at an angle to the left of the corporal, off the corporal. In order to accompany the celebrant around the altar, the thurifer may need to place the incense boat on the credence table or on its stand, according to what is most convenient at the moment. The thurifer now has both hands free to receive the censer back from the celebrant at the right-hand side of the altar. There, the thurifer takes a step back and incenses the celebrant. The thurifer bows, incenses the celebrant with three swings, and then bows again.[876] The celebrant, likewise, bows to him. The server then proceeds to incense those in the sanctuary, if anyone is present there. The server then turns to the assembly and incenses them as a group. They stand to be incensed. The server bows to them, and incenses with one swing to the center of the assembly, one to the left, and one to the right before bowing and returning the censer to its stand. At the credence table, a second server takes up the items needed to wash the celebrant's hands. In the end, it seems unlikely that the incensation of the gifts, the altar, the celebrant, and the assembly cannot be carried out gracefully without the participation of at least two servers.

875 *GIRM*, 190.

876 *GIRM*, 277; *CB*, 91–92.

Incense at the Elevations

Connected to the incensation of the gifts, altar, cross, and celebrant is the incensation of both the Sacred Host and Precious Blood after their respective consecrations. When incense is used at the elevations, the server adds more incense to the censer in the sacristy immediately after the washing of the hands. During the singing of the *Sanctus*, the server exits the sacristy by way of the church, holding the censer by the length of its chain in his right hand. The server may stand at the entrance of the sanctuary at the center, directly before the altar, or he may exit the sacristy and enter the sanctuary to stand at the end of the altar to the right of the priest without passing through the church. This is the customary position in the Requiem Mass found in the missals prior to 1969.[877] This position has the advantage of being closer to the sacristy, where the censer will be loaded. It may also be less disruptive for the server to kneel at the right side of the altar than to walk through the church in order to position himself in the middle of the sanctuary facing the altar.[878] At the conclusion of the *Sanctus*, the server kneels when all kneel.

At the elevation of the Body of the Lord, the server, still kneeling, bows from the waist and then incenses the Blessed Sacrament with three swings using his right hand at the height of his face. He bows profoundly once again at the waist. A second server rings the handbells if this is the custom. The same procedure is repeated after the consecration of the Precious Blood. At the doxology which concludes the Eucharistic Prayer, the server returns to the sacristy.[879] The censer is put away and will not be used again during Mass. Again, it will not be possible to use incense at the elevations and handbells without the participation of at least two servers.

Communion

If the number of communicants is small, and there is no extraordinary minister to offer the chalice the faithful, the celebrant himself may do so after ministering Communion under the species of bread. He places the ciborium on the altar, and takes the chalice or another cup in the right hand and a purificator in the left. He stands at the entrance of the sanctuary once again, on the lowest step. Those who wish to receive from the chalice approach him in a kind of procession for a second time. After each communicant, he wipes the rim of the chalice with the purificator and turns the chalice a quarter turn for the next communicant.

877 Fortescue, O'Connell, and Reid, *The Ceremonies of the Roman Rite Described*, 159.

878 Mutel and Freeman, *Cérémonial de la sainte messe*, 130.

879 Elliott, *Ceremonies of the Modern Roman Rite*, 149.

The Sunday Vespers in Small Congregations

The primary parish celebration of the Liturgy of the Hours is Sunday Vespers. The following description assumes the presence of one priest as the celebrant and one or two servers, along with one or more cantors. The requisites include:

In the sacristy:

- Cope (optional) and stole for the priest celebrant[880]

In the sanctuary:

- A lectern before the presidential chair, covered with an antependium in the color of the Office
- Censer, incense, and stand
- A book containing the *Liturgy of the Hours* at the presidential chair for the reading and the prayers
- Six matching candles, or at least four, on or near the altar
- The dust cover is removed from the altar.

Once all is ready, the celebrant, server(s), and cantor(s) bow to the sacristy crucifix and proceed to the sanctuary. If there are two servers, they can carry processional candles, their outside hands on the nodes and the inside hands on the bases. Organ music accompanies the procession. A hymn is not sung. Upon arriving before the altar, all bow to the altar or genuflect to the Blessed Sacrament if the tabernacle is located in the sanctuary. During the course of Vespers, all will genuflect to the Blessed Sacrament reserved in the sanctuary whenever passing before it.[881] At Vespers, the servers place their candles on either side of the lowest step of the altar or, if necessary, on either side of the lowest step of the sanctuary.[882] If this is impractical, they can place their candles at the rear corners of the credence table, as at Mass. The celebrant goes up to the altar and kisses it, and then goes to the chair.

880 *GILH*, 255.

881 The prescription to bow to the altar rather than genuflect to the Blessed Sacrament in the tabernacle whenever passing before both pertains specifically to the celebration of Mass. See *GIRM*, 274. This rubric is not found in any other liturgical book.

882 Peter J. Elliott, *Ceremonies Explained for Servers According to the Roman Rite: A Manual for Altar Servers, Acolytes, Sacristans, and Masters of Ceremonies* (San Francisco: Ignatius Press, 2019), 188; Elliott, *Ceremonies of the Modern Roman Rite*, 268.

Local custom determines the manner of singing of the psalms. For a complete description, see chapter 28. The psalm prayers after each psalm always remain optional. If a psalm prayer is said or sung after each psalm, all stand after the antiphon has been repeated. The celebrant says, "Let us pray," with hands joined, then offers the prayer with hands extended in the *orans* position.[883] The Office book rests on the lectern before his chair. The psalm prayer concludes with the short ending "Through Christ Our Lord," and all answer, "Amen." Then all sit for the singing of the next psalm or the New Testament canticle.

After the New Testament canticle, the celebrant stands to proclaim the reading from the lectern before him. The priest may preach at the chair or at the ambo, or at some other suitable place. Then a short responsory or some other chant may be sung while all remain seated, or silence may be observed instead.[884]

Incense may be used during the Gospel canticle of Evening Prayer.[885] Therefore, when the antiphon to the Magnificat is intoned, the thurifer brings the incense to the chair. Another server may move the lectern temporarily to the side. The thurifer bows to the celebrant, then kneels. The celebrant imposes incense seated. The server kneels before the celebrant with the censer. After the celebrant imposes and blesses incense, saying nothing, he returns the incense boat to the thurifer. The thurifer stands and bows to the celebrant. If convenient, the thurifer may place the boat on a nearby incense stand in order to have both hands free. The thurifer goes to the altar just to the right of where the priest will stand at the middle. As the Magnificat itself begins, all stand, including the celebrant, and make the Sign of the Cross at the first words.[886] The celebrant comes before the altar and bows, but does not kiss the altar. The thurifer gives the censer to the celebrant. The altar cross and altar are incensed as described in chapter 4. Having concluded the incensation of the altar at the right-hand corner of the altar, the celebrant returns the censer to the thurifer standing on his right. The celebrant and the thurifer return to the presidential chair by the most direct way.

883 Elliott, *Ceremonies of the Modern Roman Rite*, 269. *CB* 198 does not indicate any specific position for the hands during the psalm prayer. However, *CB* 205 does indicate hands extended for the concluding Collect of the hour. Finally, *CB* 104 indicates hands extended for any prayer directed to God while standing.

884 *GILH*, 49.

885 *GILH*, 261.

886 *CB*, 203; Elliott, *Ceremonies of the Modern Roman Rite*, 270; Elliott, *Ceremonies Explained for Servers*, 189.

Standing in front of the chair, the thurifer incenses the celebrant with three swings of the censer, bowing before and after.[887] Next, he goes to the front of the sanctuary, where he incenses the faithful with three swings of the censer, center, left, and right, bowing before and after. If the incensation is not completed when those present begin to sing the *Gloria Patri*, the thurifer stops in his place and turns to bow before the altar, facing it with the censer, until the doxology has been sung.[888] Then the server resumes the final incensations during the antiphon, reverences the altar, and returns the censer to the sacristy.

Meanwhile, the other server returns the lectern to its place before the celebrant. The two servers may take their candles from the lowest altar step and stand on either side of the lectern facing each other.[889] The celebrant introduces the intercessions and may offer the intentions standing at the lectern before him. The celebrant may introduce the Our Father with hands joined. He prays the Our Father with hands extended.[890] Without saying, "Let us pray," he immediately offers the Collect, with hands extended in the *orans* position, with the longer ending "Through Our Lord Jesus Christ your Son." The servers with candles turn and bow to the celebrant. They then stand at the entrance to the sanctuary, facing the altar. The celebrant turns toward the people if necessary and extends his hands toward the assembly, saying, "The Lord be with you." He blesses them in the customary way or uses one of the solemn blessings or blessings over the people.

If circumstances suggest it, the celebrant may go to the altar and kiss it. Then, he and any others with him in the sanctuary descend the altar steps and face the altar. Together, they make their reverence to the altar or the Blessed Sacrament and turn to their right to join the procession. The celebrant, cantor(s), and server(s) depart in the same order as in the opening procession.

An even simpler form of Evening Prayer or Morning Prayer might not include the use of incense at all. The hymn might be sung in unison, without a cantor, but the psalms and canticles may need to be recited. In that case, the recitation of the psalms and canticles can alternate between the two sides of the church or between the celebrant on the one hand and the entire assembly on the other.

[887] Fortescue, O'Connell, and Reid, *The Ceremonies of the Roman Rite Described*, 256.

[888] Fortescue, O'Connell, and Reid, *The Ceremonies of the Roman Rite Described*, 256.

[889] Elliott, *Ceremonies Explained for Servers*, 190.

[890] Contrary to Elliott, *Ceremonies of the Modern Roman Rite*, 272, *CB* 104 indicates hands extended whenever the bishop or the priest addresses a prayer to God while standing.

32

Presentation of the Lord (February 2)

WHEN THE FEAST of the Presentation of the Lord falls on a Sunday, it can be assumed that there will be a sufficient number of ministers for the celebration. For a complete description of Mass on the feast of the Presentation of the Lord, see chapter 14. In most years however, the Presentation of the Lord falls on a weekday. In that case, there may only be one server and one reader, with no one to lead the singing. Under those circumstances, a number of choices and adaptations need to be made in order to carry out the liturgy with a measure of decorum and dignity. The following description assumes two servers are assisting the celebrant. It provides indications on what can be done when there is no instrumental music and no one to lead the singing.

In addition to what is usually needed for Mass, whether on a Sunday or a weekday, the following items need to be prepared:

At the entrance of the church:

- Candles for all present as they arrive

In the sacristy:

- A white chasuble for the celebrant in the case of the solemn entrance; white chasuble or white cope for the celebrant in the case of the procession

At the place where the procession will begin:

- Candles for the celebrant and others on a tray, covered with a white cloth; the tray itself is placed on a table covered with a white cloth

- Holy water and aspergillum on that same table
- A wick from which to light the candles of those present and a source of fire on that same table
- Censer with burning coals and incense boat on its stand
- A lectern to the left of the table with candles and holy water; the lectern is covered in a white fall
- A second missal on that same lectern
- A card with the antiphons for the procession on that same lectern

At the chair in the sanctuary:

- A table for the celebrant's candle and for the card with the processional antiphons
- The missal, open to the proper page, on the table next to the chair
- White chasuble, in the case when the white cope is used for the procession; the chasuble can be draped over the presider's chair or placed on a stand behind it

The Mass on February 2 can begin either with a procession properly speaking or with the solemn entrance. Contrary to the provision made for the simple entrance on Palm Sunday, it appears that there is no possibility for beginning Mass for the Presentation of the Lord without the blessing of candles and without either the procession or solemn entrance which follows.

In the case of the procession, all or most of the faithful gather in a location outside the body of the church, either in another chapel, or a hall, or the narthex, or even outdoors, weather permitting. In the case of the solemn entrance, the assembly gathers inside the body of the church. A representative group of the faithful joins the celebrant and ministers just inside the door of the church or just outside it. When the procession begins outside the body of the church, the celebrant may wear the chasuble for Mass or a white cope. When the procession begins at the door of the church, he wears the chasuble. All hold unlit candles. The cross bearer, second server, and celebrant make their way from the sacristy to the location where the blessing of candles will take place.

If there is an altar in the location where the procession will begin, all the ministers bow to it or genuflect if the Blessed Sacrament is reserved upon arriving there. To conduct the blessing, the celebrant stands either on the epistle side of the altar, if there is one, or directly before the table prepared with the candles, facing the assembly. If there is no altar where the procession will begin, a station is created whereby the processional cross itself become the focal point of the liturgical assembly. The celebrant stands facing both the processional cross and the table with the candles in this case.[891] Therefore, as the ministers arrive in a location where there is no altar, the cross bearer positions himself or herself in such a way that the celebrant faces the cross, the candles, and those gathered.

Upon arriving at the place where the procession will begin, the celebrant and a second server bow to the altar or to the processional cross. That same server removes the veil covering the candles to be blessed on the table before the celebrant. The server then lights the candles of all present with the lighter and wick prepared for that purpose. While this is going on, the celebrant reads the proper antiphon from the missal placed on the lectern to his left. One of the faithful near the celebrant holds the lit candle destined for the celebrant until both his hands are free to take a candle. The celebrant begins with the Sign of the Cross and the greeting. After the address to the faithful and invitation to prayer, he says the prayer of blessing with hands outstretched, palms down, over the candles. The priest may invite the faithful to raise their candles in their hands for the blessing. The celebrant makes the Sign of the Cross over the candles in the form of a Greek cross with the right hand during the prayer in the first case or at the end of the prayer in the second case, the left hand resting on his chest. He then sprinkles the candles, saying nothing. With the holy water on the table in front of him, the celebrant can sprinkle the candles of everyone present standing in the same location, sprinkling the center, left, and then right of the assembly. Or, the celebrant may sprinkle the candles by walking through the assembly, with the server holding the holy water to his left. The sprinkling concluded, the second server stands with the censer and incense boat before the celebrant. The celebrant, holding the incense boat in his left hand and the spoon in his right, imposes incense three times in the usual way. Still holding the incense boat and spoon in his left hand, the celebrant blesses the incense in the form of a Greek cross with his right hand, saying nothing. The celebrant returns the boat and spoon to the thurifer. The thurifer stands behind the cross bearer, ready to turn to his right, to lead the procession or entrance into the church. The celebrant

[891] André Philippe M. Mutel and Peter Freeman, *Cérémonial de la sainte messe à l'usage ordinaire des paroisses suivant le missel romain de 2002 et la pratique léguée du rit romain*, 2nd ed. (Perpignan, France: Éditions Artège, 2012), 235.

then invites the procession to begin, and takes his candle in his right hand from the member of the faithful who has been holding it for him. The faithful also hold their candles in the right hand. All bow to the altar, or to the cross in its absence, and the procession to the sanctuary begins.

In the procession, the celebrant follows the thurifer and the cross bearer.[892] The faithful follow behind the celebrant.[893] All in the procession carry burning candles in their outside hands. When there is no singing, the celebrant can recite the various antiphons from the missal printed on a card which was placed on the lectern prepared where the procession began.

Upon arriving at the sanctuary, the celebrant and servers make the usual reverence to the altar, or to the Blessed Sacrament if it is reserved there.[894] At the chair, the celebrant extinguishes his candle. He places both the candle and the card from which he has been reading the processional antiphons on the table next to his chair. The celebrant is now free to remove the cope, if he is wearing it, and to take the chasuble.[895] Vested for Mass, he proceeds to the altar, kisses it, and incenses it if he wishes. He may prefer simply to use incense for the procession itself and to not incense the altar. The faithful may extinguish their candles upon arriving at their seats.[896] A server picks up the missal placed on the chair near the celebrant and holds it open in both hands before the celebrant at the chair. The missal should be open to the Introit for Mass, which the celebrant reads with hands joined. The celebrant then immediately begins the Gloria, the penitential act and *Kyrie* being entirely omitted. After the Gloria, the celebrant says, "Let us pray," with hands joined, and offers the Collect with hands extended. After the Collect, Mass continues without any other modifications.

892 In the case where there is only one server available, it will be necessary to omit the use of incense. See Adrian Fortescue, J. B. O'Connell, and Alcuin Reid, eds., *The Ceremonies of the Roman Rite Described*, 15th ed. (New York: Bloomsbury, 2009), 315–316, and Léon-Michel Le Vavasseur, *Cérémonial à l'usage des petites églises de paroisse selon le rite romain*, 2nd ed., (Paris: Éditions Lecoffre, 1864), 185, no. 47. In that case, it would be better to begin with the solemn entrance, rather than with the procession. If by some fortunate circumstance four servers are available, two of them can carry processional candles on either side of the processional cross. See Fortescue, O'Connell, and Reid, *The Ceremonies of the Roman Rite Described*, 317, and Le Vavasseur, *Cérémonial à l'usage des petites églises*, 185, no. 47. These same processional candles can be the source of the flame for one of the servers to light the candles of all those present.

893 *CB*, 246.

894 Mutel and Freeman, *Cérémonial de la sainte messe*, 240.

895 Mutel and Freeman, *Cérémonial de la sainte messe*, 240, n. 33.

896 Mutel and Freeman, *Cérémonial de la sainte messe*, 240.

33

Ash Wednesday

THE IMPOSITION OF ashes is the distinctive mark of the Mass celebrated on the Wednesday prior to the first Sunday of Lent. The blessing and imposition of ashes on the ministers and faithful take place after the homily and before the Prayer of the Faithful. For a more complete description, see chapter 15. At an early morning Mass on Ash Wednesday, it may not be possible to assemble the full complement of ministers which may be available at an evening Mass, for example. The following description assumes that one server is assisting the celebrant and no one is present to lead the singing of the faithful.

Prior to the celebration, in addition to everything needed for the celebration of Mass, the following items will also need to be prepared:

At the credence table:

- Pitcher, bowl, soap, towel for washing the hands after the distribution of the ashes

Near the chair:

- A table, covered by a white cloth
- The vessels of ashes, covered or veiled in violet, on this table
- Cards with the formula for imposing ashes, if needed, on this table
- The vessel of holy water and aspergillum, on this table as well
- A second missal open to the blessing of the ashes, on a lectern to the immediate left of this table

After the homily, the celebrant returns to the chair and sits in silence for some time. Then he rises and goes to the table nearby prepared with the ashes. All stand. Everything is carried out by the celebrant facing the assembly across the table.[897] The server removes the covers for the vessels of ashes or the purple veil placed over them before the celebrant begins the prayer of blessing.[898] The celebrant faces the assembly when addressing them, keeping his eyes on the missal to his left as needed. [899] The celebrant addresses the assembly with hands joined. He pauses for a moment of silent prayer. He may close his eyes and bow his head during this time. He prays the blessing of the ashes with hands extended, making the Sign of the Cross at the point indicated in the prayer of blessing. His left hand rests on his chest when making the Sign of the Cross with his extended right hand; he then joins his hands. The server offers the celebrant the aspergillum in his right hand. The celebrant sprinkles the ashes three times, center, left, and right, saying nothing. He returns the aspergillum to the server.

Once the ashes are blessed, the celebrant first imposes ashes on himself. The server or any other lay minister may not impose ashes on the celebrant. The server holds the vessel of ashes for the celebrant,[900] or the celebrant may find it more convenient to hold the vessel of ashes in his left hand.[901] The celebrant imposes ashes on himself using the thumb of his right hand, the rest of the fingers of the hand extended and joined. He makes the Sign of the Cross on his own forehead, saying nothing.[902] He does so standing at the chair, or even standing at the altar while facing it.[903] The celebrant then reads one of the antiphons in the missal that is intended to accompany the imposition of ashes before proceeding to impose ashes on others.[904]

The celebrant begins by imposing ashes on the server and any other clergy or laity in the sanctuary. These receive the ashes standing and bowing slightly. In

[897] Peter J. Elliott, *Ceremonies of the Liturgical Year According to the Modern Roman Rite: A Manual for Clergy and All Involved in Liturgical Ministries* (San Francisco: Ignatius Press, 2002), 57.

[898] Adrian Fortescue, J. B. O'Connell, and Alcuin Reid, eds., *The Ceremonies of the Roman Rite Described*, 15th ed. (New York: Bloomsbury, 2009), 319.

[899] Elliott, *Ceremonies of the Liturgical Year*, 57.

[900] Fortescue, O'Connell, and Reid, *The Ceremonies of the Roman Rite Described*, 320.

[901] Elliott, *Ceremonies of the Liturgical Year*, 57, n. 12; Léon-Michel Le Vavasseur, *Cérémonial à l'usage des petites églises de paroisse selon le rit romain*, 2nd ed. (Paris: Éditions Lecoffre, 1864), 193, no. 70.

[902] Fortescue, O'Connell, and Reid, *The Ceremonies of the Roman Rite Described*, 320.

[903] Fortescue, O'Connell, and Reid, *The Ceremonies of the Roman Rite Described*, 320.

[904] Fortescue, O'Connell, and Reid, *The Ceremonies of the Roman Rite Described*, 323; Le Vavasseur, *Cérémonial à l'usage des petites églises*, 193, no. 72.

some locations, the sacred ministers and servers kneel to receive the ashes.[905] The celebrant may take some ashes between his index finger and thumb of the right hand and sprinkle them on the crown of the head in the Sign of the Cross, or he may dip the thumb of his right hand in the ashes and trace the Sign of the Cross on the forehead. The server may hold the bowl of ashes in the right hand and a card with the formula for the imposition of ashes in the left hand. The server stands to the celebrant's left, facing him as he imposes ashes on all in the sanctuary. The celebrant then goes to the entrance of the sanctuary to impose ashes on the faithful in the same way. They may approach in one or two lines in a kind of procession. Or, they may stand, bowing slightly, or kneel across the front of the sanctuary to receive the ashes.[906] The celebrant imposes ashes on them moving from left to right.

When the imposition of ashes is completed, the server returns the vessel of ashes to the credence table and covers it once again. The celebrant also goes to the credence table, bowing to the altar whenever he passes before it. He stands there to wash and dry and his hands.[907] After washing and drying his hands, the celebrant returns to the chair and stands, with hands joined, facing the assembly, to introduce the Prayer of the Faithful. The server holds the open missal in both hands before the celebrant at the chair. The Liturgy of the Eucharist takes place without any further modifications. At the end of Mass, the celebrant prays the prayer over the people, as described in chapter 15.

905 Fortescue, O'Connell, and Reid, *The Ceremonies of the Roman Rite Described*, 320.

906 Elliott, *Ceremonies of the Liturgical Year*, 58, n. 13.

907 Peter J. Elliott, *Ceremonies Explained for Servers According to the Roman Rite: A Manual for Altar Servers, Acolytes, Sacristans, and Masters of Ceremonies* (San Francisco: Ignatius Press, 2019), 202; Fortescue, O'Connell, and Reid, *The Ceremonies of the Roman Rite Described*, 319.

34

Palm Sunday of the Passion of the Lord

The Three Forms of the Entrance

THE CELEBRATION OF Mass on Palm Sunday of the Passion of the Lord can begin in one of three different ways, either with a procession of the entire assembly, or with the solemn entrance of the ministers and a representative group of the faithful, or with the simple entrance of the ministers of the Mass alone as usual. For a more complete description of Palm Sunday Mass, see chapter 15. At a Saturday evening Mass or early Sunday morning Mass, it may not be possible to have all the ministers required for the full form of the celebration of Palm Sunday of the Passion. In that case, certain accommodations can be made. The description below will assume that two servers and one reader assist the celebrant.[908] It also assumes that there is no one present to lead the singing of the faithful.

In addition to all the usual items needed for Mass, the sacristan will need to prepare the following on Palm Sunday:

At the location where the procession or the solemn entrance begins:

- Palms for the faithful, servers, and celebrant. The palm designated for the celebrant is often decorated or larger than others. These palms are placed on a tray and may be covered with a red veil.
- Palms to attach to the processional cross after the blessing, even if the cross veiled in purple
- Holy water in its vessel with aspergillum

[908] If by chance two more servers are available, they can carry processional candles on either side of the processional cross.

- A table, covered in white, placed in the center or slightly to the left (as the celebrant faces the assembly) for the palms and holy water
- On a second table, covered in white, placed to one side, a second set of pitcher, bowl, and towel, if the celebrant washes his hands after distributing the blessed palms
- A lectern, covered in a red antependium, to the left of the table with palms
- A missal, open to the proper page, placed on this lectern
- A card with the texts of the processional chants, also on this lectern
- Censer with burning coals and incense on a stand nearby

In the sanctuary:

- A second missal near the presidential chair
- A table next to the celebrant's chair to receive his palm branch
- The red chasuble draped over the presidential chair, if the celebrant has worn the red cope for the procession

In the case of the procession, all or most of the faithful gather in a location outside the body of the church, either in another chapel, or a hall, or the narthex. The procession may also begin outdoors, weather permitting. In the case of the solemn entrance, the assembly gathers inside the body of the church. A representative group gathers with the celebrant and ministers just inside or just outside the door of the church for the entrance rite. When the procession begins outside the body of the church, the celebrant may wear the chasuble for Mass or a red cope. When the solemn entrance begins just inside or just outside the door of the church, he wears the red chasuble. All hold palm branches in their hands unless these will be distributed after the blessing.

If there is an altar in the location where the procession begins, all the ministers bow to it upon arriving or genuflect if the Blessed Sacrament is reserved there. The celebrant stands on the epistle side of the altar to conduct the blessing or at the chair, if there is one, facing the assembly. If there is no altar where the procession will begin, a station is created whereby the processional cross itself becomes the focal point of the liturgical assembly. The celebrant stands facing both the processional cross and the faithful in this case. Therefore, as the cross arrives, it is placed in such a way that the celebrant and server bow to it and face the cross as well as those gathered.

Upon arriving at the location where the procession begins, the celebrant stands facing the assembly at the table prepared with the palms. A server removes the red veil covering the palms on the table.[909] The palm branch designated for the celebrant is placed there, as is the holy water. A lectern stands to the celebrant's left for the missal.[910] The celebrant begins by reading the initial antiphon, "Hosanna to the Son or David," then makes the Sign of the Cross and offers the greeting. After the invitation, the celebrant says the prayer of blessing with arms extended in the *orans* position. The celebrant may invite the faithful to raise their palms in their hands for the blessing and sprinkling. The celebrant makes the Sign of the Cross in the form of a Greek cross over the palms during the prayer in the first case, or at the end of the prayer in the second case, his left hand resting on his chest. He then sprinkles the palms, center, left, and right, saying nothing. He can do so standing in the same location, sprinkling the center, left, and then right of the assembly, or by walking through the assembly, with the server holding the holy water walking on his left.[911] At this point, the celebrant may stand in the center and distribute palm branches to any who need to receive them. A member of the faithful holds the celebrant's palm branch until the beginning of the procession. After distributing the palms and before proceeding, the celebrant may want to wash his hands at a second table, prepared at the side for this purpose. Although the current liturgical books are silent on this practice, this washing of the hands after the distribution of the palms is part of the historical practice on Palm Sunday.[912]

The sprinkling with holy water and the distribution of the palms concluded, the thurifer stands before the celebrant, who imposes incense in the usual way in preparation for the reading of the Gospel of the Lord's entry into Jerusalem. The celebrant bows low before the altar or the processional cross to pray the prayer of preparation. The celebrant returns to the lectern to the left of the table prepared for the palms and reads the appointed Gospel from the missal placed there. If there are two additional servers serving as candle bearers, they may stand on either side of this lectern, facing each other, during the reading of the Gospel. The celebrant greets the faithful, announces the Gospel, and signs himself. Then, he takes the censer, bows, and incenses

909 André Philippe M. Mutel and Peter Freeman, *Cérémonial de la sainte messe à l'usage ordinaire des paroisses suivant le missel romain de 2002 et la pratique léguée du rit romain*, 2nd ed. (Perpignan, France: Éditions Artège, 2012), 247; Adrian Fortescue, J. B. O'Connell, and Alcuin Reid, eds., *The Ceremonies of the Roman Rite Described*, 15th ed. (New York: Bloomsbury, 2009), 324.

910 Fortescue, O'Connell, and Reid, *The Ceremonies of the Roman Rite Described*, 329.

911 Mutel and Freeman, *Cérémonial de la sainte messe*, 248.

912 Mutel and Freeman, *Cérémonial de la sainte messe*, 249.

the Gospel three times, center, left, and right, before bowing again and returning the censer to the thurifer. He reads the Gospel and announces its conclusion with hands joined. Afterwards, the celebrant kisses the text of the Gospel, as usual. The missal remains, there since a second missal is prepared at the presidential chair in the church. The celebrant may preach a homily if he wishes.

Then, the preparations for the beginning of the procession take place. If necessary, the celebrant may impose incense again. The celebrant receives the blessed palm prepared for him in his right hand. All carry palms in their right hands. Reading from the missal on the lectern, the celebrant then invites the procession to begin. All bow to the altar or to the processional cross in its absence, and the procession to the sanctuary of the church begins. The celebrant takes with him a card, on which is printed the texts of the various chants for the procession properly speaking. He will read these chants out loud during the time of the procession, since there is no one present to lead the singing. In the procession, the thurifer goes first, followed by the cross and perhaps even two candles walking together in a line, and then the celebrant. Finally, the faithful follow the behind the celebrant.[913]

Upon arriving at the sanctuary, the celebrant makes the usual reverence to the altar, or to the Blessed Sacrament if it is reserved there.[914] The celebrant is now free to remove the cope, if he is wearing it, and to take the chasuble. Normally, this is done at the chair, rather than in the nave or the entrance to the sanctuary.[915] The celebrant puts down his palm branch and the card with the chants on a table near his chair, and changes from the cope into the chasuble if necessary. The palm branches are not used again during the course of Mass. A server stands directly in front of the celebrant or slightly to his left, holding the missal open to the proper page. If the celebrant has not already done so as he entered the church, he now reads the chant which accompanies the arrival in the church or sanctuary, "As the Lord entered the holy city."[916] The opening prayer takes place immediately after this entrance chant, unless the celebrant prefers that the *Kyrie* follow the chant and precede the Collect.[917]

The third form of the beginning of Mass on Palm Sunday is the simple entrance.[918] It is perhaps less well known. This form is designed for the situation

[913] *CB*, 270.

[914] Mutel and Freeman, *Cérémonial de la sainte messe*, 252.

[915] Mutel and Freeman, *Cérémonial de la sainte messe*, 240, n. 33.

[916] *RM*, Palm Sunday, no. 10

[917] *RM*, Palm Sunday, no. 15.

[918] *RM*, Palm Sunday, nos. 16–17.

where neither the procession nor the solemn entrance can take place. According to the simple entrance, Mass on Palm Sunday begins in exactly the same manner as Mass on any other day. In this case, the entrance antiphon with its psalm verses may be recited by a reader at the beginning of the Mass as the celebrant approaches the altar.[919] The entrance antiphon on Palm Sunday is particularly important, since it recalls Christ's triumphal entry into Jerusalem. Or, the celebrant himself will read the entrance antiphon immediately upon arriving at the chair, before making the Sign of the Cross. Or, the celebrant may read the entrance antiphon after making the Sign of the Cross and greeting those present, but before introducing the penitential act.[920] A server holds the missal before him at the chair.

The simple entrance does not include the blessing of palms. The blessing of palms takes place in the other two forms because those walking in procession carry blessed palms, recalling those who welcomed Christ to Jerusalem. When no procession takes place, there is no blessing of the palms either. However, for the sake of fostering the devotion of the faithful, pastors will want to have palms blessed at a previous Mass available at the entrance of the church whenever Mass begins with the simple entrance.

The Proclamation of the Passion

The Passion can be read by the celebrant alone, either in the longer or shorter form. He does so at the ambo, which remains uncovered. Neither incense nor candles accompany the readings of the Passion. However, if they are available, two servers, side by side, do accompany the celebrant and stand on either side of the ambo with hands joined, facing each other. The celebrant announces the Passion without any greeting and without signing himself. During the reading of the Passion, all turn in their places to face the ambo. The Passion is read with hands joined. At the mention of the death of the Lord, all kneel. The celebrant kneels in his place, facing the ambo.[921] All rise for the final section of the Passion. The celebrant concludes the Passion with the usual acclamation, but without kissing the book. The servers return to their places. Mass continues without any further modifications.

[919] *RM*, Palm Sunday, no. 17a.

[920] *RM*, Palm Sunday, no. 17b; *GIRM*, 48.

[921] Mutel and Freeman, *Cérémonial de la sainte messe*, 256.

35

Holy Thursday in Small Congregations

The Paschal Triduum begins with the Evening Mass of the Lord's Supper. The Paschal Triduum forms the high point of the entire liturgical year. By its very nature, the celebration of the Triduum demands the greatest effort possible from a parish in striving toward the fullest form of the celebration. For a more complete description of the Evening Mass of the Lord's Supper, see chapter 16. Even in small congregations, singing should not be absent from Mass on Holy Thursday. Parishes need to ensure that a small schola or at least a cantor can lead the assembly in singing liturgical music familiar to them. All Masses without a congregation are forbidden on Holy Thursday. Therefore, it is common for the Evening Mass of the Lord's Supper to be concelebrated. If a parish is fortunate enough to have a concelebrating priest join them for the Evening Mass of the Lord's Supper, that concelebrant can be of great assistance to the principal celebrant. In addition, there are distinct features of the opening rites for Mass on Holy Thursday. Mass that evening may include the washing of feet as well. Finally, Mass always ends with a procession to the place of reposition of the Blessed Sacrament for a period of adoration before midnight. The washing of the feet and the transfer of the Blessed Sacrament to the repository can only be accomplished with a minimum of four servers. If a parish cannot count on someone to lead the singing or this minimum number of servers, it should consider joining a neighboring parish for the celebration of Mass on Holy Thursday, so that the minimum requirements of the liturgy can be fulfilled in a more dignified way. The following description will assume the participation of one concelebrant, four servers, one reader, and a schola to lead the singing.

The Requisites for Mass

In the sacristy:

- Six or four torches, or at least two

At the credence table:

- Everything usually needed for Mass
- A ciborium with hosts that are to be consecrated for Communion on Good Friday
- A white veil for the ciborium
- A wooden clapper or rattle (the crotalus)
- A white humeral veil

At the altar:

- Six matching candles
- The altar cross may be veiled in white rather than purple.[922]
- The Gospel book, flat, face down at the center of the altar

At the place for the foot washing in the nave or in the sanctuary:

- A gremial, or in its absence an amice, for the celebrant
- Benches or seats for those having their feet washed
- A pitcher of water and basin
- A basket with towels for drying the feet, one for each person
- A cushion for the celebrant to kneel upon, if necessary

In a convenient place in the sanctuary:

- A second set of pitcher, bowel, towel, and soap, to wash the celebrant's hands after the foot washing

[922] André Philippe M. Mutel and Peter Freeman, *Cérémonial de la sainte messe à l'usage ordinaire des paroisses suivant le missel romain de 2002 et la pratique léguée du rit romain*, 2nd ed. (Perpignan, France: Éditions Artège, 2012), 259; Adrian Fortescue, J. B. O'Connell, and Alcuin Reid, eds., *The Ceremonies of the Roman Rite Described*, 15th ed. (New York: Bloomsbury, 2009), 337.

- Candles for all those in the sanctuary
- One censer with burning charcoals, incense boat, and stand[923]

In the narthex:

- Candles for all those in the church

In the chapel where the Blessed Sacrament will be kept:

- The repository for the Blessed Sacrament
- Candles, flowers, and other suitable decorations

The Opening Rites

Mass on Holy Thursday begins with the tabernacle of the church completely empty and therefore unveiled. The sanctuary lamp is not lit and is often removed. The door to the tabernacle is left open. Well prior to the beginning of the evening Mass, the Hosts which were reserved there are transferred to a repository outside the church, distinct from the repository which will serve for adoration following Mass.[924] Often, this secret repository is located in the sacristy. Since the tabernacle is empty at the beginning of Mass, there are no genuflections to be made as the procession arrives at the sanctuary. Servers and the concelebrant will need to be reminded of this.

The thurifer can lead the procession as usual. Upon arriving at the sanctuary, the servers carrying the censer, the cross, perhaps veiled in purple, and the processional candles bow their heads to the altar. Any other servers present make a profound bow from the waist to the altar upon arriving at the sanctuary and then go to their places. The concelebrant bows profoundly, kisses the altar, and goes to his seat or waits to kiss the altar with the principal celebrant. Next, the celebrant goes up to the altar and kisses the altar, with both hands resting on the altar. The celebrant may incense the altar. (See chapter 4.) Then, the celebrant goes to his chair by the most direct route.

During the Gloria, the bells of the church are rung. According to custom, servers also ring one or more sets of handbells during this time. If necessary, due to the lack of servers, members of faithful can carry out this function. From that

[923] Although two thurifers are indicated on Holy Thursday, it is permitted to use one out of necessity. Fortescue, O'Connell, and Reid, *The Ceremonies of the Roman Rite Described*, 343.

[924] Mutel and Freeman, *Cérémonial de la sainte messe*, 258.

point on, the ringing of any bells is suspended until the Gloria of the Easter Vigil. In place of the bells, some locations instead use a wooden clapper or rattle (the crotalus) at the usual points of Mass.[925] Similarly, the use of the pipe organ is suspended until the Gloria of the Easter Vigil.[926]

The Liturgy of the Word

If a concelebrant is present on Holy Thursday, it is more fitting for him to proclaim the Gospel rather than the celebrant. He does not seek the blessing from the celebrant, but goes directly from his seat to the altar. He bows profoundly to say the prayer of preparation and picks up the Gospel book in both hands, holding it as indicated in chapter 6. No fewer than three servers are required for a proper Gospel procession. Those are the thurifer and two candle bearers. If trained servers are lacking, it may be necessary to omit the Gospel procession altogether, including omitting the use of the Gospel book. In that case, the concelebrant, or even the celebrant himself, stands when the Alleluia begins, goes to the altar, bows profoundly to say the prayer of preparation, and then goes to the ambo. He reads the Gospel from the lectionary in the usual way.

The Washing of the Feet

The washing of the feet is optional on Holy Thursday during the celebration of the Mass of the Lord's Supper. Small congregations that cannot provide the minimum number of servers to accomplish this liturgical action in a dignified way should consider omitting it from Mass. The missal does not indicate the number of persons, men or women, who are selected to have their feet washed. Historically, they have numbered eleven, twelve, or even thirteen.[927] A small congregation may prefer to designate fewer persons to have their feet washed.

Immediately following the homily, the celebrant returns to the chair. There, he removes the chasuble and places it face down on the back of his chair. A server brings him a gremial, holding it by its two corners. The celebrant receives the gremial. He passes its ribbons behind his back and draws them to his waist, where he ties them with the slipknot at the front. Meanwhile, a server goes to the persons selected to lead them from the nave to their places in the sanctuary. Long benches, or individual stools or seats if necessary, are prepared in the sanctuary for them.

[925] Fortescue, O'Connell, and Reid, *The Ceremonies of the Roman Rite Described*, 337.

[926] Mutel and Freeman, *Cérémonial de la sainte messe*, 257.

[927] Mutel and Freeman, *Cérémonial de la sainte messe*, 263.

Ideally, these would be placed in such a way that two rows face each other across the sanctuary in the manner of a choir. However, it is often easier for the celebrant to wash the feet of those chosen if he kneels on a step in front of those seated. That may require the seats to be placed across the front of the sanctuary. Unless the benches or seats can be placed in the proper location before Mass begins in such a way that they do not hinder the opening rites and the Liturgy of the Word, servers will need to bring out the benches or seats after the homily.

Upon arriving at their places, those chosen to have their feet washed remove the shoes and socks from their right feet. Once those selected are in their places, the celebrant leaves the chair and goes to them. If they are facing each other in two rows in the sanctuary, the celebrant normally begins with those on the left side of the sanctuary as one faces the sanctuary, starting with the person closest to the altar. He then does the same with those seated on the right side of the sanctuary as one faces the sanctuary, again beginning with the person seated closest to the altar. If those chosen are seated rather in a straight line across the front of the sanctuary, the celebrant generally moves from left to right. One server kneels to his immediate right with the basin. A second server stands also to the right with the pitcher of water. In case of necessity, a concelebrant may stand to the celebrant's right holding the pitcher of water in the place of a missing server. To the celebrant's left stands a server with a basket of clean towels, one for each person whose feet will be washed. Finally, if the celebrant will kneel on a hard surface, it may be helpful for the fourth server to move a cushion to each successive person for the celebrant to kneel upon, unless the celebrant decides to move the cushion himself.

The celebrant kneels to wash and dry the foot of each person. The first server is responsible for placing the basin beneath the foot of each person. The first server also receives the pitcher from the second server or the concelebrant and presents it to the celebrant and takes it back from him when the celebrant wipes each foot. The first server takes care to pick up and move the basin from person to person. That server does not slide the basin from one person to another. A more experienced server standing to the celebrant's left is responsible for passing the celebrant a clean towel for each person. That person himself or herself can finish completely drying the foot once the celebrant has done so initially. The celebrant rises each time after washing and drying a foot, and kneels again to repeat the process with the next person. The rubrics no longer obligate the celebrant to kiss each foot after washing and drying it. The fourth server can move the cushion upon which the celebrant kneels each time.

After washing and drying the foot of the last person, the celebrant washes his hands at a second credence table set up for that purpose.[928] Such a table is more conveniently located near the last person to have his or her feet washed. The celebrant may also remove the gremial there. Meanwhile, the third server returns to each person with the empty basket to retrieve the towel with which he or she finished drying his or her feet. Another server leads the designated persons back to their places in the nave. After washing and drying his hands, the celebrant returns to the chair, bowing when he passes in front of the altar, and puts on the chasuble once again. With the help of a concelebrant perhaps, he takes the chasuble from the back of his chair, and facing the chair, puts it on once again. The concelebrant assists by adjusting the chasuble as needed. Mass continues immediately with the Prayer of the Faithful.

The Eucharistic Prayer

According to the traditional practice, bells are not rung during the Triduum from the Gloria on Holy Thursday until the Gloria at the Easter Vigil on Holy Saturday. In place of the bells, some churches use a wooden clapper or rattle (the crotalus).[929] These are struck during the Eucharistic Prayer and even prior to Communion, at the same points one would ring hand bells. A member of the assembly may carry out this function if necessary.

The Procession to the Repository

During the distribution of Holy Communion, a server brings the ciborium cover with its veil to the altar, placing it outside the corporal. Another server removes the missal and places it near the celebrant's chair. Since the Blessed Sacrament is reposing on the altar during this time, both servers genuflect to the Blessed Sacrament upon approaching and departing from the altar. Once the distribution of Holy Communion is completed, the Precious Blood that remains is consumed at the altar, facing any side of the altar. The celebrant or a concelebrant places the Hosts that remain in the ciborium prepared with Hosts to be consecrated for Good Friday in the center of the corporal. He then covers the ciborium and veils it. He genuflects, and returns to his chair. All genuflect when passing in front of

[928] Mutel and Freeman, *Cérémonial de la sainte messe*, 339, 344.

[929] Peter J. Elliott, *Ceremonies of the Liturgical Year According to the Modern Roman Rite: A Manual for Clergy and All Involved in Liturgical Ministries* (San Francisco: Ignatius Press, 2002), 103, n. 24; Mutel and Freeman, *Cérémonial de la sainte messe*, 266; Fortescue, O'Connell, and Reid, *The Ceremonies of the Roman Rite Described*, 337.

the altar, or whether approaching or departing from it on the sides. Any vessels used in the distribution of Communion are brought to the credence table to be purified over corporals.[930] Meanwhile, all in the sanctuary and in the nave take candles in hand. Servers assist in lighting everyone's candles in the sanctuary and in the nave. Designated parishioners go to the sacristy to take up four or six torches for the concluding procession with the Blessed Sacrament to the repository.

The celebrant, standing at his chair, says the Post-Communion prayer there. It is not permitted to say the Post-Communion prayer standing at the altar on Holy Thursday.[931] The concluding rites are completely omitted. At this point, the cross bearer takes a position in the center aisle, facing the altar. In practice, however, it may be more helpful to have the cross bearer stand in the center aisle *before* the Post-Communion prayer, while the purifications are taking place, so that the procession can begin without delay. The torch bearers could be positioned at the same time, either across the front of the sanctuary, as they usually are, or in two rows facing each other across the center aisle. In that position, they can easily flank the celebrant carrying the Blessed Sacrament when he departs from the altar.[932] Finally, it may be better for a concelebrant to remain in the sanctuary, so that he can kneel at his place.

Then, the celebrant and the thurifer go before the altar steps, genuflect, and rise. Depending on the disposition of the sanctuary, they may face liturgical east or may face the assembly. All in the sanctuary and in the church, except the cross bearer, kneel. The celebrant turns to his right to face the thurifer, who presents him with the open incense boat. The celebrant takes the incense boat in this left hand, and using his right hand imposes incense three times on the burning coals of the open censer, held before him slightly below eye level. Returning the spoon to the incense boat in his left hand, the celebrant makes a Greek cross over the incense with his right hand, saying nothing. He closes the incense boat and returns it to the thurifer, who now holds both the censer and the incense boat. The thurifer holds the incense boat and the ring of the chains of the censer in the left hand. The thurifer holds the chains near the bowl of the censer in the right hand. The celebrant and those near him kneel. The thurifer puts the incense boat down on the step in front of him momentarily. Using the right hand, the thurifer places the chains of the censer in the left hand of the celebrant. The thurifer uses his left

930 Elliott, *Ceremonies of the Liturgical Year*, 104.

931 *RM*, Mass of the Lord's Supper, no. 35.

932 Elliott, *Ceremonies of the Liturgical Year*, 104.

hand to place the bowl of the censer in the celebrant's right hand. The celebrant elevates the bowl of the censer in the right hand to a position slightly below eye level. He incenses the Blessed Sacrament in silence from a kneeling position with three double swings, bowing before and after.[933] All those kneeling with the celebrant bow from a kneeling position at the same time he does. The celebrant then returns the censer to the thurifer. The thurifer makes sure to take up the incense boat from the step in front of him. The thurifer now holds both the censer and the incense boat once again. When all are in the proper position to begin the procession, a third server stands behind the kneeling celebrant and places the humeral veil on his shoulders. This third and fourth servers, who may have been holding the missal for the Post-Communion prayer, walk on either side of the celebrant for the length of the procession. The celebrant goes up to the altar and genuflects there. The celebrant covers the ciborium and his hands with the humeral veil. The concelebrant and any other servers stand from the kneeling position and then genuflect, as a eucharistic chant, "Pange Lingua," for example, begins.[934] The procession is now ready to set off.

The cross bearer alone leads the procession,[935] followed by the concelebrant holding a burning candle in his right hand. Then follows the thurifer, walking immediately in front of the celebrant, always facing forward.[936] The thurifer holds the chain of the censer in the right hand, the left hand resting on his chest, holding the incense boat. Then follow the celebrant holding the Blessed Sacrament, two assisting servers walking on either side of him, and torch bearers, also walking in two rows on either side of the Blessed Sacrament. They hold the torches in their outside hands, their inside hands resting on their chests. The faithful, or at least a representative group of the faithful, walk behind the celebrant. The choir may be the first among them. All hold lighted candles in their outside hands. Those who do not join the procession remain kneeling until the Blessed Sacrament has left the church or until it has been reposed in a chapel within view of the nave.[937]

If the procession to the repository passes outdoors, some churches maintain the use of the *umbrellino*, held over the celebrant by a member of the assembly walking behind him, or even the use of the baldachin, held by four laypersons,

933 *CB*, 306; *RM*, Holy Thursday, no. 37; Elliott, *Ceremonies of the Liturgical Year*, 105.

934 Mutel and Freeman, *Cérémonial de la sainte messe*, 272.

935 Commentators acknowledge that when servers are lacking, the processional candles can be omitted. See Fortescue, O'Connell, and Reid, *The Ceremonies of the Roman Rite Described*, 345.

936 Mutel and Freeman, *Cérémonial de la sainte messe*, 273, n. 133.

937 Elliott, *Ceremonies of the Liturgical Year*, 213.

with the celebrant walking beneath it and the torch bearers on either side.[938] In many locations, the baldachin or the umbrellino is used only for the portion of the procession that takes place outdoors. If a baldachin is used, those carrying it wait just outside the doors of the church.[939] The celebrant and those assisting him walk under it as they emerge from the church. The torch bearers walk on either side of those supporting the baldachin. Upon arriving at the location of the repository, those supporting the baldachin or the umbrellino during the portion of the procession outdoors allow the torch bearers and the celebrant with his assisting servers to enter the church or chapel while they remain outside.

Arriving at the altar of repose, the cross bearer moves to one side of the entrance to the temporary sanctuary and faces the altar. The concelebrant passes the cross and enters the temporary sanctuary to kneel at the celebrant's side. The torch bearers take their usual positions on either side of the entrance of the sanctuary in a row. The torch bearers kneel. The thurifer, the celebrant, and the assisting servers enter the sanctuary. The thurifer kneels to the right of where the celebrant will eventually kneel. The assisting servers kneel slightly behind the celebrant on either side of him. Upon arriving, the celebrant places the veiled ciborium in the repository, keeping its door open, or he places the ciborium on the corporal on the table of the altar of reposition. Then, the celebrant genuflects the altar and kneels on the lowest step. The third server who has been accompanying the celebrant stands behind the kneeling celebrant to remove the humeral veil. That server places the humeral veil aside or folds it over his left arm if there is no credence table available.

Customarily, the Blessed Sacrament is incensed during the final verse of the hymn "Pange Lingua,"[940] that is, at *Genitori genitoque*. Thus, during the preceding verse, *Tantum ergo*, it is customary to bow together from a kneeling position at the words *veneremur cernui*, after which the celebrant and the thurifer rise in order to prepare the incense from a standing position.[941] After preparing the incense, the celebrant hands the boat to the thurifer. All kneel. The thurifer places the boat on the step of the altar. With the right hand, the thurifer places the chains of the censer in the celebrant's left hand. With the left hand, the thurifer places the bowl of the censer in the celebrant's right hand. Holding the bowl of

938 Mutel and Freeman, *Cérémonial de la sainte messe*, 268, n. 122.

939 The use of the baldachin is optional according to no. 388 of the *Ceremonial of Bishops*.

940 *CB*, 308; *RM*, Holy Thursday, no. 39.

941 Fortescue, O'Connell, and Reid, *The Ceremonies of the Roman Rite Described*, 299.

the censer slightly below eye level in the right hand, the celebrant incenses the Blessed Sacrament with three double swings, bowing before and after.

After the incensation, the concelebrant or even the celebrant himself goes up to the altar. He places the ciborium in the repository if necessary, genuflects, and closes and locks the door. The concelebrant returns to the side of the celebrant. After a period of prayer, all in the sanctuary rise with the celebrant and genuflect. They extinguish the candles they hold. They return in silence to the sacristy in the usual order, led by the thurifer and cross bearer.[942]

[942] Elliott, *Ceremonies of the Liturgical Year*, 108.

36

Good Friday in Small Congregations

The Celebration of the Lord's Passion on Good Friday is comprised of three principal parts: The Liturgy of the Word, the adoration of the cross, and Holy Communion. In the Roman Missal of Paul VI, the structure of this service is greatly simplified compared to the past. In small congregations, whether of a rural or urban nature, it will not be possible to simplify the ritual beyond what is required. See chapter 17 for a complete description of the Celebration of the Lord's Passion on Good Friday. The description below assumes that one reader and four servers join the celebrant. It also assumes that the faithful will sing the necessary chants, led by a cantor or a small schola. If a parish is not able to provide the minimum number of ministers required, it may be best for the parish to join a neighboring parish for the celebration, in order to guarantee the necessary level of decorum and dignity for one of the holiest days of the year.

Before the Service

The following items need to be prepared in advance. Although the Celebration of the Lord's Passion is marked by great simplicity, it nevertheless demands a wide range of items in order to be carried out with dignity.

In the sacristy:

- Red Mass vestments for the priest celebrant

In a convenient place or in the sacristy itself:

- The cross, veiled in purple if the first form of veneration is used

- A stand for the cross, or a pillow on which it rests
- One or two purificators to wipe the cross
- Two candlesticks

In the chapel of reposition:

- A corporal, unfolded in front of the repository
- A red or white humeral veil[943]
- Two candlesticks

In the sanctuary:

- The credence table is covered with a cloth that extends only to the edges of its top without falling on either side.
- The chair for the celebrant is bare, without cushions.
- A lectern, uncovered, before the chair of the celebrant, if servers are lacking
- Red cushion for the celebrant, which can be placed at the steps at the entrance of the sanctuary
- The missal is placed near the celebrant's chair or on the lectern before it.
- The lectionary is placed open at the bare ambo.
- The proper text for the Universal Prayer or a second missal is placed near the ambo.

On the credence table:

- An altar cloth of a size which covers only the table (*mensa*) of the altar
- A bare stand for the missal
- A red burse with a corporal or several corporals, as needed
- Empty ciboria or patens, as needed
- An ablution bowl and finger towel
- A purificator
- A cruet of water if needed to purify the vessels

943 *CB*, 315.

- A wooden rattle or clapper (the crotalus)
- The stand to receive the cross after veneration

Even in small congregations, the Service of the Lord's Passion begins in the same manner described in chapter 17.

The Liturgy of the Word

The designated reader and cantor proclaim the readings and chants before the Passion in the usual manner. The celebrant alone reads the Passion from the lectionary on the ambo. After a brief homily, the solemn intercessions take place. The celebrant stands at the chair, with a server holding the missal directly in front of him or slightly to his left, according to the circumstances. The celebrant may also stand at the altar with the missal on its stand at the center of the altar before him.[944] This may be preferable if servers are lacking. Historically, the missal did not lay on the altar unless it was adorned with cloth, candles, and crucifix. Perhaps in this case, it is better to vest the altar with its cloth before putting the missal and its stand upon it.[945] Normally, a reader stands at the ambo to offer the introduction to each intention,[946] unless the celebrant prefers to offer the introductions himself. Thus, for the general intercessions, two missals may be needed, one at the chair or altar and one at the ambo. In any event, the one announcing each intention faces the assembly to do so. The lay minister offers the invitation to prayer with hands joined. The celebrant prays each Collect with hands extended, facing the altar if at all possible. When a lay minister offers the introductions to each intention, it is more fitting for the celebrant himself to invite the people to kneel and stand, since directions such as these are never offered by lay ministers to the assembled faithful. After each intention is announced by the reader, the celebrant says, "Let us kneel." All kneel in their places for a brief period. The reader kneels facing the ambo. The celebrant kneels at the chair or at the altar. After a period of silent prayer, the celebrant stands and says, "Let us stand." The server holding the missal in front of the celebrant at the chair remains standing throughout. When the faithful kneel, this server can bow his or her head and close his or her eyes to join them in silent prayer. Alternatively, the people may kneel or stand through the entire period of the solemn intercessions.

944 *RM*, Good Friday, no. 11.

945 Adrian Fortescue, J. B. O'Connell, and Alcuin Reid, eds., *The Ceremonies of the Roman Rite Described*, 15th ed. (New York: Bloomsbury, 2009), 356.

946 *RM*, Good Friday, no. 11.

The Showing and Veneration of the Cross

For a complete description, see chapter 17. Three servers can assure the first form of showing the veiled cross. One goes to the sacristy to take up the veiled cross. Two others accompany that server with candles on either side. The celebrant himself carries the unveiled cross through the church in the second form of showing the cross. He is accompanied by two servers with candles on either side.

The Rite of Holy Communion

For a complete description, see chapter 17. The priest celebrant himself goes to the place of reposition to bring the Blessed Sacrament to the altar. He is accompanied by two servers. If another priest or a deacon is present, it is preferable that the priest or deacon in attendance fulfill that function. As soon as the celebrant departs for the repository, the two servers who remain in the sanctuary prepare the altar with its cloth, corporal (s), additional vessels for Communion as needed, and the missal with its stand. Once at the place of reposition, one of the two servers places the red or white humeral veil on the shoulders of the celebrant before both servers take up the processional candles waiting there. The priest celebrant then takes up the ciborium from the repository and covers it in the ends of the humeral veil. The transfer of the Blessed Sacrament to the altar and the distribution of Communion take place as described in chapter 17.

Once the distribution of Communion is completed, the Blessed Sacrament is normally returned to the repository. If necessary, however, the Blessed Sacrament can be reserved temporarily in the tabernacle in the sanctuary.[947] In that case, a server lights the sanctuary lamp and veils the tabernacle in red after the celebrant has reserved the Blessed Sacrament there rather than at the repository. A server folds and removes the corporal from the altar. The celebrant prays the Post-Communion prayer and the prayer over the people either at the chair or at the altar. If the Post-Communion prayer takes place at the altar, the server places the missal straight, in the center of the altar with the bottom of the missal parallel to the edge of the altar.[948] The Post-Communion prayer is offered with hands extended in the *orans* position. The prayer over the people is offered with hands

947 *RM*, Good Friday, no. 29.

948 André Philippe M. Mutel and Peter Freeman, *Cérémonial de la sainte messe à l'usage ordinaire des paroisses suivant le missel romain de 2002 et la pratique léguée du rit romain*, 2nd ed. (Perpignan, France: Éditions Artège, 2012), 303, n. 217; Fortescue, O'Connell, and Reid, *The Ceremonies of the Roman Rite Described*, 353, 358.

outstretched, palms down, over the people. The priest says, "Let us pray," before the Post-Communion prayer.[949] He does not say, "The Lord be with you," prior to the prayer over the people, but he may say, "Bow down for the blessing," prior to the prayer over the people.[950] There is no actual blessing with the Sign of the Cross at the conclusion of the Service of the Lord's Passion on Good Friday.

After the Service of the Lord's Passion

If the Blessed Sacrament has been reserved in the tabernacle of the sanctuary, it is now transferred to the repository, either in the place of reposition for Holy Thursday, if this remains out of sight from those in the nave, or at the secret repository, usually in the sacristy. This takes place without ceremony. The priest wears the humeral veil. He is accompanied by at least one server with a torch.[951] The veil is removed from the tabernacle, and the sanctuary lamp is extinguished. Servers return to the church to remove the altar cloth without ceremony. Usually, they begin by bringing the edges of the cloth toward the middle of the altar, and then again once or twice as needed. What remains is folded one final time from front to back. They may roll the altar cloth on a tube, from right to left. Any veils over other crosses in the church or in the sacristy are removed. The veils over statues remain until the beginning of the Easter Vigil.[952]

[949] *RM*, Good Friday, no. 30.

[950] *RM*, Good Friday, no. 31.

[951] Mutel and Freeman, *Cérémonial de la sainte messe*, 302.

[952] Mutel and Freeman, *Cérémonial de la sainte messe*, 303, n. 221.

37

The Easter Vigil in Small Congregations

The Easter Vigil is comprised of four parts: the service of light, the Liturgy of the Word, in some cases the rites of Christian initiation as well as the renewal of baptismal promises, and the Liturgy of the Eucharist. For a more complete description of the Easter Vigil, see chapter 18. Even in small congregations, it is possible to celebrate the Easter Vigil in a dignified way. A schola or at least a cantor will lead the singing of the faithful. More than one reader is best, given that multiple readings will be proclaimed. However, the cantor of the responsorial psalm after each reading could also proclaim that reading in case of necessity. At least three servers are needed to assist the priest celebrant.

Requisites for the Celebration

For the blessing of the fire:

- Everything needed to light and extinguish the fire
- A tray with the five grains of incense, stylus, charcoals, tongs, a follower for the Easter candle, a candle for the celebrant
- Some means of lighting the Easter candle from the new fire
- Candles for those taking part, unless these are distributed elsewhere
- A table, covered in a white cloth, for all the items above
- A second missal on a bare lectern

In the sacristy:

- The Easter candle
- Censer without charcoals and incense boat

In the sanctuary:

- Everything usually needed for Mass
- The text of the Exsultet placed at the ambo or at a lectern
- The processional cross and candles for the recessional
- A stand for the Easter candle to the right of the ambo or in the center of the sanctuary
- A lectern, veiled in white, near the stand for the Easter candle if this cannot be placed near the ambo. This same lectern can be used to hold the ritual for the celebration of Confirmation and renewal of baptismal promises if servers are lacking.
- The Gospel book, flat, face down on the altar at the center
- White veil for the tabernacle
- Some means of lighting the sanctuary lamp after Communion
- Chrism for Confirmation, unless it remains in the ambry in the baptistry
- Cotton balls, bread, or lemons to cleanse the celebrant's hands after the Confirmations, along with a pitcher of water, bowl, and towel

At the baptismal font or in the baptistry:

- A means of pouring water for the Baptisms, towels
- White garments for the newly baptized, if used in the case of adults
- Baptismal candles for the newly baptized adults
- Chrism, unless it is placed beforehand where the Confirmations will take place
- A vessel to receive the blessed water, aspergillum
- A table, covered with a white cloth, for all the items above
- The rituals for the Christian initiation of adults or children as needed; a second missal if the Baptism of infants alone takes place
- A lectern, covered with a white cloth, for the rituals for adults or children

At the place of reservation of the Blessed Sacrament:

- White humeral veil
- Two processional candles

Prior to the beginning of the Easter Vigil, the veils on any statues have been removed. The holy water stoups remain empty. The tabernacle of the church remains completely empty and unveiled; the door is left open. A sanctuary candle is prepared, but remains unlit. The church may be illuminated in low light. The lights in the sacristy can remain on for as long as it is occupied. All the lights in the sacristy and the church are extinguished just before the Vigil begins. If the blessing of the new fire takes place outdoors, the light from the new fire may be sufficient for the celebrant to read by even without any exterior lighting. If the blessing of the new fire and the preparation and lighting of the Easter candle take place in the narthex of the church rather than outside, the lights in the narthex alone can remain on so that the celebrant will have sufficient light to read from the missal and to prepare the Easter candle. The lights in the narthex can be extinguished once the Easter candle is lit and the celebrant has read the formula "May the light of Christ rising in glory."[953] At that point, the lights are no longer needed, since there are no further texts to read. The celebrant will prepare the incense by the light of the new fire and of the Easter candle alone.

At the appointed time, the celebrant and servers make their way from the sacristy to the place where the new fire will be blessed by means of a secondary door rather than the main door of the church. Once everyone has gathered outside, the main doors of the church are opened. The processional cross and candles are not carried; they are placed in the sanctuary for use at the end of Mass. The Gospel book is not carried. If used for Mass, the Gospel book can be placed face down at the center of the altar prior to the beginning of the Easter Vigil. The thurifer carries the censer without charcoals and the incense boat as well. A senior server carries the Easter candle. All follow the server carrying the Easter candle.[954] The ministers make their way from the sacristy to the new fire in an orderly way, but not in procession. The procession properly speaking will begin from the new fire rather than from the sacristy.

The Service of Light

The celebrant and servers gather at the place where the new fire will be blessed. If outdoors, the celebrant stands with his back to the door of the church, with the new fire between him and the assembled faithful. If the service of light begins in

953 Adrian Fortescue, J. B. O'Connell, and Alcuin Reid, eds., *The Ceremonies of the Roman Rite Described*, 15th ed. (New York: Bloomsbury, 2009), 371.

954 *CB*, 338.

the narthex with most people inside the church, the celebrant again stands facing the faithful in the church with the new fire between them.[955] A bare lectern with the missal stands to the celebrant's left. The server with the candle stands to his left also. The items needed to light the incense and the candle are placed on a table to his right. The thurifer also stands to the celebrant's right. Upon arrival, the thurifer uses tongs to place the unlit coals into the new fire, unless this has already been done by the sacristan.

The celebrant begins with the Sign of the Cross. He extends his hands for the greeting and joins his hands for the instruction "Dear brethren, on this most sacred night." He extends both hands in the *orans* position to bless the fire, eventually joining his hands briefly, and then making the Sign of the Cross with his right hand over it at the point indicated in the text, his left hand resting on his chest. He then joins both hands before continuing with hands extended as before. He joins his hands once again at the conclusion, "Through Christ Our Lord."

The celebrant then prepares the Easter candle. From the tray on the table to his right, the celebrant takes a stylus and traces the cross, the alpha and the omega, and the date on the Easter candle, which the minister on his left holds upright for him. The server holding the Easter candle stands immediately next to the lectern with the missal, so that the celebrant can easily read the texts which accompany the preparation of the candle. Once finished, the celebrant returns the stylus to the table to his right. The celebrant places the each of the five grains of incense into the candle in the shape of a cross, fixing each one in place with a nail. In many churches, these acts of preparation are carried out ahead of time in the sacristy.[956] If so, the celebrant, holding the stylus in the right hand, simply traces the stylus over the figures already in place on the candle while saying the required formulas. He can touch the nails previously affixed with the joined fingers of his right hand while saying the required formulas.

The celebrant takes a taper from the table to his right and lights the Easter candle from the new fire with his right hand, saying the formula "May the light of Christ."[957] The celebrant may grasp the candle with his left hand or rest his left hand on his chest while doing so. In some churches, during the day of Saturday, the sacristan often lights the candle briefly ahead of time, so that the wick will

[955] André Philippe M. Mutel and Peter Freeman, *Cérémonial de la sainte messe à l'usage ordinaire des paroisses suivant le missel romain de 2002 et la pratique léguée du rit romain*, 2nd ed. (Perpignan, France: Éditions Artège, 2012), 318.

[956] Mutel and Freeman, *Cérémonial de la sainte messe*, 319, n. 263.

[957] Mutel and Freeman, *Cérémonial de la sainte messe*, 320.

burn more easily at the Vigil itself. In many churches, the celebrant then takes the brass or glass follower from the table to his right and places it over the Easter candle. A server may retain the taper lit until the Easter candle is shielded from the wind. Meanwhile, the senior server holding the Easter candle goes to stand in the doorway of the church. If at any time the wind blows out the Easter candle, it is relit by the celebrant from the taper or from the blessed fire itself while repeating the required formula. Conversely, if all are gathered in the narthex, those lights are now extinguished. It will not be necessary to retain a lit taper. The thurifer retrieves the burning coals from the new fire with tongs and places them in the censer. The thurifer goes to the celebrant so that he may impose incense in the usual manner. The celebrant takes an unlit candle from the table to his right and holds the candle in his right hand. An usher remains behind to make sure the Easter fire is extinguished once all have entered the church.

The thurifer leads the procession into the body of the church, followed by the senior server bearing the Easter candle and the celebrant.[958] Any other servers present follow behind the celebrant. The faithful follow behind the liturgical ministers; the choir may be the first among them. At the door of the church or even just inside, the senior server stops, facing forward into the church. The senior server raises the candle as the celebrant sings in a low tone, "The light of Christ," and all respond.[959] The celebrant alone lights his candle from the Easter candle at this point.

After the first acclamation of "The light of Christ," and the lighting of the celebrant's candle, the procession continues into the church. At the middle of the church, the senior server stops, still facing forward. The senior server raises the candle as the celebrant sings in a higher tone, "The light of Christ," a second time. The entire assembly lights their candles at this point. Historically, the clergy and servers alone lit their candles at this point. In order not to delay the procession, the procession may resume once these the clergy and servers *begin* to light the candles of the assembly behind them and next to them in procession.[960]

Finally, at the steps of the sanctuary, the senior server turns to face the assembly as the celebrant sings in a higher tone, "The light of Christ," one final time.[961] At this point, any and all candles in the church itself may be lit. These would include the

958 *RM*, Easter Vigil, no. 15.

959 Peter J. Elliott, *Ceremonies of the Liturgical Year According to the Modern Roman Rite: A Manual for Clergy and All Involved in Liturgical Ministries* (San Francisco: Ignatius Press, 2002), 138; Mutel and Freeman, *Cérémonial de la sainte messe*, 322.

960 Mutel and Freeman, *Cérémonial de la sainte messe*, 322, n. 269.

961 *RM*, Easter Vigil, no. 17.

candles in the dedication crosses, candles at any minor altars, candles and lamps located in various shrines, and any other candles set up in the sanctuary. However, the candles at the main altar itself and the sanctuary lamp itself are not lit at this point. The candles at the main altar will be lit at the Gloria. The sanctuary lamp will be lit only once reservation in the tabernacle resumes, after the conclusion of Communion. In addition, the few electric lights needed simply for the Exsultet, the readings, the chants, and the Collects, can be turned on at this point. Any lights turned on due to necessity remain lit throughout the Vigil. Electric lights are not turned or and turned off in succession throughout the course of the Vigil. It may be better to delay turning on all or most the lights of the church until after the Exsultet, or even until the Gloria, as is the custom currently in some churches.[962] Otherwise, the words of the Exsultet, "This is the night," contradict the truth of the circumstances when the interior of the church is already as bright as day when this is sung! It may even be possible for servers holding lit candles to stand around the lectern, ambo, and chair in turn such that no electric lighting may be needed until later.

All who enter the sanctuary bow profoundly to the altar. The server carrying the Easter candle and the thurifer carrying the censer bow their heads instead. There is no mention in any of the revised books of the celebrant kissing the altar upon entering the sanctuary. The senior server goes and places the Easter candle in its stand with the inscriptions on the candle facing forward. The stand for the Easter candle is placed near the ambo,[963] normally to its right, unless the circumstances dictate otherwise. If it is not possible for the Easter candle to be placed next to the ambo for some reason, the Easter candle and its stand can alternatively be located in the center of the sanctuary. In that case, a lectern covered in white, from which the celebrant himself or a cantor will sing the Exsultet, stands turned toward the assembly, slightly to the left of the Easter candle as one faces the assembly.[964] The thurifer and a server ready to hold the celebrant's candle stand at the celebrant's right at the presidential chair. The book bearer stands at the celebrant's left at the presidential chair.

Once all have their candles lit and have taken their places, the thurifer comes before the celebrant for the imposition of incense. The celebrant hands his candle to a server. The celebrant imposes and blesses incense in the usual way. The celebrant and the thurifer then go together to the altar and bow. The celebrant, still bowing

[962] Elliott, *Ceremonies of the Liturgical Year*, 280; Mutel and Freeman, *Cérémonial de la sainte messe*, 325, n. 278.

[963] *CB*, 336.

[964] *RM*, Easter Vigil, no. 19; Fortescue, O'Connell, and Reid, *The Ceremonies of the Roman Rite Described*, 364.

profoundly before the altar, prays the prayer of preparation for the Easter proclamation. The celebrant rises, and he and the thurifer go to the Easter candle. The celebrant, following the thurifer, goes to the ambo or to the temporary lectern, where he will sing the Exsultet. He receives the censer from the thurifer and incenses the book with three swings, center, left, and right, bowing before and after, saying nothing. He then incenses the Easter candle by walking around it in a counterclockwise direction, bowing before and after.[965] If the placement of the Easter candle makes it impossible to walk around it while incensing it, the celebrant may simply incense the Easter candle from a standing position with three swings, bowing before and after. The celebrant sings the Easter proclamation with hands joined. The book is illuminated by the light of the Easter candle and by the candles of those standing near the celebrant. In addition, some electric lights may be needed. A cantor may sing the proclamation in the place of the celebrant. The cantor does not ask for the celebrant's blessing beforehand and does not incense the candle or the book. A layperson sings the modified form of the Exsultet. In the case where a cantor sings the Exsultet, the celebrant may incense the candle himself prior to the Exsultet. Then, he returns to the chair and holds his candle in his right hand during the singing of the Exsultet.

After singing the Exsultet, the celebrant returns to his seat. A server removes the lectern if one is used. The celebrant signals everyone to extinguish their candles, and all are seated, as described in the missal.[966] On the other hand, following the custom in some churches, all may retain their candles lit until the Gloria, keeping their lamps lit, so to speak, for the coming of the Bridegroom. In that case, a server will need to take the candle from the celebrant each time he prays a Collect.[967] The lights of the church, or a significant portion of them, can be turned on at this point, if they were already not turned on before the Exsultet.[968] The celebrant, standing at the chair, faces the assembly to invite them to listen to the readings. A server holds the missal before him for this invitation.

[965] Mutel and Freeman, *Cérémonial de la sainte messe*, 326.

[966] *RM*, Easter Vigil no. 22.

[967] Mutel and Freeman, *Cérémonial de la sainte messe*, 327.

[968] Formerly, the lamps of the church were lit *during* the Exsultet. See Léon-Michael Le Vavasseur, *Cérémonial à l'usage des petites églises de paroisse selon the rite romain*, 2nd ed. (Paris: Éditions Lecoffre, 1864), 253, no. 250. The rubrics of the revised Easter Vigil in 1951 indicated that the lights of the church were turned on before the *beginning* of the Exsultet so that there would be sufficient light to sing the text. See Fortescue, O'Connell, and Reid, *The Ceremonies of the Roman Rite Described*, 364. This coincided with moving the time of the Easter Vigil from the morning, when additional lighting would not be necessary in order to sing the Exsultet, to the evening, when it would be needed. Thus, the timing for lighting the lamps of the church at the Easter Vigil has varied somewhat over the last century.

The Liturgy of the Word

The Liturgy of the Word at the Easter Vigil comprises up to seven readings from the Law and the Prophets, an epistle, an extended Gospel Acclamation, and a Gospel passage. Fewer are permitted. Each of the Old Testament readings is followed by a responsorial psalm and Collect. It is possible to replace each responsorial psalm with silence, concluding with the Collect nonetheless. Where readers are lacking, the cantor of each psalm can always read the preceding reading in the place of the absent reader. After the conclusion of the first of the readings and its psalm, the celebrant stands at the chair and turns to the faithful to say, "Let us pray," with hands joined. Then, facing the missal, held directly in front of him by a server, he prays the Collect with hands extended in the *orans* position. The celebrant then sits for the next reading. The celebrant prays a Collect in the same way after each of the Old Testament readings. After the Collect that concludes the final Old Testament reading, he remains standing for the Gloria and the Collect of the Mass.

At the Gloria, the organ sounds once again for the first time since the Gloria on Holy Thursday evening. Servers light the altar candles from the Easter candle. In some churches, once the altar candles are lit, the celebrant comes from his chair, bows before the altar, and kisses it, before returning immediately to his place, in order to mark the beginning of the Vigil Mass properly speaking. If any additional electric lights still need to be turned on, especially in the sanctuary, that takes place at this point. The bells of the church are rung, and servers ring handbells with either their right or left hands.

After the Gloria, the celebrant, standing at the chair, prays the Collect of the Mass in the usual way. The celebrant is seated for the epistle which follows. Immediately after the epistle, an extended Gospel Acclamation, one with a triple introduction of the Alleluia and three verses, precedes the Gospel. Historically, the Alleluia is sung three times in successively higher tones, before any verses are sung. This Alleluia is intoned by the celebrant, with the people responding. A cantor may assist the celebrant in intoning the triple Alleluia or may intone them himself or herself if the celebrant is unable to do so. The celebrant stands when the Alleluia is begun. The Roman Gradual provides only one verse for this acclamation. This single verse from the Roman Gradual can be sung as an alternative to the three verses found in the Lectionary for Mass. While the schola sings the verse or verses to the Alleluia, the celebrant imposes incense standing. Candles are not carried at the Gospel. The thurifer leads the Gospel procession, followed by two servers walking side by side with hands joined. The celebrant goes to the altar and bows to say the prayer of preparation. The celebrant rises and takes up the Gospel book in both hands, if it was placed there prior to the beginning of the Vigil. He then follows the thurifer and two servers with hands joined to the ambo, where he proclaims the Gospel. If the Gospel book is not used, the celebrant goes from the chair, bows to the altar to say the prayer of preparation, and then follows the thurifer and two servers to the ambo, where he reads the Gospel from the lectionary placed there. All in the Gospel procession proceed without any sign of reverence to the altar. At the ambo, the two servers stand facing each other on either side of the ambo, with hands joined. The thurifer stands to the right of the ambo throughout the entire reading of the Gospel. After the proclamation of the Gospel, all return to their places, bowing to the altar when passing in front of it. The homily follows, either at the chair, or at the ambo, or at another suitable place, depending on the circumstances.

The Celebration of Baptism and Confirmation

Since the number of servers will be limited, all the items needed for Baptism, and perhaps for Confirmation, are placed on a table near the font. The rituals of initiation of adults and of Baptism for children can be placed on a lectern near the font. If needed for the Baptism of infants, a second copy of the Roman Missal can also be placed on the lectern near the font first. If a server is not capable of carrying the Easter candle in procession from the sanctuary to the baptistry, a member of the faithful present in the nave can be invited to do so. One server is needed to carry the holy water from the baptistry to the place where the renewal of baptismal promises will take place. Another may be needed to carry the chrism used to anoint the heads of infants at the font to the place where Confirmation of adults will take place. Upon arrival in the sanctuary, a third server can move a lectern into place at the center to hold the ritual of adult initiation for Confirmation and the renewal of baptismal promises. The rites of Christian initiation, whether of adults or children, take place as described in chapter 18.

The Liturgy of the Eucharist and Concluding Rites

After the celebration of Confirmation or the renewal of baptismal promises as the case may be, Mass continues. The solemn blessing always concludes the Easter Vigil. The celebrant should make every effort to sing the proper dismissal with the double alleluias. After the conclusion of Mass and following the recessional, the reposition of the Blessed Sacrament from the secret repository to the tabernacle of the church takes place in the manner described in chapter 18.

38

Corpus Christi in Small Congregations

Small congregations with limited resources may find it difficult to coordinate a eucharistic procession on Corpus Christi Sunday at the conclusion of Mass. It may be easier for them to muster the various participants needed at another time that same day, as suggested in the Ceremonial and the ritual. The following description will assume that a procession takes place apart from Mass later in the day of Corpus Christi with a Host consecrated at the parish Mass that immediately preceded the procession itself. It presumes the absence of a deacon and concelebrants, but requires the participation of four servers, along with a larger number of volunteers taken from the faithful in attendance.

The following are needed at the Mass which precedes the procession but takes place earlier that day:

On the credence table:

- On the paten, a second host to be consecrated for the procession, unless this second host will be consecrated directly in the lunette
- The empty lunette to receive the consecrated Host
- The custodia to receive the lunette with the consecrated Host

During the course of Mass, the host to be used for the procession later in the day is consecrated along with the hosts for the Communion of the faithful. Normally, it is placed in the lunette to be consecrated and brought to the altar with the other gifts at the preparation of the altar.[969] If the host to be consecrated is placed in the lunette from the beginning of the preparation of the gifts, the lunette is opened and closed by the celebrant at the same time as the covers to the ciboria are removed and replaced. Alternatively, at the fraction rite, the Host consecrated at that Mass, on a paten along with the principal Host for that Mass, is placed in the lunette brought to the altar by a server.[970] In either case, the lunette containing the Host consecrated for the procession is left on the corporal during the entire time of Communion.[971] During this time, all genuflect whenever approaching the altar, or departing from it, even at the side, as if the Blessed Sacrament were already exposed in the monstrance.[972] Naturally, those carrying the Blessed Sacrament in their hands during the time of Communion omit this sign of reverence. At the conclusion of Communion, a server brings the custodia from the credence table to the altar. The celebrant places the lunette in the custodia and brings the custodia with the Host consecrated for the procession to the tabernacle, along with the Hosts that remain from the distribution of Communion. He places the custodia and the ciborium in the tabernacle, genuflects, then closes and locks the tabernacle door. Mass proceeds in the usual way.

Later that same day, the following items are prepared for the eucharistic procession:

In the sacristy:

- White cope and stole for the priest celebrant
- Processional cross and candles

On or near the altar:

- Six candles, or at least four
- White burse with one corporal
- Monstrance veiled in white

969 Adrian Fortescue, J. B. O'Connell, and Alcuin Reid, eds., *The Ceremonies of the Roman Rite Described*, 15th ed. (New York: Bloomsbury, 2009), 389.

970 Peter J. Elliott, *Ceremonies of the Modern Roman Rite: The Eucharist and the Liturgy of the Hours*, rev. ed. (San Francisco: Ignatius Press, 1995), 258.

971 Elliott, *Ceremonies of the Modern Roman Rite*, 258.

972 André Philippe M. Mutel and Peter Freeman, *Cérémonial de la sainte messe à l'usage ordinaire des paroisses suivant le missel romain de 2002 et la pratique léguée du rit romain*, 2nd ed. (Perpignan, France: Éditions Artège, 2012), 268.

At the steps of the altar or nearby:

- One censer with burning coals, incense boat and stand[973]
- White humeral veil

In a convenient place:

- Four or six torches, or at least two
- Hand candles for all those present
- The canopy or baldachin (optional)

In the place where the procession will conclude:

- A second custodia to receive the lunette on the altar to the right
- A veil for the monstrance
- A corporal opened upon the altar
- A burse, on the right side of the altar, to receive the corporal
- *Holy Communion and Worship of the Eucharist Outside Mass,* or at least a card with the necessary prayers
- A second stand for the censer and incense boat, on the right side of the sanctuary
- Handbells, if used

The white burse with one corporal is placed at the center of the altar, its opening facing away from the assembly. To the left of the center of the altar, perpendicular to its front edge, is the monstrance, veiled in white.[974] A stand holding a censer with burning coals and incense is placed to the far-right of the center of the steps of the altar. Normally, the celebrant kneels on the bare steps. The use of a cushion or kneeler at adoration was formerly reserved to bishops and prelates.[975]

The rite of exposition begins as the ministers make their way from the sacristy to the sanctuary. Instrumental music or singing may accompany the

[973] Although two thurifers are normally required for the procession on Corpus Christi, one is permitted in case of necessity. See Fortescue, O'Connell, and Reid, *The Ceremonies of the Roman Rite Described,* 343.

[974] Fortescue, O'Connell, and Reid, *The Ceremonies of the Roman Rite Described,* 297.

[975] Fortescue, O'Connell, and Reid, *The Ceremonies of the Roman Rite Described,* 295.

procession to the altar.[976] Two servers with candles flank the processional cross and its bearer. These servers carry the candlesticks in their outside hands at the nodes, with their other hands resting on the bases of the candlesticks.[977] The fourth server and the celebrant follow the cross and candles. Upon arriving in the sanctuary, the servers place their candles on either side of the lowest step of the altar.[978] If this is impractical, they can place their candles at the rear corners of the credence table, as at Mass. The cross bearer puts the cross aside for the time being. The celebrant and servers genuflect before the steps of the sanctuary to the Blessed Sacrament reserved there and then kneel on the first step of the altar. All kneel. The celebrant does not kneel after genuflecting, but goes first to the altar and unfolds the corporal from the burse in the same way as one would do at Mass, leaving the burse flat on the right-hand side of the altar. The opening of the burse faces away from the assembly. Then, the celebrant unveils the monstrance, placing it on the corporal on the altar, perpendicular to the front of the altar and to the left side of the corporal, with its door open. In some churches, the unveiled monstrance is already placed on the altar in this position before the entrance of the ministers. Meanwhile, all in the sanctuary and in the nave take candles in hand. Servers assist in lighting everyone's candles in the sanctuary and in the nave. Designated parishioners go to the sacristy to take up four or six or at least two torches for the procession with the Blessed Sacrament.

The celebrant then proceeds to the tabernacle in the sanctuary. He opens the door and genuflects. He takes the custodia and places it on a corporal outside the tabernacle in order to close the door. He then takes the custodia in both hands and makes his way to the altar. Once at the altar, he places the custodia down on the corporal on the altar and opens it. He reverently places the lunette with his right hand into the monstrance and closes the door. He then closes the empty custodia and sets it aside to the right of the corporal.[979] He then reverently places the monstrance at the center of the corporal on the altar or on the throne on the altar, facing the assembly. He genuflects on one knee, with both hands resting on

[976] *HCWEOM*, 93.

[977] Elliott, *Ceremonies of the Modern Roman Rite*, 248.

[978] Peter J. Elliott, *Ceremonies Explained for Servers According to the Roman Rite: A Manual for Altar Servers, Acolytes, Sacristans, and Masters of Ceremonies* (San Francisco: Ignatius Press, 2019), 188; Elliott, *Ceremonies of the Modern Roman Rite*, 268.

[979] Elliott, *Ceremonies of the Modern Roman Rite*, 249.

the altar outside the corporal.[980] The celebrant returns to his place at the bottom step of the altar and kneels.

Additional accommodations must be made if the Blessed Sacrament is reserved in a location outside the sanctuary where the procession will begin. Upon arriving, the candle bearers place their candles down before them on the lowest step of the altar or, if necessary, on the lowest step of the sanctuary. The cross bearer places the processional cross aside. All bow to the altar and kneel. All in the assembly kneel. The celebrant prepares the corporal(s) and monstrance as indicated above, and then returns to kneel in front of the altar. Standing behind the priest, the fourth server places the white humeral veil on his shoulders. The celebrant and the two candle bearers then stand. The two servers now carrying candles once again flank the celebrant, as he goes to the place of reservation to retrieve the Blessed Sacrament and brings the Host to the altar in the custodia. After placing the Host in the monstrance in the manner described above, and genuflecting and returning to his place at the bottom step, the priest gives up the humeral veil from a kneeling position.

At once, the celebrant and those kneeling with him bow from the waist and stand. The celebrant turns to his right. The celebrant receives the incense boat from the fourth server, now acting as the thurifer. The thurifer faces the celebrant and presents him with the open censer with the spoon. The celebrant opens the incense boat and holds it in his left hand. He imposes incense three times on the burning coals with the right hand. He blesses the incense in the form of a Greek cross with his right hand, saying nothing, his left hand resting on his chest and holding the incense boat. The celebrant returns the incense boat to the thurifer. The celebrant then turns to his left, in order to face the altar once again from the middle of the sanctuary steps, and kneels. The thurifer, to his right, also kneels with the censer and incense boat. The thurifer can place the incense boat temporarily on the altar step. From a kneeling position, the thurifer places the rings of the chain in the left hand of the celebrant by using his own right hand. The thurifer places the chains near the bowl of the censer into the right hand of the celebrant with his own left hand. If necessary, the thurifer may then hold back the edge of the celebrant's cope with his left hand, his right hand resting on his chest.

[980] *CB*, 1103. According to the revised liturgical books all genuflections, either during Mass, or made to the Blessed Sacrament in the tabernacle, or made to the Blessed Sacrament exposed, are made on one knee (*HCWEOM*, 84). Some churches have preserved the custom of genuflecting momentarily on both knees in the presence of the Blessed Sacrament exposed.

Holding the bowl of the censer in the right hand slightly below eye level, the celebrant incenses the Blessed Sacrament with three double swings, bowing before and after from a kneeling position. All those kneeling next to the celebrant bow with him from a kneeling position at the same time he does. The celebrant then returns the censer to the thurifer, who makes sure to take up the incense boat once again. The thurifer momentarily places both the censer and the incense boat on its stand nearby. Then the thurifer stands behind the kneeling celebrant and places the humeral veil on his shoulders, genuflects, and takes up the censer and boat from its stand once again. The celebrant goes up to the altar and genuflects there. He takes the monstrance in his veiled hands, with the front of the monstrance facing outward. All in the sanctuary stand from the kneeling position, genuflect, and the eucharistic chant, for example "Pange Lingua" (excluding the last two verses), begins.[981] The procession is now ready to set off. For the order of procession, see figure 8.

The cross bearer and two candle bearers lead the procession, walking together. Then follows the thurifer, always facing forward.[982] The thurifer holds the chain of the censer in the right hand, the left hand resting on his chest, holding the incense boat. Then follows the celebrant, holding the Blessed Sacrament, with the torch bearers also walking in two rows on either side of the Blessed Sacrament. They hold the torches in their outside hands, their inside hands resting on their chests. The faithful, or at least a representative group of the faithful, walk behind the celebrant. The choir may be the first among them. All hold lighted candles in their outside hands. Those present but not participating in the procession remain kneeling as the Blessed Sacrament passes by.[983]

If the procession to the passes outdoors, some churches maintain the use of the umbrellino, held over the celebrant by a member of the faithful walking behind him, or even the use of the baldachin, held by four laypersons, with the celebrant walking beneath it and the torch bearers on either side.[984] In many locations, the baldachin or the umbrellino is used only for the portion of the procession that takes place outdoors. Those carrying it wait just outside the doors of the church.[985] The celebrant walks under it as he emerges from the church. The torch bearers walk on either side of those supporting the baldachin.

981 Mutel and Freeman, *Cérémonial de la sainte messe*, 272.
982 Mutel and Freeman, *Cérémonial de la sainte messe*, 273, n. 133.
983 Elliott, *Ceremonies of the Liturgical Year*, 213.
984 Mutel and Freeman, *Cérémonial de la sainte messe*, 268, n. 122.
985 The use of the baldachin is optional according to no. 388 of the *Ceremonial of Bishops*.

Normally, the procession on Corpus Christi begins in the sanctuary of one church and concludes in the sanctuary of a second church or a distinct chapel of the original church.[986] In some cases, it may only be possible for the procession to proceed outdoors for some distance before returning to the sanctuary of the same church. The procession is not intended to take place entirely within the walls of a single church. A eucharistic procession on public streets requires the permission of the diocesan bishop.[987] The procession may be arranged with stations at which the Blessed Sacrament rests on an altar and hymns and prayers can be offered. At these altars, the "Tantum Ergo" or some other eucharistic song is sung, the Blessed Sacrament is incensed from a kneeling position as usual, and the Collect is offered, perhaps preceded by the usual versicle and response. Strictly speaking, benediction should not be given. In the past, benediction at the stations was in fact tolerated, if such was the custom and it took place no more than twice during the procession.[988] Upon arriving at the location where the procession will conclude, those supporting the baldachin or the umbrellino for the portion of the procession outside allow the torch bearers and the celebrant to enter the church or chapel while they remain outside.

Arriving at the sanctuary, the cross bearer and candle bearers move together as a group to the right side of the sanctuary and stand to face the altar in a row. The torch bearers take their usual positions on either side of the entrance of the sanctuary in a row; they kneel. The thurifer and the celebrant enter the sanctuary. The thurifer momentarily places the censer and boat on its stand and kneels to the celebrant's right. The celebrant places the monstrance on the altar with its front facing the assembly. Then, the celebrant genuflects before the altar and kneels on the lowest step, as he did prior to the procession. The thurifer, standing behind the celebrant, removes the humeral veil and sets it aside for the time being.

The celebrant allows time for all those who participated in the procession to arrive at the place of its conclusion and kneel. Once all have arrived in place, the schola can begin singing the last two verses of the "Pange Lingua." This will be the signal to the celebrant to begin the incensation of the Blessed Sacrament. Normally, the Blessed Sacrament is incensed during the final verse,[989] that is, at *Genitori genitoque*. Thus, during the preceding verse, *Tantum ergo*, it is customary for the ministers to

986 *CB*, 393.

987 *HCWEOM*, 101–102.

988 Fortescue, O'Connell, and Reid, *The Ceremonies of the Roman Rite Described*, 387–388, 391.

989 *CB*, 391.

bow together from a kneeling position at the words *veneremur cernui*, after which the celebrant and the thurifer rise to prepare the incense.[990] The Blessed Sacrament is incensed from a kneeling position, bowing before and after incensing. The hymn and the incensation concluded, the celebrant alone rises, without bowing. The ritual, *Holy Communion and Worship of the Eucharist Outside Mass*, or at least a card with the necessary prayers, can be placed near the center of the altar steps where the celebrant will kneel and stand. He holds the text in his hands when standing. Bowing his head, he intones the Collect with "Let us pray." Then, after a period of silence, he sings the Collect.[991] After the Collect, the celebrant kneels and places the text of the Collect on the step in front of him. The thurifer returns with the humeral veil and comes behind him to place it over his shoulders once again. The celebrant secures it in the front and stands to go up directly to the altar without any further reverence. It is often more convenient to give the blessing from the side of the altar closest to the assembly. The celebrant may also go around the altar to face the assembly and give the blessing from there as well. As he approaches the altar, the celebrant may enfold his joined hands in the humeral veil in order to lift its edges and avoiding tripping on it.

Once at the altar, the celebrant frees his hands, places them flat on the altar outside the corporal, and genuflects. The celebrant then covers his hands with the humeral veil once again to take the monstrance, with its front facing forward. The celebrant can hold the monstrance with the right hand at the node, and the left hand steadying its base, or he can take it at the node with both hands. The celebrant turns to his right if he is not already facing the assembly. He makes the Sign of the Cross once over the people, saying nothing. The celebrant keeps his eyes fixed on the Blessed Sacrament throughout this action. He begins by raising the monstrance slightly above eye level.[992] He lowers the monstrance, with its base no lower than the table of the altar, and raises it again halfway, at about eye level. Turning to the left, not beyond his left shoulder, he makes a straight line to the right, again not beyond his right shoulder and not moving his feet.

During the time of the blessing, the thurifer may incense the Blessed Sacrament with three double swings, bowing from a kneeling position before and after. The thurifer may do so either at the center of the sanctuary steps, or from the right-hand side of the altar.[993] If it is the custom, a member of the faithful may

[990] Fortescue, O'Connell, and Reid, *The Ceremonies of the Roman Rite Described*, 299.
[991] *CB*, 1113.
[992] Elliott, *Ceremonies of the Modern Roman Rite*, 252.
[993] Elliott, *Ceremonies of the Modern Roman Rite*, 253.

ring the handbells three separate times during the course of the blessing. Historically, it was usual to ring the bells once as the celebrant turned to the people, once at the middle of the blessing, and once as he turned back to the altar.[994] If the celebrant is already facing the assembly when he imparts the blessing, perhaps this custom could be adapted. The volunteer could first ring the handbells to accompany the raising of the monstrance for the blessing. That person could ring them a second time when the monstrance moves from the center to the left, and a third time when the monstrance moves from the center to the right. The thurifer incensing the Blessed Sacrament could coordinate the swings of the censers with the three rings of the handbells during the blessing.[995] In some locations, all those present bow while kneeling at their places in order to receive the blessing. They may also sign themselves once with the Sign of the Cross.

Having completed the blessing, the celebrant returns the monstrance to the center and pauses, before turning to his right to the altar if necessary, completing the circle, lowering the monstrance to place it on the corporal. The celebrant repositions the monstrance on the corporal so that the front of the monstrance is once again facing the assembly. After genuflecting at the altar, the celebrant returns to his place at the center of the sanctuary steps and kneels. The thurifer places the censer on its stand and then removes the humeral veil from the kneeling celebrant. In some locations, the Divine Praises are said at this point before proceeding with reposition.[996] If not, the celebrant can remain at the altar and proceed directly with reposition, after relinquishing the humeral veil. Meanwhile, as the reposition begins, all sing a hymn, such as "Holy God We Praise Thy Name," or an acclamation as reposition is taking place.[997]

After the blessing or after the Divine Praises, as the case may be, the celebrant begins reposition by placing the monstrance perpendicular to the front of the altar, toward the left, yet still on the corporal. He moves the custodia which will receive the lunette onto the corporal and opens it. He then removes the lunette from the monstrance, places it in the custodia, and closes its cover. He closes the door to the monstrance and moves the monstrance off the corporal to his left, still perpendicular to the front of the altar. He then takes the custodia in both hands and places it in the tabernacle in the sanctuary, genuflecting before closing

994 Fortescue, O'Connell, and Reid, *The Ceremonies of the Roman Rite Described*, 300.

995 Elliott, *Ceremonies of the Modern Roman Rite*, 253.

996 Elliott, *Ceremonies of the Modern Roman Rite*, 253–254.

997 *CB*, 1114; *HCWEOM*, 100; Elliott, *Ceremonies of the Modern Roman Rite*, 254.

the door and locking it. Customarily, all stand when the door to the tabernacle is closed or when the singing which accompanied reposition ends. In some churches, all being singing a Marian antiphon at this point. The celebrant may then return briefly to the altar, bowing when he approaches it and departs from it, to veil the monstrance, and to fold the corporal and place it in its burse. The burse is placed at the center of the altar, with its closed edge facing the assembly. All genuflect in their places before the lowest step of the sanctuary before departing and returning to the sacristy in the usual order.

Additional accommodations must be made if the Blessed Sacrament is normally reserved in a location outside the sanctuary where benediction just took place. After the blessing, still wearing the humeral veil, or perhaps after the Divine Praises, having received the humeral veil from the fourth server once again, the celebrant goes up to the altar, genuflects before the Blessed Sacrament, and removes the lunette from the monstrance as described above. With the custodia containing the lunette and his hands covered by the ends of the humeral veil, he returns to the place of reservation, flanked by two torch bearers who served in the procession.[998] Upon returning to the sanctuary, the celebrant gives up the humeral veil from a kneeling position. He may return to the altar to veil the monstrance and fold the corporal and place it in its burse. The burse is placed at the center of the altar, with its closed edge facing the assembly. Then, all stand and bow to the altar, and return to the sacristy in the same manner as at the beginning of exposition described above.

[998] Elliott, *Ceremonies of the Modern Roman Rite*, 248.

APPENDIX

Diagrams

Diagram Key

[Source: Peter J. Elliott, "Code for Diagrams," *Ceremonies of the Modern Roman Rite: The Eucharist and the Liturgy of the Hours*, rev. ed. (San Francisco: Ignatius Press, 1995), 337, no. 1 (388).]

CODE FOR DIAGRAMS

B	Bishop	† **cr**	cross bearer
C	Celebrant	**cb**	candle bearer
Cc	Concelebrant	**bb**	book bearer
D	Deacon	**th**	thurifer
AD	Assistant Deacon	**bo**	boat bearer
Ac	Acolyte	**tb**	torch bearer
Lc	Lector	**mr**	miter bearer
Mc	Master of Ceremonies	**cz**	crozier bearer

Figure 1: Incensing the Freestanding Altar

[Source: "Ordo Incensationis Altaris: Quod Commode Circuiri Potest," *Missale Romanum* [Roman Missal] (New York: Catholic Book Publishing Company, 1964), lxxi.]

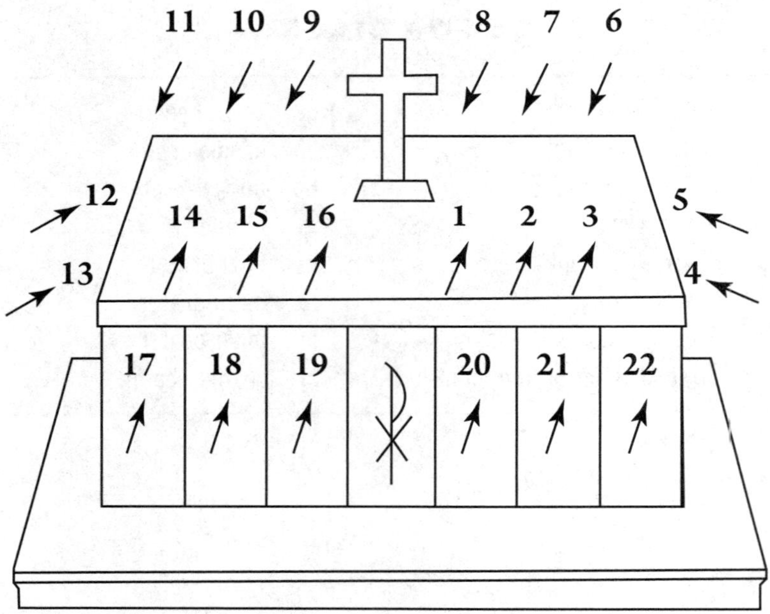

The incensing of the cross (and relics or images) having proceeded, there follow 22 swings, of which numbers 1–3 and 14–16 are above the table of the altar, and numbers 4–13 and 17–22 are below and from the side.

Figure 2: Incensing the Offerings

[Source: Peter J. Elliott, "Incensing the Offerings," *Ceremonies of the Modern Roman Rite: The Eucharist and the Liturgy of the Hours*, rev. ed. (San Francisco: Ignatius Press, 1995), 340, (397).]

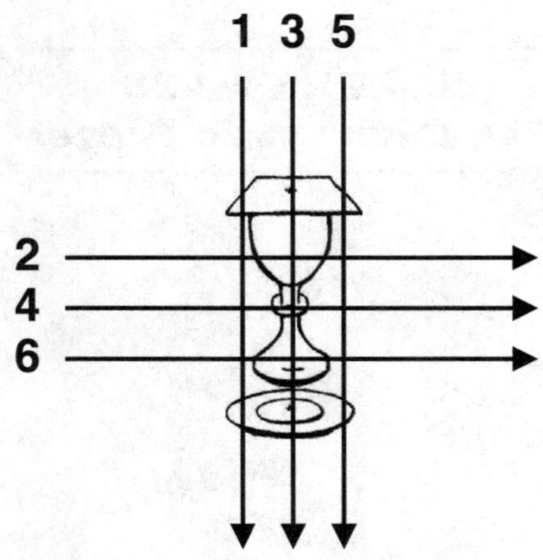

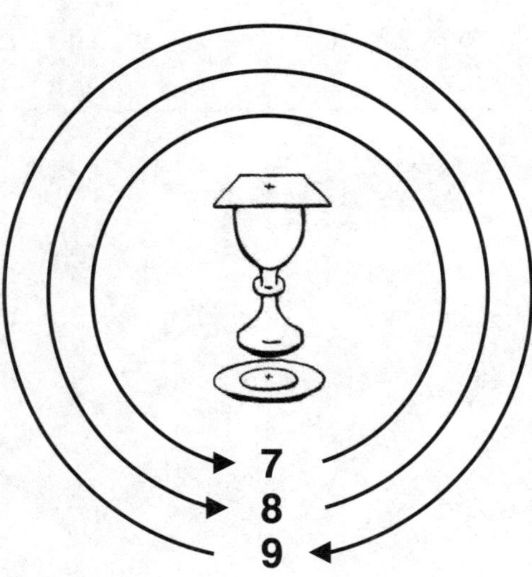

Figure 3: Incensing at the Elevations; Concelebrants Standing at the Altar

[Source: Peter J. Elliott, "Solemn Mass: The Eucharistic Prayer," *Ceremonies of the Modern Roman Rite: The Eucharist and the Liturgy of the Hours*, rev. ed. (San Francisco: Ignatius Press, 1995), 338, no. 4 (402, 403).]

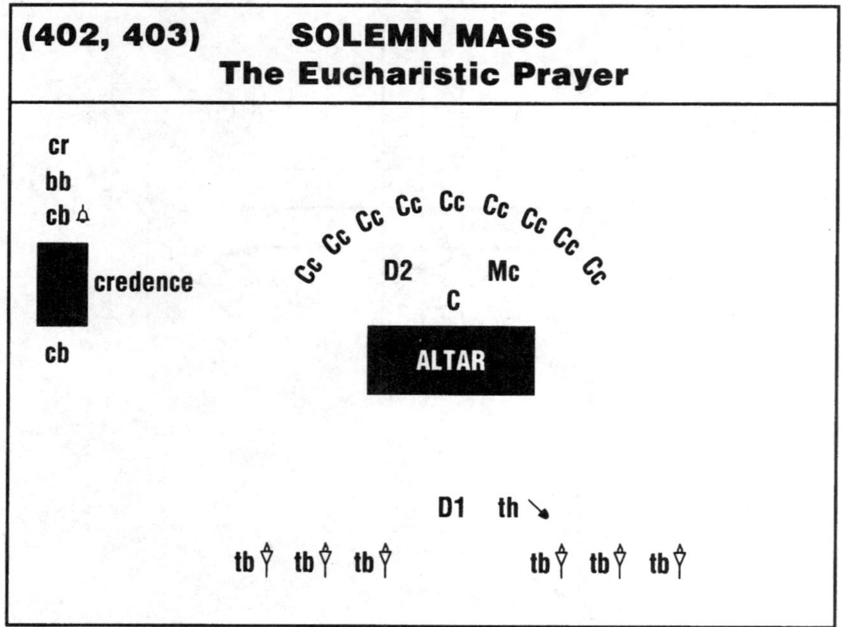

Figure 4: The Entrance Procession

[Source: Peter J. Elliott, "Solemn Mass: Entrance Procession," *Ceremonies of the Modern Roman Rite: The Eucharist and the Liturgy of the Hours*, rev. ed. (San Francisco: Ignatius Press, 1995), 337, no. 2 (376).]

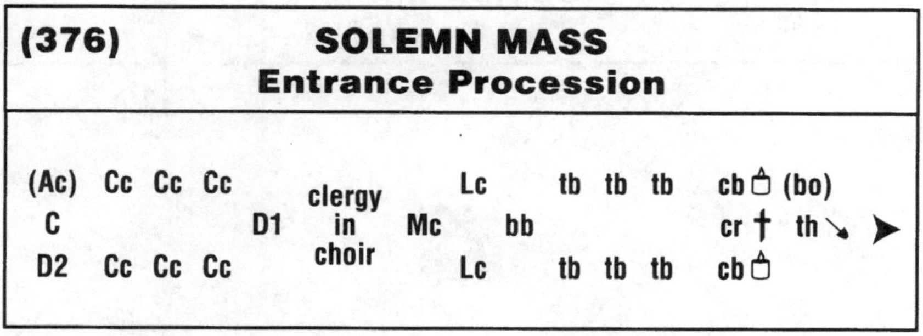

(376) SOLEMN MASS
Entrance Procession

(Ac)	Cc	Cc	Cc		clergy		Lc		tb	tb	tb	cb 🕯	(bo)	
C				D1	in	Mc		bb				cr †	th ↘	➤
D2	Cc	Cc	Cc		choir		Lc		tb	tb	tb	cb 🕯		

Figure 5: Proclaiming the Gospel

[Source: Peter J. Elliott, "Solemn Mass: The Gospel," *Ceremonies of the Modern Roman Rite: The Eucharist and the Liturgy of the Hours,* rev. ed. (San Francisco: Ignatius Press, 1995), 337, no. 3 (388).]

(388) **SOLEMN MASS**
The Gospel

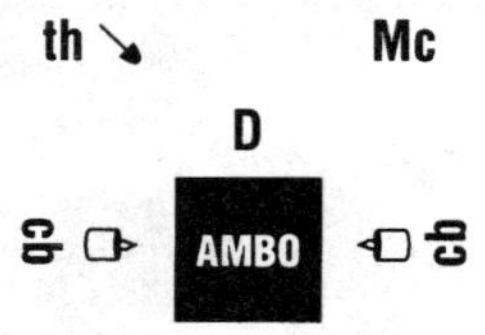

th ↘ Mc

D

cb AMBO cb

Figure 6: The Corporal

[Source: Peter J. Elliott, "Unfolding the Corporal," *Ceremonies Explained for Servers According to the Roman Rite: A Manual for Altar Servers, Acolytes, Sacristans, and Masters of Ceremonies* (San Francisco: Ignatius Press, 2019), 64].

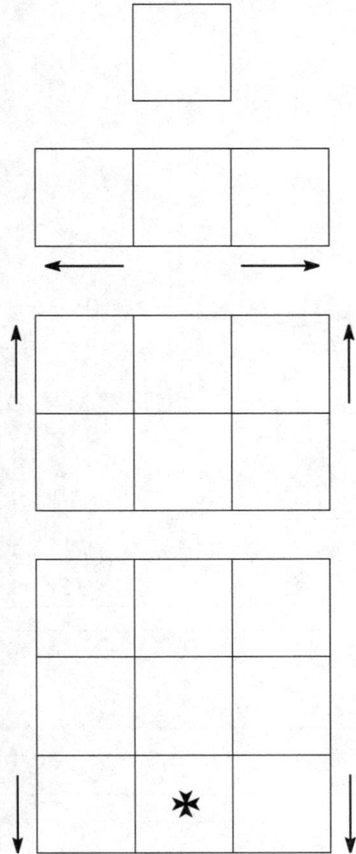

Figure 7: Incensing an Altar from One Side Only

[Source: "Ordo Incensationis Altaris: Iuxta Rubricas Missalis Romani," *Missale Romanum* [Roman Missal] (New York: Catholic Book Publishing Companry, 1964), lxx.]

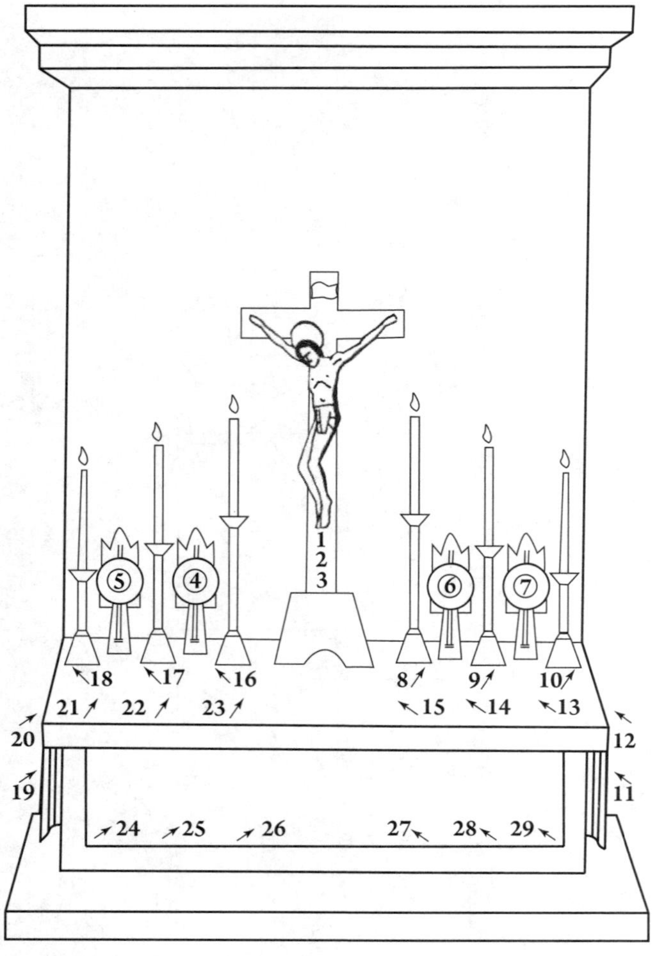

If the relics or images of the Saints are not present on the altar, their incensing is omitted, which is indicated under nn. 4. 5. 6. 7 (rites to be observed IV, 5) and immediately incense the cross (nn. 1, 2, 3), proceed to incense the altar according to order nn. 8, 9, ect. to 29.

Figure 8: Corpus Christi Procession

[Source: Peter J. Elliott, "A Eucharistic Procession," *Ceremonies of the Modern Roman Rite: The Eucharist and the Liturgy of the Hours*, rev. ed. (San Francisco: Ignatius Press, 1995), 339, no. 7 (704).]

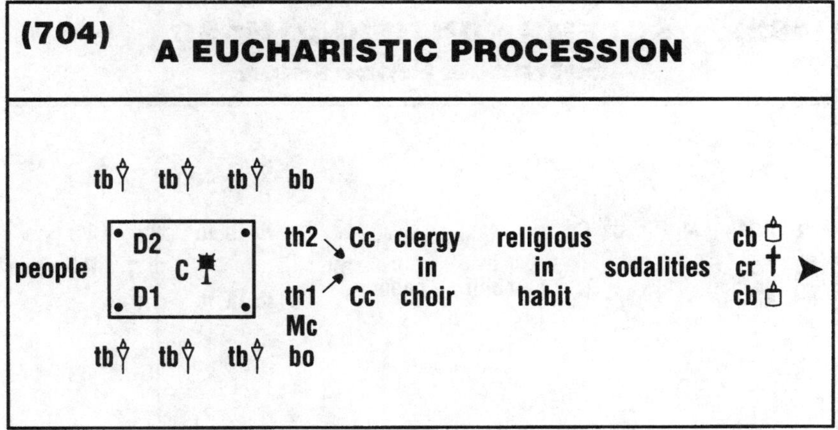

Figure 9: Mass with the Bishop

[Source: Peter J. Elliott, "Solemn Pontifical Mass: Entrance Procession," *Ceremonies of the Modern Roman Rite: The Eucharist and the Liturgy of the Hours*, rev. ed. (San Francisco: Ignatius Press, 1995), 338, no. 5 (482).]

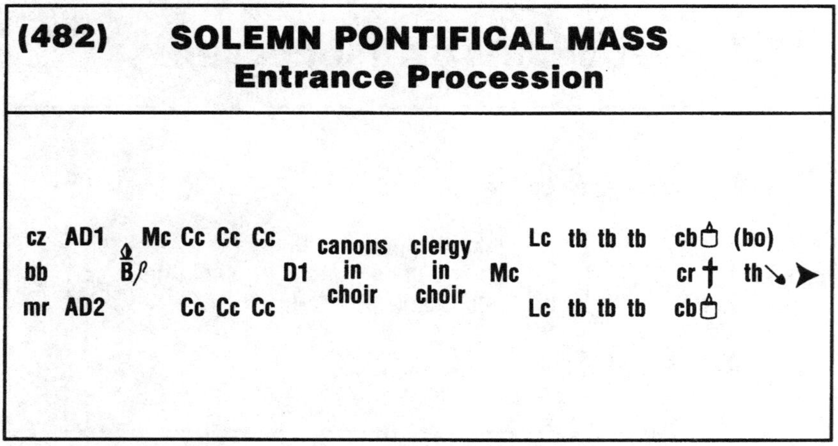

(482) SOLEMN PONTIFICAL MASS
Entrance Procession

cz	AD1		Mc Cc Cc Cc		canons	clergy		Lc tb tb tb	cb	(bo)
bb		B		D1	in	in	Mc		cr †	th ➤
mr	AD2		Cc Cc Cc		choir	choir		Lc tb tb tb	cb	

Bibliography

Crouan, Denis. *L'art de célébrer: Guide liturgique à l'usage des paroisses*. Lille, France: Éditions Librim Concept, 2015.

Elliott, Peter J. *Ceremonies Explained for Servers According to the Roman Rite: A Manual for Altar Servers, Acolytes, Sacristans, and Masters of Ceremonies*. San Francisco: Ignatius Press, 2019.

———. *Ceremonies of the Liturgical Year According to the Modern Roman Rite: A Manual for Clergy and All Involved in Liturgical Ministries*. San Francisco: Ignatius Press, 2002.

———. *Ceremonies of the Modern Roman Rite: The Eucharist and the Liturgy of the Hours*. Rev. ed. San Francisco: Ignatius Press, 1995.

Fortescue, Adrian, J. B. O'Connell, and Alcuin Reid, eds. *The Ceremonies of the Roman Rite Described*. 15th ed. New York: Bloomsbury, 2009.

Le Vavasseur, Léon-Michel. *Cérémonial à l'usage des petites églises de paroisse selon le rite romain*. 2nd ed. Paris: Lecoffre, 1864.

Le Vavasseur, Léon-Michel, Joseph Haegy, and Louis Stercky. *Manuel de liturgie et cérémonial selon le rit romain*. 2 vols. 16th ed. Paris: Éditions Gabalda, 1935.

Martinucci, Pio, and J. B. Menghini. *Manuale sacrarum caeremoniarum*. Regensburg: Pustet, 1911–1915.

McManus, Frederick R. *Handbook for the New Rubrics*. London: Geoffrey Chapman, 1961.

Mutel, André Philippe M., and Peter Freeman. *Cérémonial de la sainte messe à l'usage ordinaire des paroisses suivant le missel romain de 2002 et la pratique léguée du rit romain.* 2nd ed. Perpignan, France: Éditions Artège, 2012.

O'Connell, J. B. *The Celebration of Mass: A Study of the Rubrics of the Roman Missal.* Milwaukee: Bruce, 1964.

O'Connell, Laurence, and Walter J. Schmitz. *The Book of Ceremonies.* Milwaukee: Bruce, 1956.

Wapelhorst, Innocent. *Compendium sacrae liturgiae juxta Ritum Romanum.* New York: Benziger, 1931.

Wuest, Joseph, Thomas W. Mullaney, and William T. Barry. *Matters Liturgical.* New York: Pustet, 1956.

Author Bio

MSGR. MARC B. CARON is a priest of the Diocese of Portland, Maine. He holds a licentiate degree in Liturgical Studies from The Catholic University of America and a doctorate in sacred theology from the University of St. Mary of the Lake/ Mundelein Seminary. For fourteen years he has served as diocesan master of ceremonies. Over the same period, he has held positions as diocesan Chancellor, director of the Department of Ministerial Services, Moderator of the Curia, and Vicar General. In addition, he has served as the parochial vicar and pastor of a number of parishes in Maine, as well as university chaplain. For four years, he was a member of the formation faculty of St. John's Seminary, Brighton, Massachusetts, and director of liturgy. He has published articles on liturgical topics and priestly spirituality in *The Jurist, Worship, Homiletic and Pastoral Review, The Catechumenate,* and *Adoremus Bulletin.*

Sophia Institute

Sophia Institute is a nonprofit institution that seeks to nurture the spiritual, moral, and cultural life of souls and to spread the Gospel of Christ in conformity with the authentic teachings of the Roman Catholic Church.

Sophia Institute Press fulfills this mission by offering translations, reprints, and new publications that afford readers a rich source of the enduring wisdom of mankind.

Sophia Institute also operates the popular online Catholic resource CatholicExchange.com. *Catholic Exchange* provides world news from a Catholic perspective as well as daily devotionals and articles that will help readers to grow in holiness and live a life consistent with the teachings of the Church.

In 2013, Sophia Institute launched Sophia Institute for Teachers to renew and rebuild Catholic culture through service to Catholic education. With the goal of nurturing the spiritual, moral, and cultural life of souls, and an abiding respect for the role and work of teachers, we strive to provide materials and programs that are at once enlightening to the mind and ennobling to the heart; faithful and complete, as well as useful and practical.

Sophia Institute gratefully recognizes the Solidarity Association for preserving and encouraging the growth of our apostolate over the course of many years. Without their generous and timely support, this book would not be in your hands.

www.SophiaInstitute.com
www.CatholicExchange.com
www.SophiaInstituteforTeachers.org

Sophia Institute Press® is a registered trademark of Sophia Institute.
Sophia Institute is a tax-exempt institution as defined by the
Internal Revenue Code, Section 501(c)(3). Tax I.D. 22-2548708.